P9-EEA-902

THE LOEB CLASSICAL LIBRARY

FOUNDED BY JAMES LOEB, LL.D.

EDITED BY

G. P. GOOLD, PH.D.

PREVIOUS EDITORS

† T. E. PAGE, C.H., LITT.D.   † E. CAPPS, PH.D., LL.D.

† W. H. D. ROUSE. LITT.D.   † L. A. POST, L.H.D.

E. H. WARMINGTON, M.A., F.R.HIST.SOC.

CICERO

IV

DE ORATORE III
DE FATO
PARADOXA STOICORUM
DE PARTITIONE ORATORIA

CICERO

IN TWENTY-EIGHT VOLUMES

IV

DE ORATORE
BOOK III

DE FATO
PARADOXA STOICORUM
DE PARTITIONE ORATORIA

WITH AN ENGLISH TRANSLATION BY

H. RACKHAM, M.A.
FELLOW OF CHRIST'S COLLEGE, CAMBRIDGE

CAMBRIDGE, MASSACHUSETTS
HARVARD UNIVERSITY PRESS
LONDON
WILLIAM HEINEMANN LTD
MCMLXXVII

American
ISBN 0-674-99384-5

British
ISBN 0 434 99349 2

First printed 1942
Reprinted 1948, 1960, 1968, 1977

v al 4

PA
6156
.C5

31,686

Printed in Great Britain

CAMROSE LUTHERAN COLLEGE
LIBRARY

CONTENTS

PAGE

List of Cicero's Works vii

DE ORATORE

Text and Translation—

Book III 2

DE FATO

Introduction 189

Text and Translation 192

PARADOXA STOICORUM

Introduction 252

Text and Translation 254

DE PARTITIONE ORATORIA

Introduction 306

Text and Translation 310

CONTENTS

PAGE

INDEXES

To *De Oratore* 423

To *De Fato* 433

To *Paradoxa Stoicorum* 435

To *De Partitione Oratoria* 437

LIST OF CICERO'S WORKS

SHOWING THEIR DIVISION INTO VOLUMES IN THIS EDITION

VOLUME

Λ. RHETORICAL TREATISES. 5 VOLUMES

  I. [Cicero], Rhetorica ad Herennium

  II. De Inventione
     De Optimo Genere Oratorum
     Topica

  III. De Oratore, Books I-II

  IV. De Oratore, Book III
     De Fato
     Paradoxa Stoicorum
     De Partitione Oratoria

  V. Brutus
    Orator

LIST OF CICERO'S WORKS

VOLUME

B. ORATIONS.   10 VOLUMES

VI. Pro Quinctio
Pro Roscio Amerino
Pro Roscio Comoedo
De Lege Agraria Contra Rullum I-III

VII. The Verrine Orations I :
In Q. Caecilium
In C. Verrem Actio I
In C. Verrem Actio II, Books I-II

VIII. The Verrine Orations II :
In C. Verrem Actio II, Books III-V

IX. De Imperio Cn. Pompei (Pro Lege Manilia)
Pro Caecina
Pro Cluentio
Pro Rabirio Perduellionis Reo

X. In Catilinam I-IV
Pro Murena
Pro Sulla
Pro Flacco

XI. Pro Archia
Post Reditum in Senatu
Post Reditum ad Quirites

LIST OF CICERO'S WORKS

VOLUME

De Domo Sua
De Haruspicum Responsis
Pro Cn. Plancio

XII. Pro Sestio
In Vatinium

XIII. Pro Caelio
De Provinciis Consularibus
Pro Balbo

XIV. Pro Milone
In Pisonem
Pro Scauro
Pro Fonteio
Pro Rabirio Postumo
Pro Marcello
Pro Ligario
Pro Rege Deiotaro

XV. Philippics I-XIV

C. PHILOSOPHICAL TREATISES   6 VOLUMES

XVI. De Re Publica
De Legibus

XVII. De Finibus Bonorum et Malorum

LIST OF CICERO'S WORKS

VOLUME

XVIII. Tusculan Disputations

XIX. De Natura Deorum
Academica I and II

XX. Cato Maior de Senectute
Laelius de Amicitia
De Divinatione

XXI. De Officiis

D. LETTERS. 7 VOLUMES

XXII. Letters to Atticus, Books I-VI

XXIII. Letters to Atticus, Books VII-XI

XXIV. Letters to Atticus, Books XII-XVI

XXV. Letters to His Friends, Books I-VI

XXVI. Letters to His Friends, Books VII-XII

XXVII Letters to His Friends, Books XIII-XVI

XXVIII. Letters to His Brother Quintus
Letters to Brutus
Commentariolum Petitionis
Epistula ad Octavianum

DE ORATORE

BOOK III

M. TULLII CICERONIS

DE ORATORE

DIALOGUS SEU LIBER TERTIUS

1   I. Instituenti mihi, Quinte frater, eum sermonem
referre et mandare huic tertio libro, quem post
Antonii disputationem Crassus habuisset, acerba sane
recordatio veterem animi curam molestiamque re-
novavit. Nam illud immortalitate dignum ingenium,
illa humanitas, illa virtus L. Crassi morte exstincta
subita est vix diebus decem post eum diem qui hoc
2 et superiore libro continetur. Ut enim Romam rediit
extremo scenicorum ludorum die, vehementer com-
motus ea oratione quae ferebatur habita esse in contione a Philippo, quem dixisse constabat videndum
sibi aliud esse consilium, illo senatu se rempublicam
gerere non posse, mane idibus Septembribus et ille et
senatus frequens vocatu Drusi in curiam venit. Ibi
cum Drusus multa de Philippo questus esset, rettulit
ad senatum de illo ipso quod consul in eum ordinem
3 tam graviter in contione esset invectus. Hic, ut
saepe inter homines sapientissimos constare vidi

2

MARCUS TULLIUS CICERO

THE MAKING OF AN ORATOR

BOOK THE THIRD

1 I. When I set about recalling and embodying in this
Third Volume the discourse of Crassus that followed
the remarks made by Antonius, I confess, brother
Quintus, that the recollection was painful to me, re-
newing as it did an old sorrow and distress. For it
was little more than a week after the day described in
this and the preceding volume when that genius so
deserving of immortality, the humane and virtuous
Lucius Crassus, was snatched away by sudden death.

2 Crassus had gone back to Rome on the concluding
day of the dramatic festival, feeling deeply stirred by
the speech reported to have been delivered at a
meeting by Philip, who, it was said, had declared it to
be incumbent on him to devise some other plan of
action, as it was impossible for him to carry on the
government with the present Senate ; and on the
morning of September 13, at the summons of Drusus
he and a crowd of members came to the senate-
house, where Drusus, after a long series of complaints
against Philip, moved for a vote of the Senate on the
definite issue that a consul had in public assembly
delivered an extremely violent attack upon their
3 order. Hereupon, as I have frequently known men of
great accomplishments to agree, although whenever

Introduc-
tion : death
of Crassus
soon after
this
discussion.

3

quanquam hoc Crasso, cum aliquid accuratius dixisset, semper fere contigisset, ut nunquam dixisse melius putaretur, tamen omnium consensu sic esse tum iudicatum, ceteros a Crasso semper omnes, illo autem die etiam ipsum a sese superatum. Deploravit enim casum atque orbitatem senatus, cuius ordinis a consule, qui quasi parens bonus aut tutor fidelis esse deberet, tanquam ab aliquo nefario praedone diriperetur patrimonium dignitatis : neque vero esse mirandum si, cum suis consiliis rempublicam profligasset, consilium senatus a republica repudiaret. Hic cum homini et vehementi et diserto et in primis forti ad resistendum Philippo quasi quasdam verborum faces ammovisset, non tulit ille et graviter exarsit pignoribusque ablatis Crassum instituit coercere. Quo quidem ipso in loco multa a Crasso divinitus dicta esse ferebantur, cum sibi illum consulem esse negaret cui senator ipse non esset : An tu, cum omnem auctoritatem universi ordinis pro pignore putaris eamque in conspectu populi Romani concideris, me his pignoribus existimas posse terreri ? Non tibi illa sunt caedenda si Crassum vis coercere : haec tibi est excidenda lingua ; qua vel evulsa spiritu ipso libidinem tuam libertas mea refutabit.

---

^a Property seized as security for payment of a fine, or as a pledge to enforce obedience to an order ; in the latter case it might be restored on compliance or destroyed as a punishment for refusal. The present seems to be the only known case of its being used or threatened as a punishment for language used in debate.

Crassus delivered a specially prepared oration he almost invariably succeeded in giving the impression that he had never spoken better, nevertheless it was the unanimous verdict now that one who had always surpassed all the rest of the speakers had on this occasion surpassed even himself. He deplored the disaster and the bereavement that had befallen the senatorial order, whose hereditary dignities a consul whose duty it was to be its fostering parent or faithful guardian was plundering like some unprincipled brigand ; but that nevertheless it was no matter for wonder if after his own policy had inflicted a disastrous blow on the state he was endeavouring to oust the wisdom of the Senate from the direction 4 of public affairs. Philip was a headstrong person, a fluent orator and one of the most courageous of adversaries ; and when Crassus's eloquence had put a match to the tinder, it was more than he could stand : he flared out violently, and took steps to coerce Crassus by seizing a pledge *a* from him. At this particular juncture, it was reported, Crassus said a great deal that showed extraordinary sagacity. He protested that a consul who would not recognize him as a member of the Senate was to him no consul at all. " What, when you have reckoned all the authority of our whole order as a forfeited pledge and in the sight of the nation have destroyed it, do you imagine that these pledges can have any terrors for me ? If your wish is to coerce Lucius Crassus, it is not those pledges that you have to destroy : you must cut out this tongue of mine—although even when this has been torn from my throat, my breath of itself will serve my liberty for the refutation of your licence."

5

5 II. Permulta tum vehementissima contentione animi, ingenii, virium ab eo dicta esse constabat ; sententiamque eam quam senatus frequens secutus est ornatissimis et gravissimis verbis : ' Ut populo Romano satisfieret, nunquam senatus neque consilium reipublicae neque fidem defuisse,' ab eo dictam ; et eundem (id quod in auctoritatibus perscriptis[1] exstat) scribendo adfuisse.

6 Illa tanquam cycnea fuit divini hominis vox et oratio, quam quasi exspectantes post eius interitum veniebamus in curiam ut vestigium illud ipsum in quo ille postremum institisset contueremur ; namque tum latus ei dicenti condoluisse sudoremque multum consecutum esse audiebamus ; ex quo cum cohorruisset, cum febri domum rediit dieque septimo

7 lateris dolore consumptus est. O fallacem hominum spem fragilemque fortunam, et inanes nostras contentiones, quae medio in spatio saepe franguntur et corruunt et ante in ipso cursu obruuntur quam portum conspicere potuerunt ! Nam quamdiu Crassi fuit ambitionis labore vita districta, tamdiu privatis magis officiis et ingenii laude floruit quam fructu amplitudinis aut reipublicae dignitate : qui autem ei annus primus ab honorum perfunctione aditum omnium concessu ad summam auctoritatem dabat, is eius omnem spem atque omnia vitae consilia morte

---

[1] *v.l.* praescriptis.

5 II. This was followed by a great deal more, which was universally admitted to display a superlative energy of spirit, intellect and force ; and Crassus moved a resolution expressed in most polished and dignified terms, which was passed by a crowded house : " That the nation should be assured that neither the advice nor the loyalty of the Senate had ever failed to support the state " ; and it was said that he personally witnessed the minuting of the resolution, as appears in the list of resolutions recorded.

6 That oration was the swan-song of this inspired genius, the sound of whose voice we almost expected to hear when we used to come into the Senate-house after his death in order to gaze upon the spot on which he had stood for the last time ; for while actually speaking on this occasion, we used to be told, he was seized with a violent pain in the side, followed by profuse perspiration ; after which he trembled all over, and went back home with a fever,

7 and a week later was carried off by pleurisy. Ah, how treacherous are men's hopes, how insecure their fortunes ! How hollow are our endeavours, which often break down and come to grief in the middle of the race, or are shipwrecked in full sail before they have been able to sight the harbour ! For throughout all the time that his life was racked by the toils of ambition, Crassus stood higher in point of his private services and his distinguished talents than in regard to the emoluments of high estate or public eminence ; but the first year after the completion of his official career, the year which offered him by universal consent access to the highest grade of power, at one stroke overthrew by death all his hopes and all his

7

8 pervertit. Fuit hoc luctuosum suis, acerbum patriae, grave bonis omnibus ; sed ei tamen reipublicae casus secuti sunt ut mihi non erepta L. Crasso a diis immortalibus vita sed donata mors esse videatur. Non vidit flagrantem bello Italiam, non ardentem invidia senatum, non sceleris nefarii principes civitatis reos, non luctum filiae, non exsilium generi, non acerbissimam C. Mari fugam, non illam post reditum eius caedem omnium crudelissimam, non denique in omni genere deformatam eam civitatem in qua ipse florentissima multum omnibus[1] praestitisset.

9 III. Sed quoniam attigi cogitatione vim varietatemque fortunae, non vagabitur oratio mea longius atque eis fere ipsis definietur viris qui hoc sermone quem referre suscepimus continentur. Quis enim non iure beatam L. Crassi mortem illam, quae est a multis saepe defleta, dixerit cum horum ipsorum sit qui tum cum illo postremum fere collocuti sunt eventum recordatus ? Tenemus enim memoria Q. Catulum virum omni laude praestantem, cum sibi non incolumem fortunam sed exsilium et fugam deprecaretur, esse coactum ut vita se ipse privaret. Iam

10 M. Antoni, in eis ipsis rostris in quibus ille rempublicam constantissime consul defenderat quaeque censor imperatoriis manubiis ornarat, positum caput illud fuit a quo erant multorum civium capita servata ; neque vero longe ab eo C. Iulii caput hospitis Etrusci

[1] *v.l.* omnibus gloria.

---

[a] See Introduction, vol. i. p. xiii.
[b] See *ibid.* p. xiv.

8

8 plans of life. This brought lamentation to his friends, sorrow to his country and regret to all good men ; but the national disasters that followed have been such as to make me feel that the powers above did not rob Lucius Crassus *a* of life but vouchsafed to him the gift of death. He did not see Italy ablaze with war, the Senate inflamed with passion, the leading citizens arraigned for a nefarious crime, his daughter's grief, her husband's exile, the utterly lamentable flight of Gaius Marius, the massacre unparalleled in savagery that followed his return, nor in fine the utter corruption in every respect of a country in which at the period of its supreme prosperity he had himself held by far the highest position.

9 III. But now that I have reached these reflections on the might and mutability of fortune, my discourse shall not roam further, but shall restrict itself for the most part to the actual persons figuring in the dialogue that we have undertaken to record. Many have often deplored the death of Lucius Crassus, but who will not be bound to pronounce it a happy end when he recalls the fate of these very persons who were in conversation with him almost for the last time on this occasion ! It remains in our memory that Quintus Catulus, *b* a man of eminent distinction, prayed to be granted not acquittal but exile and 10 flight, and then was forced to take his own life. Next Marcus Antonius, on the very platform on which as consul he had most resolutely championed the cause of the state and which as censor he had decorated with the trophies of his military command, laid down the life that had preserved the lives of many men ; and indeed at no great distance from that spot lay the head of Gaius Julius, betrayed by the crime of his

Fate of the other characters.

9

scelere proditum cum L. Iulii fratris capite iacuit,
ut ille, qui haec non vidit, et vixisse cum republica
pariter et cum illa simul exstinctus esse videatur.
Neque enim propinquum suum, maximi animi virum,
P. Crassum suapte interfectum manu neque collegae
sui pontificis maximi sanguine simulacrum Vestae
respersum esse vidit—cui maerori, qua mente ille in
patriam fuit, etiam C. Carbonis inimicissimi hominis
11 eodem illo die mors nefaria fuisset ; non vidit eorum
ipsorum qui tum adolescentes Crasso se dicarant
horribiles miserosque casus—ex quibus Cotta, quem
ille florentem reliquerat, paucis diebus post mortem
Crassi depulsus per invidiam tribunatu, non multis ab
eo tempore mensibus eiectus est e civitate ; Sulpicius
autem, qui in eadem invidiae flamma fuisset, quibuscum privatus coniunctissime vixerat hos in tribunatu spoliare instituit omni dignitate ; cui quidem
ad summam gloriam eloquentiae florescenti ferro
erepta vita est et poena temeritatis non sine magno
reipublicae malo constituta.
12   Ego vero te, Crasse, cum vitae flore, tum mortis
opportunitate divino consilio et ornatum[1] et exstinc-
tum esse arbitror ; nam tibi aut pro virtute animi
constantiaque tua civilis ferri subeunda fuit crude-
litas aut, si qua te fortuna ab atrocitate mortis vin-
dicasset, eadem esse te funerum patriae spectatorem
coegisset ; neque solum tibi improborum dominatus

---

[1] *v.l.* ortum.

Tuscan host, side by side with the head of his brother
Lucius Julius, so that Gaius, who did not witness
these events, may be deemed to have spent his life
with the republic still living and to have passed out of
existence together with her passing. For he did not
see his gallant kinsman Publius Crassus dispatched
by his own hand, nor Vesta's image splashed with the
blood of his colleague the chief pontiff—who patriot
as he was would have mourned the wicked murder on
the very same day of his bitter enemy Gaius Carbo
11 also ; he did not see the awful and pitiable disasters
that befell even the men who on that occasion had
pledged their youthful loyalty to Crassus—of whom
Cotta, whom he had left prosperous, owing to personal
animosity was a few days after the death of Crassus
expelled from his office of tribune, and a few months
later banished from the country ; while Sulpicius,
although he had been involved in the same outburst
of hatred, in his tribuneship set about robbing of
every honourable office the very persons with whom
before he rose to office he had associated on the closest
terms of intimacy ; yet he indeed, when just achieving the highest distinction in eloquence, lost his life
by the sword and met the penalty of his rashness, not
without great loss to the state.
12   But in my opinion, Crassus, both the brilliant life
vouchsafed to you and the timely death that ended
your career display the working of a wise providence ;
for either your courage and resolution would have
made you fall a victim to the cruel blade of civil war,
or else, if some chance had rescued you from an awful
death, that same chance would have forced you to be
a spectator of fatal blows dealt to your country ; and
you would have had to lament not only the domina-

sed etiam propter admixtam civium caedem bonorum
victoria maerori fuisset.

13 IV. Mihi quidem, Quinte frater, et eorum casus
de quibus ante dixi et ea quae nosmet ipsi ob amorem
in rempublicam incredibilem et singularem pertuli-
mus ac sensimus cogitanti sententia saepe tua vera
ac sapiens videri solet, qui propter tot, tantos, tamque
praecipites casus clarissimorum hominum atque op-
timorum virorum me semper ab omni contentione ac
14 dimicatione revocasti. Sed quoniam haec iam neque
in integro nobis esse possunt et summi labores nostri
magna compensati gloria mitigantur, pergamus ad
ea solatia quae non modo sedatis molestiis iucunda
sed etiam haerentibus salutaria nobis esse possunt,
sermonemque L. Crassi reliquum ac paene postremum memoriae prodamus, atque ei etsi nequa-
quam parem illius ingenio at pro nostro tamen studio
15 meritam gratiam debitamque referamus. Neque
enim quisquam nostrum, cum libros Platonis mira-
biliter scriptos legit in quibus omnibus fere Socrates
exprimitur, non, quanquam illa scripta sunt divinitus,
tamen maius quiddam de illo de quo scripta sunt
suspicatur; quod item nos postulamus non a te quidem qui nobis omnia summa tribuis sed a ceteris qui
haec in manus sument, ut maius quiddam de L.
Crasso quam quantum a nobis exprimetur suspicen-
16 tur. Nos enim, qui ipsi sermoni non interfuissemus

tion of the wicked but also the victory of the righteous, as it involved the massacre of your countrymen.

13   IV. For my own part, brother Quintus, when I think of the disasters of the persons I have spoken of before and also the reverses that an incredible and unparalleled patriotism has prompted me myself to undergo, I am often inclined to think that your judgement has been true and wise, when in view of all the violent and crushing disasters that have befallen persons of the highest distinction and men of superlative merit, you have constantly urged me to desist 14 from all controversy and competition. But as these matters can no longer be for me an issue still open, and as my efforts, intense as they were, have been lightened by the compensation of great renown, let me press forward to the consolations that have the capacity not only to delight me when my troubles are allayed, but also to cheer me while they still persist ; and let me place on record the remaining and almost the final discourse of Lucius Crassus, and repay him the gratitude due to his deserts, which if it by no means comes up to his genius yet is the best that my 15 devotion can achieve. In point of fact, when reading the admirable volumes of Plato, almost all of them containing a picture of Socrates, there is not one of us who, although they are works of genius, yet does not imagine something on a larger scale in regard to the personality that is their subject ; and I make a similar claim not indeed upon yourself, who pay me the highest possible consideration, but upon everybody else who takes this work into his hands, that he shall form a mental picture of Lucius Crassus on a 16 larger scale than the sketch that I shall draw. For I was not myself present at the conversation, and have

et quibus C. Cotta tantummodo locos ac sententias huius disputationis tradidisset, quo in genere orationis utrumque oratorem cognoveramus, id ipsum sumus in eorum sermone adumbrare conati ; quod si quis erit qui ductus opinione vulgi aut Antonium ieiuniorem aut Crassum pleniorem fuisse putet quam quomodo a nobis uterque inductus est, is erit ex eis qui aut illos non audierint aut iudicare non possint. Nam fuit uterque, ut exposui antea, cum studio atque ingenio et doctrina praestans omnibus, tum in suo genere perfectus, ut neque in Antonio deesset hic ornatus orationis neque in Crasso redundaret.

17 V. Ut igitur ante meridiem discesserunt paululumque requierunt, in primis hoc a se Cotta animadversum esse dicebat, omne illud tempus meridianum Crassum in acerrima atque attentissima cogitatione posuisse, seseque, qui vultum eius cum ei dicendum esset obtutumque oculorum in cogitando probe nosset atque in maximis causis saepe vidisset, tum dedita opera quiescentibus aliis in eam exhedram venisse in qua Crassus lectulo posito recubuisset, cumque eum in cogitatione defixum esse sensisset, statim recessisse, atque in eo silentio duas horas fere esse consumptas. Deinde cum omnes inclinato iam in pomeridianum tempus die venissent ad Crassum,

only received a report from Gaius Cotta of the general
lines of argument and opinions expressed in this
debate ; and it is just this that I have attempted to
indicate in the discourses of the two orators, merely
the class of oratory in which each of them was actually
known to me ; and if there is anybody who is led by
the popular belief to think that Antonius must have
employed a plainer style or Crassus a more abundant
one than each is represented by me as using, the
critic will belong to the class of people who either
never heard these orators or else lack the capacity to
judge them. For in point of fact each of them, as I
have before explained, not only exceeded everybody
else in devotion to oratory, in natural talent and also
in learning, but also was an absolute master in his own
class, so the oratorical embellishments in question
were neither wanting in the case of Antonius nor
superabundant in that of Crassus.

17   V. Accordingly, Cotta went on to say, after they   Debate
had separated before noon to take a brief siesta,   resumed
what he chiefly noticed was that Crassus devoted all   after siesta.
this midday interval to the closest and most careful
meditation ; and that as he was well acquainted with
the look he wore when he had to make a speech
and with the fixed gaze of his eyes when he was
meditating, and had often witnessed this in important
lawsuits, on the present occasion he was careful to
wait till the others were reposing, when he came to
the alcove where Crassus was reclining on a couch
placed there for him, and as he perceived that he was
buried deep in meditation, at once retired ; and that
almost two hours were spent in this manner without
a word being spoken. Later on, when afternoon had
begun, they all joined Crassus ; and Julius said,

15

Quid est, Crasse, inquit Iulius, imusne sessum ? etsi
admonitum venimus te, non flagitatum.

18 Tum Crassus : An me tam impudentem esse
existimatis ut vobis hoc praesertim munus putem
me[1] diutius posse debere ?

Quinam igitur, inquit ille, locus ? an in media
silva placet ? Est enim is maxime et opacus et
frigidus.

Sane, inquit Crassus, etenim est in eo loco sedes
huic nostro non inopportuna sermoni.

Cum placuisset idem ceteris, in silvam venitur et
ibi magna cum audiendi exspectatione considitur.

19 Tum Crassus : Cum auctoritas atque amicitia
vestra tum Antoni facilitas eripuit, inquit, mihi in
optima mea causa libertatem recusandi ; quanquam
in partienda disputatione nostra, cum sibi de eis quae
dici ab oratore oporteret sumeret, mihi autem relinqueret ut explicarem quemadmodum illa ornari oporteret, ea divisit quae seiuncta esse non possunt. Nam
cum omnis ex re atque verbis constet oratio, neque
verba sedem habere possunt si rem subtraxeris neque
20 res lumen si verba semoveris. Ac mihi quidem
veteres illi maius quiddam animo complexi, multo
plus etiam vidisse videntur quam quantum nostrorum
ingeniorum acies intueri potest, qui omnia haec, quae
supra et subter, unum esse et una vi atque[2] consen-
sione naturae constricta esse dixerunt. Nullum est

---

[1] me *add. Lambinus.*　　　　　　　　[2] *v.l.* atque una.

" How now, Crassus ?   Shall we resume our session ?
—though we only come to give you a reminder, not
to insist."

18   " Do you think me so devoid of shame " replied
Crassus, " as to consider it possible for me to withhold
this due of all dues from you any longer ? "

" Well then," said the other, " what is to be our
place of session ?   Would you like somewhere in the
middle of the plantation ?   There it is the shadiest
and coolest."

" Quite so," said Crassus, " in fact there is a seat in
the place you suggest that will not do badly for this
colloquy of ours."

The proposal was carried unanimously, and we went
into the plantation and took our seats there, all agog
to listen.

19   Thereupon Crassus said, " Your influence over me
and your friendship for me, no less than the prompt-
ness of Antonius, have deprived me of all excuse for
refusing the task, although I have an excellent case
for doing so ; all the same, when in arranging our
shares in the debate he took for himself the subject
of the proper topics of oratory and left it to me to
expound the proper method of embellishing them, he
separated from one another things that cannot really
stand apart.   Every speech consists of matter and
words, and the words cannot fall into place if you
remove the matter, nor can the matter have clarity

20 if you withdraw the words.   And in my own view the
great men of the past, having a wider mental grasp,
had also a far deeper insight than our mind's eye can
achieve, when they asserted that all this universe
above us and below is one single whole, and is held
together by a single force and harmony of nature ;

*Crassus
begins his
exposition:
style and
matter not
separable,
and
eloquence
a single art,
to whatever
subject
applied.*

17

enim genus rerum quod aut avulsum a ceteris per se ipsum constare aut quo cetera si careant, vim suam atque aeternitatem conservare possint.

21 VI. Sed si haec maior esse ratio videtur quam ut hominum possit sensu aut cogitatione comprehendi, est etiam illa Platonis vera et tibi, Catule, certe non inaudita vox. Omnem doctrinam harum ingenuarum et humanarum artium uno quodam societatis vinculo contineri : ubi enim perspecta vis est rationis eius qua causae rerum atque exitus cognoscuntur, mirus quidam omnium quasi consensus 22 doctrinarum concentusque reperitur. Sed si hoc quoque videtur esse altius quam ut id nos humi strati suspicere possimus, illud certe tamen quod amplexi sumus, quod profitemur, quod suscepimus, nosse et tenere debemus.

Una est enim, quod et ego hesterno die dixi et aliquot locis antemeridiano sermone significavit Antonius, eloquentia, quascumque in oras disputationis 23 regionesve delata est ; nam sive de caeli natura loquitur sive de terrae, sive de divina vi sive de humana, sive ex inferiore loco sive ex aequo sive ex superiore, sive ut impellat homines sive ut doceat sive ut deterreat sive ut concitet sive ut reflectat, sive ut incendat sive ut leniat, sive ad paucos sive ad multos, sive inter alienos sive cum suis sive secum, rivis est diducta oratio, non fontibus, et quocumque ingreditur eodem est instructu ornatuque comitata.

18

for there exists no class of things which can stand by itself, severed from the rest, or which the rest can dispense with and yet be able to preserve their own force and everlasting existence.

21   VI. " But if this appears to be too vast a theory for the senses or the thought of human beings to be able to grasp it, there is also the truth enunciated by Plato, which you, Catulus, have undoubtedly heard, that the whole of the content of the liberal and humane sciences is comprised within a single bond of union ; since, when we grasp the meaning of the theory that explains the causes and issues of things, we discover that a marvellous agreement and harmony underlies all branches of knowledge.

22 But if this truth also seems too lofty for the sight of us lowly earthlings to be able to rise to it, nevertheless it is unquestionably our duty to know and to hold to the system that we have embraced and profess and have undertaken to maintain.

   " For, as I said yesterday, and also Antonius indicated in some passages of his discourse this morning, eloquence is one, into whatever shores or realms of dis-

23 course it ranges. Whether its subject is the nature of the heavens or of the earth, the power of gods or men, whether it speaks from the well of the court or the floor of the house or from the bench or rostrum, whether its object is to move men to action or to instruct them or to deter them, to excite them or to curb them, to fire them or to calm them down, whether it be delivered to few or to many, among strangers or among friends or by oneself, the flow of language though running in different channels does not spring from different sources, and wherever it goes, the same supply of matter and equipment of

19

24 Sed quoniam oppressi iam sumus opinionibus non
modo vulgi verum etiam hominum leviter eruditorum, qui quae complecti tota nequeunt haec facilius divulsa et quasi discerpta contrectant, et qui
tanquam ab animo corpus sic a sententiis verba
seiungunt, quorum sine interitu fieri neutrum potest,
non suscipiam oratione mea plus quam mihi imponi-
tur : tantum significabo brevi, neque verborum
ornatum inveniri posse non partis[1] expressisque sententiis neque esse ullam sententiam illustrem sine
luce verborum.

25   Sed priusquam illa conor attingere quibus orationem ornari atque illuminari putem, proponam
breviter quid sentiam de universo genere dicendi.

VII. Natura nulla est, ut mihi videtur, quae non
habeat in suo genere res complures dissimiles inter
se, quae tamen consimili laude dignentur ; nam et
auribus multa percipimus quae etsi nos vocibus delectant tamen ita sunt varia saepe ut id quod proxi-
mum audias iucundissimum esse videatur ; et oculis
colliguntur paene innumerabiles voluptates quae nos
ita capiunt ut unum sensum in[2] dissimili genere
delectent ; et reliquos sensus voluptates oblectant
dispares, ut sit difficile iudicium excellentis maxime

26 suavitatis.   Atque[3] hoc idem quod est in naturis rerum transferri potest etiam ad artes.   Una fingendi

---

[1] *Lambinus :* partitis.   [2] in *add. Sorof.*
                    [3] *Kayser :* at.

24 style go with it. But as nowadays we are deluged not only with the notions of the vulgar but also with the opinions of the half-educated, who find it easier to deal with matters that they cannot grasp in their entirety if they split them up and take them piece-meal, and who separate words from thoughts as one might sever body from mind—and neither process can take place without disaster,—I will not under-take more in my speech than is placed upon me : I will only give briefly my opinion, that it is impossible to achieve an ornate style without first procuring ideas and putting them into shape, and at the same time that no idea can possess distinction without lucidity of style.

25 " But before attempting to deal with the qualities that seem to me to give ornament and brilliance to a discourse, I will briefly put forward my views on the subject of oratory as a whole.

VII. " Among natural objects, as it seems to me, there is none which does not comprise in its own kind a multiplicity of things that are different from one another and yet are esteemed as having a similar value : for instance, our ears convey to us a number of perceptions which, while consisting in sounds that give us pleasure, are nevertheless frequently so different from one another that you think the one you hear last the most agreeable ; also our eyes collect for us an almost countless number of pleasures, whose charm consists in their delighting a single sense in a variety of different ways ; and the rest of the senses enjoy gratifications of various kinds, making it diffi-
26 cult to decide which is the most agreeable. Moreover this observation in the sphere of natural objects can also be transferred to the arts as well. There is a

The senses receive different impressions and artists have different styles, but all may give pleasure ;

21

est ars, in qua praestantes fuerunt Myro, Polyclitus,
Lysippus, qui omnes inter se dissimiles fuerunt, sed
ita tamen ut neminem sui velis esse dissimilem. Una
est ars ratioque picturae, dissimillimique tamen inter
se Zeuxis, Aglaophon, Apelles, neque eorum quisquam est cui quidquam in arte sua deesse videatur.
Et si hoc in his quasi mutis artibus est mirandum et
tamen verum, quanto admirabilius in oratione atque
in lingua ! Quae cum in eisdem sententiis verbisque
versetur, summas habet dissimilitudines non sic ut
alii vituperandi sint, sed ut ei quos constet esse laudandos in dispari tamen genere laudentur.

27   Atque id primum in poetis cerni licet, quibus est
proxima cognatio cum oratoribus, quam sint inter
sese Ennius, Pacuvius Acciusque dissimiles ; quam
apud Graecos Aeschylus, Sophocles, Euripides, quanquam omnibus par paene laus in dissimili scribendi
gcncrc tribuatur.

28   Aspicite nunc eos homines atque intuemini
quorum de facultate quaerimus [quid intersit inter
oratorum studia atque naturas].[1] Suavitatem Isocrates, subtilitatem Lysias, acumen Hyperides, soni-
tum Aeschines, vim Demosthenes habuit : quis
eorum non egregius ? tamen quis cuiusquam nisi sui
similis ? Gravitatem Africanus, lenitatem Laelius,
asperitatem Galba, profluens quiddam habuit Carbo

[1] *secl. Kayser.*

---

[a] Presumably an interpolation.

single art of sculpture, in which eminence was
attained by Myron, Polyclitus and Lysippus, all of
whom were different from one another, yet without
the consequence of our desiring any one of them to
be different from what he was. There is a single art
and method of painting, and nevertheless there is an
extreme dissimilarity between Zeuxis, Aglaophon
and Apelles, while at the same time there is not one
among them who can be thought to lack any factor
in his art. And if this be surprising and nevertheless true in the case of what may be called the silent
arts, how much more remarkable it is in oratory and
in language ! This art is occupied with the same
supply of ideas and expressions, and yet it comprises
extreme dissimilarities—not in the sense that some
speakers deserve praise and others blame, but that
the ones admittedly deserving of praise nevertheless
achieve it in a variety of styles.

27 " This can in the first instance be observed in the
case of poetry, poets being the next of kin to orators ;
what a difference there is between Ennius, Pacuvius
and Accius, and in Greece between Aeschylus,
Sophocles and Euripides, although all of them win
almost equal applause in their various styles of
writing.

28 " Now turn your attention to consider the people
whose department we are investigating [the difference between the interests and the natures of
orators].[a] Isocrates had grace of style, Lysias precision, Hyperides penetration, Aeschines sonorous-
ness, Demosthenes force : which of them is not
eminent ? and yet which resembles anyone but himself ? Africanus had weight, Laelius smoothness,
Galba harshness, Carbo a kind of flow and melody :

similarly different styles of oratory may all be admirable.

et canorum : quis horum non princeps temporibus illis fuit ? et suo tamen quisque in genere princeps.

29 VIII. Sed quid ego vetera conquiram, cum mihi liceat uti praesentibus exemplis atque vivis ? Quid iucundius auribus nostris unquam accidit huius oratione Catuli ? quae est pura sic ut Latine loqui paene solus videatur, sic autem gravis ut in singulari dignitate omnis tamen adsit humanitas ac lepos. Quid multa ? istum audiens equidem sic iudicare soleo, quidquid aut addideris aut mutaveris aut detraxeris, vitiosius et deterius futurum.

30 Quid, noster hic Caesar nonne novam quamdam rationem attulit orationis et dicendi genus induxit prope singulare ? Quis unquam res praeter hunc tragicas paene comice,[1] tristes remisse, severas hilare, forenses scenica prope venustate tractavit, atque ita ut neque iocus magnitudine rerum excluderetur nec

31 gravitas facetiis minueretur ? Ecce praesentes duo prope aequales Sulpicius et Cotta : quid tam inter se dissimile ? quid tam in suo genere praestans ? Limatus alter et subtilis, rem explicans propriis aptisque verbis, haeret in causa semper et, quid iudici probandum sit cum acutissime vidit, omissis ceteris argumentis in eo mentem orationemque defigit, Sulpicius autem fortissimo quodam animi impetu, plenissima et maxima voce, summa contentione corporis et

---

[1] tragicas paene comice *secl. edd. nonnulli.*

---

[a] This doubtful compliment to the orator's style has been suspected to be an interpolation.

which of these in the old days was not eminent ? and yet each eminent in his own particular style.

29   VIII. " But why should I ransack past history for instances, when it is open to me to use examples living at the present day ?   What greater treat have our ears ever had than the eloquence of our friend Catulus ?   Its style is so pure that he seems almost the only person that speaks sound Latin, and while weighty, its unique dignity nevertheless includes complete urbanity and charm.   In brief, for my own part when listening to him my regular verdict is that any addition or alteration or subtraction you might make would be inferior—an alteration for the worse.

30   " Again, has not our friend Caesar here contributed quite a novel method of oratory and introduced a style that is almost unique ?   Whoever beside Caesar has handled tragic themes in a manner almost proper to comedy,[a] gloomy topics lightheartedly, severe ones cheerfully, and the business of the courts with a charm suggestive of the stage ? and this without allowing the importance of the subject to preclude a jest or the touches of humour to impair the dignity of

31   the style.   In present company, consider Sulpicius and Cotta, who stand almost on a level : what greater difference could there be between two orators, and yet what greater eminence in their respective styles ? The one accurate and precise, unfolding the matter in language appropriate and suitable to it—he always sticks to his brief, and having discerned with supreme acumen the point that has to be proved to the court, he lays all other matters on one side and rivets his thoughts and utterances to this ; Sulpicius on the other hand combines extreme boldness and energy, a very loud and resonant voice, and unrivalled vigour

25

dignitate motus, verborum quoque ea gravitate et
copia est ut unus ad dicendum instructissimus a
natura esse videatur.

32 IX. Ad nosmet ipsos iam revertor, quoniam sic
fuimus semper comparati ut hominum sermonibus
quasi in aliquod contentionis iudicium vocaremur :
quid tam dissimile quam ego in dicendo et Antonius ?
cum ille is sit orator ut nihil eo possit esse
praestantius, ego autem, quanquam memet mei
poenitet, cum hoc maxime tamen in comparatione
coniungar. Videtisne genus hoc quod sit Antoni ?
Forte, vehemens, commotum in agendo, praemuni-
tum et ex omni parte causae septum, acre, acutum,
enucleatum, in una[1] quaque re commorans, honeste
cedens, acriter insequens, terrens, supplicans, summa
orationis varietate, nulla nostrarum aurium satietate.

33 Nos autem, quicumque in dicendo sumus (quoniam
esse aliquo in numero vobis videmur), certe tamen
ab huius multum genere distamus ; quod quale sit
non est meum dicere, propterea quod minime sibi
quisque notus est et difficillime de se quisque sentit ;
sed tamen dissimilitudo intellegi potest et ex motus
mei mediocritate et ex eo quod, quibus vestigiis
primum institi, in eis fere soleo perorare, et quod
aliquanto me maior in verbis[2] eligendis quam eum
labo   cura torquet, verentem ne si paulo obsoletior

---

[1] *v.l.* in sua.
[2] in verbis quam in sententiis *codd.*, quam in sententiis
secl. Wilkins.

of bearing and dignity of gesture with a weight and flow of language that make us think him Nature's nonpareil of orators !

32 IX. " I now come back to ourselves, as comparison has so constantly been made between us that the talk of the town seemed to summon us to appear in competition before a court of critics. What two styles of oratory can be more unlike than mine and Antonius's ? although he is an orator of unsurpassable eminence, while I, although far from satisfied with my achievements, am nevertheless especially coupled with Antonius for comparison. Do you not see what this style of Antonius's is ? it is bold, vehement, vigorous in delivery, carefully prepared and safeguarded in respect of every aspect of the case, keen, penetrating, precise, dwelling upon each separate point, making courteous concessions and gallant onsets, intimidating, imploring, employing a vast variety of styles without
33 ever exhausting the appetite of the audience. I on the other hand, whatever my status as an orator may be—as you are pleased to deem me of some account—, nevertheless unquestionably stand at a wide distance removed from the class to which our friend here belongs ; what the nature of the difference may be, it is not my business to say, for the reason that everybody is very little acquainted with himself and has the greatest difficulty in forming an opinion about himself ; but nevertheless the dissimilarity can be inferred both from my moderation in the employment of action and my almost invariable practice of ending a speech standing exactly where I first took up my position, and from my being tormented by considerably more anxiety and trouble in regard to choice of vocabulary than he is, as I am afraid lest if I employ

fuerit oratio non digna exspectatione et silentio fuisse
34 videatur. Quod si in nobis qui adsumus tantae dissimilitudines sunt,[1] tam certae res cuiusque propriae,
et in ea varietate fere melius a deteriore facultate
magis quam genere distinguitur, atque omne laudatur quod in suo genere perfectum est, quid censetis
si omnes qui ubique sunt aut fuerunt oratores
amplecti voluerimus ? nonne fore ut quot oratores,
totidem paene reperiantur genera dicendi ?

Ex qua mea disputatione forsitan occurrat illud,
si paene innumerabiles sint quasi formae figuraeque
dicendi, specie dispares, genere laudabiles, non posse
ea quae inter se discrepant eisdem praeceptis atque
35 in una institutione formari. Quod non est ita, dili-
gentissimeque hoc est eis qui instituunt aliquos atque
erudiunt videndum quo sua quemque natura maxime
ferre videatur. Etenim videmus ex eodem quasi
ludo summorum in suo cuiusque genere artificum et
magistrorum exisse discipulos dissimiles inter se, attamen laudandos, cum ad cuiusque naturam insti-
36 tutio doctoris accommodaretur. Cuius est vel
maxime insigne illud exemplum (ut ceteras artes
omittamus) quod dicebat Isocrates doctor singularis
se calcaribus in Ephoro, contra autem in Theopompo
frenis uti solere : alterum enim exsultantem ver-

[1] sunt *add. Bakius.*

too old-fashioned a style my speech may be thought to have been unworthy of the hushed attention of
34 the audience. And if such wide differences exist between us who are present and each of us has such clearly marked characteristics, and if in this variety the superior is distinguished from the inferior almost more by capacity than by style, and everything is applauded that is perfect in its own style, what do you not suppose the result will be if we choose to take into consideration all the orators past and present of all countries ? do you not expect that we shall find almost as many styles of oratory as orators ?

"This assertion on my part may possibly suggest the objection that, if the ideal types of oratory, different in form but each in its own kind praiseworthy, are almost countless in number, it is impossible that things thus differing from one another should be regulated by the same rules and belong to
35 a single system. This is not the case, and it is the duty of professors who train pupils, to be most careful to observe the direction in which each seems to be specially carried by his own nature. For as a matter of fact we notice that pupils have emerged from the same school, kept by experts and masters of supreme eminence in their respective styles, who though quite unlike one another are yet worthy of commendation, in cases when the teacher's curriculum has been
36 adapted to the nature of the individual pupil. A most outstanding instance of this (to leave out the other systems) is the saying of the eminent professor Isocrates, that he made a practice of employing the spur with Ephorus and the bridle with Theopompus— meaning that he used to check the one's exuberance

29

borum audacia reprimebat, alterum cunctantem et quasi verecundantem incitabat. Neque eos similes effecit inter se, sed tantum alteri affinxit, de altero limavit, ut id conformaret in utroque quod utriusque natura pateretur.

37 X. Haec eo mihi praedicenda fuerunt ut, si non omnia quae proponerentur a me ad omnium vestrum studium et ad genus id quod quisque vestrum in dicendo probaret adhaerescerent, id a me genus exprimi sentiretis quod maxime mihi ipsi probaretur.

Ergo haec et agenda sunt ab oratore quae explicavit Antonius et dicenda quodam modo. Quinam igitur dicendi est modus melior—nam de actione post videro—quam ut Latine, ut plane, ut ornate, ut ad id quodcumque agetur apte congruenterque dica- 38 mus ? Atque eorum quidem quae duo prima dixi rationem non arbitror exspectari a me, puri dilucidique sermonis : neque enim conamur docere eum dicere qui loqui nesciat, nec sperare qui Latine non possit hunc ornate esse dicturum, neque vero qui non dicat quod intellegamus hunc posse quod admiremur dicere. Linquamus igitur haec, quae cognitionem habent facilem, usum necessarium : nam alterum traditur litteris doctrinaque puerili, alterum adhibetur ob eam causam ut intellegatur quid quisque dicat : quod videmus ita esse necessarium ut tamen eo minus 39 nihil esse possit. Sed omnis loquendi elegantia

and boldness of style and spur on the hesitation and diffidence of the other. Not that he turned them out like one another, but he grafted on to the one, and pruned away from the other, exactly the right amount to produce in each the configuration that the nature of each permitted.

37 X. " I had to make these prefatory observations, in order that, in case the considerations I put forward should not all be adapted to the taste of all of you and to the kind of oratory that you severally favour, you may understand that the kind I am describing is the one that I most approve of myself.

" Well then, it is the business of an orator both to argue the points that Antonius has enumerated and also to express them in a particular style. Now what better style of expression can there be—I will consider delivery later—than that our language should be correct, lucid, ornate and suitably appropriate to the particular matter under consideration ?

38 Now as to the two first-mentioned qualities, I do not suppose that I shall be expected to give an account of purity and lucidity of language, as it is not our task to teach oratory to a person who does not know the language, nor to hope that one who cannot speak correct Latin should speak ornately, nor yet that one who does not say something that we can understand can possibly say something that we shall admire. Let us therefore leave these qualities, which are easy to learn and indispensable ; for one of them is conveyed by books and by elementary education, and the other is employed for the purpose of making an individual's statements understood, which obviously while indispensable is at the same time the
39 merest minimum. But all correct choice of diction,

Four requisites of style for oratory (§§ 37-90) : (1) correct diction, (2) lucidity

quanquam expolitur scientia litterarum, tamen augetur legendis oratoribus et poetis. Sunt enim illi
veteres, qui ornare nondum poterant ea quae dicebant, omnes prope praeclare locuti : quorum sermone assuefacti qui erunt, ne cupientes quidem
poterunt loqui nisi Latine. Neque tamen erit utendum verbis eis quibus iam consuetudo nostra non
utitur, nisi quando ornandi causa, parce, quod osten-
dam ; sed usitatis ita poterit uti lectissimis ut utatur
is qui in veteribus erit scriptis studiose et multum
volutatus.

40 XI. Atque ut Latine loquamur non solum videndum est ut et verba efferamus ea quae nemo iure
reprehendat, et ea sic et casibus et temporibus et
genere et numero conservemus ut ne quid pertur-
batum ac discrepans aut praeposterum sit, sed etiam
lingua et spiritus et vocis sonus est ipse moderandus.

41 Nolo exprimi litteras putidius, nolo obscurari negle-
gentius ; nolo verba exiliter exanimata exire, nolo
inflata et quasi anhelata gravius. Nam de voce nondum ea dico quae sunt actionis, sed hoc quod mihi
cum sermone quasi coniunctum videtur : sunt enim
certa vitia quae nemo est quin effugere cupiat—
mollis vox aut muliebris aut quasi extra modum

42 absona atque absurda. Est autem vitium quod nonnulli de industria consectantur : rustica vox et agrestis quosdam delectat, quo magis antiquitatem, si

32

although it is formed by knowledge of literature, is nevertheless increased by reading the orators and poets ; for the old masters, who did not yet possess the ability to embellish their utterances, almost all of them had an eminently clear style, and those who have made themselves familiar with their language, will be unable to speak anything but good Latin, even if they want to. All the same they must not employ words that are no longer in customary use, except occasionally and sparingly, for the sake of decoration, as I will explain ; but one who has diligently steeped himself in the old writings while employing words in current usage will be able to employ the choicest among them.

40   XI. " And in order to speak correctly we must not Pronuncia tion. only be careful both to produce words that no one can justly object to and to arrange them in respect of cases, tenses, gender and number in such a manner that there may be no confusion and false concord or wrong order, but we must also regulate our tongue

41 and breath and actual tone of voice. I want neither excessive precision nor yet slackness in the pronunciation of the letters, neither faintness and feebleness nor yet excessive fullness and volume in the utterance of the words. For on the question of voice I am not yet speaking of points that concern delivery, but about a matter that seems to me to be connected with utterance as such : there are certain faults which everyone without exception desires to escape—a soft or effeminate tone of voice,

42 or one that is unmusical and out of tune. But there is one fault that some persons deliberately affect : certain people enjoy using a rustic countrified pronunciation, with the object that if their speech is in

ita sonet, eorum sermo retinere videatur : ut tuus,
Catule, sodalis L. Cotta gaudere mihi videtur gravitate linguae sonoque vocis agresti, et illud quod
loquitur priscum visum iri putat si plane fuerit rusti-
canum. Me autem tuus sonus et subtilitas ista
delectat—omitto verborum, quanquam est caput,
verum id affert ratio, docent litterae, confirmat consuetudo et legendi et loquendi—sed hanc dico suavitatem quae exit ex ore : quae quidem ut apud
Graecos Atticorum, sic in Latino sermone, huius

43 est urbis maxime propria : Athenis iam diu doctrina
ipsorum Atheniensium interiit, domicilium tantum in
illa urbe remanet studiorum quibus vacant cives,
peregrini fruuntur capti quodammodo nomine urbis
et auctoritate ; tamen eruditissimos homines Asia-
ticos quivis Atheniensis indoctus non verbis sed sono
vocis nec tam bene quam suaviter loquendo facile
superabit. Nostri minus student litteris quam
Latini ; tamen ex istis quos nostis urbanis, in quibus
minimum est litterarum, nemo est quin litteratis-
simum togatorum omnium Q. Valerium Soranum
lenitate vocis atque ipso oris pressu et sono facile
vincat.

44 XII. Quare cum sit quaedam certa vox Romani
generis urbisque propria, in qua nihil offendi, nihil

this tone it may seem to preserve a greater flavour of
antiquity ; just as your friend Lucius Cotta, Catulus,
appears to me to take pleasure in a heavy tone and
a rustic pronunciation, and thinks that what he says
will seem to have a flavour of the good old days
if it is downright countrified. I on the contrary
like your tone of voice and delicate precision—I do
not at the moment mean precision of language,
though that is of chief importance, but it is the
product of method, and learnt from literature, and
strengthened by practice in reading and in speaking,
—but I mean actual **charm** of utterance, a merit
which as among the Greeks it is peculiar to Attica
so in Latin speech is specially the attribute of this
43 city. At Athens erudition among the Athenians
themselves has long ago perished, and that city now
only continues to supply a lodging for studies from
which the citizens are entirely aloof, and which are
enjoyed by foreign visitors who are under the spell
of the city's name and authority ; nevertheless any
uneducated Athenian will easily surpass the most
cultivated Asiatics not in vocabulary but in tone
of voice, and not so much in the correctness as
in the charm of his way of speaking. Our citizens
study literature less than the people of Latium, and
yet there is not one of the fine gentlemen of your
acquaintance, virtually devoid as they are of literature, who does not easily beat Q. Valerius Soranus,
the most erudite *littérateur* of all who have the
Roman citizenship, in smoothness of voice and in
actual distinctness of pronunciation and tone.

44 XII. " Consequently as there is a particular accent
peculiar to the Roman race and to our city, involving
no possibility of stumbling or causing offence or
35

displicere, nihil animadverti possit, nihil sonare aut
olere peregrinum, hanc sequamur, neque solum rusti-
cam asperitatem sed etiam peregrinam insolentiam
45 fugere discamus. Equidem cum audio socrum meam
Laeliam—facilius enim mulieres incorruptam antiquitatem conservant, quod multorum sermonis ex-
pertes ea tenent semper quae prima didicerunt—sed
eam sic audio ut Plautum mihi aut Naevium videar
audire : sono ipso vocis ita recto et simplici est ut
nihil ostentationis aut imitationis afferre videatur; ex
quo sic locutum esse eius patrem iudico, sic maiores,
non aspere, ut ille quem dixi, non vaste, non rustice,
non hiulce, sed presse et aequabiliter et leniter.
46 Quare Cotta noster, cuius tu illa lata, Sulpici, nonnunquam imitaris ut iota litteram tollas et E plenis-
simum dicas, non mihi oratores antiquos sed messores
videtur imitari.

Hic cum arrisisset ipse Sulpicius, Sic agam vobiscum, inquit Crassus, ut, quoniam me loqui
voluistis, aliquid de vestris vitiis audiatis.

Utinam quidem ! inquit ille, id enim ipsum volumus, idque si feceris, multa, ut arbitror, hic hodie
vitia ponemus.

47 At enim non sine meo periculo, Crassus inquit,
possum, Sulpici, te reprehendere, quoniam Antonius
mihi te simillimum dixit sibi videri.

Tum ille : Tu vero, quod[1] monuit idem ut ea
quae in quoque maxima essent imitaremur : ex quo

---

[1] *Schütz :* Tum quod.

unpleasantness or objection, no note or flavour of
provincialism, let us make this accent our model, and
learn to avoid not only rustic roughness but also
45 provincial solecisms. For my own part when I hear
my wife's mother Laelia—since it is easier for women
to keep the old pronunciation unspoiled, as they do
not converse with a number of people and so always
retain the accents they heard first—well, I listen to
her with the feeling that I am listening to Plautus or
Naevius : the actual sound of her voice is so un-
affected and natural that she seems to introduce no
trace of display or affectation ; and I consequently
infer that that was how her father and her ancestors
used to speak—not harshly, like the person I mentioned, nor with a broad or countrified or jerky
pronunciation, but neatly and evenly and smoothly.
46 Consequently our friend Cotta, whose broad pronunciation referred to before [a] you occasionally copy,
Sulpicius, in dropping the letter I and substituting a
very full E, is in my opinion copying not the orators
of old days but the farm-labourers."

This made even Sulpicius laugh ; and Crassus went
on : "You gentlemen wanted me to speak, and so
I will deal with you in such a way as to let you hear
something about your own faults."

" I only hope we may ! " said the other, " as that
is just what we do want, and if you do so I am sure
we shall get rid of a lot of faults here to-day."

47   " All the same," said Crassus, " I can't find fault
with you without running some risk on my own
account, because Antonius said that in his view you
and I are extremely like one another."

" O yes you can," rejoined the other, " as he
advised us each to copy the other's strongest points,

vereor ne nihil sim tui nisi supplosionem pedis imi-
tatus et pauca quaedam verba et aliquem, si forte,
motum.

Ergo ista, inquit Crassus, quae habes a me
non reprehendo, ne me ipsum irrideam—sunt autem
ea multo et plura et maiora quam dicis ; quae
autem sunt aut tua plane aut imitatione ex aliquo
expressa, de his te, si qui me forte locus ad-
48 monuerit, commonebo. XIII. Praetereamus igitur
praecepta Latine loquendi, quae puerilis doctrina
tradit et subtilior cognitio ac ratio litterarum alit aut
consuetudo sermonis quotidiani ac domestici, libri
confirmant et lectio veterum oratorum et poetarum ;
neque vero in illo altero diutius commoremur, ut disputemus quibus rebus assequi possimus ut ea quae
49 dicamus intellegantur : Latine scilicet dicendo, verbis
usitatis ac proprie demonstrantibus ea quae significari ac declarari volemus sine ambiguo verbo aut
sermone, non nimis longa continuatione verborum,
non valde productis eis quae similitudinis causa ex
aliis rebus transferuntur, non discerptis sententiis,
non praeposteris temporibus, non confusis personis,
non perturbato ordine. Quid multa ? tam facilis est
tota res ut mihi permirum saepe videatur cum diffi-
cilius intellegatur quid patronus velit dicere quam si
50 ipse ille qui patronum adhibet de re sua diceret. Isti
enim qui ad nos causas deferunt ita nos plerumque

38

—which makes me afraid that I have copied nothing of yours except the stamp of the foot and a few turns of language, and possibly some gestures."

" Well then," said Crassus, " I won't find fault with the tricks in you that you have got from me, or my ridicule will fall on myself—and indeed these features are much more numerous and more marked than you say ; but, if some occasion happens to prompt me, I will enumerate the qualities that are either absolutely your own or that you have copied by imitation 48 from somebody else. XIII. Therefore let us pass over the rules of correct Latin style, which are imparted by education in boyhood and fostered by a more intensive and systematic study of literature, or else by the habit of daily conversation in the family circle, and confirmed by books and by reading the old orators and poets ; and do not let us linger any longer over the second topic either, to discuss by what means we can attain to ensuring that what we say 49 may be understood : obviously this will be by talking correct Latin, and employing words in customary use that indicate literally the meaning that we desire to be conveyed and made clear, without ambiguity of language or style, avoiding excessively long periodic structure, not spinning out metaphors drawn from other things, not breaking the structure of the sentences, not using the wrong tenses, not mixing up the persons, not perverting the order. In short, the whole affair is so easy that it often strikes me as astonishing when it is harder to understand the case as put by an advocate than it would be if the client who has retained him put his own case for himself. 50 In fact the members of the public who entrust their lawsuits to us usually give us such satisfactory

ipsi docent ut non desideres planius dici ; easdem
res autem simul ac Fufius aut vester aequalis Pomponius agere coepit, non aeque quid dicant nisi admodum attendi intellego : ita confusa est oratio, ita
perturbata nihil ut sit primum, nihil ut secundum,
tantaque insolentia ac turba verborum ut oratio, quae
lumen adhibere rebus debet, ea obscuritatem et
tenebras afferat atque ut quodam modo ipsi sibi in
51 dicendo obstrepere videantur.   Verum si placet, quoniam haec satis spero vobis quidem certe maiora
exspectantibus[1] molesta et putida videri, ad reliqua
aliquanto odiosiora pergamus.

XIV. Atqui vides, inquit Antonius, quam alias
res agamus, qui adduci possumus—de me enim
coniicio—relictis ut rebus omnibus te sectemur : ita
de horridis rebus nitida, de ieiunis plena, de pervul-
gatis nova quaedam est oratio tua !

52 Faciles enim, inquit, Antoni, partes eae fuerunt
duae quas modo percurri, vel potius paene prae-
terii, Latine loquendi planeque dicendi: reliquae
sunt magnae, implicatae, variae, graves, quibus
omnis admiratio ingeni, omnis laus eloquentiae continetur ; nemo enim unquam est oratorem quod
Latine loqueretur admiratus : si est aliter, irrident,
neque eum oratorem tantummodo sed hominem non
putant ; nemo extulit eum verbis qui ita dixisset ut

[1] *Reid ? :* certe maioribus.

instructions themselves that one could not want it to be put more clearly; whereas the moment Fufius or you gentlemen's contemporary Pomponius begins to plead, unless I pay fairly close attention I do not understand their meaning so well—their speeches are so muddled up and inverted that there is no head or tail to them, and they use such a flood of out-of-the-way words that oratory, the proper function of which is to throw light on the facts, only contributes additional darkness, and that they actually seem in a sort of way to be shouting themselves 51 down in their own speeches. But as I hope that you at all events who undoubtedly have higher requirements consider these tricks of style to be tiresome and in bad taste, please let us go on to the considerably more objectionable ones that remain."

XIV. "All the same," said Antonius, "you see how inattentive we are, when you are able to induce us —as I infer from my own case—to follow your discourse to the exclusion of everything else; so successful is your eloquence in giving charm to subjects that are unattractive, fullness to what is dry, and some degree of novelty to what is hackneyed."

52 "Yes, Antonius," he replied, "that is because the two departments I have just run through, or rather almost passed over, are quite easy—the subjects of correctness of style and lucidity; but the remaining ones are big matters, involved, shifting and difficult, and on them depends all success in winning credit for talent and applause for eloquence; for nobody ever admired an orator for correct grammar, they only laugh at him if his grammar is bad, and not only think him no orator but not even a human being; no one ever sang the praises of a speaker whose style

Value of oratory.

qui adessent intellegerent quid diceret, sed contemp-
53 sit eum qui minus id facere potuisset.   In quo igitur
homines exhorrescunt ? quem stupefacti dicentem
intuentur ? in quo exclamant ? quem deum, ut ita
dicam, inter homines putant ? Qui distincte, qui
explicate, qui abundanter, qui illuminate et rebus et
verbis dicunt, et in ipsa oratione quasi quemdam
numerum versumque conficiunt—id est quod dico
ornate.   Qui idem ita moderantur ut rerum, ut personarum dignitates ferunt, ei sunt in eo genere laudandi laudis quod ego aptum et congruens nomino.
54 Qui ita dicerent, eos negavit adhuc se vidisse Antonius, et eis hoc nomen dixit eloquentiae solis esse
tribuendum.   Quare omnes istos me auctore deridete
atque contemnite qui se horum qui nunc ita appellantur rhetorum praeceptis omnem oratoriam[1] vim
complexos esse arbitrantur, neque adhuc quam per-
sonam teneant aut quid profiteantur intellegere potuerunt.   Vero enim oratori quae sunt in hominum
vita, quandoquidem in ea versatur orator atque ea est
ei subiecta materies, omnia quaesita, audita, lecta,
55 disputata, tractata, agitata esse debent.   Est enim
eloquentia una quaedam de summis virtutibus—
quanquam sunt omnes virtutes aequales et pares,
sed tamen est specie[2] alia magis alia formosa et
illustris, sicut haec vis quae scientiam complexa re-

---

[1] *Bakius :* oratorum.
[2] *Kayser :* species.

succeeded in making his meaning intelligible to his
audience, but only despised one deficient in capacity
53 to do so. Who then is the man who gives people a
thrill? whom do they stare at in amazement when
he speaks? who is interrupted by applause? who
is thought to be so to say a god among men? It
is those whose speeches are clear, explicit and full,
perspicuous in matter and in language, and who in
the actual delivery achieve a sort of rhythm and
cadence—that is, those whose style is what I call
artistic. Those who manage this same artistry as
the relative importance of the facts and persons
concerned directs, deserve to be applauded on the
score of the sort of distinction that I designate appro-
54 priateness and suitability of style. Speakers of this
kind Antonius declared that he had never so far encountered, and he said that they were the only ones
that merit this title of eloquence. Consequently if
you take my advice you must treat with derision and
contempt all those persons who suppose that the rules
laid down by these rhetoricians, now so called, have
enabled them to compass the whole range of oratorical
power, but who have not so far succeeded in understanding what character they are appearing in or
what it is that they profess. For the genuine orator
must have investigated and heard and read and discussed and handled the whole of the
contents of the life of mankind, inasmuch as that is
the field of the orator's activity, the subject matter
55 of his study. For eloquence is one of the supreme
virtues—although all the virtues are equal and on a
par, but nevertheless one has more beauty and distinction in outward appearance than another, as is
the case with this faculty, which, after compassing

rum, sensa mentis et consilia sic verbis explicat ut eos
qui audiant quocumque incubuerit possit impellere ;
quae quo maior est vis, hoc est magis probitate
iungenda summaque prudentia ; quarum virtutum
expertibus si dicendi copiam tradiderimus, non eos
quidem oratores effecerimus, sed furentibus quaedam
56 arma dederimus. XV. Hanc, inquam, cogitandi pro-
nuntiandique rationem vimque dicendi veteres Graeci
sapientiam nominabant ; hinc illi Lycurgi, hinc
Pittaci, hinc Solones, atque ab hac similitudine Coruncanii nostri, Fabricii, Catones, Scipiones fuerunt,
non tam fortasse docti sed impetu mentis simili et
voluntate. Eadem autem alii prudentia sed consilio
ad vitae studia dispari quietem atque otium secuti,
ut Pythagoras, Democritus, Anaxagoras, a regendis
civitatibus totos se ad cognitionem rerum trans-
tulerunt : quae vita propter tranquillitatem et
propter ipsius scientiae suavitatem, qua nihil est
hominibus iucundius, plures quam utile fuit rebus
57 publicis delectavit. Itaque ut ei studio se excel-
lentissimis ingeniis homines dediderunt, ex ea summa
facultate vacui ac liberi temporis, multo plura quam
erat necesse doctissimi homines otio nimio et ingeniis

44

a knowledge of facts, gives verbal expression to
the thoughts and purposes of the mind in such a
manner as to have the power of driving the hearers
forward in any direction in which it has applied its
weight; and the stronger this faculty is, the more
necessary it is for it to be combined with integrity
and supreme wisdom, and if we bestow fluency of
speech on persons devoid of those virtues, we shall
not have made orators of them but shall have put
56 weapons into the hands of madmen. XV. This
method of attaining and of expressing thought, this
faculty of speaking, was, I say, designated by the
ancient Greeks wisdom; this was the source that
produced men like Lycurgus and Pittacus and Solon
of old, and after their likeness came the Coruncanii
and Fabricii, the Catos and Scipios of Rome, not so
much perhaps as the result of instruction but owing
to a similarity of intention and of will. Others again
with the same wisdom but a different principle as
to life's purposes pursued tranquillity and leisure—
for instance Pythagoras, Democritus and Anaxagoras, and these abandoned the sphere of government and gave themselves entirely to study; and
owing to its tranquillity and to the intrinsic attract-
iveness of knowledge, which is the sweetest of
human pleasures, this life of study laid its charm on a
larger number of persons than was advantageous to
57 the commonwealth. Consequently when men of outstanding intellectual ability devoted themselves to
this pursuit, as a result of this unlimited command of
unoccupied free time, persons of very great learning,
being supplied with over-abundant leisure and extreme fertility of intellect, formed the opinion that
it was their duty to devote themselves to the pursuit

Relation of oratory to philo-sophy.

uberrimis affluentes curanda sibi esse ac quaerenda
et investiganda duxerunt. Nam vetus quidem illa
doctrina eadem videtur et recte faciendi et bene
dicendi magistra, neque disiuncti doctores sed eidem
erant vivendi praeceptores atque dicendi : ut ille
apud Homerum Phoenix qui se a Peleo patre Achilli
iuveni comitem esse datum dicit ad bellum ut illum
efficeret ' oratorem verborum actoremque rerum.'
58 Sed ut homines labore assiduo et quotidiano assueti,
cum tempestatis causa opere prohibentur, ad pilam
se aut ad talos aut ad tesseras conferunt aut etiam
novum sibi aliquem excogitant in otio ludum, sic illi
a negotiis publicis tanquam ab opere aut temporibus
exclusi aut voluntate sua feriati totos se alii ad poetas,
alii ad geometras, alii ad musicos contulerunt, alii
etiam ut dialectici novum sibi ipsi studium ludumque
pepererunt atque in eis artibus quae repertae sunt
ut puerorum mentes ad humanitatem fingerentur
atque virtutem omne tempus atque aetates suas
59 consumpserunt. XVI. Sed quod erant quidam eique
multi qui aut in republica propter ancipitem quae
non potest esse seiuncta faciendi dicendique sapientiam florerent, ut Themistocles, ut Pericles, ut Theramenes, aut qui minus ipsi in republica versarentur
sed huius tamen eiusdem sapientiae doctores essent,
ut Gorgias, Thrasymachus, Isocrates, inventi sunt

---

[a] *Il.* ix. 443 μύθων τε ῥητῆρ' ἐμέναι πρακτῆρά τε ἔργων.

of far more numerous lines of investigation than was really necessary. For in old days at all events the same system of instruction seems to have imparted education both in right conduct and in good speech ; nor were the professors in two separate groups, but the same masters gave instruction both in ethics and in rhetoric, for instance the great Phoenix in Homer, who says that he was assigned to the young Achilles by his father Peleus to accompany him to the wars in order to make him 'an orator and man of action too.' [a]

58 But just as persons usually engaged in constant daily employment, when debarred from work because of the weather, betake themselves to tennis or gambling or dicing or even devise for themselves some novel game to occupy their leisure, so when the persons in question have been debarred from their work of politics by the circumstances of the time or have chosen to take a vacation, some of them have devoted themselves entirely to poetry, others to mathematics and others to music, and others also have created for themselves a new interest and amusement as dialecticians, and have spent the whole of their time and their lives in the sciences that were invented for the purpose of moulding the minds of the young on

59 the lines of culture and of virtue. XVI. But as there have been certain persons and those a considerable number who either held a high position on account of their twofold wisdom, as men of action and as orators—two careers that are inseparable—, for instance Themistocles and Pericles and Theramenes, or other persons who were not themselves so much engaged in public life but were professional teachers of this same wisdom, for instance Gorgias, Thrasymachus, Isocrates, persons have been found who

47

qui cum ipsi doctrina et ingeniis abundarent, a re
autem civili et a negotiis animi quodam iudicio abhor-
rerent, hanc dicendi exercitationem exagitarent
60 atque contemnerent. Quorum princeps Socrates fuit,
is qui omnium eruditorum testimonio totiusque
iudicio Graeciae cum prudentia et acumine et venustate et subtilitate, tum vero eloquentia, varietate,
copia quam se cumque in partem dedisset omnium fuit
facile princeps ; is eis qui haec quae nos nunc quaerimus tractarent, agerent, docerent, cum nomine
appellarentur uno quod omnis rerum optimarum
cognitio atque in eis exercitatio philosophia nomi-
naretur, hoc commune nomen eripuit, sapienterque
sentiendi et ornate dicendi scientiam re cohaerentes
disputationibus suis separavit ; cuius ingenium vari-
osque sermones immortalitati scriptis suis Plato
tradidit, cum ipse litteram Socrates nullam reliquisset.
61 Hinc discidium illud exstitit quasi linguae atque
cordis, absurdum sane et inutile et reprehendendum,
ut alii nos sapere, alii dicere docerent. Nam cum
essent plures orti fere a Socrate, quod ex illius variis
et diversis et in omnem partem diffusis disputationibus alius aliud apprehenderat, proseminatae
sunt quasi familiae dissentientes inter se et multum
disiunctae et dispares, cum tamen omnes se philosophi
Socraticos et dici vellent et esse arbitrarentur.
48

being themselves copiously furnished with learning and with talent, but yet shrinking on deliberate principle from politics and affairs, scouted and scorned 60 this practice of oratory. The chief of these was Socrates, the person who on the evidence of all men of learning and the verdict of the whole of Greece, owing not only to his wisdom and penetration and charm and subtlety but also to his eloquence and variety and fertility easily came out top whatever side in a debate he took up ; and whereas the persons engaged in handling and pursuing and teaching the subjects that we are now investigating were designated by a single title, the whole study and practice of the liberal sciences being entitled philosophy, Socrates robbed them of this general designation, and in his discussions separated the science of wise thinking from that of elegant speaking, though in reality they are closely linked together ; and the genius and varied discourses of Socrates have been immortally enshrined in the compositions of Plato, Socrates himself not having left a single scrap of writing. 61 This is the source from which has sprung the undoubtedly absurd and unprofitable and reprehensible severance between the tongue and the brain, leading to our having one set of professors to teach us to think and another to teach us to speak. For because of the plurality of schools that virtually sprang from Socrates, owing to the fact that out of his various and diverse discussions, ranging in every direction, one pupil had picked up one doctrine and another another, there were engendered families at discord with one another and widely separated and unlike, although all philosophers claimed and sincerely claimed the title of followers of Socrates.

49

62 XVII. Ac primo ab ipso Platone Aristoteles et
Xenocrates, quorum alter Peripateticorum, alter
Academiae nomen obtinuit; deinde ab Antisthene,
qui patientiam et duritiam in Socratico sermone
maxime adamarat, Cynici primum, deinde Stoici;
tum ab Aristippo, quem illae magis voluptariae disputationes delectarant, Cyrenaica philosophia mana-
vit quam ille et eius posteri simpliciter defenderunt:
ei qui nunc voluptate omnia metiuntur, dum vere-
cundius id agunt, nec dignitati satisfaciunt quam
non aspernantur nec voluptatem tuentur quam am-
plexari volunt. Fuerunt etiam alia genera philosophorum qui se omnes fere Socraticos esse dicerent,
Eretricorum, Erilliorum, Megaricorum, Pyrrhone-
orum, sed ea horum vi et disputationibus sunt iam diu
63 fracta et exstincta. Ex illis autem quae remanent
ea philosophia quae suscepit patrocinium voluptatis,
etsi cui vera videatur, procul abest tamen ab eo viro
quem quaerimus et quem auctorem publici consilii
et regendae civitatis ducem et sententiae atque
eloquentiae principem in senatu, in populo, in causis
publicis esse volumus. Nec ulla tamen ei philosophiae
fiet iniuria a nobis; non enim repelletur inde quo
aggredi cupiet,[1] sed in hortulis quiescet suis ubi vult,
ubi etiam recubans molliter ac delicate nos avocat

---

[1] ⟨non⟩ cupiet *Matthiae.*

62   XVII. " And in the first place from Plato himself
sprang Aristotle and Xenophon, on one of whom was
bestowed the name of the Peripatetic School and on
the other that of the Academy ; and next from
Antisthenes, who in the Socratic discourse had been
captivated chiefly by the ideal of endurance and
hardness, came first the Cynics and next the Stoics ;
and then from Aristippus, who had taken delight
rather in the Socratic discussions on the subject of
pleasure, was derived the Cyrenaic philosophy, which
Aristippus and his successors maintained without
modification, whereas the contemporary thinkers that
make pleasure the sole standard of value, in doing so
with greater modesty neither satisfy the claims of
virtue, which they do not despise, nor successfully
defend pleasure, which they wish to embrace.   There
have also been other groups of philosophers who
almost all professed to be followers of Socrates, the
Eretrians, the pupils of Erillus, the Megareans, the
school of Pyrrho, but these have long ago been routed
out of existence by the forceful arguments of the
63 aforesaid schools.   But from among the systems still
surviving, the philosophy that has undertaken the
championship of pleasure, although some may accept
it as true, is nevertheless quite remote from the man
whom we are seeking and whom we wish to be
the political leader of the nation, guiding the government and pre-eminent for wisdom and eloquence in
the Senate, in the assembly of the people and in
public causes.   And nevertheless no wrong will be
done to that philosophy by us, for we shall not be de-
barring it from a position that it aspires to occupy,
but it will be reposing where it wishes to be, in its own
charming gardens, where moreover as it reclines it

51

a rostris, a iudiciis, a curia, fortasse sapienter, hac
64 praesertim republica. Verum ego non quaero nunc
quae sit philosophia verissima sed quae oratori coniuncta maxime. Quare istos sine ulla contumelia
dimittamus, sunt enim et boni viri et, quoniam sibi
ita videntur, beati, tantumque eos admoneamus ut
illud, etiam si sit verissimum, tacitum tamen tanquam mysterium teneant, quod negant versari in
republica esse sapientis : nam si hoc nobis atque
optimo cuique persuaserint, non poterunt ipsi esse,
id quod maxime cupiunt, otiosi.

65　XVIII. Stoicos autem, quos minime improbo, di-
mitto tamen, nec eos iratos vereor quoniam omnino
irasci nesciunt, atque hanc eis habeo gratiam, quod
soli ex omnibus eloquentiam virtutem ac sapientiam
esse dixerunt. Sed nimirum[1] est in his quod ab hoc
quem instruimus oratore valde abhorreat : vel quod
omnes qui sapientes non sint servos, latrones, hostes,
insanos esse dicunt, neque tamen quemquam esse
sapientem—valde autem est absurdum ei concionem
aut senatum aut ullum coetum hominum committere
cui nemo illorum qui adsint sanus, nemo civis, nemo
66 liber esse videatur. Accedit quod orationis etiam
genus habent fortasse subtile et certe acutum, sed,
ut in oratore, exile, inusitatum, abhorrens ab auribus
vulgi, obscurum, inane, ieiunum, attamen eius modi

[1] *v.l.* sed utrumque : sed utcunque est *Ellendt.*

gently and tactfully appeals to us to abandon the platform and the courts and parliament,—perhaps a wise invitation, particularly in the present state of public 64 affairs. However for my part my present inquiry is not which system of philosophy is the truest but which is the most fully akin to the orator. Consequently let us dismiss the masters in question, without any derogatory comment, as they are excellent fellows and happy in their belief in their own happiness, and only let us warn them to keep to themselves as a holy secret, though it may be extremely true, their doctrine that it is not the business of a wise man to take part in politics—for if they convince us and all our best men of the truth of this they themselves will not be able to live the life of leisure which is their ideal.

65 XVIII. " Moreover, the Stoics, of whom I by no means disapprove, I nevertheless dismiss—and I do not fear their anger, because anger is quite unknown to them, and I am grateful to them for being the only one of all the schools that has pronounced eloquence to be a virtue and a form of wisdom. But clearly there is something in them that is quite out of keeping with the orator whom we are depicting: in the first place their assertion that all those who are not wise are slaves, brigands, enemies, madmen, and that all the same nobody is wise—yet it would be the height of folly to place a public meeting or the Senate or any assembly of people under the direction of a person who holds the view that not one of those 66 present is sane, or a citizen, or a free man. There is the further point that even the style of their discourse, though possibly subtle and undoubtedly penetrating, yet for an orator is bald, unfamiliar, jarring on the ear of the public, devoid of clarity, fullness

quo uti ad vulgus nullo modo possit ; alia enim et
bona et mala videntur Stoicis et ceteris civibus vel
potius gentibus, alia vis ' honoris,' ' ignominiae,'
' praemii,' ' supplicii '—vere an secus nihil ad hoc
tempus, sed ea si sequamur, nullam unquam rem
dicendo expedire possimus.

67   Reliqui sunt Peripatetici et Academici, quanquam
Academicorum nomen est unum, sententiae duae.
Nam Speusippus Platonis sororis filius et Xenocrates qui Platonem audierat et qui Xenocratem
Polemo et Crantor nihil ab Aristotele, qui una
audierat Platonem, magnopere dissenserunt,[1] copia
fortasse et varietate dicendi pares non fuerunt ;
Arcesilas primum qui Polemonem audierat ex variis
Platonis libris sermonibusque Socraticis hoc maxime arripuit, nihil esse certi quod aut sensibus aut
animo percipi possit ; quem ferunt eximio quodam
usu lepore dicendi aspernatum esse omne animi
sensusque iudicium primumque instituisse—quanquam id fuit Socraticum maxime—non quid ipse
sentiret ostendere sed contra id quod quisque se
68 sentire dixisset disputare.   Hinc haec recentior Academia emanavit, in qua exstitit divina quadam celeri-
tate ingenii dicendique copia Carneades ; cuius ego
etsi multos auditores cognovi Athenis, tamen auctores certissimos laudare possum et socerum meum

---

[1] *Lambinus :* dissensit.

and spirit, while at the same time of a character that makes it quite impossible to employ it in public speaking; for the Stoics hold a different view of good and bad from all their fellow-citizens or rather from all other nations, and give a different meaning to 'honour,' 'disgrace,' 'reward,' 'punishment'—whether correctly or otherwise does not concern us now, but if we were to adopt their terminology, we should never be able to express our meaning intelligibly about anything.

67 "There remain the Peripatetics and the Academics, though the latter are really two schools of thought under one name. For Plato's nephew Speusippus and his pupil Xenocrates and Xenocrates' pupils Polemo and Crantor did not seriously disagree on any point of opinion from Aristotle, their fellow-pupil under Plato, although possibly they were not his equals in fullness and variety of style; whereas Polemo's pupil Arcesilas, to begin with, selected for adoption from the various writings of Plato and the Socratic dialogues the dogma that nothing can be apprehended with certainty either by the senses or by the mind; and he is said to have employed a remarkably attractive style of discourse in rejecting mental and sensory judgement entirely and to have initiated the practice—an entirely Socratic one it is true—of not stating his own opinion but arguing against the

68 opinions put forward by everyone else. From this source descended the more recent Academy of our day, in which the almost inspired intellectual acumen and rhetorical fluency of Carneades have made him the leading figure; and though at Athens I got to know a number of his pupils, I myself nevertheless can recommend as entirely reliable authorities my

c   55

Scaevolam qui eum Romae audivit adolescens et
Q. Metellum L. filium familiarem meum, clarissimum virum, qui illum a se adolescente Athenis iam
affectum senectute multos dies auditum esse dicebat.

69   XIX. Haec autem, ut ex Apennino fluminum,
sic ex communi sapientium iugo sunt doctrinarum
facta divortia, ut philosophi tanquam in superum
mare[1] defluerent Graecum quoddam et portuosum,
oratores autem in inferum hoc Tuscum et barbarum,
scopulosum atque infestum, laberentur, in quo etiam
70 ipse Ulysses errasset. Quare si hac eloquentia atque hoc oratore contenti sumus qui sciat aut negare
oportere quod arguare aut si id non possis tum
ostendere quod is fecerit qui insimuletur aut recte
factum aut alterius culpa aut iniuria aut ex lege aut
non contra legem aut imprudentia aut necessario,
aut non eo nomine usurpandum quo arguatur, aut
non ita agi ut debuerit ac licuerit ; et, si satis esse
putatis ea quae isti scriptores artis docent discere,
quae multo tamen ornatius quam ab illis dicuntur
et uberius explicavit Antonius—sed, si his contenti
estis atque eis etiam quae dici voluistis a me, ex
ingenti quodam oratorem immensoque campo in
71 exiguum sane gyrum compellitis. Sin veterem illum
Periclem aut hunc etiam, qui familiarior nobis propter
scriptorum multitudinem est, Demosthenem sequi

----

[1] *Kayser :* mare Ionium.

----

father-in-law Scaevola, who in his youth heard
Carneades at Rome, and my friend the distinguished
Quintus Metellus, son of Lucius, who used to say that
as a young man he heard him on many occasions at
Athens when he was already showing signs of age.

69   XIX. " However, the streams of learning flowing *Eloquence*
from the common watershed of wisdom, as rivers do *needs more*
than
from the Apennines, divided in two, the philosophers *rhetorical*
theory.
flowing down into the entirely Greek waters of the
Eastern Mediterranean with its plentiful supply of
harbours, while the orators glided into the rocky and
inhospitable Western seas of our outlandish Tuscany,

70   where even Ulysses himself lost his bearings.   Consequently if we are contented with this degree of
eloquence, and with the orator who knows that one
must either deny the charge brought against one,
or if one cannot do that then prove that the action
of the accused party was either a right action, or due
to someone else's fault or transgression, or legal, or
not illegal, or inadvertent, or inevitable, or incorrectly
designated in the charge, or that the proceedings
being taken are irregular and illegal ; and if you
people think it sufficient to learn the instructions
drawn up by your writers on the science of rhetoric,
instructions nevertheless that have been expounded [a]
by Antonius in a much more graceful and more
copious form than they are enunciated by the authors
in question—well, if you are content with these rules
and also the ones you have desired me to state, you
are making the orator abandon a vast, immeasurable
plain and confine himself to quite a narrow circle.

1 If on the other hand you chose to follow the famous
Pericles of old, or even our friend Demosthenes with
whom his many writings have made us better ac-

vultis et si illam praeclaram et eximiam speciem
oratoris perfecti et pulchritudinem adamastis, aut
vobis haec Carneadia aut illa Aristotelia vis compre-
72 hendenda est. Namque, ut ante dixi, veteres illi
usque ad Socratem omnem omnium rerum quae ad
mores hominum, quae ad vitam, quae ad virtutem,
quae ad rempublicam pertinebant cognitionem et
scientiam cum dicendi ratione iungebant ; postea
dissociati, ut exposui, a Socrate[1] et deinceps a
Socraticis item omnibus, philosophi eloquentiam
despexerunt, oratores sapientiam, neque quidquam
ex alterius parte tetigerunt nisi quod illi ab his aut
ab illis hi mutuarentur ; ex quo promiscue haurirent
73 si manere in pristina communione voluissent. Sed
ut pontifices veteres propter sacrificiorum multitudinem tres viros epulones esse voluerunt, cum
essent ipsi a Numa ut etiam illud ludorum epulare
sacrificium facerent instituti, sic Socratici a se causarum actores et a communi philosophiae nomine
separaverunt, cum veteres dicendi et intellegendi
mirificam societatem esse voluissent.
74   XX. Quae cum ita sint, paululum equidem de me
deprecabor, et petam a vobis ut ea quae dicam non
de memet ipso sed de oratore dicere putetis. Ego
enim sum is qui cum summo studio patris in pueritia

_____
[1] *Müller :* Socrate diserti a doctis.

CAMROSE LUTHERAN COLLEGE
LIBRARY

quainted, and if you have grown to love that glorious
and supreme ideal, that thing of beauty, the perfect
orator, you are bound to accept either the modern
dialectic of Carneades or the earlier method of
72 Aristotle. For, as I said before, the older masters
down to Socrates used to combine with their theory
of rhetoric the whole of the study and the science
of everything that concerns morals and conduct and
ethics and politics ; it was subsequently, as I have
explained, that the two groups of students were
separated from one another, by Socrates and then
similarly by all the Socratic schools, and the philosophers looked down on eloquence and the orators
on wisdom, and never touched anything from the side
of the other study except what this group borrowed
from that one, or that one from this ; whereas they
would have drawn from the common supply indiffer-
ently if they had been willing to remain in the partner-
73 ship of early days. But just as the old pontiffs owing
to the vast number of sacrifices decided to have
a Banquet Committee of three members, though
they had themselves been appointed by Numa for
the purpose among others of holding the great
Sacrificial Banquet of the Games, so the followers of
Socrates cut connexion with the practising lawyers
and detached these from the common title of philosophy, although the old masters had intended there
to be a marvellously close alliance between oratory
and philosophy.

4 XX. " This being so, I will enter a brief plea on my
own behalf, and will beg you to believe that what
I say is not said about myself personally but about
the orator as such. For I myself am a person who,
having been given by my father an extremely careful

*Value of
oratory
resumed :
the orator
needs wide
culture;*

doctus essem et in forum ingenii tantum quantum ipse
sentio, non tantum quantum[1] forsitan vobis videar
detulissem, non possim dicere me haec quae nunc
complector perinde ut dicam discenda esse didicisse :
quippe qui omnium maturrime ad publicas causas
accesserim annosque natus unum et viginti nobilis-
simum hominem et eloquentissimum in iudicium
vocarim—cui disciplina fuerit forum, magister usus
et leges et instituta populi Romani mosque maiorum.
75 Paulum sitiens istarum artium de quibus loquor gus-
tavi, quaestor in Asia cum essem, aequalem fere
meum ex Academia rhetorem nactus Metrodorum
illum de cuius memoria commemoravit Antonius ;
et inde decedens Athenis, ubi ego diutius essem mora-
tus nisi Atheniensibus quod mysteria non referrent
ad quae biduo serius veneram succensuissem ; quare
hoc quod complector tantam scientiam vimque doctrinae non modo non pro me sed contra me est potius
—non enim quid ego sed quid orator possit disputo—
atque hos omnes qui artes rhetoricas exponunt per-
ridiculos ; scribunt enim de litium genere et de prin-
76 cipiis et de narrationibus ; illa vis autem eloquentiae
tanta est ut omnium rerum, virtutum, officiorum

[1] *Ernesti :* quantum ipse.

[a] C. Carbo, see Book I, § 40.
[b] Book II, § 360.

education in my youth, and having brought into
public life an amount of talent of which I am myself
conscious, although not the amount with which you
perhaps credit me, cannot assert that I pursued the
studies with which I am now dealing exactly in the
manner in which I am going to say they ought to
be pursued : inasmuch as I came forward as a public
advocate at an extremely early age, and when only
one and twenty conducted the impeachment of a
very eloquent and very distinguished man,[a]—in fact
public life was my education, and practical experience of the laws and institutions of the state and the
75 custom of the country was my schoolmaster. Though
thirsty for those accomplishments of yours of which
I am speaking I had only a small taste of them, having
during my quaestorship in Asia secured the services
of a professor of rhetoric from the Academy, a person
of about the same age as myself, the great Metrodorus whose memory Antonius recalled[b] ; and also
on my way home from Asia, at Athens, where I
should have made a longer stay if I had not been so
angry with the authorities there for refusing to repeat
the celebration of the mysteries, for which I had
arrived two days late ; and consequently the fact
that I include in my treatment this extensive and
important field of learning is not only not in my
favour but rather tells against me—for my subject
is not what I myself can achieve but what the
orator as such can—and against these exponents of
the science of rhetoric, who are exceedingly foolish
persons, as they only write about the classification
of cases and the elementary rules and the methods
76 of stating the facts ; whereas eloquence is so potent
a force that it embraces the origin and operation and

omnisque naturae quae mores hominum, quae animos,
quae vitam continet originem, vim mutationesque
teneat, eadem mores, leges, iura describat, rempublicam regat, omniaque ad quamcumque rem per-
77 tineant ornate copioseque dicat. In quo genere nos
quidem versamur tantum quantum possumus, quantum ingenio, quantum mediocri doctrina, quantum
usu valemus; neque tamen istis qui in una philosophia quasi tabernaculum vitae suae collocarunt
multum sane in disputatione concedimus.

78 XXI. Quid enim meus familiaris C. Velleius
afferre potest quam ob rem voluptas sit summum
bonum, quod ego non copiosius possim vel tutari si
velim vel refellere ex illis locis quos exposuit Antonius,
hac dicendi exercitatione in qua Velleius est rudis,
unusquisque nostrum versatus? Quid est quod aut
Sext. Pompeius aut duo Balbi aut meus amicus qui
cum Panaetio vixit M. Vigellius de virtute hominum[1]
Stoici possint dicere, qua in disputatione ego his
79 debeam aut vestrum quisquam concedere? Non est
enim philosophia similis artium reliquarum: nam
quid faciet in geometria qui non didicerit? quid in
musicis? aut taceat oportebit aut ne sanus quidem
iudicetur; haec vero quae sunt in philosophia ingeniis
eruuntur ad id quod in quoque verisimile est elicien-
dum acutis atque acribus eaque exercitata oratione
poliuntur. Hic noster vulgaris orator, si minus erit

---

[1] *v.l.* homines : [hominum Stoici] *Kayser.*

developments of all things, all the virtues and duties, all the natural principles governing the morals and minds and life of mankind, and also determines their customs and laws and rights, and controls the government of the state, and expresses everything that concerns whatever topic in a graceful and flowing style.
77 In this field I for my part occupy myself to the best of my ability, and with such capacity as is supplied me by my natural talents, my limited studies and my practical experience ; though all the same I really do not yield much ground in debate to those who have pitched their camp for their lifetime solely in this province of philosophy.

78 XXI. " For what proof can our friend Gaius Velleius bring to show that pleasure is the chief good, which I on my side am not able with greater fertility either to maintain if I choose or to rebut, by drawing on the arguments set out by Antonius, thanks to this practice in oratory in which Velleius is a tiro but every one of us an expert ? For what is there that can be said on the subject of virtue by Stoics such as Sextus Pompeius or the two Balbi or my friend Marcus Vigellius who lived with Panaetius, to make it necessary either for me or for any one of
79 you to give ground to them in debate ? For philosophy does not resemble the other sciences—for what good will a man be in geometry if he has not studied it ? or in music ? he will either have to hold his tongue or be set down as a positive lunatic ; whereas the contents of philosophy are discovered by intellects of the keenest acumen in eliciting the probable answer to every problem, and the results are elaborated with practised eloquence. In this situation our popular orator, though perhaps in-

doctus, attamen in dicendo exercitatus, hac ipsa exercitatione communi istos quidem[1] verberabit neque
80 se ab eis contemni ac despici sinet ; sin aliquis ex-
stiterit aliquando qui Aristotelio more de omnibus
rebus in utramque sententiam possit dicere et in
omni causa duas contrarias orationes praeceptis illius
cognitis explicare, aut hoc Arcesilae modo et Car-
neadis contra omne quod propositum sit disserat,
quique ad eam rationem adiungat hunc usum[2] ex-
ercitationemque dicendi, is sit[3] verus, is perfectus,
is solus orator.   Nam neque sine forensibus nervis
satis vehemens et gravis nec sine varietate doctrinae
81 satis politus et sapiens esse orator potest.   Quare
Coracem istum veterem[4] patiamur nos quidem pullos
suos excludere in nido qui evolent clamatores odiosi
ac molesti, Pamphilumque nescio quem sinamus in
infulis tantam rem tanquam pueriles delicias aliquas
depingere, nosque ipsi hac tam exigua disputatione
hesterni et hodierni diei totum oratoris munus ex-
plicemus, dummodo illa res tanta sit ut omnibus
philosophorum libris, quos nemo[5] istorum unquam
attigit, comprehensa esse videatur.
82   XXII. Tum Catulus : Haudquaquam hercle,
inquit, Crasse, mirandum est esse in te tantam
dicendi vel vim vel suavitatem vel copiam ; quem

[1] *Ernesti :* quidem nostros (quidem doctos *Sorof*).
[2] *Edd. :* hunc rhetoricum usum moremque.
[3] is erit *Bakius.*
[4] *Bakius :* vestrum.
[5] *Ellendt :* nemo oratorum.

---

[a] See Book I, § 91.
[b] Quintilian iii. 6. 34 mentions a rhetorician of this name.
The exact nature of his *memoria technica* here alluded to it
does not seem possible to discover. Reid thinks *deliciae*

adequately schooled, having nevertheless had experience in speaking, will anyway be enabled merely by that ordinary experience to give those persons a sound drubbing, and will not allow them to despise

80 and look down on him; whereas if there has really ever been a person who was able in Aristotelian fashion to speak on both sides about every subject and by means of knowing Aristotle's rules to reel off two speeches on opposite sides on every case, or in the manner of Arcesilas and Carneades argue against every statement put forward, and who to that method adds the experience and practice in speaking indicated, he would be the one and only true and perfect orator. For an orator cannot have sufficient cogency and weight if he lacks the vigour that public speaking demands, and cannot be adequately polished and profound if he lacks width of

81 culture. Consequently let us for our part allow your old Mr. Raven [a] to hatch out his own chicks in the nest, so that they may fly abroad as annoying and tiresome bawlers, and permit some Pamphilus [b] or other to sketch out a subject of this importance on his tapes, like a nursery game, and let us for our part within the narrow limits of the debate of yesterday and to-day unfold the function of the orator in its entirety, provided it be granted that the subject is so extensive that it might be supposed to fill all the volumes of the philosophers, books which none of those gentlemen have ever had in their hands."

82 XXII. Catulus then said: " I declare, Crassus, it is not in the least surprising that you possess so forcible and attractive and fluent a style of speaking. *but his studies must be limited to their practical object.*

means 'pets,' because Catullus uses the word of Lesbia's sparrow.

quidem antea natura rebar ita dicere ut mihi non solum orator summus sed etiam sapientissimus homo viderere: nunc intellego illa te semper etiam potiora duxisse quae ad sapientiam spectarent atque ex his hanc dicendi copiam fluxisse. Sed tamen cum omnes gradus aetatis recordor tuae cumque vitam tuam ac studia considero, neque quo tempore ista didiceris video nec magnopere te istis studiis, hominibus, libris intellego deditum. Neque tamen possum statuere utrum magis mirer te illa quae mihi persuades maxima esse adiumenta potuisse in tuis tantis occupationibus perdiscere, an, si non potueris, posse isto modo dicere.

83 Hic Crassus : Hoc tibi, inquit, Catule, primum persuadeas velim, me non multo secus facere cum de oratore disputem ac facerem si esset mihi de histrione dicendum. Negarem enim posse eum satis facere in gestu nisi palaestram, nisi saltare didicisset : neque ea cum dicerem me esse histrionem necesse esset, sed fortasse non stultum alieni artificii existi-

84 matorem. Similiter nunc de oratore vestro impulsu loquor, summo scilicet, semper enim, quacumque de arte aut facultate quaeritur, de absoluta et perfecta quaeri solet. Quare si iam me vultis esse oratorem,

In fact even before this I used to think you had
natural gifts as a speaker which made me consider
you not merely a consummate orator but also an
accomplished philosopher, but now I realize that you
have always thought matters relating to philosophy
more important, and that these are the source from
which this oratorical fluency has been derived. But
all the same when I recall all the stages of your
career, and when I contemplate your life and pursuits,
I cannot see at what period you learnt the facts in
question and I do not observe that you have paid any
considerable attention to those studies or persons
or books. And nevertheless I am unable to decide
whether I am more surprised at your having been
able among all your occupations to familiarize yourself with the subjects which you assure me constitute very valuable auxiliaries, or at your ability to
speak as you do if you have not been able to do so."

83 " In the first place, Catulus," rejoined Crassus, " I
do wish you would assure yourself that I do not take
a very different line when I am discussing the orator
from the line I should take if I had to speak about
the actor. For I should assert it to be impossible
for him to come up to the mark in point of gesture
if he had not had lessons in wrestling and in dancing ;
and in saying this I should not need to be an actor
myself, but perhaps a not quite incompetent critic
84 of an accomplishment that was not my own. The
same applies now when at your instigation I am
talking about the orator—the ideal orator, I assume,
as whatever science or accomplishment is under
examination, it is customary to examine a finished
and perfect specimen of it. Consequently if on the
present occasion you will have it that I am myself an

si etiam sat bonum, si bonum denique, non repugnabo;
quid enim nunc sim ineptus ? ita me existimari scio.
Quod si ita est, summus tamen certe non sum ; neque
enim apud homines res est ulla difficilior neque maior
neque quae plura adiumenta doctrinae desideret.
85 Attamen quoniam de oratore nobis disputandum est,
de summo oratore dicam necesse est ; vis enim et
natura rei nisi perfecta ante oculos ponitur, qualis
et quanta sit intellegi non potest.   Me autem, Catule,
fateor neque hodie in istis libris et cum istis hominibus
vivere, nec vero, id quod tu recte commeministi,
ullum unquam habuisse sepositum tempus ad discendum, ac tantum tribuisse doctrinae temporis
quantum mihi puerilis aetas, forenses feriae conces-
serint.

86   XXIII. Ac, si quaeris, Catule, de doctrina ista quid
ego sentiam, non tantum ingenioso homini et ei qui
forum, qui curiam, qui causas, qui rempublicam
spectet opus esse arbitror temporis quantum sibi ei
sumpserunt quos discentes vita defecit.   Omnes
enim artes aliter ab eis tractantur qui eas ad usum
transferunt, aliter ab eis qui ipsarum artium tractatu
delectati nihil in vita sunt aliud acturi.   Magister
hic Samnitium summa iam senectute est et quo-

orator, and even that I am a fairly good or even a good orator, I will raise no objection ; for what need is there here for affecting modesty ? I know this is what is thought of me. But though this is the case, all the same it is certain that I am not a supremely good orator ; for in fact there is nothing in human life which is more difficult or bulks larger 85 or which requires more subsidiary training. And nevertheless, as our debate is to be about the orator, I am bound to speak of the supreme orator ; for it is impossible to understand the character and magnitude of a thing's essential nature unless a perfect specimen of it is set before our eyes. For my own part however, Catulus, I confess that nowadays I do not pass my life among the books and in company with the persons in question, and moreover, as you have correctly recalled, that I have never had any time set apart for study, and have only given so much time to the acquisition of knowledge as was allowed me by my boyhood and by holidays from public business. 86 XXIII. " Moreover, Catulus, if you ask me my personal opinion as to the study in question, I do not think that a person of ability, and acquainted at first hand with public life and procedure in parliament and the law-courts, requires as much time as has been taken for themselves by those who have spent the whole term of their life in study. For all branches of knowledge are handled by those who apply them to practice in a different manner from that in which they are handled by those who take their pleasure in the pursuit of the sciences themselves and have no intention of following any other career. Our trainer of gladiators here has now reached extreme old age and practises every day, as it is his only

tidie commentatur ; nihil enim curat aliud : at Q.
Velocius puer addidicerat, sed quod erat aptus ad
illud totumque cognorat, fuit, ut est apud Lucilium,

> Quamvis bonus ipse
> Samnis in ludo, ac rudibus cuivis satis asper ;

sed plus operae foro tribuebat, amicis, rei familiari.
Valerius quotidie cantabat; erat enim scenicus: quid
87 faceret aliud ? at Numerius Furius noster familiaris
cum est commodum cantat ; est enim paterfamilias,
est eques Romanus ; puer didicit quod discendum
fuit. Eadem ratio est harum artium maximarum ;
dies et noctes virum summa virtute et prudentia
videbamus philosopho cum operam daret, Q. Tubero-
nem ; at eius avunculum vix intellegeres id agere,
cum ageret tamen, Africanum. Ista discuntur facile
si et tantum sumas quantum opus sit et habeas qui
docere fideliter possit et scias ipse etiam discere.
88 Sed si tota vita nihil velis aliud agere, ipsa tractatio
et quaestio cotidie ex se gignit aliquid quod cum
desidiosa delectatione vestiges. Ita fit ut agitatio
rerum sit infinita, cognitio facilis, si usus doctrinam
confirmet, mediocris opera tribuatur, memoria studi-
umque permaneat. Libet autem semper discere :
ut si velim ego talis optime ludere aut pilae studio
tenear, etiam fortasse si assequi non possim ; at alii

---

a *Remains of Old Latin* (L.C.L.), iii. pp. 58 f., Marx,
Lucilius 1283-1284.

interest in life : whereas Quintus Velocius had only
had fencing as one of his lessons in boyhood, but
having a natural capacity for it and having gone
through the whole course he was in Lucilius's words

> Himself as good a fencer as you please,
> A tough match with the foils for any man—[a]

but he devoted more of his attention to public life and
to his friends and his estate. Valerius used to sing
87 every day, and naturally so, being a professional ; but
our friend Numerius Furius sings when it suits him,
for he is a head of a household and a Knight of Rome ;
he learnt what was necessary when he was a boy.
The same is the case in regard to these master
sciences : we used to see that excellent and sagacious
gentleman, Quintus Tubero, occupied with his professor for whole days and nights, whereas one would
scarcely guess that his uncle Africanus was engaged
in study at all, when nevertheless he actually was so
occupied. The subjects in question are easily learnt
if one only takes up so much of them as one really
needs and if one has a reliable tutor and also knows
88 how to study by himself. But if one wants to
devote the whole of one's life to study and to nothing
else, the actual process of investigation every day
produces spontaneously some question for one to
follow up with leisurely delight. The consequence
is that the pursuit of facts is unlimited, and their
acquisition easy if study is reinforced by practice and
a moderate amount of diligence is bestowed on it,
and if memory and interest endure. However to
learn a thing is always amusing—for instance if I
took a fancy to excel at playing dice or were a devotee
of tennis, even though possibly unable to achieve

quia praeclare faciunt vehementius quam causa
postulat delectantur, ut Titius pila, Brulla talis.
89 Quare nihil est quod quisquam magnitudinem artium
ex eo quod senes discunt pertimescat, namque aut
senes ad eas accesserunt, aut usque ad senectutem
in studiis detinentur, aut sunt tardissimi. Res
quidem se mea sententia sic habet ut, nisi quod
quisque cito potuerit, nunquam omnino possit perdiscere.

90　　XXIV. Iam, iam, inquit Catulus, intellego, Crasse,
quid dicas ; et hercule assentior. Satis video tibi
homini ad perdiscendum acerrimo ad ea cognoscenda
quae dicis fuisse temporis.

　　Pergisne, inquit Crassus, me quae dicam de me,
non de re putare dicere ? Sed iam, si placet, ad
instituta redeamus.

　　Mihi vero, Catulus inquit, placet.

91　　Tum Crassus : Quorsum igitur haec spectat, inquit, tam longa et tam alte repetita oratio ? Hae
duae partes quae mihi supersunt illustrandae orationis ac totius eloquentiae cumulandae, quarum
altera dici postulat ornate, altera apte, hanc habent
vim, ut sit quam maxime iucunda, quam maxime in
sensus eorum qui audiunt influat, et quam plurimis
92 sit rebus instructa. Instrumentum autem hoc forense, litigiosum, acre, tractum ex vulgi opinionibus

---

ª See § 37.

success ; but other men, because they are distinguished performers, take a keener delight in such amusements—for instance Titius in tennis and Brulla 89 in dice—than the situation demands. Consequently nobody need be afraid of the magnitude of the sciences on the ground that old men are studying them, for either they have come to them in old age, or their interest in their studies has lasted on to old age, or they are very slow learners. In fact my view of the situation is that unless a man is able to learn a subject quickly he will never be able to learn it thoroughly at all."

90 XXIV. " At last," said Catulus, " at last I take your meaning, Crassus ; and I vow I agree with you. It is clear enough to me that you as an extremely keen and thorough student have had enough time to get to know the things that you are saying."

" Do you persist in thinking," said Crassus, " that what I am saying refers to myself and not to the fact of the matter ? But now if you please let us go back to our subject."

" Why certainly," said Catulus.

91 Crassus proceeded : " Well then, what is the purport of this long and recondite discourse ? The two divisions [a] of the subject of beauty of style and complete elaboration of oratory that now remain to me, one the requirement that the language should be ornate and the other that it should be appropriate, amount to this, that the style must be in the highest possible degree pleasing and calculated to find its way to the attention of the audience, and that it must 92 have the fullest possible supply of facts. But the stock of ideas employed in our ordinary public life of contention and criticism, derived as it is from

The requisites of oratory continued : (3) ornament and (4) appropriateness of style.

exiguum sane atque mendicum est; illud rursus
ipsum quod tradunt isti qui profitentur se dicendi
magistros non multum est maius quam illud vulgare
ac forense : apparatu nobis opus est et rebus ex-
quisitis undique et collectis, arcessitis, comportatis,
ut tibi, Caesar, faciendum est ad annum, ut ego in
aedilitate laboravi, quod quotidianis et vernaculis
rebus satisfacere me posse huic populo non puta-
93 bam. Verborum eligendorum et collocandorum et
concludendorum facilis est vel ratio vel sine ratione
ipsa exercitatio; rerum est silva magna, quam cum
Graeci iam non tenerent ob eamque causam iuventus
nostra dedisceret paene discendo, etiam Latini, si
dis placet, hoc biennio magistri dicendi exstiterunt;
quos ego censor edicto meo sustuleram, non quo,
ut nescio quos dicere aiebant, acui ingenia adoles-
centium nollem, sed contra ingenia obtundi nolui,
94 corroborari impudentiam. Nam apud Graecos,
cuicuimodi essent, videbam tamen esse praeter
hanc exercitationem linguae doctrinam aliquam et
humanitate dignam scientiam,[1] hos vero novos
magistros nihil intellegebam posse docere nisi ut
auderent; quod etiam cum bonis rebus coniunctum
per se ipsum est magnopere fugiendum : hoc cum

---

[1] *Lambinus :* humanitatem dignam scientia.

---

[a] Caesar was now aedile elect.

the notions of the common people, is an altogether meagre and beggarly affair ; and again even the style imparted by your professional teachers of rhetoric is not on much larger lines than the popular oratory of the courts ; whereas what we require is elaboration, and the accumulation and acquisition from all sources of a collection of recondite topics, which will be your task, Caesar, in a year's time,[a] and which was my own diligent occupation when I was aedile, because I felt it was not possible for me to satisfy our public with the commonplaces of an 93 everyday style. There is no difficulty about the theory, or if you prefer the purely practical problem, of the choice of words and their position in sentences and combination to form periods ; and there is a large stock of ideas, which were no longer kept to themselves by the Greeks, with the result that our young students virtually unlearned them in the process of learning them, so that in the last two years there actually arose, heaven help us ! Latin professors of rhetoric ; but these I had used my authority as censor to abolish by edict, my motive not being the one that was said to be attributed to me in certain quarters, unwillingness to let the rising generation sharpen their wits, but on the contrary I was unwilling for their wits to be blunted and their 94 conceit increased. For I was aware that whatever the demerits of the Greek professors, they did nevertheless possess some sort of system and knowledge not unworthy of the humanities, in addition to this practice in tongue-wagging, but so far as I could see these new masters had no capacity to teach anything except audacity, which even when combined with qualities of value is in itself to be carefully

unum traderetur et cum impudentiae ludus esset,
putavi esse censoris ne longius id serperet providere.
95 Quanquam non haec ita statuo atque decerno ut
desperem Latine ea de quibus disputavimus tradi
ac perpoliri[1] : patitur enim et lingua nostra et
natura rerum veterem illam excellentemque prudentiam Graecorum ad nostrum usum moremque
transferri ; sed hominibus opus est eruditis, qui
adhuc in hoc quidem genere nostri nulli fuerunt ;
sin quando exstiterint, etiam Graecis erunt ante-
ponendi.

96   XXV. Ornatur igitur oratio genere primum et
quasi colore quodam et suco suo ; nam ut gravis, ut
suavis, ut erudita sit, ut liberalis, ut admirabilis, ut
polita, ut sensus, ut dolores habeat quantum opus sit,
non est singulorum articulorum : in toto spectantur
haec corpore.   Ut porro conspersa sit quasi verborum
sententiarumque floribus, id non debet esse fusum
aequabiliter per omnem orationem sed ita distinctum
ut sint quasi in ornatu disposita quaedam insignia et
97 lumina.   Genus igitur dicendi est eligendum quod
maxime teneat eos qui audiant et quod non solum
delectet sed etiam sine satietate delectet—non enim
a me iam exspectari puto ut moneam ut caveatis ne

----

[1] perpoliri ⟨posse⟩ *Pearce.*

avoided, but as this was the only thing that they imparted, and as their school was a seminary of conceit, I decided that it was a censor's duty to take measures to prevent the movement from spreading 95 further. Albeit my verdict and judgement on this matter is not such as to make me give up hope of conveying the topics of our discussion with complete elegance of style, for the importation of the time-honoured and outstanding wisdom of the Greeks for our habitual employment is permitted both by language and by the nature of things ; but it needs persons of advanced learning, of whom so far we have had none, at all events in this department ; whereas if they do ever arise, they will deserve to rank above even the Greeks.

96 XXV. " Well then, the embellishment of oratory is achieved in the first place by general style and by a sort of inherent colour and flavour ; for that it shall be weighty and pleasing and scholarly and gentlemanly and attractive and polished, and shall possess the requisite amount of feeling and pathos, is not a matter of particular divisions of the framework, but these qualities must be visible in the whole of the structure. But further, in order to embellish it with flowers of language and gems of thought, it is not necessary for this ornamentation to be spread evenly over the entire speech, but it must be so distributed that there may be brilliant jewels placed at various points as a sort of decoration. 97 Consequently it is necessary to choose the style of oratory best calculated to hold the attention of the audience, and not merely to give them pleasure but also to do so without giving them too much of it—for I do not imagine that you look to me

Rules for ornate style

exilis, ne inculta sit vestra oratio, ne vulgaris, ne
obsoleta : aliud quiddam maius et ingenia me hor-
tantur vestra et aetates.

98 Difficile enim dictu est quaenam causa sit cur
ea quae maxime sensus nostros impellunt voluptate
et specie prima acerrime commovent, ab eis celerrime
fastidio quodam et satietate abalienemur. Quanto
colorum pulchritudine et varietate floridiora sunt in
picturis novis pleraque quam in veteribus ! quae
tamen, etiamsi primo aspectu nos ceperunt, diutius
non delectant, cum eidem nos in antiquis tabulis illo
ipso horrido obsoletoque teneamur. Quanto mol-
liores sunt et delicatiores in cantu flexiones et falsae
voculae quam certae et severae ! quibus tamen non
modo austeri sed si saepius fiunt multitudo ipsa re-
99 clamat. Licet hoc videre in reliquis sensibus—un-
guentis minus diu nos delectari summa et acerrima
suavitate conditis quam his moderatis, et magis
laudari quod terram[1] quam quod crocum olere[2]
videatur, in ipso tactu esse modum et mollitudinis et
levitatis. Quin etiam gustatus, qui est sensus ex
omnibus maxime voluptarius quique dulcitudine
praeter ceteros sensus commovetur, quam cito id
quod valde dulce est aspernatur ac respuit ! quis
potione uti aut cibo dulci diutius potest ? cum utroque
in genere ea quae leviter sensum voluptate moveant

---

[1] *Lambinus coll. Plin. N.H. xiii. 3. 4 :* ceram.
[2] sapere *Lambinus coll. eodem loco.*

at this point for the warning to avoid an impoverished
and uncultivated style, and expressions that are
vulgar or out of date ; your talents and also your ages
demand from me something more important.

98   " For it is hard to say why exactly it is that the
things which most strongly gratify our senses and
excite them most vigorously at their first appearance, are the ones from which we are most speedily
estranged by a feeling of disgust and satiety.   How
much more brilliant, as a rule, in beauty and variety
of colouring are the contents of new pictures than
those of old ones ! and nevertheless the new ones,
though they captivated us at first sight, later on fail
to give us pleasure—although it is also true that in
the case of old pictures the actual roughness and
old-fashioned style are an attraction.   In singing,
how much more delightful and charming are trills
and flourishes than notes firmly held ! and yet the
former meet with protest not only from persons of
severe taste but, if used too often, even from the
99 general public.   This may be observed in the case
of the rest of the senses—that perfumes com-
pounded with an extremely sweet and penetrating
scent do not give us pleasure for so long as those
that are moderately fragrant, and a thing that seems
to have the scent of earth is more esteemed than one
that suggests saffron ; and that in touch itself there
are degrees of softness and smoothness.   Taste is the
most voluptuous of all the senses and more sensitive
to sweetness than the rest, yet how quickly even
it dislikes and rejects anything extremely sweet !
who can go on taking a sweet drink or food for a long
time ? whereas in both classes things that pleasur-
ably affect the sense in a moderate degree most easily

100 facillime fugiant satietatem. Sic omnibus in rebus
voluptatibus maximis fastidium finitimum est ; quo
hoc minus in oratione miremur, in qua vel ex poetis
vel ex oratoribus possumus iudicare concinnam, dis-
tinctam, ornatam, festivam, sine intermissione, sine
reprehensione, sine varietate, quamvis claris sit
coloribus picta vel poesis vel oratio, non posse in
delectatione esse diuturna. Atque eo citius in oratoris aut in poetae cincinnis ac fuco offenditur quod
sensus in nimia voluptate natura non mente satiantur,
in scriptis et in dictis non aurium solum sed animi
101 iudicio etiam magis infucata vitia noscuntur. XXVI.
Quare ' bene ' et ' praeclare,' quamvis nobis saepe
dicatur, ' belle,' et ' festive,' nimium saepe nolo ;
quanquam illa ipsa exclamatio ' non potest melius '
sit velim crebra ; sed habeat tamen illa in dicendo
admiratio ac summa laus umbram aliquam et re-
cessum, quo magis id quod erit illuminatum exstare
102 atque eminere videatur. Nunquam agit hunc versum
Roscius eo gestu quo potest :

Nam sapiens virtuti honorem praemium, haud praedam
petit—

sed abicit prorsus, ut in proximo

Set[1] quid video ? Ferro saeptus possidet sedes sacras—

incidat, aspiciat, admiretur, stupescat. Quid ille
alter

[1] *Gruter :* proximos et.

80

100 escape causing satiety. Thus in all things the greatest pleasures are only narrowly separated from disgust; which makes this less surprising in the case of language, in which we can judge from either the poets or the orators that a style which is symmetrical, decorated, ornate and attractive, but that lacks relief or check or variety, cannot continue to give pleasure for long, however brilliantly coloured the poem or speech may be. And what makes the curls and rouge of the orator or poet jar upon us all the more quickly is, that whereas with the senses satiety in the case of excessive pleasure is an instinctive and not a deliberate reaction, in the case of writings and speeches faults of over-colouring are detected not only by the verdict of the ears but even more by that

101 of the mind. XXVI. Hence although we hope to win a ' Bravo, capital ! ' as often as possible, I don't want too much of ' Very pretty, charming ! '—albeit the actual ejaculation ' Couldn't be better ! ' is one I should like to hear frequently ; but all the same, this applause in the middle of a speech and this unlimited praise had better have some shadow and background, to make the spot of high light appear to stand out

102 more prominently. When Roscius speaks the lines

since for the wise
Honour is valour's prize and not its prey,

he never uses the action at his command, but just throws them off, so that he can put his whole weight into the next lines—

But what see I ?   A sword-girt warrior
Seated within the sanctuary shrine !

—which he delivers with a stare of stupefied surprise. Again, how quietly and gently and with what little energy the other great actor gives the line

CICERO

Quid petam praesidi ?

quam leniter, quam remisse, quam non actuose !
instat enim

O pater, o patria, o Priami domus !

in quo tanta commoveri actio non posset si esset
consumpta superiore motu et exhausta. Neque id
actores prius viderunt quam ipsi poetae, quam denique illi etiam qui fecerunt modos, a quibus utrisque
summittitur aliquid, deinde augetur, extenuatur,
103 inflatur, variatur, distinguitur. Ita sit nobis igitur
ornatus et suavis orator (nec tamen potest aliter esse)
ut suavitatem habeat austeram et solidam, non dul-
cem atque decoctam. Nam ipsa ad ornandum praecepta quae dantur eiusmodi sunt ut ea quamvis[1]
vitiosissimus orator explicare possit ; quare, ut ante
dixi, primum silva rerum[2] comparanda est, qua de
parte dixit Antonius : haec formanda filo ipso et
genere orationis, illuminanda verbis, varianda sententiis.
104 Summa autem laus eloquentiae est amplificare
rem ornando, quod valet non solum ad augendum
aliquid et tollendum altius dicendo sed etiam ad
extenuandum atque abiciendum. XXVII. Id de-
sideratur omnibus eis in locis quos ad fidem orationis
faciendam adhiberi dixit Antonius, vel cum explana-
mus aliquid vel cum conciliamus animos vel cum

---

[1] *Ellendt :* quivis (quivis vel *Sorof*).
[2] *Wilkins :* rerum ac sententiarum.

---

[a] From Ennius's *Andromache* (*Remains*, i. pp. 250 f.,
Vahlen, *Ennius* 86). The sources of the preceding quotations are not known.

What succour shall I seek ? [a]

For he presses on :

O father ! O fatherland ! O palace of Priam [b] !

—on which he could not work up such an energetic
delivery if he had used up his whole supply of energy
on the preceding gesture. Nor did the actors see
this sooner than the poets themselves did, or indeed
sooner than the composers of the musical accompani-
ments, for both poets and composers employ a definite
fall in tone and then a rise, a sinking and a swell,
103 variations, pauses. Consequently while we secure
that our orator shall have ornament and charm—
though these qualities are necessarily his—at the
same time his charm must be severe and substantial,
not sweet and luscious. For the actual rules that are
given as to decoration are of such a nature that any
speaker, even the most defective, could apply them ;
consequently as I said before, one has to begin by
accumulating a supply of matter, a department that
Antonius has dealt with [c] ; but the matter has to
receive shape from the general texture and style of
the speech, and to be embellished by the diction and
given variety by reflexions.

104   "But the highest distinction of eloquence consists
in amplification by means of ornament, which can
be used to make one's speech not only increase the
importance of a subject and raise it to a higher level,
but also to diminish and disparage it. XXVII. This
is requisite in all the lines of argument referred to by
Antonius as employed to make a speech convincing,
either when we are explaining something or winning

Methods of amplification.

  [b] *Ibid.* Ennius, *Andromache* (*Remains*, i. pp. 250 ff.).
    [c] See Bk. II, xvi., xxix. etc.

105 concitamus ; sed in hoc quod postremum dixi amplificatio potest plurimum, eaque una laus oratoris est[1]
propria maxime.   Etiam maior est[2] illa exercitatio
quam extremo sermone instruxit Antonius (primo
reiciebat), laudandi et vituperandi ; nihil est enim
ad exaggerandam et amplificandam orationem accom-
modatius quam utrumque horum cumulatissime
106 facere posse.   Consequentur etiam illi loci qui quanquam proprii causarum et inhaerentes in earum
nervis esse debent, tamen quia de universa re tractari
solent 'communes' a veteribus nominati sunt; quorum
partim habent vitiorum et peccatorum acrem quamdam cum amplificatione incusationem aut querelam
—contra quam dici nihil solet nec potest,—ut in de-
peculatorem, in proditorem, in parricidam, quibus
uti confirmatis criminibus oportet, aliter enim ieiuni
sunt atque inanes, alii autem habent deprecationem,
107 aut miserationem ; alii vero ancipites disputationes,
in quibus de universo genere in utramque partem
disseri copiose licet.   Quae exercitatio nunc propria
duarum philosophiarum de quibus ante dixi putatur,
apud antiquos erat eorum a quibus omnis de rebus
forensibus dicendi ratio et copia petebatur ; de vir-

---

[1] *Pearce :* est et.   [2] Adhibenda etiam est *Sorof.*

---

[a] The text here seems corrupt.
[b] Book II, §§ 43 ff., 342-349.   [c] § 67.
[d] Wise men such as those mentioned in § 56.

105 sympathy or arousing emotion ; but it is in the last-mentioned field that amplification is most effective, and success in this is the one distinction that most specially marks the orator. Even more important [a] is the activity which Antonius dwelt on at the end of his discourse after putting it on one side at the beginning,[b] namely laudation and censure ; for nothing is more effective for the development and amplification of a speech than to be able to use both of these in the 106 fullest abundance. There will also follow the topics which, although they ought to be specially appropriate to the cases in hand and inherent in their essential structure, nevertheless from being normally employed in dealing with general questions have received from the old writers the designation of ' commonplaces ' ; one set of these consists in a vigorous and fully developed attack or protest as to particular vices and offences—an attack usually left unanswered and indeed unanswerable—for instance charges of embezzlement or treachery or parricide, the employment of which must be supported by full proof of the accusations, as otherwise they fall quite flat, while others consist in the deprecation of such charges or 107 an appeal for mercy ; whereas others on the contrary are non-committal debates allowing copious arguments to be advanced both *pro* and *contra* in regard to the general question. The latter exercise is now considered the special province of the two schools of philosophy of which I spoke before,[c] but in early days it was the function of the persons [d] who used to be called on to furnish a complete line of argument and supply of matter for speeches on public affairs—the fact being that we orators are bound to possess the intelligence, capacity and skill to speak both *pro* and

tute enim, de officio, de aequo et bono, de dignitate, utilitate, honore, ignominia, praemio, poena simili-busque de rebus in utramque partem dicendi animos

108 et vim et artem habere debemus. Sed quoniam de nostra possessione depulsi in parvo et eo litigioso praediolo relicti sumus et aliorum patroni nostra tenere tuerique non potuimus, ab eis, quod indignis-simum est, qui in nostrum patrimonium irruperunt quod opus est nobis mutuemur.

109 XXVIII. Dicunt igitur nunc quidem illi qui ex particula parva urbis ac loci nomen habent et ' Peri-patetici' philosophi aut 'Academici' nominantur, olim autem propter eximiam rerum maximarum scientiam a Graecis politici philosophi appellati universarum rerum publicarum nomine vocabantur, omnem civilem orationem in horum alterutro genere versari : aut de finita controversia[1] certis temporibus ac reis, hoc modo, placeatne a Carthaginiensibus captivos nostros red-ditis suis recuperari ? aut infinite de universo genere quaerentis quid omnino de captivo statuendum sit ? Atque horum superius illud genus ' causam ' aut ' controversiam ' appellant eamque tribus, lite aut deliberatione aut laudatione, definiunt; haec autem altera quaestio infinita et quasi proposita ' consulta-

110 tio' nominatur. Atque [hactenus loquuntur][2] etiam hac in instituendo divisione utuntur, sed ita, non ut iure aut iudicio, vi[3] denique recuperare amissam pos-

---

[1] definitae controversiae *Pearce.*
[2] *Kayser.*   [3] *Madvig :* ut.

---

[a] *Quasi proposita* is a translation of θέσις.

contra on the topics of virtue, duty, equity and good,
moral worth and utility, honour and disgrace, reward
108 and punishment, and like matters. But now we have
been ousted from our own estate and left in occupation
of a trifling little property, and that contested, and
we who are the defenders of other people have been
unable to hold and to safeguard our own possessions ;
so let us put our pride in our pocket and borrow what
we need from those who have trespassed on our
heritage.

109 XXVIII. "Well then, it is now asserted by the (*a*) As to
philosophers who are designated by names derived general
from a small section of the city or district 'Peripatetic' principles :
or 'Academic,' but who once upon a time owing to
their exceptional knowledge of important affairs were
styled by the Greeks 'political philosophers' and
thus bore a title covering the entire field of public
affairs—these now assert that the whole of political
discourse is employed in one or other of these two
departments : either on an issue limited by fixed
dates and particular parties, thus—is it agreed to
obtain restitution of our captured fellow-countrymen from the Carthaginians by returning theirs ? or
else, an unlimited inquiry about a general issue :
what is the proper general rule and opinion about a
prisoner of war ? And of these two classes of problem they designate the former kind a 'case' or
'controversy,' and limit it to three occasions, a lawsuit, a debate or a panegyric ; but the second class,
propounding *a* an unlimited subject of inquiry, is
110 named a 'deliberation.' And they also employ the
second division in establishing their system, but in
such a manner as to appear not to be recovering a
lost property by legal proceedings, in fact by force,

sessionem, sed ut [iure civili][1] surculo defringendo
usurpare videantur. Nam illud alterum genus quod
est temporibus, locis, reis definitum obtinent, atque
id ipsum lacinia—nunc enim apud Philonem, quem
in Academia maxime[2] vigere audio, etiam harum
iam causarum cognitio exercitatioque celebratur—,
alterum vero tantummodo in prima arte tradenda
nominant et oratoris esse dicunt, sed neque vim
neque naturam eius nec partes nec genera proponunt
—ut praeteriri omnino fuerit satius quam attentatum
deseri : nunc enim inopia reticere intelleguntur,
tum iudicio viderentur.

111   XXIX. Omnis igitur res eamdem habet naturam
ambigendi de qua quaeri et disceptari potest, sive
in infinitis consultationibus disceptatur sive in eis
causis quae in civitate et in forensi disceptatione
versantur ; neque est ulla quae non aut ad cognos-
cendi aut ad agendi vim rationemque referatur ;
112 nam aut ipsa cognitio rei scientiaque perquiritur, ut
virtus suamne propter dignitatem an propter fructus
aliquos expetatur, aut agendi consilium exquiritur,
113 ut sitne sapienti capessenda respublica. Cognitionis autem tres modi, coniectura, definitio et, ut
ita dicam, consecutio ; nam quid in re sit coniectura
quaeritur, ut illud, sitne in humano genere sapientia ;

[1] *Ellendt.*   [2] maxime *v.l. om.*

88

but asserting their claim to it by the formality of
breaking off a twig. For they retain their hold upon
the former of the two classes, the one limited by
dates and places and parties, and this itself they
hold on to merely by the fringe—for at the present
time the study and practice of these cases also is
pursued in the school of Philo, who I am told is in
high esteem at the Academy—but the latter they
only just mention when imparting the elements
of their system, specifying it as belonging to the
orator but not setting out its importance or nature
nor its divisions and classes—so that it would have
been more satisfactory for it to be passed over entirely
than to be just touched on and then dropped ; for
as it is, their silence is interpreted as due to lack of
matter, whereas in the other case it would have
appeared to be deliberate.

11 XXIX. " Accordingly every matter that can be the three lines
subject of inquiry and discussion involves the same of argument
kind of issue, whether the discussion falls in the class able.
of abstract deliberations or of things within the range
of political and legal debate ; and there is none which
has not for its object either the acquisition of know-
12 ledge or the performance of action ; for the object
of the inquiry is either the actual ascertainment and
knowledge of a fact, for instance whether virtue is
desired for its own intrinsic value or for the sake of
some result, or else some principle of action, for
instance whether it is proper for the wise man to
3 engage in politics. Now of acquiring knowledge
there are three modes, inference, definition and
thirdly what I may designate deduction : for we
employ inference to discover the essential content
of a thing, for instance supposing the question to

89

quam autem vim quaeque res habeat definitio explicat, ut si quaeratur quid sit sapientia; consecutio autem tractatur cum quid quamque rem sequatur inquiritur, ut illud, sitne aliquando mentiri

114 boni viri. Redeunt rursus ad coniecturam eamque in quattuor genera dispertiunt; nam aut quid sit quaeritur, hoc modo, naturane sit ius inter homines an[1] opinionibus; aut quae sit origo cuiusque rei, ut quod sit initium legum aut rerum publicarum; aut causa et ratio, ut si quaeratur cur doctissimi homines de maximis rebus dissentiant; aut de immutatione, ut si disputetur num interire virtus in homine aut num in vitium possit converti.

115 Definitionis autem sunt disceptationes, aut cum quaeritur quid in communi mente quasi impressum sit, ut si disseratur idne sit ius quod maximae parti sit utile; aut cum quid cuiusque sit proprium exquiritur, ut ornate dicere propriumne sit oratoris an id etiam aliquis praeterea possit; aut cum res distribuitur in partes, ut si quaeratur quot sint genera rerum expetendarum, ut sintne tria, corporis, animi, externarumque rerum; aut cum quae forma et quasi naturalis nota cuiusque sit describitur, ut si quaeratur avari species, seditiosi, gloriosi.

116 Consecutionis autem duo prima quaestionum

---

[1] an in *Wilkins.*

be, is wisdom an essential attribute of the human race? definition explains the force possessed by a particular thing, for instance it is asked, what is wisdom? while deduction is the procedure when we are investigating a particular thing's consequence, for instance, is it occasionally the duty of a good 114 man to tell a lie? Reverting to inference, they divide it into four classes, the question being either what actually exists, as for instance does justice exist between mankind by nature or is it merely a matter of opinion? or what is the origin of something, for example what is the source of law and government? or the cause and reason of things, for instance the question what causes the difference of opinion existing among very learned persons about matters of very great importance; or it deals with change, for instance the debate whether virtue can perish in a man or whether it can change into vice.

115 " Then disputes as to definition arise either on the question of what is the conviction generally prevalent, for instance supposing the point under discussion to be whether right is the interest of the majority; or on the question of the essential property of something, for instance is elegant speaking the peculiar property of the orator or is it also in the power of somebody beside; or when a thing is divided into parts, for instance if it is asked how many classes there are of things desirable, for example are there three, goods of the body, goods of the mind, external goods; or on the problem of defining the special form and natural mark of a particular thing, for instance supposing we are investigating the specific character of the miser, or the rebel, or the braggart.

116 " Under the head of deduction fall two main classes

genera ponuntur ; nam aut simplex est disceptatio, ut si disseratur expetendane sit gloria, aut ex comparatione, laus an divitiae magis expetendae sint. Simplicium autem sunt tres modi : de expetendis fugiendisve rebus, ut expetendine honores sint, num fugienda paupertas ; de aequo aut iniquo, ut aequumne sit ulcisci iniurias etiam propinquorum ; de honesto aut turpi, ut hoc, sitne honestum gloriae

117 causa mortem obire.   Comparationis autem duo sunt modi : unus cum idemne sit an aliquid intersit quaeritur, ut metuere et vereri, ut rex et tyrannus, ut assentator et amicus ; alter cum quid praestet aliud alii quaeritur, ut illud, optimine cuiusque sapientes an populari laude ducantur.   Atque eae quidem disceptationes quae ad cognitionem referuntur sic fere a doctissimis hominibus describuntur.

118   XXX. Quae vero referuntur ad agendum, aut in officii disceptatione versantur—quo in genere quid rectum faciendumque sit quaeritur, cui loco omnis virtutum et vitiorum est silva subiecta—aut in animorum aliqua permotione aut gignenda aut sedanda tollendave tractantur.   Huic generi subiectae sunt cohortationes, obiurgationes, consolationes, miserationes, omnisque ad omnem animi motum et impulsio et, si ita res feret, mitigatio.

119   Explicatis igitur his generibus ac modis disceptationum omnium nihil sane ad rem pertinet si qua

of inquiry : either the question considered is a simple one, for instance if the debate is whether fame is desirable ; or it involves a comparison— whether praise or wealth is the more desirable ? Of simple questions there are three modes—concerning things to be desired or to be avoided, as whether honours are desirable, whether poverty is to be avoided ; concerning right or wrong, as whether it is right to retaliate even for injuries done by relatives ; and concerning the honourable and base, for instance the question, is it honourable to face death for the 117 sake of glory ? Of comparison on the other hand there are two modes, one when it is asked whether two things—for example fear and reverence, king and tyrant, flatterer and friend—are the same or whether there is a difference between them, and the other when it is asked which of two things is pre- ferable, for example, are wise men attracted by the approval of eminent individuals or by popular applause ? This virtually is the classification made by persons eminent for learning of discussions as to matters of knowledge.

118 XXX. "Those referring to conduct either deal with (b) As to the discussion of duty—the department that asks particular what action is right and proper, a topic comprising problems of conduct: the whole subject of the virtues and vices—or are employed either in producing or in allaying or re- moving some emotion. This class comprises modes of exhortation, reproach, consolation, compassion and every method of exciting, and also, if so indicated by the situation, of allaying all the emotions.

19 "Now therefore that we have explained these classes and modes of every form of discussion, it is obviously a matter of no consequence if our classi-

in re discrepavit ab Antoni divisione nostra partitio :
eadem enim sunt membra in utriusque disputationibus, sed paulo secus a me atque ab illo partita ac
distributa. Nunc ad reliqua progrediar meque ad
meum munus pensumque revocabo. Nam ex illis
locis quos exposuit Antonius omnia sunt ad quaeque
genera quaestionum argumenta sumenda sed aliis
generibus alii loci magis erunt apti ; de quo, non tam
quia longum est quam quia perspicuum, dici nihil
est necesse.

120   Ornatissimae sunt igitur orationes eae quae latissime vagantur et a singulari[1] controversia se ad
universi generis vim explicandam conferunt et con-
vertunt, ut ei qui audiant natura et genere et universa
re cognita de singulis reis et criminibus et litibus
121 statuere possint. Hanc ad consuetudinem exercitationis vos adolescentes est cohortatus Antonius
atque a minutis angustisque concertationibus ad
omnem vim varietatemque vos disserendi traducendos
putavit ; quare non est paucorum libellorum hoc
munus, ut ei qui scripserunt de dicendi ratione arbi-
trati sunt, neque Tusculani atque huius ambulationis
antemeridianae aut nostrae pomeridianae sessionis ;
non enim solum acuenda nobis neque procudenda
lingua est, sed onerandum complendumque pectus
maximarum rerum et plurimarum suavitate, copia,
varietate.

122   XXXI. Nostra est enim—si modo nos oratores,
si in civium disceptationibus, si in periculis, si in

---

[1] *Kayser :* a privata ac a singulari (a privata *Sorof*).

---

[a] Book II, §§ 133 ff.

fication has differed in any point from the divisions
made by Antonius; both our treatments of the subject contain the same component parts, but they have
been somewhat differently divided and arranged by
me and by him. I will now go on to the remaining
subjects and will recall myself to the particular task
assigned to me. For from the topics set out by
Antonius all the arguments applicable to each class
of problem have to be taken, but different topics
will be more suitable for different classes; however,
nothing need be said about this, not so much because
it is a lengthy matter as because it is obvious.

120 "Well then, the most ornate speeches are those
which take the widest range and which turn aside
from the particular matter in dispute to engage in
an explanation of the meaning of the general issue,
so as to enable the audience to base their verdict
in regard to the particular parties and charges and
actions in question on a knowledge of the nature and
121 character of the matter as a whole. The regular
practice of this exercise has been urged upon you
juniors by Antonius,[a] who thought it proper to lead
you away from narrow pettifogging argumentation to
the whole expanse and diversity of discourse; and in
consequence this is not a task to be performed by a
few handbooks, as the authors of systems of rhetoric
imagine, nor an occupation for a country holiday
and for our morning walk or afternoon session in
the colonnade; for we require not merely to forge
a sharp edge to our tongue, but to load and charge
our mind with a delightful and plentiful variety of
high matters in the greatest number.

122 XXXI. "For to us belong—assuming that we are
really orators, that is, persons competent to be re-

how to apply general principles.

deliberationibus publicis adhibendi auctores et principes sumus—nostra est, inquam, omnis ista prudentiae doctrinaeque possessio, in quam homines
quasi caducam atque vacuam abundantes otio nobis
occupatis involaverunt, atque etiam aut irridentes
oratorem ut ille in Gorgia Socrates cavillantur aut
aliquid de oratoris arte paucis praecipiunt libellis
eosque rhetoricos inscribunt, quasi non illa sint
propria rhetorum quae ab eisdem de iustitia, de
officio, de civitatibus instituendis et regendis, de omni
123 vivendi ratione[1] dicuntur.   Quae quoniam iam aliunde non possumus, sumenda sunt nobis ab eis ipsis
a quibus expilati sumus ; dummodo illa ad hanc
civilem scientiam quo pertinent et quam intuentur
transferamus, neque, ut ante dixi, omnem teramus
in his discendis rebus aetatem, sed cum fontes videri-
mus, quos nisi qui celeriter cognorit nunquam cog-
noscet omnino, tum quotiescumque opus erit ex eis
124 tantum quantum res petet hauriamus—nam neque
tam est acris acies in naturis hominum et ingeniis ut
res tantas quisquam nisi monstratas possit videre,
neque tanta tamen in rebus obscuritas ut eas non
penitus acri vir ingenio cernat si modo aspexerit.
In hoc igitur tanto tam immensoque campo cum
liceat oratori vagari libere atque ubicumque con-

[1] *Bakius :* vivendi denique etiam de naturae ratione.

tained as leaders and principals in civil actions and criminal trials and public debates—to us, I say, belong the broad estates of wisdom and of learning, which having been allowed to lapse and become derelict during our absorption in affairs, have been invaded by persons too generously supplied with leisure, persons who actually either banter and ridicule the orator after the manner of Socrates in Plato's *Gorgias*, or else write a few little manuals of instruction in the art of oratory and label them with the title of *Rhetoric*—just as if the province of the rhetoricians did not include their pronouncements on the subjects of justice and duty and the constitution and government of states, in short, the entire field 123 of practical philosophy. As we can now no longer obtain these principles from elsewhere, we have to take them from the very persons who plundered us : only provided that we carry them over into the field of political science to which they belong and with which they are concerned, and, as I said before, avoid spending an entire lifetime in acquiring them, but after we have beheld the fountain-heads, which one who does not get to know them quickly will never get to know at all, then draw from these sources, whenever necessary, as much as the subject demands 124 —for mankind is not endowed by nature with such keenness of intellect that anyone can discern these great matters without having had them pointed out to him, nor all the same do they involve so much obscurity that a man of keen intelligence cannot see to the bottom of them, provided he has looked closely at them. Consequently as the orator has the liberty to roam freely in so wide and measureless a field and wherever he takes his stand to find himself on his

stiterit consistere in suo, facile suppeditat omnis
125 apparatus ornatusque dicendi ; rerum enim copia
verborum copiam gignit, et si est honestas in rebus
ipsis de quibus dicitur, exsistit[1] naturalis quidam
splendor in verbis. Sit modo is qui dicet aut scribet
institutus liberaliter educatione doctrinaque puerili
et flagret studio et a natura adiuvetur et in univer-
sorum generum infinitis disceptationibus exercitatus
ornatissimos scriptores oratoresque ad cognoscendum
imitandumque delegerit, nae ille haud sane quemadmodum verba struat et illuminet a magistris istis
requiret ; ita facile in rerum abundantia ad orationis
ornamenta sine duce natura ipsa, si modo est exercitata, labetur.[2]

126   XXXII. Hic Catulus : Di immortales ! inquit,
quantam rerum varietatem, quantam vim, quantam
copiam, Crasse, complexus es quantisque ex angustiis
oratorem educere ausus es et in maiorum suorum
regno collocare ! Namque illos veteres doctores
auctoresque dicendi nullum genus disputationis a se
alienum putasse accepimus semperque esse in omni
127 orationis ratione versatos ; ex quibus Eleus Hippias
cum Olympiam venisset maxima illa quinquennali
celebritate ludorum, gloriatus est cuncta paene
audiente Graecia nihil esse ulla in arte rerum omnium

---

[1] *Wilkins :* exsistit ex re.
[2] *Bétolaud* (excitata labetur *Ellendt*) *:* delabetur.

own ground, all the resources and embellishments
125 of oratory are readily available ; for a full supply
of facts begets a full supply of words, and if the subjects discussed are themselves of an elevated character this produces a spontaneous brilliance in the
language. Only let the intending speaker or writer,
thanks to the training given by a liberal education
in boyhood, possess a glowing enthusiasm as well as
the assistance of good natural endowments, and,
having had practice in the abstract discussions of
general principles, have selected the most accomplished writers and orators for study and imitation :
then of a certainty such a one will not have to come
to your professors to be shown how to put words together and how to invest them with brilliance of style ;
so easily will nature of herself, if only she has received
training, given a plentiful supply of matter, find her
way without any guidance to the adornments of
oratory."

126   XXXII. Here Catulus broke in : " Good heavens," The
he said, " what an enormous variety of important sophists
considerations you have covered, Crassus, and out rhetoric
of what narrow limitations you have been bold ambitious
enough to rescue the orator and elevate him to the
throne of his ancestors ! For in the good old days,
as we are told, the professors and masters of rhetoric
considered no kind of discourse to lie outside their
province, and continually occupied themselves with
127 every system of oratory ; one of them, Hippias of
Elis, visiting Olympia on the occasion of the quad-
rennial celebration of the famous games, boasted
before an audience containing virtually the whole of
Greece that there was not a single fact included in
any system of encyclopaedic knowledge with which

quod ipse nesciret, nec solum has artes quibus
liberales doctrinae atque ingenuae continerentur,
geometriam, musicam, litterarum cognitionem et
poetarum, atque illa quae de naturis rerum, quae de
hominum moribus, quae de rebus publicis dicerentur
se tenere,[1] sed anulum quem haberet, pallium quo
amictus, soccos quibus indutus esset, se sua manu
128 confecisse. Scilicet nimis hic quidem est progressus,
sed ex eo ipso est coniectura facilis quantum sibi illi
ipsi oratores de praeclarissimis artibus appetierint
qui ne sordidiores quidem repudiarint. Quid de
Prodico Ceo, quid de Thrasymacho Chalcedonio,
de Protagora Abderita loquar ? quorum unusquisque
plurimum ut[2] temporibus illis etiam de natura rerum
129 et disseruit et scripsit. Ipse ille Leontinus Gorgias
quo patrono, ut Plato voluit, philosopho succubuit
orator—qui aut non est victus unquam a Socrate
neque sermo ille Platonis verus est, aut si est victus,
eloquentior videlicet fuit et disertior Socrates et ut
tu appellas copiosior et melior orator—sed hic in illo
ipso Platonis libro de omni re quaecumque in disceptationem quaestionemque vocetur se copiosissime
dicturum esse profitetur ; isque princeps ex omnibus
ausus est in conventu poscere qua de re quisque vellet
audire ; cui tantus honos habitus est a Graecia, soli
ut ex omnibus Delphis non inaurata statua sed aurea
statueretur.
130 Sed hi quos nominavi multique praeterea summi

---

[1] se tenere *add. Campius.*
[2] ut *add. Campius.*

---

[a] The Sicilian professor of oratory who figures in Plato's
Gorgias as arguing, against Socrates, that rhetoric is the
supreme science.
[b] *Cf.* Book I, § 47.

he was not acquainted ; and that he had not only acquired the accomplishments that form the basis of the liberal education of a gentleman, mathematics, music, knowledge of literature and poetry, and the doctrines of natural science, ethics and political science, but had made with his own hand the ring he had on, the cloak he was dressed in and the boots 128 he was wearing. No doubt Hippias went too far, but the story of itself makes it easy for us to guess how keen an appetite the orators of old had for the most distinguished accomplishments, if they did not spurn even the meaner ones. What shall I say about Prodicus of Ceos or Thrasymachus of Chalcedon or Protagoras of Abdera ? each of whom both lectured and wrote what was considering their period a great 129 amount on natural science as well. Even the famous Gorgias [a] of Leontini, who according to Plato appeared as advocate for the orator when he lost his case against the philosopher,—an adversary who either in reality never was defeated by Socrates and Plato's famous dialogue is untrue, or if defeated he was, obviously Socrates was more eloquent and fluent and, to use your own description,[b] a fuller and better orator—well, Gorgias in the very volume of Plato in question gives it out that he will speak with exhaustive fullness on every subject brought forward for discussion and investigation ; and he was the first of all persons who was bold enough in conference to ask what subject each of the party wished to hear him speak on. And he was held in such honour by Greece that to him alone of all men a statue was erected at Delphi that was not gilt but made of solid gold.

130 "But these whom I have named and many eminent

dicendi auctores uno tempore fuerunt : **ex** quibus
intellegi potest ita se rem habere ut tu, Crasse, dicis,
' oratorisque ' nomen apud antiquos in Graecia maiore
131 quadam vel copia vel gloria floruisse.   Quo quidem
magis dubito, tibine plus laudis an Graecis vitupera-
tionis esse tribuendum statuam : cum tu in alia lingua
ac moribus natus occupatissima in civitate vel privatorum negotiis paene omnibus vel orbis terrae pro-
curatione ac summi imperii gubernatione districtus
tantam **vim** rerum cognitionemque comprehenderis,
eamque omnem cum eius qui consilio et oratione in
civitate valeat scientia atque exercitatione sociaris,
illi nati in litteris ardentesque his studiis, otio vero
diffluentes, non modo nihil acquisierint sed ne relictum quidem et traditum et suum conservaverint.

132   XXXIII. Tum Crassus : Non in hac, inquit, una,
Catule, **re** sed **in** aliis etiam compluribus distributione partium **ac** separatione magnitudines sunt
artium diminutae. **An** tu existimas, cum esset
Hippocrates ille Cous, fuisse tum alios medicos qui
morbis, alios qui vulneribus, alios qui oculis mede-
rentur ? num geometriam Euclide aut Archimede,
num musicam Damone aut Aristoxeno, num ipsas
litteras Aristophane aut Callimacho tractante tam
discerptas fuisse **ut** nemo genus universum com-

authorities on oratory besides were all contemporaries; and they are evidence that what you say, Crassus, is the case—a larger or perhaps more famous list adorned the name of 'orator' in Greece
131 in the old days. This indeed makes me the more doubtful whether to decide that more praise is to be assigned to you or more blame to the Greeks; inasmuch as you who have another native language and were born under a different form of society, in spite of your dwelling in an extremely busy community and being engrossed in almost every sort of private business or else in the government of the entire world and the administration of a vast empire, have succeeded in acquiring and grasping so vast a range of facts, and have coupled with all this the knowledge and the practical activity of one whose wisdom and oratory give him influence in the state ; whereas the Greeks, though born in a world of literature and enthusiasts for these studies, are yet demoralized by sloth and have not only made no further acquisitions but have not even preserved their own heritage that came down to them."

132 XXXIII. " That is not the only loss," Crassus rejoined, " but there are a great many others also that have been inflicted on the wide domain of science by its being split up into separate departments. Do you really suppose that in the time of the great Hippocrates of Cos there were some physicians who specialized in medicine and others in surgery and others in ophthalmic cases? or that mathematics in the hands of Euclid or Archimedes, or music with Damon or Aristoxenus, or even literature with Aristophanes or Callimachus were such entirely separate subjects that nobody embraced culture as a whole, but instead

Great oratory avoids narrow specialization.

103

plecteretur atque ut alius aliam sibi partem in qua
133 elaboraret seponeret ? Equidem saepe hoc audivi
de patre et de socero meo, nostros quoque homines
qui excellere sapientiae gloria vellent omnia quae
quidem tum haec civitas nosset solitos esse complecti.
Meminerant illi Sex. Aelium ; M'. vero Manilium
nos etiam vidimus transverso ambulantem foro,
quod erat insigne eum qui id faceret facere civibus
omnibus consilii sui copiam ; ad quos olim et ita
ambulantes et in solio sedentes domi sic adibatur
non solum ut de iure civili ad eos verum etiam de filia
collocanda, de fundo emendo, de agro colendo, de
omni denique aut officio aut negotio referretur.
134 Haec fuit P. Crassi illius veteris, haec Ti. Coruncani,
haec proavi generi mei Scipionis prudentissimi
hominis sapientia, qui omnes pontifices maximi
fuerunt, ut ad eos de omnibus divinis atque humanis
rebus referretur ; eidemque et in senatu et apud
populum et in causis amicorum et domi et militiae
135 consilium suum fidemque praestabant. Quid enim
M. Catoni praeter hanc politissimam doctrinam
transmarinam atque adventitiam defuit ? num quia
ius civile didicerat causas non dicebat ? aut quia
poterat dicere iuris scientiam neglegebat ? At
utroque in genere et laboravit et praestitit. Num
propter hanc ex privatorum negotiis collectam
gratiam tardior in republica capessenda fuit ? Nemo

of that everybody chose for himself a different division
133 to work in ? For my part I have often heard my
own father and my wife's father say that our people
too who desired to win high distinction in philosophy
used to embrace all the subjects that at all events at
that period were known in our country. They could
recollect Sextus Aelius, while we have actually seen
Manius Manilius walking across the forum, and the
remarkable thing was that in doing this he was putting
his wisdom at the service of all his fellow-citizens ;
and in old days persons resorted to these men both
when they were going a walk as described and when
seated in their chairs of state at home, not only to
consult them on points of law but also about marrying
off a daughter, buying a farm, tilling their estates,
134 and in short every sort of liability or business. Such
was the wisdom of the old Publius Crassus, of Titus
Coruncanius and of that most sagacious person Scipio,
my wife's great-great-grandfather, all of whom were
Supreme Pontiffs, that they were consulted about
every kind of business, religious or secular ; and
what is more they proferred the services of their
wisdom and loyalty in the Senate and the popular
assembly, in their friends' lawsuits, at home and on
135 foreign service. For what did Marcus Cato lack
except our present-day super-refinement of culture
which we have imported from overseas ? Did his study
of the law cause him to refrain from appearing in
court ? did his ability as a pleader make him neglect
the science of jurisprudence ? No, he was an ardent
worker in both fields, and won distinction in both.
Did the influence thus acquired from doing the business of private clients make him backward in taking
part in public life ? No one had more influence in

apud populum fortior, nemo melior senator, idem
facile optimus imperator ; denique nihil in hac
civitate temporibus illis sciri discive potuit quod ille
non cum investigarit et scierit, tum etiam conscrip-
136 serit. Nunc contra plerique ad honores adipiscendos
et ad rempublicam gerendam nudi veniunt atque
inermes, nulla cognitione rerum, nulla scientia ornati.
Sin aliquis excellit unus e multis, effert se si unum
aliquid affert, aut bellicam virtutem et[1] usum
aliquem militarem, quae sane nunc quidem obsole-
verunt, aut iuris scientiam, ne eius quidem universi,
nam pontificium quod est coniunctum nemo discit ;
aut eloquentiam, quam in clamore et in verborum
cursu positam putant ; omnium vero bonarum artium,
denique virtutum ipsarum societatem cognationem-
que non norunt.

137 XXXIV. Sed ut ad Graecos referam orationem,
quibus carere hoc quidem in sermonis genere non
possumus—nam ut virtutis a nostris, sic doctrinae
sunt ab illis exempla repetenda—septem fuisse
dicuntur uno tempore qui ' sapientes ' et haberentur
et vocarentur : hi omnes praeter Milesium Thalen
civitatibus suis praefuerunt. Quis doctior eisdem illis
temporibus aut cuius eloquentia litteris instructior
fuisse traditur quam Pisistrati ? qui primus Homeri

[1] *Rackham :* aut.

the Assembly of the People, no one was a better member of the Senate, and at the same time he was also easily our most competent military commander—in fine there was nothing that at that period could possibly be known or learned that he had not studied and acquired, and, what is more, 136 written about. Nowadays on the contrary men usually come to the pursuit of office and to positions in the government quite naked and unarmed, not equipped with any acquaintance with affairs or knowledge. Or if a single one among many stands out as an exception, he is proud of himself if he brings to his duties a single qualification, either soldierly valour and some military experience—these no doubt being things that are quite out of date nowadays,—or knowledge of law—and not even then of the whole of the law, for nobody studies ecclesiastical law, which is connected with civil law,—or eloquence, which they fancy to consist in shouting and in a flow of words ; but as for familiarity and kinship with the whole of the liberal sciences and in fine with the virtues themselves—this lies outside their ken.

137 XXXIV. " But to bring round my discourse to the Greeks—with whom in this class of discussion at all events we cannot dispense, for just as we have to go to our fellow-countrymen for examples of virtue so we have to turn to the Greeks for models of learning— it is said that there existed seven persons at one time who were deemed and actually styled ' wise men ' ; all these excepting Thales of Miletus were the heads of their states. Who is recorded to have been wiser, at that same period, or better equipped with eloquence informed by learning than Pisistratus ? He is said to have been the first person who arranged

The Greek statesmen were men of culture.

libros confusos antea sic disposuisse dicitur ut nunc
habemus. Non fuit ille quidem civibus suis utilis,
sed ita eloquentia floruit ut litteris doctrinaque prae-
138 staret. Quid Pericles ? de cuius dicendi copia sic
accepimus ut, cum contra voluntatem Atheniensium
loqueretur pro salute patriae severius, tamen id
ipsum quod ille contra populares homines diceret
populare omnibus et iucundum videretur : cuius in
labris veteres comici, etiam cum illi male dicerent
—quod tum Athenis fieri licebat—leporem habitasse
dixerunt, tantamque in eo vim fuisse ut in eorum
mentibus qui audissent quasi aculeos quosdam relinqueret. At hunc non clamator aliqui ad clep-
sydram latrare docuerat sed, ut accepimus, Clazo-
menius ille Anaxagoras, vir summus in maximarum
rerum scientia : itaque hic doctrina, consilio, eloquentia excellens quadraginta annos praefuit Athenis
139 et urbanis eodem tempore et bellicis rebus. Quid
Critias ? quid Alcibiades ? civibus[1] quidem suis
non boni sed certe docti atque eloquentes nonne
Socraticis erant disputationibus eruditi ? Quis
Dionem Syracusium doctrinis omnibus expolivit ?
non Plato ? atque eum idem ille non linguae solum
verum etiam animi ac virtutis magister ad liberandam
patriam impulit, instruxit, armavit. Aliisne igitur

[1] *Warmington :* civitatibus.

---

[a] Πειθώ τις ἐπεκάθιζεν ἐπὶ τοῖς χείλεσιν·
οὕτως ἐκήλει καὶ μόνος τῶν ῥητόρων
τὸ κέντρον ἐγκατέλειπε τοῖς ἀκροωμένοις.
Eupolis fr. 94.

the previously disordered books of Homer in the order
in which now we have them. Pisistratus it is true
did no service to his fellow-citizens, but he was so
distinguished for his eloquence that he was an out-
138 standing figure in literature and learning. What of
Pericles ? as to whose oratorical powers we are told
that although he used to speak with some degree of
sternness in opposition to the wishes of the Athenians
when the national safety required, nevertheless
the very fact that he spoke against the popular
leaders appeared to be popular and acceptable to
everyone ; and there was a saying *a* of the play-
wrights of the Old Comedy, even although they
used to abuse him—which in those days was permitted at Athens—, that charm dwelt in his lips,
and that he possessed so much force as to leave a
sting in the minds of his hearers. But Pericles'
teacher had not been some bawler giving lessons in
vociferating against the clock, but, as we are told, it
was the great Anaxagoras of Clazomenae, a man distinguished for his knowledge of the highest sciences ;
and consequently Pericles was eminent in learning,
wisdom and eloquence, and for forty years was supreme at Athens both in politics and at the same time
139 in the conduct of war. What of Critias ? and Alcibiades ? these though not benefactors of their fellow-
citizens were undoubtedly learned and eloquent ;
and did they not owe their training to the discussions
of Socrates ? Who put the final polish on the education of Dio of Syracuse in every department of learning ? was it not Plato ? and it was that same teacher
not only of eloquence but also of wisdom and virtue
who instigated Dio to win freedom for his native land
and equipped him with weapons for the task. Were

artibus hunc Dionem instituit Plato, aliis Isocrates
clarissimum virum Timotheum, Cononis praestantis-
simi imperatoris filium, summum ipsum imperatorem
hominemque doctissimum ? aut aliis Pythagoreus
ille Lysis Thebanum Epaminondam, haud scio an
summum virum unum omnis Graeciae ? aut Xenophon Agesilaum aut Philolaus Archytam Tarentinum?
aut ipse Pythagoras totam illam veterem Italiae
Graeciam quae quondam Magna vocitata est ?
140 Equidem non arbitror; XXXV. sic enim video, unam
quamdam omnium rerum quae essent homine erudito
dignae atque eo qui in republica vellet excellere
fuisse doctrinam, quam qui accepissent, si eidem
ingenio ad pronuntiandam[1] valuissent et se ad
dicendum quoque non repugnante natura dedissent,
141 eloquentia praestitisse. Itaque ipse Aristoteles cum
florere Isocratem nobilitate discipulorum videret
quod[2] suas disputationes a causis forensibus et civi-
libus ad inanem sermonis elegantiam transtulisset,
mutavit repente totam formam prope disciplinae
suae versumque quemdam Philoctetae paulo secus
dixit : ille enim turpe sibi ait esse tacere cum bar-
baros, hic autem cum Isocratem pateretur dicere ;
itaque ornavit et illustravit doctrinam illam omnem
rerumque cognitionem cum orationis exercitatione
coniunxit. Neque vero hoc fugit sapientissimum
regem Philippum, qui hunc Alexandro filio doctorem

---

[1] *Rackham :* pronuntiandum.
[2] *Wilkins :* quod ipse.

---

[a] Αἰσχρὸν σιωπᾶν βαρβάρους δ' ἐᾶν λέγειν Plutarch, *adv.
Colot.* 1108 в, perhaps from Euripides, *Philoctetes.*
[b] *Turpe esse tacere et Isocratem pati dicere* Quintilian
iii. 1. 4, schol. αἰσχρὸν σιωπᾶν 'Ισοκράτην δ' ἐᾶν λέγειν.

any other subjects then employed by Plato for the education of Dio, or by Isocrates with the famous commander Conon's most distinguished son Timotheus,
himself a consummate soldier and an erudite scholar ?
or by the great Pythagorean philosopher Lysis with
Epaminondas of Thebes, perhaps the most outstanding
figure in Greek history ? or Xenophon with Agesilaus ?
or Philolaus with Archytas of Taranto ? or Pythagoras
himself with the whole of the old Greek district of
Italy that in former times bore the name of Magna
140 Graecia ?   That is not my own opinion ; XXXV. for
what I observe is, that there was one particular course
of education, including all the subjects worthy of a
man of culture and of political ambition, which enabled
persons who had received it, provided that they also
had the talent enabling them to express it in words,
and moreover had practised themselves in speaking
and were not hampered by any natural incapacity,
141 to come to the front in oratory.   Accordingly when
Aristotle observed that Isocrates succeeded in obtaining a distinguished set of pupils by means of abandon-
ing legal and political subjects and devoting his
discourses to empty elegance of style, he himself
suddenly altered almost the whole of his own system
of training, and quoted a line from *Philoctetes* with a
slight modification : the hero in the tragedy said
that it was a disgrace for him to keep silent and suffer
barbarians to speak,[a] but Aristotle put it ' suffer
Isocrates to speak '[b] ; and consequently he put the
whole of his system of philosophy in a polished and
brilliant form, and linked the scientific study of facts
with practice in style.   Nor indeed did this escape
the notice of that extremely sagacious monarch
Philip, who summoned Aristotle to be the tutor of

accierit, a quo eodem ille et agendi acciperet praecepta et loquendi.

142 Nunc sive qui volet, eum philosophum qui copiam
nobis rerum orationisque tradat per me appellet
oratorem licet, sive hunc oratorem quem ego dico
sapientiam iunctam habere eloquentiae philosophum
appellare malit, non impediam : dummodo hoc
constet, neque infantiam eius qui rem norit sed eam
explicare dicendo non queat, neque inscientiam
illius cui res non suppetat, verba non desint, esse
laudandam. Quorum si alterum sit optandum, malim
equidem indisertam prudentiam quam stultitiam
143 loquacem ; sin quaerimus quid unum excellat ex
omnibus, docto oratori palma danda est. Quem si
patiuntur eundem esse philosophum, sublata controversia est ; sin eos diiungent, hoc erunt inferiores
quod in oratore perfecto inest illorum omnis scientia,
in philosophorum autem cognitione non continuo
inest eloquentia ; quae quamvis contemnatur ab eis,
necesse est tamen aliquem cumulum illorum artibus
afferre videatur.

Haec cum Crassus dixisset, parumper et ipse con-
ticuit et ceteris silentium fuit.

144 XXXVI. Tum Cotta : Equidem, inquit, Crasse,
non possum queri quod mihi videare aliud quid-

his son Alexander, and to impart to him the principles both of conduct and of oratory.

142 "At this stage I give full leave to anybody who wishes, to apply the title of orator to a philosopher who imparts to us an abundant command of facts and of language, or alternatively I shall raise no obstacle if he prefers to designate as a philosopher the orator whom I on my side am now describing as possessing wisdom combined with eloquence : only provided it be agreed that neither the tongue-tied silence of the man who knows the facts but cannot explain them in language, nor the ignorance of the person who is deficient in facts but has no lack of words, is deserving of praise. And if one had to choose between them, for my own part I should prefer wisdom lacking

143 power of expression to talkative folly ; but if on the contrary we are trying to find the one thing that stands top of the whole list, the prize must go to the orator who possesses learning. And if they allow him also to be a philosopher, that is the end of the dispute ; but if they keep the two separate, they will come off second best in this, that the consummate orator possesses all the knowledge of the philosophers, but the range of philosophers does not necessarily include eloquence ; and although they look down on it, it cannot but be deemed to add a crowning embellishment to their sciences."

After saying this Crassus himself was silent for a space, and nothing was said by any of the others either.

144 XXXVI. Then Cotta spoke : " For my own part, Crassus," he said, " I cannot grumble at your having discussed a different subject, as it seems to me, and not

Marginal notes: Even philosophers require style.

That orators need culture disputed.

dam et non id quod susceperis disputasse. Plus
enim aliquanto attulisti quam tibi esset tributum a
nobis ac denuntiatum ; sed certe ut eae partes fuerunt tuae de illustranda oratione ut diceres, et eras
ipse iam ingressus atque in quatuor partes omnem
orationis laudem discripseras, cum de duabus[1] primis
nobis quidem satis, sed, ut ipse dicebas, celeriter
exigueque dixisses, duas tibi reliquas feceras, quemadmodum primum ornate, deinde etiam apte
145 diceremus ; quo cum ingressus esses, repente te
quasi quidam aestus ingenii tui procul a terra abripuit
atque in altum a conspectu paene omnium abstraxit.
Omnem enim rerum scientiam complexus non tu
quidem eam nobis tradidisti, neque enim fuit tam
exigui temporis, sed apud hos quid profeceris nescio,
me quidem in Academiam totum compulisti. In
qua velim sit illud quod saepe posuisti, ut non necesse
sit consumere aetatem atque ut possit is illa omnia
cernere qui tantummodo aspexerit : sed etiamsi est
aliquanto[2] spissius aut si ego sum tardior, profecto
nunquam conquiescam neque defatigabor ante quam
illorum ancipites vias rationesque et pro omnibus et
contra omnia disputandi percepero.

146 Tum Caesar : Unum, inquit, me ex tuo ser-

---

[1] *Kayser :* cumque duabus.
[2] *v.l.* aliquando.

---

[a] § 37.

the one that you undertook to discuss. For you have contributed considerably more than had been assigned to you and requisitioned by us; but assuredly, whereas you were cast for the part of speaking about stylistic embellishment, and you had actually started and had divided [a] the whole subject of excellence of style into four parts, although you had treated the first two of them (adequately, it is true, for the purpose of our investigation, but, as you yourself admitted, rapidly and on a small scale), you had left the two others still to be dealt with—the questions how we are to secure (a) elegance and (b) appropriate-
145 ness of style; and after starting on this, you were suddenly caught by the flood-tide of your genius and carried away from land out to deep sea, almost out of everybody's sight. For you embraced the whole of knowledge, and though it is true you did not convey it to us, which was indeed impossible in so short a space of time, nevertheless, although I do not know how you succeeded with our friends, in my own case anyway you forced me to come over entirely to the side of the Academy. And I should be glad to think that your frequent assertion holds good—that it is not indispensable to spend a lifetime in that school, and that it is possible to gain a complete purview of the system by a mere glance; but even if it is a considerably slower business than that, or if I myself am rather a slow-coach, unquestionably I shall never come to a standstill or give up from exhaustion before I have a full grasp of the school's twofold method and its system of arguing both *pro* and *contra* about every proposition."

146 " One thing in your discourse particularly struck me, Crassus," interposed Caesar, " your assertion that

mone maxime, Crasse, commovit, quod eum negasti
qui non cito quid didicisset unquam omnino posse
perdiscere : ut mihi non sit difficile periclitari et aut
statim percipere ista quae tu verbis ad caelum ex-
tulisti, aut, si non potuerim, tempus non perdere,
cum tamen his nostris possim esse contentus.

147 Hic Sulpicius : Ego vero, inquit, Crasse, neque
Aristotelem istum neque Carneadem nec philosophorum quemquam desidero. Vel me licet existimes
desperare ista posse perdiscere vel, id quod facio,
contemnere ; mihi rerum forensium et communium
vulgaris haec cognitio satis magna est ad eam quam
specto eloquentiam ; ex qua ipsa tamen permulta
nescio, quae tum denique cum causa aliqua quae a
me dicenda est desiderat quaero. Quam ob rem nisi
forte es iam defessus et si tibi non graves sumus,
refer ad illa te quae ad ipsius orationis laudem splen-
doremque pertinent : quae ego ex te audire volui
non ut desperarem me eloquentiam consequi posse
sed ut aliquid addiscerem.

148 XXXVII. Tum Crassus : Pervulgatas res requiris, inquit, et tibi non incognitas, Sulpici ;
quis enim de isto genere non docuit, non instituit,
non etiam scriptum reliquit ? Sed geram morem
et ea dumtaxat quae mihi nota sunt breviter exponam tibi ; censebo tamen ad eos qui auctores et

a person who does not succeed in learning a thing quickly will never be able to learn it thoroughly at all ; so that I need make no bones about trying my luck, and either fully grasping the principles you have extolled so highly at one stroke, or, if I prove unable, not wasting my time, as all the same I am quite able to rest content with these faculties that belong to our race."

47 Hereat Sulpicius said : " I on the contrary, Crassus, have no use for your Aristotle or Carneades or any other philosopher. You are welcome to assume either that I have no hope of being able to master those doctrines of yours or that I despise them—as in fact I do ; but for my own part our ordinary acquaintance with legal and public affairs is extensive enough for the eloquence that I have in view ; though even it contains a great deal that I do not know, and this I only look up when it is necessary for some case that I have to plead. Consequently, if you are not perhaps by this time tired out, and if we are not boring you, go back to the qualities that contribute to distinction and brilliance in oratory itself ; which for my part I wanted to hear from you not in order to make me lose all hope of being able to attain eloquence myself, but for the purpose of adding to my stock of knowledge."

XXXVII. " The matters you inquire about are extremely familiar," rejoined Crassus, " and not unknown to yourself, Sulpicius ; for who has not given lessons and even left essays on the branch of the subject you allude to ? However, I will humour you by giving you a brief lecture on at all events the points that I am acquainted with ; although my real opinion will be that the proper method is to go back

The ornate style in detail :

inventores sunt harum sane minutarum rerum re-
vertendum.

149 Omnis igitur oratio conficitur ex verbis, quorum
primum nobis ratio simpliciter videnda est, deinde
coniuncte ; nam est quidam ornatus orationis qui ex
singulis verbis est, alius qui ex continuatis[1] constat.
Ergo utimur verbis aut eis quae propria sunt et certa
quasi vocabula rerum paene una nata cum rebus
ipsis ; aut eis quae transferuntur et quasi alieno in
loco collocantur ; aut eis quae novamus et facimus
150 ipsi. In propriis est igitur[2] illa laus oratoris ut ab-
iecta atque obsoleta fugiat, lectis atque illustribus
utatur in quibus plenum quiddam et sonans inesse
videatur. Sed in hoc verborum genere[3] delectus est
quidam habendus atque is aurium quodam iudicio
ponderandus : in quo consuetudo etiam bene lo-
151 quendi valet plurimum. Itaque hoc quod vulgo de
oratoribus ab imperitis dici solet, ' Bonis hic verbis,'
aut ' Aliquis non bonis utitur,' non arte aliqua per-
penditur sed quodam quasi naturali sensu iudicatur :
in quo non magna laus est vitare vitium, quanquam
id est magnum, verum hoc quasi solum quoddam
atque fundamentum est, verborum usus et copia
152 bonorum. Sed quid ipse aedificet orator et in quo
adiungat artem, id esse a nobis quaerendum[4] videtur.

XXXVIII. Tria sunt igitur in verbo simplici quae
orator afferat ad illustrandam atque exornandam

---

[1] *Kayser :* continuatis coniunctis.
[2] *v.l.* igitur verbis.
[3] *Kayser :* genere propriorum.
[4] *v.l.* quaerendum atque explicandum.

to those who on these undoubted niceties rank as original authorities.

149 "Well then, all oratory is made up of words, and we must examine the principle of these first when they stand independently and then when in combination; for grace of style is of two kinds, one derived from the separate words and another from their combinations. The words we employ then are either the proper and definite designations of things, which were almost born at the same time as the things themselves; or terms used metaphorically and placed in a connexion not really belonging to them; or new 50 coinages invented by ourselves. In the case of proper words therefore it is the distinction of an orator to avoid what is commonplace and hackneyed and to employ select and distinguished terms that seem to have some fullness and sonority in them. But in this class of words a certain choice must be exercised, and this choice must be weighed by a critical faculty of ear—in which process the habit of speaking well 51 also has very great value. Consequently the common remark of the ordinary layman about orators, 'A's vocabulary is good' or 'B's vocabulary is not good,' is not a definitely scientific judgement but a sort of instinctive commonsense verdict; and in this department it is no great distinction to avoid mistakes, although that is important; the basic foundation is the employment of a good and copious vocabulary. 2 But it appears that what we have to discover is, what superstructure does the orator himself build, and in what does he apply his skill?

XXXVIII. "There are then three things which the orator contributes in the matter of mere vocabulary towards the decoration and embellishment of his

(a) Vocabulary:

orationem, aut inusitatum verbum aut novatum aut
153 translatum.   Inusitata sunt prisca fere ac vetusta
et ab usu quotidiani sermonis iamdiu intermissa ;
quae sunt poetarum licentiae liberiora quam nostrae,
sed tamen raro habet etiam in oratione poeticum
aliquod verbum dignitatem ;   neque enim illud
fugerim dicere, ut Coelius, ' Qua tempestate Poenus
in Italiam venit,' nec ' prolem,' aut ' sobolem,' aut
' effari,' aut ' nuncupare ' ; aut, ut tu soles, Catule,
' non rebar,' aut ' opinabar ' ;   et alia multa quibus
loco positis grandior atque antiquior oratio saepe
154 videri solet.   Novantur autem verba quae ab eo qui
dicit ipso gignuntur ac fiunt, vel coniungendis verbis,
ut haec :

Tum pavor sapientiam omnem mihi exanimato expectorat.

et[1]

   Num non vis huius me versutiloquas malitias . . . ?

—Videtis enim et ' versutiloquas ' et ' expectorat ' ex
coniunctione facta esse verba, non nata ; vel saepe[2]
sine coniunctione verba novantur, ut ille ' senius
desertus,' ut ' dii genitales,' ut ' bacarum ubertate
incurvescere.'
155   Tertius ille modus transferendi verbi late patet ;
quem necessitas genuit inopia coacta et angustiis,
post autem delectatio iucunditasque celebravit.   Nam

---

[1] et *add. Warmington.*
[2] *v.l.* sed saepe vel.

---

[a] From Ennius, *Alcmeo* (*Remains,* i. pp. 230 f., Vahlen,
Ennius, Scenica 23).
[b] From an unknown tragedy.

style—rare words, new coinages, and words used
153 metaphorically. Rare words are usually archaisms   are words
which because of their antiquity have long passed
out of use in everyday speech. These are more
freely allowed to the licence of poets than to ourselves, but nevertheless on rare occasions even in
oratory a poetic word has dignity. Indeed I should
not be afraid to use Coelius's phrase ' what time the
Carthaginian came into Italy,' nor the word ' off-
spring ' or ' progeny,' or ' utter ' or ' pronounce,' or
your favourite expressions, Catulus, ' I did not deem '
or ' I opined '; or many others that if used in the
proper context often seem to have a way of adding
154 grandeur and antiquity to the style. New coinages   new
are words invented and created by the actual speaker,   coinages,
either by combining words together, like the instances :

> Then fear from out my fainting consciousness
> Outbosoms all wisdom [a]:

and

> Surely thou would'st not have
> This fellow's twisty-speaking artfulness [b] . . .

—for you all of you notice that the words ' twisty-
speaking ' and ' outbosoms ' are artificial combinations and not a natural growth—; or often new
words are coined without the use of combination, for
instance the expression ' derelict oldster,' or ' genital
gods,' or ' to crookbow with their plenteous load of
berries.'

155   " The third method in our list, the use of metaphor,   metaphors.
is of wide application ; it sprang from necessity due
to the pressure of poverty and deficiency, but it has
been subsequently made popular by its agreeable and
entertaining quality. For just as clothes were first

ut vestis frigoris depellendi causa reperta primo, post adhiberi coepta est ad ornatum etiam corporis et dignitatem, sic verbi translatio instituta est inopiae causa, frequentata delectationis. Nam 'gemmare vites,' ' luxuriem esse in herbis,' ' laetas esse segetes ' etiam rustici dicunt. Quod enim declarari vix verbo proprio potest, id translato cum est dictum, illustrat id quod intellegi volumus eius rei quam alieno verbo posuimus similitudo. Ergo hae translationes quasi mutuationes sunt, cum quod non habeas aliunde sumas ; illae paulo audaciores quae non inopiam indicant sed orationi splendoris aliquid arcessunt : quarum ego quid vobis aut inveniendi rationem aut genera exponam ?[1]   XXXIX. [Similitudinis est ad verbum unum contracta brevitas, quod verbum in alieno loco tanquam in suo positum si agnoscitur, delectat, si simile nihil habet, repudiatur.][2]   Sed ea transferri oportet quae aut clariorem faciunt rem, ut illa[3] :

Inhorrescit mare,
Tenebrae conduplicantur, noctisque et nimbum occaecat nigror,
Flamma inter nubes coruscat, caelum tonitru contremit,
Grando mixta imbri largifluo subita praecipitans cadit,
Undique omnes venti erumpunt, saevi exsistunt turbines ;
Fervit aestu pelagus. . . .

—omnia fere quo essent clariora translatis per simi-

<hr />

[1] *Rackham :* ponam.
[2] *Sorof.*   [3] *Ellendt :* illa omnia.

<hr />

[a] This irrelevant explanation of the difference between a simile and a metaphor is clearly an interpolation.

[b] Also quoted *De Div.* i. 24, as from Pacuvius—perhaps his *Dulorestes* or his *Teucer.* *Cf. Remains,* ii. pp. 294 f., Ribbeck 411. The metaphors here are in the verbs.

invented to protect us against cold and afterwards
began to be used for the sake of adornment and dignity
as well, so the metaphorical employment of words
was begun because of poverty, but was brought into
common use for the sake of entertainment. For even
country people speak of ' jewelled vines,' ' luxuri-
ous herbage,' ' joyful harvests.' The explanation is
that when something that can scarcely be conveyed
by the proper term is expressed metaphorically, the
meaning we desire to convey is made clear by the
resemblance of the thing that we have expressed by
156 the word that does not belong. Consequently the
metaphors in which you take what you have not got
from somewhere else are a sort of borrowing ; but
there is another somewhat bolder kind that do not
indicate poverty but convey some degree of brilliance
to the style. However there is no need for me to
give you a lecture on the method of inventing these
157 or on their classification. XXXIX. [ᵃA metaphor is
a short form of simile, contracted into one word ;
this word is put in a position not belonging to it
as if it were its own place, and if it is recognizable
it gives pleasure, but if it contains no similarity it is
rejected.] But only such metaphors should be used
as either make the meaning clearer, as for instance
the following ᵇ :

> A shivering takes the sea,
> Darkness is doubled, and the murk of night
> And stormclouds blinds the sight, flame 'mid the clouds
> Quivers, the heavens shudder with thunderclaps,
> A sudden hail with bounteous rain commingled
> Falls headlong, all the winds from every quarter
> Burst forth, and savage whirlwinds rise ; the sea
> Surges and boils. . . .

—to make them clearer almost all the details are

158 litudinem verbis dicta sunt—, aut quo significatur magis res tota sive facti alicuius sive consilii, ut ille qui occultantem consulto ne id quod ageretur intellegi posset duobus translatis verbis similitudine ipsa indicat :

Quandoquidem is se circumvestit dictis sepit se dolo.

Nonnunquam etiam brevitas translatione conficitur, ut illud ' Si telum manu fugit ' : imprudentia teli emissi brevius propriis verbis exponi non potuit quam est uno significata translato.

159 Hoc in genere persaepe mihi admirandum videtur quid sit quod omnes translatis et alienis magis delectantur verbis quam propriis et suis. XL. Nam si res suum nomen et proprium vocabulum non habet, ut 'pes' in navi, ut 'nexum' quod per libram agitur, ut in uxore ' divortium,' necessitas cogit quod non habeas aliunde sumere; sed in suorum verborum maxima copia tamen homines aliena multo magis, si sunt

160 ratione translata, delectant. Id ideo[1] accidere credo vel quod ingenii specimen est quoddam transilire ante pedes posita et alia longe repetita sumere ; vel quod is qui audit alio ducitur cogitatione neque tamen

---

[1] ideo *add. Rackham.*

[a] Probably from Accius, perhaps his *Armorum Iudicium*, or else his *Antigone,* as the line suggests Sophocles, *Ant.* 241 εὖ γε στοχάζει κἀποφράγνυσαι κύκλῳ τὸ πρᾶγμα.
[b] Law as to homicide in *The Twelve Tables* (*Remains,* iii. pp. 492 f.).

expressed by metaphors based upon resemblance—,
158 or such as better convey the whole meaning of the
matter, whether it consists in an action or a thought,
like the man in the play who by means of two words
used metaphorically indicates by mere resemblance
a person purposely using concealment in order to
make it impossible to understand what was going
on :

> Since he employs a cloak of words, a fence
> Of guilefulness.[a]

Occasionally also metaphors serve to achieve brevity,
for instance ' If the weapon slipped from his hand ' [b] :
it was not possible to express the unintentional nature
of the discharge of the missile more briefly by employing the proper words than it is conveyed by a
single word used metaphorically.

159 "Under this heading I very often feel it a
curious point to inquire why it is that everybody
derives more pleasure from words used metaphorically and not in their proper sense than from the
proper names belonging to the objects. XL. For if a
thing has not got a proper name and designation of
its own, for example a ' sheet ' in a ship, a ' bond ' in
the sense of a contract made with a pair of scales, a
' separation ' in the case of a wife, necessity compels
one to borrow what one has not got from somewhere
else ; but even in cases where there are plenty of
specific words available, metaphorical terms give
people much more pleasure, if the metaphor is a good
160 one. I suppose the cause of this is either that it is
a mark of cleverness of a kind to jump over things
that are obvious and choose other things that are
far-fetched ; or because the hearer's thoughts are
led to something else and yet without going astray,

aberrat, quae maxima est delectatio ; vel quod singulis verbis res ac totum simile conficitur ; vel quod
omnis translatio, quae quidem sumpta ratione est,
ad sensus ipsos admovetur, maxime oculorum, qui
161 est sensus acerrimus : nam et ' odor urbanitatis '
et ' mollitudo humanitatis ' et ' murmur maris ' et
' dulcedo orationis ' sunt ducta a ceteris sensibus,
illa vero oculorum multo acriora, quae ponunt paene
in conspectu animi quae cernere et videre non possumus.   Nihil est enim in rerum natura cuius nos
non in aliis rebus possimus uti vocabulo et nomine :
unde enim simile duci potest (potest autem ex omnibus), indidem verbum unum quod similitudinem
continet translatum lumen affert orationi.

162   Quo in genere primum fugienda est dissimilitudo :
' coeli ingentes fornices ' : quamvis sphaeram in
scenam, ut dicitur, attulerit Ennius, tamen in sphaera
fornicis similitudo inesse non potest.

> . . . Vive, Ulyxes, dum licet !
> Oculis postremum lumen radiatum rape !

Non dixit ' cape,' non ' pete,' haberet enim moram
sperantis diutius esse sese victurum, sed ' rape ' : hoc
verbum est ad id aptatum quod ante dixerat, ' dum
licet.'
163   XLI. Deinde videndum est ne longe simile sit
ductum. ' Syrtim patrimonii ' : ' scopulum ' libentius dixerim, ' Charybdim bonorum ' ' voraginem '

---

^a Perhaps from *Ajax*.

which is a very great pleasure ; or because a single word in each case suggests the thing and a picture of the whole ; or because every metaphor, provided it be a good one, has a direct appeal to the senses, especially the sense of sight, which is the keenest :

161 for while the rest of the senses supply such metaphors as ' the fragrance of good manners,' ' the softness of a humane spirit,' ' the roar of the waves,' ' a sweet style of speaking,' the metaphors drawn from the sense of sight are much more vivid, virtually placing within the range of our mental vision objects not actually visible to our sight. For there is nothing in the world the name or designation of which cannot be used in connexion with other things ; with anything that can supply a simile—and a simile can be drawn from everything—a single word supplied by it that comprises the similarity, if used metaphorically, will give brilliance to the style.

162 " In this department the first thing is to eschew a metaphor where there is no real resemblance : ' the vasty vaults of heaven.' It is true that an actual sphere was brought on to the boards, so it is said, by Ennius, but all the same a sphere possesses no possible resemblance to a vault.

> Live, Ulysses, while thou mayest !
> Snatch with thine eyes thy latest ray of light ! [a]

he did not say ' seek ' or ' take,' for these would imply the delay of a person who had hopes of living longer, but ' snatch '—this word fits with what went before it, ' while thou mayest.'

163 XLI. " Then we must see that the resemblance is not too far-fetched : ' the Syrtis of his heritage ' I should rather call the ' rock,' and for a ' Charybdis

potius : facilius enim ad ea quae visa quam ad illa quae audita sunt mentis oculi feruntur. Et quoniam haec vel summa laus est verbi transferendi ut sensum feriat id quod translatum sit, fugienda est omnis turpitudo earum rerum ad quas eorum animos qui

164 audiunt trahet similitudo. Nolo dici morte Africani 'castratam' esse rempublicam, nolo 'stercus curiae' dici Glauciam : quamvis sit simile, tamen est in utroque deformis cogitatio similitudinis. Nolo esse aut maius quam res postulet, 'tempestas comissationis,' aut minus, 'comissatio tempestatis'; nolo esse verbum angustius id quod translatum sit quam fuisset illud proprium ac suum :

> Quidnam est, obsecro ? Quid te adirier abnutas ?

Melius esset ' vetas,' ' prohibes,' ' absterres,' quoniam ille dixerat :

> Ilico istic,
> Ne contagio mea bonis umbrave obsit. . . .

165 Atque etiam, si vereare ne paulo durior translatio esse videatur, mollienda est praeposito saepe verbo : ut si olim M. Catone mortuo ' pupillum ' senatum quis relictum diceret, paulo durius, sin ' ut ita dicam, pupillum,' aliquanto mitius ; etenim verecunda debet esse translatio, ut deducta esse in alienum locum, non

---

a From Ennius, *Thyestes* (*Remains*, i. pp. 352 f.) ; the reply of the chorus to the words of Thyestes next quoted : he has tasted the flesh of his children served up to him by Atreus and forbids anyone to approach him for fear of sharing in the curse that has fallen on him.

of wealth' I should prefer 'whirlpool'; for the mind's eye is carried more easily to things we have seen than to things we have heard of. And as perhaps the highest merit in the employment of metaphor is when the metaphorical expression directly hits our senses, one must avoid all unseemliness in the things to which the comparison will lead the hearers'

164 minds. I deprecate the expression that the death of Africanus 'left the state gelt,' or that Glaucia was 'the excrement of the House of Lords'; there may be a likeness, but all the same in each case the resemblance contains an ugly idea. I deprecate a metaphor that is on a bigger scale than the thing requires—'a hurricane of revelry,' or on a smaller scale—'the revelling of the hurricane'; I deprecate the metaphorical term being narrower in scope than the literal and proper word would have been :

> What is't, I pray ? Why shakest thou thy head
> At mine approach ? [a]—

'forbid' or 'prohibit' or 'deter' would be better, as the other had said—

> Hold, stay !
> Lest my mere touch or shadow harm the righteous.

165 And moreover, if one is afraid of the metaphor's appearing a little too harsh, it should be softened down with a word of introduction, as is frequently done ; for instance if in the old days somebody had spoken of the Senate as 'left an orphan' by the death of Marcus Cato, it would have been a little too harsh, whereas 'what I may call an orphan' would have been a little easier ; in fact the metaphor ought to have an apologetic air, so as to look as if it had entered a place that does not belong to it with a proper introduction, not

irruisse atque ut precario, non vi venisse videatur.
166 Modus autem nullus est florentior in singulis verbis
nec qui plus luminis afferat orationi ; nam illud quod
ex hoc genere profluit non est in uno verbo translato
sed ex pluribus continuatis connectitur, ut aliud
dicatur, aliud intellegendum sit :

> . . . . neque me patiar
> Iterum ad unum scopulum ut olim classem Achivum
> offendere ;

atque illud,

> Erras, erras ; nam exsultantem te et praefidentem tibi
> Repriment validae legum habenae atque imperi insistent
> iugo.

Sumpta re simili verba eius rei propria deinceps in
167 rem aliam, ut dixi, transferuntur.   XLII. Est hoc
magnum ornamentum orationis.   In quo obscuritas
fugienda est : etenim ex hoc genere fiunt ea quae
dicuntur aenigmata ; non est autem in verbo modus
hic sed in oratione, id est, in continuatione verborum.
Ne illa quidem traductio atque immutatio in verbo
quamdam fabricationem habet [sed in oratione][1] :

> Africa terribili tremit horrida terra tumultu ;

[Pro ' Afris ' est sumpta ' Africa,'][2] neque factum
verbum est, ut ' mare saxifragis undis,' neque trans-

----

[1] *Schütz.*   [2] *Kayser.*

----

[a] A translation of ἀλληγορία.   The source of these two
quotations is unknown.

[b] *i.e.* ' Africa ' is used by metonymy to mean ' the
Africans,' as below ' Rome ' means ' the Romans.' The
line is from Ennius's *Annales* (*Remains*, i. pp. 114 f., Vahlen,
Ennius, Annals 310); it refers to the landing of Scipio in
Africa before the battle of Zama.

taken it by storm, and as if it had come with per-
166 mission, not forced its way in. But there is no
mode of speech more effective in the case of single
words, and none that adds more brilliance to the
style ; for from this class of expression comes a development not consisting in the metaphorical use of
a single word but in a chain of words linked together,
so that something other than what is said has to be
understood [a] :

> Neither will I endure that I make shipwreck,
> Like the Achaean fleet in days gone by,
> A second time upon the self-same rock ;

and the passage :

> Thou err'st, thou err'st ; for as thou rear'st thy head
> In over-confidence, the law's strong rein
> Shall curb thee, and shall bring thee to a stand
> Beneath authority's yoke.

Something resembling the real thing is taken, and
the words that properly belong to it are then, as
I said, applied metaphorically to the other thing.
167 XLII. This is a valuable stylistic ornament ; but care
must be taken to avoid obscurity—and in fact it is
usually the way in which what are called riddles
are constructed ; but this mode does not turn on
a single word but consists in the general style, that
is, in a series of words. Nor yet does the figure
of substitution or metonymy involve an innovation
in a word :

> The rugged realm of Africa [b]
> With dire disorder trembles— ;

nor is a word invented, as

> The sea with its rockrupting waves—

latum, ut ' mollitur mare,' sed ornandi causa proprium proprio commutatum :

> Desine, Roma, tuos hostes ..

et

> Testes sunt Campi Magni .

Gravis est modus in ornatu orationis et saepe sumendus ; ex quo genere haec sunt, ' Martem belli ' esse ' communem,' ' Cererem ' pro frugibus, ' Liberum ' appellare pro vino, ' Neptunum ' pro mari, ' curiam ' pro senatu, ' campum ' pro comitiis, ' togam ' pro 168 pace, ' arma ' ac ' tela ' pro bello. Quo item in genere et virtutes et vitia pro ipsis in quibus illa sunt appellantur :

> Luxuries quam in domum irrupit,

et ' quo avaritia penetravit,' aut ' fides valuit,' ' iustitia confecit.' Videtis profecto genus hoc totum, cum inflexo commutatoque verbo res eadem enuntiatur ornatius. Cui sunt finitima illa minus ornata sed tamen non ignoranda, cum intellegi volumus aliquid aut ex parte totum, ut pro ' aedificiis ' cum ' parietes ' aut ' tecta ' dicimus ; aut ex toto partem, ut cum unam turmam ' equitatam Populi Romani ' dicimus ; aut ex uno plures :

> At Romanus homo, tamen etsi res bene gesta est,
> Corde suo trepidat ;

---

[a] *i.e.* ' Roma ' for ' Romani,' ' Campi Magni,' a place in Africa (Livy xxx. 8), for Africa itself. From Ennius's *Scipio*, see *Remains*, i. pp. 398 f.

[b] Apparently a verse quotation, but source unknown.

nor employed metaphorically, as

> The sea is softened— :

but for the sake of ornament one proper name is sub-
stituted for another[a] :

> Cease, Rome, thy foes . . .

and

> The Great Veldt is my witness . .

The method is effective in ornamenting the style,
and should often be adopted ; and to the same class
belong the phrase ' the impartiality of the War-god '
and the use of the terms ' Ceres ' for corn, ' Liber ' for
wine, ' Neptune ' for the sea, ' the House ' for parliament, ' the polling booth ' for elections, ' civilian
168 dress ' for peace, ' arms ' or ' guns ' for war ; and
also in the same class is the use of the names of
the virtues and vices to stand for the people who
possess them—

> The dwelling whereinto Extravagance
> Hath forced an entry[b]—

and ' where avarice has found its way,' or ' loyalty
has prevailed,' ' justice has achieved.' You see
what I mean—this whole class of expressions in
which the same meaning is conveyed more elegantly
by modifying or altering a word. And akin to it are
the less decorative but nevertheless not negligible
figures employed when we desire a part to be understood to mean a whole, for instance when for ' houses '
we say ' walls ' or ' roofs '; or else a whole to mean a
part, for instance when we call a single squadron of
horse ' the cavalry of Rome '; or one thing to mean
several :

> But though the day is won, the Roman's heart
> Trembles—

aut cum ex pluribus intellegitur unum :

> Nos sumu' Romani qui fuimus ante Rudini ;

aut quocumque modo non ut dictum est in eo genere
intellegitur sed ut sensum est.

169 XLIII. Abutimur saepe etiam verbo non tam
eleganter quam in transferendo, sed, etiamsi licentius,
tamen interdum non impudenter : ut cum ' grandem '
orationem pro ' magna,' ' minutum ' animum pro
' parvo ' dicimus. Verum illa videtisne esse non
verbi sed orationis, quae ex pluribus, ut exposui,
translationibus connexa sunt ? haec autem quae
aut immutata esse dixi aut aliter intellegenda ac
dicerentur, sunt translata quodam modo.

170 Ita fit ut omnis singulorum verborum virtus atque
laus tribus exsistat ex rebus : si aut vetustum verbum
sit, quod tamen consuetudo ferre possit, aut factum
vel coniunctione vel novitate, in quo item est auribus
consuetudinique parcendum, aut translatum, quod
maxime tanquam stellis quibusdam notat et illuminat
orationem.

171 Sequitur continuatio verborum, quae duas res
maxime, collocationem primum, deinde modum
quemdam formamque desiderat. Collocationis est
componere et struere verba sic ut neve asper eorum
concursus neve hiulcus sit, sed quodam modo coag-

---

^a Both quotations are from Ennius (see *Remains*, i. pp.
434 f., Vahlen, *Ennius, Annals* 545); in the latter (quoted to
illustrate the use of ' we ' for ' I ') he speaks of himself—he
was born at Rudiae in Calabria and afterwards received the
Roman citizenship.

^b *i.e.* metonymy.

^c Literally ' full-grown,' ' tall.'

or when several mean one :

> We now are Romans who were erst Rudini [a]—

or in whatever way a word is used not in its literal
meaning but in a suggested sense.

169   XLIII. "Often also we use [b] a word out of its
literal sense in a less elegant manner than when it is
used metaphorically, but this even though rather a
loose use is nevertheless sometimes unobjectionable :
for instance when we say a ' full-length ' [c] speech
instead of a ' long' speech, and a ' petty ' mind for a
'small' mind. But the figure previously mentioned [d]
consisting, as I explained, of a series of several metaphorical terms strung together, is a matter, do you
notice, not of a word but of a sentence ; whilst the
figure now in question, consisting of words used as
I said metonymously or in what is not their literal
meaning, is a metaphor of a sort.

170   " It follows that all merit and distinction in the use
of words singly arises from three factors : the word
may either be archaic but at the same time acceptable
to habitual usage; or a coinage made by compounding
two words, or inventing a new one—and here similarly consideration must be paid to what our ears are
used to ; or used metaphorically—a most effective
way of introducing spots of high light to give brilliance
to the style.

171   " There follows the question of periodic structure,
which involves two things in particular, first arrangement and then rhythm and balance. It belongs to
arrangement to place the words together in such
a structure as not to have any harsh clash of consonants or hiatus of vowels, but a sort of connexion

(b) Struc-
ture of the
sentence :
(1) syntax,

---

[d] *i.e.* allegory, § 166.

mentatus et laevis ; in quo[1] in soceri mei persona lusit is qui elegantissime id facere potuit[1] :

> Quam lepide λέξεις compostae ! ut tesserulae omnes
> Arte pavimento atque emblemate vermiculato.

Quae cum dixisset in Albucium illudens, ne a me quidem abstinuit :

> Crassum habeo generum, ne rhetoricoterus tu sis.

Quid ergo ? iste Crassus, quoniam eius abuteris nomine, quid efficit ? Idem illud—scilicet, ut ille volt et ego vellem, melius aliquanto quam Albucius : 172 verum in me quidem lusit ille, ut solet. Sed est tamen haec collocatio conservanda verborum de qua loquor, quae iunctam[2] orationem efficit, quae cohaerentem, quae lenem, quae aequabiliter fluentem ; id assequemini si verba extrema cum consequentibus primis ita iungetis ut ne aspere concurrant neve vastius diducantur.

173   XLIV. Hanc diligentiam subsequitur modus etiam et forma verborum, quod iam vereor ne huic Catulo videatur esse puerile ; versus enim veteres illi in hac soluta oratione propemodum, hoc est, numeros quosdam nobis esse adhibendos putaverunt. Interspirationis enim, non defatigationis nostrae neque librariorum notis sed verborum et sententiarum modo interpunctas clausulas in orationibus esse voluerunt ;

---

[1] in quo lepide *et* potuit Lucilius *codd.:* lepide *et* Lucilius *secl. Kayser.*
[2] vinctam *Friedrich.*

---

[a] The copyists have correctly identified the author in question as Lucilius.   [b] Scaevola.

[c] This rendering is by Wilkins.

[d] The speaker. See *Remains,* iii. pp. 28 f., Marx, *Lucilius* 84-86.

and smoothness ; as to which a jest was made by the author [a] most capable of doing it neatly—the character speaking is my wife's father [b] :

How charmingly he *fait ses phrases*—set in order, like the lines
Of mosaic in a pavement, and his inlaid work he twines.[c]

And after this hit at Albucius he did not keep his tongue off me either :

I've a son-in-law named Crassus [d] so don't be too oratorical.

What then ? what is the achievement of this Mr. Crassus (as you drag in his name, Lucilius) ? Just the one in question—no doubt considerably better done by him than it was by Albucius : that is what Scaevola in the poem means and I myself hope ; however the hit against me was only a joke of his, as 172 his way is. But nevertheless it is important to pay attention to this matter of order of words which I am speaking of—it produces a well-knit, connected style, with a smooth and even flow ; this you will achieve if the ends of the words join on to the beginning of the words that follow in such a way as to avoid either harsh collision or awkward hiatus.

173 XLIV. " After attention to this matter comes also (2) rhythm. the consideration of the rhythm and shape of the words, a point which I am afraid Catulus here may consider childish ; for the old Greek masters held the view that in this prose style it is proper for us to use something almost amounting to versification, that is, certain definite rhythms. For they thought that in speeches the close of the period ought to come not when we are tired out but where we may take breath, and to be marked not by the punctuation of the copying clerks but by the arrangement of the

137

idque princeps Isocrates instituisse fertur ut incon-
ditam antiquorum dicendi consuetudinem delectationis atque aurium causa, quemadmodum scribit
discipulus eius Naucrates, numeris astringeret.

174 Namque haec duo musici, qui erant quondam eidem
poetae, machinati ad voluptatem sunt, versum atque
cantum, ut et verborum numero et vocum modo
delectatione vincerent aurium satietatem. Haec
igitur duo, vocis dico moderationem et verborum
conclusionem, quoad orationis severitas pati possit,
a poetica ad eloquentiam traducenda duxerunt.

175 In quo illud est maximum,[1] quod versus in oratione
si efficitur coniunctione verborum, vitium est, et
tamen eam coniunctionem, sicuti versum, numerose
cadere et quadrare et perfici volumus : neque est ex
multis res una quae magis oratorem ab imperito
dicendi ignaroque distinguat quam quod ille rudis
incondite fundit quantum potest et id quod dicit
spiritu, non arte, determinat, orator autem sic illigat
sententiam verbis ut eam numero quodam complec-

176 tatur et astricto et soluto. Nam cum vinxit modis
et forma, relaxat et liberat immutatione ordinis, ut
verba neque alligata sint quasi certa aliqua lege
versus neque ita soluta ut vagentur.

[1] *v.l.* vel maximum.

words and of the thought; and it is said that Isocrates first introduced the practice of tightening up the irregular style of oratory which belonged to the early days, so his pupil Naucrates writes, by means of an element of rhythm, designed to give pleasure to 174 the ear. For two contrivances to give pleasure were devised by the musicians, who in the old days were also the poets, verse and melody, with the intention of overcoming satiety in the hearer by delighting the ear with the rhythm of the words and the mode of the notes. These two things therefore, I mean the modulation of the voice and the arrangement of words in periods, they thought proper to transfer from poetry to rhetoric, so far as was compatible with the severe character of oratory.

175 " In this matter an extremely important point is, that although it is a fault in oratory if the connexion of the words produces verse, nevertheless we at the same time desire the word-order to resemble verse in having a rhythmical cadence, and to fit in neatly and be rounded off; nor among the many marks of an orator is there one that more distinguishes him from an inexperienced and ignorant speaker, than that the tiro pours out disorderly stuff as fast as he can with no arrangement, and ends a sentence not from artistic considerations but when his breath gives out, whereas the orator links words and meaning together in such a manner as to unfold his thought 76 in a rhythm that is at once bound and free. For after enclosing it in the bonds of form and balance, he loosens and releases it by altering the order, so that the words are neither tied together by a definite metrical law nor left so free as to wander uncontrolled.

XLV. Quonam igitur modo tantum munus insistemus, ut arbitremur nos hanc vim numerose dicendi consequi posse ? Non est res tam difficilis quam necessaria ; nihil est enim tam tenerum neque tam flexibile neque quod tam facile sequatur quocumque ducas quam oratio. Ex hac versus, ex eadem dispares numeri conficiuntur ; ex hac haec etiam soluta variis modis multorumque generum oratio ; non enim sunt alia sermonis, alia contentionis verba, neque ex alio genere ad usum quotidianum, alio ad scenam pompamque sumuntur, sed ea nos cum iacentia sustulimus e medio, sicut mollissimam ceram ad nostrum arbitrium formamus et fingimus. Itaque tum graves sumus, tum subtiles, tum medium quiddam tenemus : sic institutam nostram sententiam sequitur orationis genus, idque ad omnem et aurium voluptatem et animorum motum mutatur et vertitur. Sed ut in plerisque rebus incredibiliter hoc natura est ipsa fabricata, sic in oratione, ut ea quae maximam utilitatem in se continerent eadem haberent plurimum vel dignitatis vel saepe etiam venustatis. Incolumitatis ac salutis omnium causa videmus hunc statum esse huius totius mundi atque naturae, rotundum ut caelum terraque ut media sit eaque sua vi nutuque teneatur ; sol ut eam[1] circum feratur, ut accedat ad brumale signum et inde sensim ascendat in diversam partem ; ut luna accessu et recessu [suo][2] solis lumen accipiat ; ut eadem spatia quinque stellae dispari

177

178

---

[1] eam *add. Friedrich.*   [2] *v.l. om.*

---

[a] The sun's apparent course sinks to the sign of Capricornus at midwinter (Wilkins).

[b] *i.e.* the planets Mercury, Venus, Mars, Jupiter, Saturn.

XLV. " How then pray shall we enter on so great
an undertaking with confidence in our ability to
attain this capacity of rhythmical utterance ? The
difficulty of the thing is not as great as its importance ; for there is nothing so delicate or flexible,
or that follows so easily wherever one leads it,
177 as speech. Speech is the material used alike for
making verses and irregular rhythms. Also it is the
material for prose of various styles and many kinds ;
for the vocabulary of conversation is the same as that
of formal oratory, and we do not choose one class of
words for daily use and another for full-dress public
occasions, but we pick them up from common life as
they lie at our disposal, and then shape them and
mould them at our discretion, like the softest wax.
Consequently at one moment we use a dignified
style, at another a plain one, and at another we keep
a middle course between the two ; thus the style
of our oratory follows the line of thought we take,
and changes and turns to suit all the requirements
of pleasing the ear and influencing the mind of
78 the audience. But in oratory as in most matters
nature has contrived with incredible skill that the
things possessing most utility also have the greatest
amount of dignity, and indeed frequently of beauty
also. We observe that for the safety and security
of the universe this whole ordered world of nature is
so constituted that the sky is a round vault, with the
earth at its centre, held stationary by its own force
and stress ; and the sun travels round it, approaching
towards the constellation of mid-winter [a] and then
gradually rising towards the opposite direction ;
while the moon receives the sun's light as it advances
and retires ; and five stars [b] accomplish the same

179 motu cursuque conficiant. Haec tantam habent
vim ut paulum immutata cohaerere non possint,
tantam pulchritudinem ut nulla species ne excogitari
quidem possit ornatior. Referte nunc animum ad
hominum vel etiam ceterorum animantium formam
et figuram : nullam partem corporis sine aliqua
necessitate affictam totamque formam quasi per-
fectam reperietis arte, non casu. XLVI. Quid in
arboribus ? in quibus non truncus, non rami, non
folia sunt denique nisi ad suam retinendam conser-
vandamque naturam ; nusquam tamen est ulla pars
180 nisi venusta. Linquamus naturam, artesque videamus : quid tam in navigio necessarium quam latera,
quam cavernae, quam prora, quam puppis, quam
antennae, quam vela, quam mali ? quae tamen hanc
habent in specie venustatem ut non solum salutis
sed etiam voluptatis causa inventa esse videantur.
Columnae et templa et porticus sustinent, tamen
habent non plus utilitatis quam dignitatis. Capitoli
fastigium illud et ceterarum aedium non venustas
sed necessitas ipsa fabricata est ; nam cum esset
habita ratio quemadmodum ex utraque tecti parte
aqua delaberetur, utilitatem fastigii templi dignitas
consecuta est, ut etiamsi in caelo capitolium statueretur ubi imber esse non posset, nullam sine fastigio
dignitatem habiturum fuisse videatur.

181   Hoc in omnibus item partibus orationis evenit, ut
utilitatem ac prope necessitatem suavitas quaedam

---

a i.e. the same courses round the earth as the sun and
moon.

courses _a_ with different motion and on a different
179 route. This system is so powerful that a slight
modification of it would make it impossible for it to
hold together, and it is so beautiful that no lovelier
vision is even imaginable. Now carry your mind
to the form and figure of human beings or even of
the other living creatures : you will discover that the
body has no part added to its structure that is super-
fluous, and that its whole shape has the perfection
of a work of art and not of accident. XLVI. Take
trees : in these the trunk, the branches and lastly
the leaves are all without exception designed so as
to keep and to preserve their own nature, yet no-
180 where is there any part that is not beautiful. Let
us leave nature and contemplate the arts : in a ship,
what is so indispensable as the sides, the hold, the
bow, the stern, the yards, the sails and the masts ?
yet they all have such a graceful appearance that
they appear to have been invented not only for the
purpose of safety but also for the sake of giving
pleasure. In temples and colonnades the pillars are
to support the structure, yet they are as dignified in
appearance as they are useful. Yonder pediment
of the Capitol and those of the other temples are the
product not of beauty but of actual necessity ; for
it was in calculating how to make the rain-water fall
off the two sides of the roof that the dignified design
of the gables resulted as a by-product of the needs of
the structure—with the consequence that even if one
were erecting a citadel in heaven, where no rain
could fall, it would be thought certain to be entirely
lacking in dignity without a pediment.
181 " The same is the case in regard to all the divisions of a speech—virtually unavoidable practical
143

et lepos consequatur. Clausulas enim atque inter-
puncta verborum animae interclusio atque angustiae
spiritus attulerunt; id inventum ita est suave ut,
si cui sit infinitus spiritus datus, tamen eum per-
petuare verba nolimus; id enim auribus nostris
gratum est[1] quod hominum lateribus non tolerabile
182 solum sed etiam facile esse posset. XLVII. Longis-
sima est igitur complexio verborum quae volvi uno
spiritu potest, sed hic naturae modus est, artis alius.
Nam cum sint numeri plures, iambum et trochaeum
frequentem segregat ab oratore Aristoteles, Catule,
vester; qui natura tamen incurrunt ipsi in orationem
sermonemque nostrum, sed sunt insignes percus-
siones eorum numerorum et minuti pedes. Quare
primum ad heroum nos[2] pedem invitat; in quo
impune progredi licet duo dumtaxat pedes aut paulo
plus, ne plane in versum aut similitudinem versus
incidamus: ' altae sunt geminae quibus . . .' Hi
tres[3] pedes in principia continuandorum verborum
183 satis decore cadunt. Probatur autem ab eodem illo
maxime paean, qui est duplex, nam aut a longa oritur
quam tres breves consequuntur, ut haec verba,
' desinite, incipite, comprimite '; aut a brevibus
deinceps tribus, extrema producta atque longa, sicut

---

[1] *Piderit :* est inventum.
[2] *Wilkins :* nos dactyli et anapaesti et spondei.
[3] *Madvig :* tres heroi.

---

[a] The foot that we call a trochee Cicero names *choreus*
(Wilkins).
[b] Those of the heroic metre—the iambus, tribrach and
dactyl.

requirements produce charm of style as a result.
It was failure or scantiness of breath that originated
periodic structure and pauses between words, but
now that this has once been discovered, it is so
attractive, that even if a person were endowed with
breath that never failed, we should still not wish
him to deliver an unbroken flow of words ; for
our ears are only gratified by a style of delivery
which is not merely endurable but also easy for
182 the human lungs. XLVII. Consequently though the
longest group of words is that which can be reeled
off in one breath, this is the standard given by
nature ; the standard of art is different. For among
the variety of metres, a frequent use of the iambus
and the tribrach *a* is interdicted to the orator by
Aristotle, the master of your school, Catulus. Nevertheless they invade our Roman oratory and conversational style automatically ; yet these rhythms have
a very marked beat, and the foot is too short. Consequently Aristotle asks us to employ primarily the
heroic metre, in which it is quite legitimate to carry
on for the space of two feet or a little more, provided
we do not fall into downright verse or something
resembling verse :

Both of the maids are tall, and they . . .

These three feet *b* suit the beginning of a period
83 well enough. But the same authority specially
approves of the paean, of which there are two
varieties, beginning either with a long syllable followed by three short ones, like the phrases ' stóp
doing it,' ' gét on to it,' ' préss down on it,' or else
with three consecutive shorts with a long carrying
on at the end, examples of which are ' beaten them

illa sunt, ' domuerant,' ' sonipedes ; ' atque illi philosopho[1] ordiri placet a superiore paeane, posteriore
finire. Est autem paean hic posterior[2] non syllaba-
rum numero sed aurium mensura, quod est acrius
iudicium et certius, par fere Cretico, qui est ex longa
et brevi et longa, ut

> Quid petam praesidi aut exsequar ? quove nunc . . .

a quo numero exorsus est Fannius : ' Si, Quirites,
minas illius . . .' Hunc ille clausulis aptiorem putat,
quas vult longa plerumque syllaba terminari.

184   XLVIII. Neque vero haec tam acrem curam dili-
gentiamque desiderant quam est illa poetarum ;
quos necessitas cogit et ipsi numeri ac modi sic verba
versu includere ut nihil sit ne spiritu quidem minimo
brevius aut longius quam necesse est. Liberior est
oratio, et plane ut dicitur sic et est vere ' soluta,' non
ut fugiat tamen aut erret sed ut sine vinculis sibi ipsa
moderetur. Namque ego illud assentior Theo-
phrasto, qui putat orationem, quae quidem sit polita
atque facta quodam modo, non astricte sed remissius

185 numerosam esse oportere. Etenim, sicut ille suspicatur, et ex illis modis quibus hic usitatus versus
efficitur post anapaestus procerior quidam numerus
effloruit, inde ille licentior et divitior fluxit dithyrambus, cuius membra et pedes, ut ait idem, sunt in
omni locupleti oratione diffusa ; et si numerosum est

---

    [1] [philosopho] *Kayser.*   [2] [posterior] *Kayser.*

---

    [a] From Ennius, *Andromache* (*Remains*, i. pp. 250 f.,
Vahlen, *Ennius*, *Scenica* 86).

áll,' ' clatter of hoóves ' ; and the philosopher mentioned approves of using the former kind of paean at
the beginning and the latter kind at the end. But
as a matter of fact this latter paean is almost the same
—not in number of syllables but in length as it affects
the ear, which is a sharper and more reliable test—
as the cretic, which consists of long, short, long : for
instance :

Whére can Í gó for hélp ? Whát's the néxt ? Whére awáy . . .ᵃ

This was the rhythm used by Fannius at the beginning of a speech : ' Noble lords, if the threats hurled
by this . . . '   Aristotle considers this foot more
suitable for ends of clauses, which he desires to
end as a rule with a long syllable.

184   XLVIII. "These points however do not call for
such close attention and care as is practised by the
poets ; for them it is a requirement of actual necessity and of the metrical forms themselves that the
words shall be so framed in the line that there may not
be less or more by even a single breath than the length
required.   Prose is less fettered, and its designation
as ' free style ' is quite a correct one, only this does
not mean that it is free to go loose or to roam about,
but that it is not in chains and supplies its own control.   For I agree with the opinion of Theophrastus,
that at all events polished and systematic prose must
have a rhythm, though not rigid, yet fairly loose.
85 In fact, as he divines, not only have the metres
used for the verse now in vogue with us blossomed
out later into a more drawn-out metre, the anapaest,
from which has flowed the looser and more sumptuous
dithyramb, whose members and feet, as the same
writer says, occur widely in all opulent prose ; but

id in omnibus sonis atque vocibus quod habet quasdam impressiones et quod metiri possumus intervallis aequalibus, recte genus hoc numerorum, dummodo ne continuum sit,[1] in orationis laude ponetur.[2] Nam si rudis et impolita putanda est illa sine intervallis loquacitas perennis et profluens, quid est aliud causae cur repudietur nisi quod hominum auribus vocem natura modulatur ipsa ?[3] quod fieri nisi inest numerus 186 in voce non potest. Numerus autem in continuatione nullus est ; distinctio et aequalium et saepe variorum intervallorum percussio numerum conficit, quem in cadentibus guttis, quod intervallis distinguuntur, notare possumus, in amni praecipitante non possumus. Quod si continuatio verborum haec soluta multo est aptior atque iucundior si est articulis membrisque distincta quam si continuata ac producta, membra illa modificata esse debebunt : quae si in extremo breviora sunt, infringitur ille quasi verborum ambitus—sic enim has orationis conversiones Graeci nominant. Quare aut paria esse debent posteriora superioribus, extrema[4] primis, aut, quod etiam est melius et iucundius, longiora.

187 XLIX. Atque haec quidem ab eis philosophis quos tu maxime diligis, Catule, dicta sunt : quod eo saepius testificor ut auctoribus laudandis ineptiarum crimen effugiam.

Quarum tandem ? inquit Catulus, aut quid dis-

[1] *v.l.* continui sint.   [2] *v.l.* ponitur.
[3] aures vocem natura modulantur ipsae *Fritsche.*
[4] *Piderit :* et extrema.

also, if all sounds and utterances contain an element of rhythm possessing certain beats and capable of being measured by its regular intervals, it will be proper to reckon this kind of rhythm as a merit in prose, provided that it is not used in an unbroken succession. For if a continuous flow of verbiage unrelieved by intervals must be considered rough and unpolished, what other reason is there to reject it except that nature herself modulates the voice to gratify the ear of mankind ? and this cannot be achieved unless the voice contains an element of

186 rhythm. But in a continuous flow there is no rhythm ; rhythm is the product of a dividing up, that is of a beat marking equal and also frequently varying intervals,—the rhythm that we can notice in falling drops of water, because they are separated by intervals, but cannot detect in a fast flowing river. But if this continuous series of words in prose is much neater and more pleasing if it is divided up by joints and limbs than if it is carried right on without a break, the limbs in question will need management ; and if they are shorter at the end, this makes a break in the periodic structure of the words—for ' period ' is the Greek name for these turning-points of speech. Consequently the later clauses must either be equal to the preceding ones, and the last ones to the first, or they must be longer, which is even better and more pleasing.

187   XLIX. " So far these are the pronouncements of the philosophers to whom you, Catulus, are most attached —a fact that I call in evidence the more often with the object of escaping the charge of ineptitude by speaking highly of the authorities."

    " What ineptitude, pray ? " said Catulus, " or

putatione ista afferri potest elegantius aut omnino
dici subtilius ?

188   At enim vereor, inquit Crassus, ne haec aut
difficiliora istis ad persequendum esse videantur aut,
quia non tradantur[1] in vulgari ista disciplina, nos
ea maiora ac difficiliora videri velle videamur.

   Tum Catulus : Erras, inquit, Crasse, si aut me aut
horum quemquam putas a te haec opera quoti-
diana et pervagata exspectare ; ista quae dicis dici
volumus, neque tam dici quam isto dici modo. Neque
tibi hoc pro me solum sed pro his omnibus sine ulla
dubitatione respondeo.

189   Ego vero, inquit Antonius, inveni tandem[2] quem
negaram in eo quem scripsi libello me invenisse,
eloquentem ; sed eo te ne laudandi quidem causa
interpellavi ne quid de hoc tam exiguo sermonis tui
tempore verbo uno meo diminueretur.

190   Hanc igitur, Crassus inquit, ad legem cum exercitatione tum stylo, qui et alia et hoc maxime
ornat ac limat, formanda nobis oratio est. Neque
tamen hoc tanti laboris est quanti videtur, nec sunt
haec rhythmicorum ac musicorum acerrima norma
dirigenda ; efficiendum est illud modo nobis ne fluat
oratio ne vagetur, ne insistat interius, ne excurrat
longius, ut membris distinguatur, ut conversiones

---

   [1] *Rackham :* traduntur.   [2] *v.l.* inveni iam.

what could be put more elegantly or in any way expressed with greater subtlety than the exposition you have given us ? ''

188   '' O, but in fact,'' said Crassus, '' I am nervous lest either these doctrines may seem to our young friends to be too difficult to carry out in practice, or we may ourselves be thought to want them to seem grander and more difficult because they are not taught as part of their regular curriculum.''

'' You are mistaken, Crassus,'' rejoined Catulus, '' if you fancy that either I or any of the party expect you to give us these everyday hackneyed exercises. What we want to be told is what you are telling us, and we don't so much want it to be told as to be told in your style of telling ; nor have I any hesitation in making you this answer for the whole party and not for myself only.''

189   '' Well, as for me,'' said Antonius, '' I've now found what in that book of mine I said I never had found— an eloquent speaker. But my reason for not inter- rupting you even with compliments was in order that the very brief time available for your discourse might not be shortened by a single word from me.''

190   '' Well, then,'' said Crassus, '' we must make our style conform to this law of rhythm both by practice in speaking and by using the pen, which is a good tool for giving style and polish both to other forms of composition and particularly to oratory. All the same, this is not so laborious a job as it looks, nor is it necessary to regulate these matters by the strictest rule of the metricians or musicians ; all that we have to achieve is that the language shall not be diffuse and rambling, stopping short of the mark or wander- ing on too far, and that the parts of the structure

habeat absolutas. Neque semper utendum est perpetuitate et quasi conversione verborum, sed saepe partienda[1] membris minutioribus oratio est, quae
191 tamen ipsa membra sunt numeris vincienda. Neque vos paean aut herous ille conturbet : ipsi occurrent orationi, ipsi inquam, se offerent et respondebunt non vocati. Consuetudo modo illa sit scribendi atque dicendi ut sententiae verbis finiantur eorumque verborum[2] iunctio nascatur a proceris numeris ac liberis, maxime heroo aut paeane priore aut Cretico, sed varie distincteque considat, notatur enim maxime similitudo in conquiescendo ; et si primi et postremi[3] pedes sunt hac ratione servati, medii possunt latere, modo ne circuitus ipse verborum sit aut brevior quam aures exspectent aut longior quam vires atque anima
192 patiatur. L. Clausulas autem diligentius etiam servandas esse arbitror quam superiora, quod in his maxime perfectio atque absolutio iudicatur. Nam versus aeque prima et media et extrema pars attenditur, qui debilitatur in quacumque sit parte titubatum : in oratione autem prima pauci cernunt, postrema plerique ; quae quoniam apparent et intelleguntur, varianda sunt ne aut animorum iudiciis
193 repudientur aut aurium satietate. Duo enim aut tres sunt fere extremi servandi et notandi pedes, si

---

[1] partienda *Reid :* carpenda.
[2] [sententiae verbis finiantur eorumque] *Kayser.*
[3] *Wilkins :* postremi illi.

shall be distinct and the periods finished. And at the same time it is not necessary to use long sentences and periods all the time ; on the contrary, the discourse should frequently be divided up into smaller members, although these themselves should possess

191 a rhythmical unity of structure. Nor need you worry about the paeans or the dactyls we were talking about : they will turn up in prose of their own accord—yes, they will fall in and report themselves as present without being summoned. Only let your habitual practice in writing and speaking be to make the thoughts end up with the words, and the combination of the words themselves spring from good long free metres, specially the dactylic or the first paean or the cretic, though with a close of various forms and clearly marked, for similarity is particularly noticed at the close ; and if the first and last feet of the sentences are regulated on this principle, the metrical shapes of the parts in between can pass unnoticed, only provided that the actual period is not shorter than the ear expected or longer than the

192 strength and the breath can last out. L. However, the close of the sentences in my opinion requires even more careful attention than the earlier parts, because it is here that perfection of finish is chiefly tested. For with verse equal attention is given to the beginning and middle and end of a line, and a slip at any point weakens its force, but in a speech few people notice the first part of the sentences and nearly everybody the last part ; so as the ends of the sentences show up and are noticed, they must be varied, in order not to be turned down by the critical faculty

193 or by a feeling of surfeit in the ear. For there are perhaps two or three feet that ought to be kept

modo non breviora et praecisa erunt superiora ; quos aut choreos aut heroos aut alternos esse oportebit aut in paeane illo posteriore quam Aristoteles probat aut ei pari Cretico. Horum vicissitudines efficient ut neque ei satientur qui audient fastidio similitudinis nec nos id quod faciemus opera dedita facere videa-

194 mur. Quod si Antipater ille Sidonius quem tu probe, Catule, meministi solitus est versus hexametros aliosque variis modis atque numeris fundere ex tempore, tantumque hominis ingeniosi ac memoris valuit exercitatio ut cum se mente ac voluntate coniecisset in versum verba sequerentur, quanto id facilius in oratione exercitatione et consuetudine adhibita 'consequemur !

195 Illud autem ne quis admiretur, quonam modo haec vulgus imperitorum in audiendo notet, cum in omni genere, tum in hoc ipso magna quaedam est vis incredibilisque naturae. Omnes enim tacito quodam sensu sine ulla arte aut ratione quae sint in artibus ac rationibus recta ac prava diiudicant ; idque cum faciunt in picturis et in signis et in aliis operibus ad quorum intellegentiam a natura minus habent instrumenti, tum multo ostendunt magis in verborum numerorum vocumque iudicio, quod ea sunt in communibus infixa sensibus neque earum rerum quem-

196 quam funditus natura voluit esse expertem. Itaque

for sentence endings, and thrown into relief, provided the preceding rhythms are not too short and jerky ; these will have to be either trochees or dactyls, or else either trochee or dactyl alternating with the posterior paean that Aristotle approves of or with its equivalent the cretic. To ring the changes on these will prevent the audience from being bored by monotony, and we shall avoid appearing to have taken a lot of trouble to prepare for the task in front 194 of us. But if the great Antipater of Sidon, whom you, Catulus, can remember well, had a habit of pouring out hexameters and other verses of various forms and metres *impromptu*, and as he had a quick wit and a good memory, made himself such an adept by practice, that when he deliberately decided to throw his ideas into verse, words followed automatically, how much more easily shall we achieve this in prose, given practice and training !

95 " But do not let anybody wonder how these things can possibly make any impression on the unlearned crowd when it forms the audience, because in this particular department as in every other nature has a vast and indeed incredible power. For everybody is able to discriminate between what is right and what wrong in matters of art and proportion by a sort of subconscious instinct, without having any theory of art or proportion of their own ; and while they can do this in the case of pictures and statues and other works to understand which nature has given them less equipment, at the same time they display this much more in judging the rhythms and pronunciations of words, because these are rooted deep in the general sensibility, and nature has decreed that nobody shall be entirely devoid of these

Subconscious effect of general style on audience.

non solum verbis arte positis moventur omnes verum
etiam numeris ac vocibus. Quotus enim quisque
est qui teneat artem numerorum ac modorum ? at
in his si paulum modo offensum est ut aut contractione
brevius fieret aut productione longius, theatra tota
reclamant. Quid ? hoc non idem fit in vocibus, ut
a multitudine et populo non modo catervae atque
concentus sed etiam ipsi sibi singuli discrepantes
197 eiciantur ? LI. Mirabile est, cum plurimum in
faciendo intersit inter doctum et rudem, quam non
multum differat in iudicando. Ars enim cum a natura
profecta sit, nisi naturam moveat ac delectet nihil
sane egisse videatur. Nihil est autem tam cognatum
mentibus nostris quam numeri atque voces, quibus
et excitamur et incendimur et lenimur et languesci-
mus et ad hilaritatem et ad tristitiam saepe deduci-
mur ; quorum illa summa vis carminibus est aptior
et cantibus, non neglecta, ut mihi videtur, a Numa
rege doctissimo maioribusque nostris, ut epularum
solemnium fides ac tibiae Saliorumque versus indicant,
maxime autem a Graecia vetere celebrata. Quibus
utinam similibusque de rebus disputari quam de
puerilibus his verborum translationibus maluissetis ![1]

198   Verum ut in versu vulgus si est peccatum videt ;
sic si quid in nostra oratione claudicat sentit ; sed

[1] [quibus . . . maluissetis] *Schütz.*

196 faculties. And consequently everybody is influenced not only by skilful arrangement of words but also by rhythms and pronunciations. For what proportion of people understands the science of rhythm and metre ? yet all the same if only a slight slip is made in these, making the line too short by a contraction or too long by dwelling on a vowel, the audience protests to a man. Well, does not the same thing take place in the case of pronunciation, so that if there are not only discrepancies between the members of a troupe or a chorus but even inconsistency in the pronunciation of individual actors, the ordinary public

197 drives them off the stage ?   LI. It is remarkable how little difference there is between the expert and the plain man as critics, though there is a great gap between them as performers. For as art started from nature, it would certainly be deemed to have failed if it had not a natural power of affecting us and giving us pleasure ; but nothing is so akin to our own minds as rhythms and words—these rouse us up to excitement, and smooth and calm us down, and often lead us to mirth and to sorrow ; though their extremely powerful influence is more suited for poetry and song, nor was it overlooked by that very learned monarch, King Numa, and by our ancestors, as is shown by the use of the lyre and the pipes at ceremonial banquets, and by the verses of the Salii ; but it was most frequently employed by the Greece of old days. And I only wish that you people had chosen this and similar topics as the subject of our debate, instead of this childish question of verbal metaphors !

198   " However, just as the public sees a mistake in versification, so it notices a slip in our oratory ; but

poetae non ignoscit, nobis concedit, taciti[1] tamen omnes non esse illud quod diximus aptum perfectumque cernunt. Itaque illi veteres, sicut hodie etiam nonnullos videmus, cum circuitum et quasi orbem verborum conficere non possent (nam id quidem nuper vel posse vel audere coepimus), terna aut bina aut nonnulli singula etiam verba dicebant; qui in illa infantia naturale illud quod aures hominum flagitabant tenebant tamen, ut et illa essent paria quae dicerent et aequalibus interspirationibus uterentur.

199   LII. Exposui fere ut potui quae maxime ad ornatum orationis pertinere arbitrabar; dixi enim de singulorum laude verborum, dixi de coniunctione eorum, dixi de numero atque forma. Sed si habitum orationis etiam et quasi colorem aliquem requiritis, est et plena quaedam sed tamen teres, et tenuis non sine nervis ac viribus, et ea quae particeps utriusque generis quadam mediocritate laudatur. His tribus figuris insidere quidam venustatis non fuco illitus 200 sed sanguine diffusus debet color. Tum denique hic nobis orator ita conformandus est et verbis et sententiis ut ei qui in armorum tractatione versantur,[2] ut quemadmodum qui utuntur armis aut palaestra non solum sibi vitandi aut feriendi rationem esse habendam putant sed etiam ut cum venustate mo-

---

[1] *v.l.* tacite.
[2] ut ei qui . . . versantur *transponunt varie codd. et edd.*

whereas it does not forgive a poet, it makes allowances for us, although all the audience, in spite of its not saying everything, perceives that our remarks were not neatly put or finished in style. Consequently those old orators, as we see to be the case with some speakers even nowadays, being incapable of constructing a rounded period (which indeed we have only lately begun to have the capacity or the courage to do) used to make their clauses consist of three or two words, or in the case of some speakers, even a single word ; though at that speechless period they nevertheless kept to the natural practice, demanded by the human ear, of making their clauses balance each other in pairs, and also of inserting regular pauses for taking breath.

99 LII. " I have practically concluded, to the best of my ability, my account of the few factors that I deemed most important for the decoration of oratory, having discussed the value of particular words, combination of words, and rhythm and shape of sentence. But if you also want to hear about general character and tone of diction, there is the full and yet rounded style of oratory, the plain style that is not devoid of vigour and force, and the style which combines elements of either class and whose merit is to steer a middle course. These three styles should exhibit a certain charm of colouring, not as a surface varnish 200 but as permeating their arterial system. Then finally our orator must be shaped in regard to both his words and his thoughts in the same way as persons whose business is the handling of weapons are trained in style, so that just as people who practise fencing or boxing think that they must give consideration not only to avoiding or striking blows but also to

Three artistic styles.

159

veantur, sic verbis quidem ad aptam compositionem et decentiam, sententiis vero ad gravitatem orationis utatur.

Formantur autem et verba et sententiae paene innumerabiles, quod satis scio notum esse vobis ; sed inter conformationem verborum et sententiarum hoc interest, quod verborum tollitur si verba mutaris, sententiarum permanet quibuscumque verbis uti 201 velis. Quod quidem vos etsi facitis, tamen admonendos puto ne quid esse aliud oratoris putetis quod quidem sit egregium atque mirabile nisi in singulis verbis illa tria tenere, ut translatis utamur frequenter, interdum factis, raro autem etiam pervetustis. In perpetua autem oratione, cum et coniunctionis lenitatem et numerorum quam dixi rationem tenuerimus, tum est quasi luminibus distinguenda et frequentanda 202 omnis oratio sententiarum atque verborum. LIII. Nam et commoratio una in re permultum movet et illustris explanatio rerumque quasi gerantur sub aspectum paene subiectio, quae et in exponenda re plurimum valent[1] et ad illustrandum id quod exponitur et ad amplificandum, ut eis qui audient illud quod augebimus quantum efficere oratio poterit tantum esse videatur ; et huic contraria saepe praecisio est et plus ad intellegendum quam dixeris sig-

---

[1] *v.l.* valet.

[a] §§ 152, 170.

grace of movement, similarly he may aim on the one hand at neatness of structure and grace in his employment of words and on the other hand at impressiveness in expressing his thoughts.

" Now there is an almost incalculable supply both of figures of speech and of figures of thought, a thing of which I know you are perfectly well aware ; but there is this difference between the figurative character of language and of thought, that the figure suggested by the words disappears if one alters the words, but that of the thoughts remains whatever 201 words one chooses to employ. And even if as a matter of fact you do attend to this, still I think you ought to be warned not to imagine that there is anything else essential to the orator, at all events anything outstanding and remarkable, except to be careful in his vocabulary to keep to the three rules stated already,[a] to use metaphorical words frequently, new coinages occasionally, and words that are actually archaic rarely. Then again, in the general structure of the language, after we have mastered smoothness of arrangement and the principle of rhythm that I spoke of, we then must vary and intersperse all our discourse with brilliant touches both 02 of thought and of language. LIII. For a great impression is made by dwelling on a single point, and also by clear explanation and almost visual presentation of events as if practically going on— which are very effective both in stating a case and in explaining and amplifying the statement, with the object of making the fact we amplify appear to the audience as important as eloquence is able to make it ; and explanation is often countered by a rapid review, and by a suggestion that causes more to be

Lines of argument.

161

CICERO

nificatio et distincte concisa brevitas et extenuatio
et huic adiuncta illusio a praeceptis Caesaris non
203 abhorrens ; et ab re longa degressio ; in qua cum
fuerit delectatio, tum reditus ad rem aptus et con-
cinnus esse debebit ; propositioque quid sis dicturus
et ab eo quod est dictum seiunctio et reditus ad propositum et iteratio et rationis apta conclusio ; tum
augendi minuendive causa veritatis supralatio atque
traiectio ; et rogatio, atque huic finitima quasi per-
contatio, expositioque sententiae suae ; tum illa
quae maxime quasi irrepit in hominum mentes, alia
dicentis ac significantis dissimulatio, quae est periu-
cunda cum orationis[1] non contentione sed sermone
tractatur ; deinde dubitatio, tum distributio, tum
correctio vel ante vel postquam dixeris vel cum aliquid
204 a te ipse reicias ; praemunitio est etiam ad id quod
aggrediare ; et traiectio in alium ; communicatio,
quae est quasi cum eis ipsis apud quos dicas deliberatio ; morum ac vitae imitatio vel in personis vel
siue illis, magnum quoddam ornamentum orationis
et aptum ad animos conciliandos vel maxime, saepe
205 autem etiam ad commovendos ; personarum ficta inductio, vel gravissimum lumen augendi ; descriptio,
erroris inductio, ad hilaritatem impulsio, anteoccupatio ; tum duo illa quae maxime movent, similitudo
et exemplum ; digestio, interpellatio, contentio,

---

[1] *v.l.* cum in oratione.

---

[a] Book II, §§ 261 ff., 269 ff.
[b] *Veritatis supralatio atque traiectio* is a tentative rendering of ὑπερβολή.

understood than one actually says, and by concise-
ness achieved with due regard to clearness, and dis-
paragement, and coupled with it raillery kept within
203 the rules prescribed [a] by Caesar ; and digression
from the matter at issue ; and after this has supplied
entertainment, the return to the subject will have to
be neatly and tactfully effected ; and the exposition
of what one is going to say, and its distinction from
what has already been said ; and return to a point
set out already, and repetition ; and the use of
formal syllogism ; then exaggeration [b] designed to
overstate or understate the facts ; and interrogation,
and the kindred device of rhetorical question, and
the statement of one's own opinion ; then irony, or
saying one thing and meaning another, which has
a very great influence on the minds of the audience,
and which is extremely entertaining if carried on in
a conversational and not a declamatory tone ; next
hesitation, then distinction, then correction of a
statement either before or after one has made it, or
204 when one rejects its application to oneself ; also
preparation applies to what one is going on to ; and
transference of responsibility to someone else ; taking into partnership, which is a sort of consultation
with one's audience ; imitation of manners and be-
haviour, either given in character or not, is a considerable ornament of style, and extremely effective
in calming down an audience and often also in exciting
205 it ; impersonation of people, an extremely brilliant
method of amplification; picturing of results; putting
on the wrong scent ; raising a laugh ; forestalling
the other side's case ; then two extremely effective
figures, comparison and example ; division into
parts, interruption, contrast of opposites, relapse into

163

reticentia, commendatio[1]; vox quaedam libera atque etiam effrenatior augendi causa; iracundia, obiurgatio, promissio, deprecatio, obsecratio, declinatio brevis a proposito (non ut superior illa degressio); purgatio, conciliatio, laesio, optatio atque exsecratio.

206 LIV. His fere luminibus illustrant orationem sententiae.

Orationis autem ipsius, tanquam armorum, est vel ad usum comminatio et quasi petitio vel ad venustatem ipsam[2] tractatio. Nam et geminatio verborum habet interdum vim, leporem alias, et paulum immutatum verbum atque deflexum, et eiusdem verbi crebra tum a primo repetitio, tum in extremum conversio, et in eadem verba impetus et concursio, et adiunctio, et progressio, et eiusdem verbi crebrius positi quaedam distinctio, et revocatio verbi, et illa quae similiter desinunt aut quae cadunt similiter aut quae paribus paria referuntur aut quae sunt inter

207 se similia. Est etiam gradatio quaedam et conversio et verborum concinna transgressio et contrarium et dissolutum et declinatio et reprehensio et exclamatio et imminutio, et quod in multis casibus ponitur et quod de singulis rebus propositis ductum refertur ad singula, et ad propositum subiecta ratio et item in distributis supposita ratio et permissio et rursum alia dubitatio et improvisum quiddam et dinumeratio

---

[1] comminatio *Kayser*.　　　　　[2] *Reid:* ipsa.

---

[a] *Metathesis, e.g.* oportet esse ut vivas, non vivere ut edas (Wilkins). Just above the word has another sense.

[b] Not that at § 203 fin., the rhetorical statement of doubt as to action, but doubt as to which of two expressions to use.

silence, compliment ; free use of the voice and even
uncontrolled vociferation to amplify the effect; anger,
invective, promise of proof, deprecation, entreaty,
brief divergence from the subject (not on the scale of
the digression mentioned above); self-justification, in-
gratiation, hard-hitting, appeals to the powers above
206 and imprecation. LIV. These roughly are the embellishments which the line of thought can employ to
explain the meaning.

"Then as to the actual diction: this is like a Figures of
weapon either employed for use, to threaten and to speech.
attack, or simply brandished for show. For there is
sometimes force and in other cases charm in iteration
of words, in slightly changing and altering a word,
and in sometimes repeating the same word several
times at the beginning of clauses and sometimes repeating the same word several times at their end, and
starting and ending clauses with the same words, and
attachment of a word, and climax, and assigning a
different meaning to the same word used several times,
and repetition of a word, and the employment of words
that rhyme or have the same case-ending or balance
207 each other or sound alike. There is also advance step
by step, and inversion,[a] and harmonious interchange
of words, and antithesis, and omission of connecting
particles, and change of subject, and self-correction,
and exclamation, and abbreviation, and the use of a
noun in several cases, and the reference of a term derived from several things mentioned to each of them
separately, and the appending of a reason to a statement made, and also the assignment of a reason for
separate details, and concession of a point, and again
another kind of hesitation,[b] and an unexpected turn of
expression, and enumeration of points, and another

165

et alia correctio et dissipatio et quod continuatum
et interruptum, et imago et sibi ipsi responsio et
immutatio et disiunctio et ordo et relatio et digressio
208 et circumscriptio.   Haec enim sunt fere atque horum
similia—vel plura etiam esse possunt—quae sententiis orationem verborumque conformationibus
illuminant.[1]

LV. Quae quidem te, Crasse, video, inquit Cotta,
quod nota esse nobis putes, sine definitionibus et
sine exemplis effudisse.

Ego vero, inquit Crassus, ne illa quidem quae
supra dixi nova vobis esse arbitrabar, sed voluntati
209 vestrum omnium parui.   His autem de rebus sol me
ille admonuit ut brevior essem, qui ipse iam praecipitans me quoque haec praecipitem paene evolvere
coegit.   Sed tamen huius generis demonstratio est
et doctrina ipsa vulgaris ; usus autem gravissimus et
210 in hoc toto dicendi studio difficillimus.   Quam ob
rem quoniam de ornatu omni orationis sunt omnes
si non patefacti at certe commonstrati loci, nunc quid
aptum sit, hoc est, quid maxime deceat in oratione
videamus.   Quanquam id quidem perspicuum est
non omni causae nec auditori neque personae neque
211 tempori congruere orationis unum genus.   Nam et
causae capitis alium quemdam verborum sonum
requirunt, alium rerum privatarum atque parvarum ;
et aliud dicendi genus deliberationes, aliud laudationes, aliud iudicia,[2] aliud sermones, aliud consolatio,

---

[1] *Kayser :* illuminent.
[2] [aliud iudicia] *Wilkins.*

---

[a] Not that mentioned in § 203 fin., but a mere substitution
of a more correct word.

kind of correction,[a] and local distribution, and running on, and breaking off, and indication of similarity, and answering one's own question, and metonymy, and distinguishing terms, and order, and reference

208 back, and digression, and periphrasis. For these more or less are the figures—and possibly there may be even more also like them—that embellish oratory with thoughts and with arrangements of words."

LV. " And indeed, Crassus," said Cotta, " I notice that you have poured them out without giving definitions or examples, in the belief that we are familiar with them."

" O well," said Crassus, " I did not suppose that all I told you before either was new to you, but I

209 obeyed the general wish of the company. But in regard to the present subject I was warned to be brief by yonder sun, which is now rapidly setting, and which has compelled me likewise to develop this topic at an almost headlong pace. But all the same, an exposition of this sort and the doctrine itself are nothing out of the way, though practice is extremely important, and in the whole of this pursuit of oratory

210 extremely difficult. Consequently as the whole subject of decoration in oratory has now been, if not thoroughly explored, at all events fully indicated in all its departments, now let us consider the subject of appropriateness, that is, what style is most suitable in a speech. Although one point at least is obvious, that no single kind of oratory suits every cause or

211 audience or speaker or occasion. For important criminal cases need one style of language and civil actions and unimportant cases another ; and different styles are required by deliberative speeches, panegyrics, lawsuits and lectures, and for consolation,

Adaptation of style to occasion.

aliud obiurgatio, aliud disputatio, aliud historia
desiderat. Refert etiam qui audiant, senatus an
populus an iudices, frequentes an pauci an singuli,
et quales ; ipsique oratores qua sint aetate, honore,
auctoritate[1] ; tempus pacis an belli, festinationis an
212 otii. Itaque hoc loco nihil sane est quod praecipi
posse videatur nisi ut figuram orationis plenioris et
tenuioris et item illius mediocris ad id quod agemus
ccommodatam deligamus. Ornamentis eisdem uti
fere licebit alias contentius, alias summissius ; omni-
que in re posse quod deceat facere artis et naturae
est, scire quid quandoque deceat prudentiae.

213 LVI. Sed haec ipsa omnia perinde sunt ut aguntur.
Actio, inquam, in dicendo una dominatur ; sine hac
summus orator esse in numero nullo potest, mediocris
hac instructus summos saepe superare. Huic primas
dedisse Demosthenes dicitur cum rogaretur quid in
dicendo esset primum, huic secundas, huic tertias ;
quo mihi melius etiam illud ab Aeschine dictum videri
solet, qui, cum propter ignominiam iudicii cessisset
Athenis et se Rhodum contulisset, rogatus a Rhodiis,

---

[1] *Lambinus :* auctoritate debet videri.

protest, discussion and historical narrative, respectively. The audience also is important—whether it
is the lords or the commons or the bench ; a large
audience or a small one or a single person, and their
personal character ; and consideration must be given
to the age, station and office of the speakers themselves, and to the occasion, in peace time or during
212 a war, urgent or allowing plenty of time. And so
at this point it does not in fact seem possible to lay
down any rules except that we should choose a more
copious or more restrained style of rhetoric, or likewise the intermediate style that has been specified,
to suit the business before us. It will be open to us
to use almost the same ornaments of style on
some occasions in a more energetic and on others in
a more quiet manner ; and in every case while the
ability to do what is appropriate is a matter of trained
skill and of natural talent, the knowledge of what is
appropriate to a particular occasion is a matter of
practical sagacity.

213   LVI. " But the effect of all of these oratorical
devices depends on how they are delivered. Delivery, I assert, is the dominant factor in oratory ;
without delivery the best speaker cannot be of any
account at all, and a moderate speaker with a trained
delivery can often outdo the best of them. The
story goes that when Demosthenes was asked what
is the first thing in speaking, he assigned the first
rôle to delivery, and also the second, and also the
third ; and I constantly feel that this answer was
actually outdone by the remark of Aeschines. That
orator, having had a discreditable defeat in a lawsuit,
had left Athens and betaken himself to Rhodes ;
there it is said that at the request of the citizens

Delivery, including voice and gesture.

169

legisse fertur orationem illam egregiam quam in
Ctesiphontem contra Demosthenem dixerat ; qua
perlecta petitum est ab eo postridie ut legeret illam
etiam quae erat contra a Demosthene pro Ctesiphonte
edita ; quam cum suavissima et maxima voce legisset,
admirantibus omnibus, ' Quanto,' inquit, ' magis
admiraremini si audissetis ipsum ! ' ex quo satis
significavit quantum esset in actione, qui orationem
214 eamdem aliam esse putaret actore mutato.   Quid
fuit in Graccho, quem tu, Catule, melius meministi,
quod me puero tantopere efferretur ?[1]   ' Quo me
miser conferam ? quo vertam ?   In Capitoliumne ? at
fratris sanguine redundat.   An domum ? matremne
ut miseram lamentantemque videam et abiectam ? '
Quae sic ab illo acta esse constabat oculis, voce, gestu,
inimici ut lacrimas tenere non possent.

Haec ideo dico pluribus quod genus hoc totum
oratores, qui sunt veritatis ipsius actores, reliquerunt,
imitatores autem veritatis, histriones, occupaverunt.
215 LVII. Ac sine dubio in omni re vincit imitationem
veritas, et[2] ea si satis in actione efficeret ipsa per
sese, arte profecto non egeremus ; verum quia animi
permotio, quae maxime aut declaranda aut imitanda
est actione, perturbata saepe ita est ut obscuretur
ac paene obruatur, discutienda sunt ea quae obscurant

---

[1] *Lambinus :* ferretur.
[2] et *Bakius :* sed.

he read the splendid speech that he had delivered against Ctesiphon, when Demosthenes was for the defence ; and when he had read it, next day he was asked also to read the speech that had been made in reply by Demosthenes for Ctesiphon. This he did, in a very attractive and loud voice ; and when everybody expressed admiration he said, 'How much more remarkable you would have thought it if you had heard Demosthenes himself ! ' thereby clearly indicating how much depends on delivery, as he thought that the same speech with a change of

214 speaker would be a different thing. In the case of Gracchus, whom you, Catulus, remember better than I do, what was there to be so highly extolled, when I was a boy ? ' Unhappy that I am, where am I to go ? Where am I to turn ? To the Capitol ? But the Capitol drips with my brother's blood. Or to my home ? To see my unhappy mother lamenting and despondent ? ' And report says that he delivered this with such effective glances and tone of voice and gestures that even his enemies could not restrain their tears.

" My reason for dwelling on these points is because the whole of this department has been abandoned by the orators, who are the players that act real life, and has been taken over by the actors, who only

215 mimic reality. LVII. And there can be no doubt that reality beats imitation in everything ; and if reality unaided were sufficiently effective in presentation, we should have no need at all for art. But because emotion, which mostly has to be displayed or else counterfeited by action, is often so confused as to be obscured and almost smothered out of sight, we have to dispel the things that

et ea quae sunt eminentia et prompta sumenda.
216 Omnis enim motus animi suum quemdam a natura
habet vultum et sonum et gestum ; totumque corpus
hominis et eius omnis vultus omnesque voces, ut nervi
in fidibus, ita sonant ut a motu animi quoque sunt
pulsae.   Nam voces ut chordae sunt intentae quae
ad quemque tactum respondeant, acuta gravis, cita
tarda, magna parva, quas tamen inter omnes est suo
quaeque in genere mediocris ; atque etiam illa sunt
ab his delapsa plura genera, lene asperum, contractum
diffusum, continenti spiritu intermisso, fractum scis-
217 sum, flexo sono attenuatum inflatum.   Nullum est
enim horum generum quod non arte ac moderatione tractetur ; hi sunt actori, ut pictori, expositi
ad variandum colores.   LVIII. Aliud enim vocis
genus iracundia sibi sumat, acutum, incitatum, crebro
incidens :

> Ipsus hortatur me frater ut meos malis miser
> Manderem natos . . .

et ea quae tu dudum, Antoni, protulisti :

> Segregare abs te ausu's . . .

et

> Ecquis hoc animadvertit ? Vincite . . .

et Atreus fere totus.   Aliud miseratio ac moeror,
flexibile, plenum, interruptum, flebili voce :

> Quo nunc me vertam ? quod iter incipiam ingredi ?
> Domum paternamne ? anne ad Peliae filias ?

---

^a The precise meaning of these and of some of Cicero's
other technical terms of music is doubtful.
^b From Accius, *Atreus* (*Remains*, ii. pp. 390 f.).
^c Book II, § 193.
^d Ennius, *Medea* (*Remains*, i. pp. 320 f.).

obscure it and take up its prominent and striking
216 points. For nature has assigned to every emotion a
particular look and tone of voice and bearing of its
own ; and the whole of a person's frame and every
look on his face and utterance of his voice are like
the strings of a harp, and sound according as they
are struck by each successive emotion. For the tones
of the voice are keyed up like the strings of an
instrument, so as to answer to every touch, high, low,
quick, slow, *forte*, *piano*, while between all of these
in their several kinds there is a medium note ; and
there are also the various modifications derived from
these, smooth or rough, limited or full in volume,
tenuto or *staccato*, faint or harsh,[a] *diminuendo* or
217 *crescendo*. For there are none of these varieties that
cannot be regulated by the control of art ; they are
the colours available for the actor, as for the painter,
to secure variety. LVIII. For one kind of tone must
be taken by anger—shrill, hasty, with short abrupt
clauses—

> Why, my very brother bids me miserably masticate
> Mine own children [b]—

and the line you quoted some time ago,[c] Antonius—

> Hast thou dared to sunder from thee—

and

> Will no one mark this ?   Put in chains—

and almost the whole of *Atreus*. Another tone is
proper for compassion and for sorrow, wavering, full,
halting, in a mournful key :

> Whither shall I turn now ? on what path enter ?
> Seek my sire's house ? or turn to Pelias' daughters ? [d]

173

CICERO

et illa :

O pater ! O patria ! O Priami domus

et quae sequuntur :

Haec omnia vidi inflammarei,
Priamo vi vitam evitarei.

218 Aliud metus, demissum et haesitans et abiectum,

Multimodis sum[1] circumventus, morbo, exsilio atque inopia :
Tum pavor sapientiam mihi omnem exanimato expectorat ;
Mater[2] terribilem minitatur vitae cruciatum et necem,
Quae nemo est tam firmo ingenio et tanta confidentia
Quin refugiat timido sanguen atque exalbescat metu.

219 Aliud vis, contentum, vehemens, imminens quadam
incitatione gravitatis :

Iterum Thyestes Atreum attractatum advenit,
Iterum iam aggreditur me et quietum exsuscitat.
Maior mihi moles, maius miscendumst malum
Qui illius acerbum cor contundam et comprimam.

Aliud voluptas effusum, lene, tenerum, hilaratum
ac remissum :

Sed sibi cum detulit coronam ob coligandas[3] nuptias,
Tibi ferebat ; cum simulabat se sibi alacriter dare,
Tum ad te ludibunda docte et delicate detulit.

Aliud molestia, sine commiseratione grave quiddam,
et uno pressu ac sono obductum :

[1] *Müller :* multis sum modis.
[2] mater *add. Kayser.*
[3] collocandas, coiugandas *edd*₀

---

[a] Ennius, *Andromache* (*Remains*, i. pp. 250-254 ; Vahlen,
Ennius, Scenica 92, 97 f.).
[b] Ennius, *Alcmeo* (*Remains*, i. pp. 230 f.).
[c] Accius, *Atreus* (*Remains*, ii. pp. 382 f.).
[d] From an unknown source.

174

and the verse—

> O father, O my country, O Priam's palace![a]

and the lines that follow—

> All of them I saw fiercely blazing,
> And Priam's life by violence
> Of life bereft.

218 Another belongs to fear, low and hesitating and despondent :

> I am entrapped in many ways, by sickness, exile, poverty :
> Also alarm my fainting heart of every shred of wisdom robs :
> My mother menaces my life with direful torture and with death,
> And none could be so firm of spirit, none so confident of heart
> But that hereat his blood would ebb with terror and his face turn pale.[b]

219 Another denotes energy ; this is intense, vehement, eager with a sort of impressive urgency :

> Again Thyestes comes to grapple Atreus,
> Again he approaches to disturb my peace.
> More misery, more misfortune must I brew,
> Wherewith to check and crush his cruel heart.[c]

Another is that of joy, gushing, smooth, tender, cheerful and gay :

> But when she brought herself a wreath wherewith to tie the marriage knot,
> For thee she brought it ; when she feigned to give it gaily t herself,
> 'Twas but in sport, to thee she bore it with adroitness and address.[d]

Another is the tone of dejection, a heavy kind of utterance, not employing appeal to compassion, drawn out in a single articulation and note :

175

Qua tempestate Paris Helenam innuptis iunxit nuptiis,
Ego tum gravida, expletis iam fere ad pariendum mensibus;
Per idem tempus Polydorum Hecuba partu postremo parit.

220 LIX. Omnes autem hos motus subsequi debet gestus, non hic verba exprimens scenicus sed universam rem et sententiam non demonstratione sed significatione declarans, laterum inflexione hac forti ac virili non ab scena et histrionibus sed ab armis aut etiam a palaestra ; manus autem minus arguta, digitis subsequens verba, non exprimens, brachium procerius proiectum quasi quoddam telum orationis, supplosio pedis in contentionibus aut incipiendis aut 221 finiendis. Sed in ore sunt omnia, in eo autem ipso dominatus est omnis oculorum ; quo melius nostri illi senes qui personatum ne Roscium quidem magnopere laudabant. Animi est enim omnis actio, et imago animi vultus, indices oculi ; nam haec est una pars corporis quae quot animi motus sunt tot significationes et commutationes[1] possit efficere, neque vero est quisquam qui eadem conivens efficiat. Theophrastus quidem Tauriscum quemdam dixit actorem aversum solitum esse dicere qui in agendo 222 contuens aliquid pronuntiaret. Quare oculorum esto[2] magna moderatio ; nam oris non est nimium mutanda species ne aut ad ineptias aut ad pravitatem aliquam

---

[1] [et commutationes] *Wilkins.*
[2] esto *nonnulli :* est.

---

[a] Probably from Pacuvius, *Iliona* (*Remains*, ii. pp. 243 f.).

What time did Paris mate with Helen, wedlock that no wedlock was,
I was with child, and now the months were ended and my
  time was near ;
'Twas at that season Hecuba gave birth to Polydore, her last.[a]

220   LIX. "But all these emotions must be accompanied
by gesture—not this stagy gesture reproducing the
words but one conveying the general situation and
idea not by mimicry but by hints, with this vigorous
manly throwing out of the chest, borrowed not from
the stage and the theatrical profession but from the
parade ground or even from wrestling ; but the
movements of the hand must be less rapid, following
the words and not eliciting them with the fingers ;
the arm thrown out rather forward, like an elocu-
tionary missile ; a stamp of the foot in beginning or
221 ending emphatic passages.   But everything depends
on the countenance, while the countenance itself is
entirely dominated by the eyes ; hence our older
generation were better critics, who used not to
applaud even Roscius very much when he wore a
mask.   For delivery is wholly the concern of the
feelings, and these are mirrored by the face and
expressed by the eyes ; for this is the only part of
the body capable of producing as many indications
and variations as there are emotions, and there is
nobody who can produce the same effect with the
eyes shut.   Theophrastus indeed declares that a
certain Tauriscus used to speak of an actor that recited
his lines on the stage with his gaze fixed on something
222 as ' turning his back on the audience.'   Consequently
there is need of constant management of the eyes,
because the expression of the countenance ought not
to be too much altered, for fear of slipping into looks

177

deferamur ; oculi sunt, quorum tum intentione, tum remissione, tum coniectu, tum hilaritate motus animorum significemus apte cum genere ipso orationis. Est enim actio quasi sermo corporis, quo magis menti 223 congruens esse debet ; oculos autem natura nobis, ut equo et leoni iubas, caudam, aures, ad motus animorum declarandos dedit, quare in hac nostra actione secundum vocem vultus valet ; is autem oculis gubernatur. Atque in eis omnibus quae sunt actionis inest quaedam vis a natura data ; quare etiam hac imperiti, hac vulgus, hac denique barbari maxime commoventur : verba enim neminem movent nisi cum qui eiusdem linguae societate coniunctus est, sententiaeque saepe acutae non acutorum hominum sensus praetervolant : actio, quae prae se motum animi fert, omnes movet; eisdem enim omnium animi motibus concitantur et eos eisdem notis et in aliis agnoscunt et in se ipsi indicant.

224 LX. Ad actionis autem usum atque laudem maximam sine dubio partem vox obtinet, quae primum est optanda nobis, deinde quaecumque erit ea tuenda. De quo illud iam nihil ad hoc praecipiendi genus quemadmodum voci serviatur, equidem tamen magnopere censeo serviendum ; sed illud videtur ab

that are in bad taste or into some distortion ; but
it is the eyes that should be used to indicate the
emotions, by now assuming an earnest look, now re-
laxing it, now a stare, and now a merry glance, in
correspondence with the actual nature of the speech.
For by action the body talks, so it is all the more
223 necessary to make it agree with the thought ; and
nature has given us eyes, as she has given the horse
and the lion their mane and tail and ears, to indicate
the feelings of the mind, so that in the matter of
delivery which we are now considering the face is
next in importance to the voice ; and the eyes are
the dominant feature in the face. And all the
factors of delivery contain a certain force bestowed
by nature ; which moreover is the reason why it is
delivery that has most effect on the ignorant and the
mob and lastly on barbarians ; for words influence
nobody but the person allied to the speaker by sharing
the same language, and clever ideas frequently outfly
the understanding of people who are not clever,
whereas delivery, which gives the emotion of the
mind expression, influences everybody, for the same
emotions are felt by all people and they both recognize them in others and manifest them in themselves
by the same marks.

24   LX. " But for effectiveness and distinction in delivery the greatest share undoubtedly belongs to the
voice. The gift of a voice is what we should pray
for first, but then we should take care of such voice
as we may have. As to this, the proper way of caring
for the voice is no concern of the kind of instruction
that we are considering, although all the same my
own view is that very great care ought to be taken
of it ; but it does seem pertinent to the province

huius nostri sermonis officio non abhorrere quod, ut
dixi paulo ante, plurimis in rebus quod maxime est
utile id nescio quo pacto etiam decet maxime.   Nam
ad vocem obtinendam nihil est utilius quam crebra
mutatio, nihil perniciosius quam effusa sine intermis-
225 sione contentio.   Quid, ad aures nostras et actionis
suavitatem quid est vicissitudine et varietate et
commutatione aptius ?   Itaque idem Gracchus (quod
potes audire, Catule, ex Licinio cliente tuo, litterato
homine, quem servum sibi ille habuit ad manum)
cum eburneola solitus est habere fistula qui staret
occulte post ipsum cum concionaretur peritum
hominem qui inflaret celeriter eum sonum quo illum
aut remissum excitaret aut a contentione revocaret.

Audivi mehercule, inquit Catulus, et saepe sum
admiratus hominis cum diligentiam, tum etiam doctrinam et scientiam.

226   Ego vero, inquit Crassus, ac doleo quidem illos
viros in eam fraudem in republica esse delapsos ;
quanquam ea tela texitur, et ea incitatur in civitate
ratio vivendi ac posteritati ostenditur, ut eorum
civium quos nostri patres non tulerunt iam similes
habere cupiamus.

Mitte, obsecro, inquit, Crasse, Iulius, sermonem
istum et te ad Gracchi fistulam refer, cuius ego non
dum plane rationem intellego.

227   LXI. In omni voce, inquit Crassus, est quoddam medium, sed suum cuique voci : hinc gradatim

of our present discussion, that as I said a little earlier,[a] in a great many matters the thing that is most useful is also in a way the most becoming. Now for the preservation of the voice nothing is more useful than a frequent change of tone, and nothing more detrimental than continuous uninterrupted exertion. Well, what is better suited to please our ears and secure an agreeable delivery than alternation and variation and change? Accordingly, the same Gracchus (as you, Catulus, may hear from that scholarly person, your retainer Licinius, who was a slave of Gracchus and acted as his amanuensis) made a practice of having a skilled attendant to stand behind him out of sight with a little ivory flageolet when he was making a speech, in order promptly to blow a note to rouse him when he was getting slack or to check him from overstraining his voice."

" To be sure I have heard it," said Catulus, " and I have often admired both the diligence and the learning and knowledge of the person in question."

" I certainly admire him myself," said Crassus, " and I regret, it is true, that those people fell into the error they did in their public life; though the pattern being woven into the texture of our politics and the principles of public conduct being fostered and displayed to future generations are such, that we only wish that we now possessed citizens resembling the ones that our fathers would not tolerate."

" Drop that subject, Crassus, I beg of you," said Julius, " and go back to Gracchus's flageolet, the principle of which I don't yet quite understand."

LXI. " In every voice," said Crassus, " there is a mean pitch, but each voice has its own; and for the voice to rise gradually from the mean is not only

ascendere vocem[1] et suave est (nam a principio clamare agreste quiddam est) et idem illud ad firmandam est vocem salutare ; deinde est quoddam contentionis extremum, quod tamen interius est quam acutissimus clamor, quo te fistula progredi non sinet et iam ab ipsa contentione revocabit ; est item contra quoddam in remissione gravissimum quoque tanquam sonorum gradibus descenditur. Haec varietas et hic per omnes sonos vocis cursus et se tuebitur et actioni afferet suavitatem. Sed fistulatorem domi relinquetis, sensum huius consuetudinis vobiscum ad forum deferetis.

228 Edidi quae potui, non ut volui sed ut me temporis angustiae coegerunt ; scitum est enim causam conferre in tempus, cum afferre plura si cupias non queas.

Tu vero, inquit Catulus, collegisti omnia, quantum ego possum iudicare, ita divinitus ut non a Graecis didicisse sed eos ipsos haec docere posse videare. Me quidem istius sermonis participem factum esse gaudeo ; ac vellem ut meus gener, sodalis tuus Hortensius affuisset ; quem quidem ego confido omnibus istis laudibus quas tu oratione complexus es excellentem fore.

229 Et Crassus : Fore dicis ? inquit, ego vero esse iam iudico et tum iudicavi cum me consule in senatu

---

[1] *v.l.* vocem utile.

agreeable (because it is a boorish trick to shout loudly at the beginning) but also beneficial for giving it strength ; then there is an extreme point of elevation, which nevertheless falls short of the shrillest possible screech, and from this point the pipe will not allow one to go further, and will begin to call one back from the actual top note ; and on the other side there is similarly an extreme point in the lowering of the pitch, the point reached in a sort of descending scale of sounds. This variation and this passage of the voice through all the notes will both safeguard itself and add charm to the delivery. But you will leave the piper at home, and only take with you down to the house the perception that his training gives you.

28 " I have given the best exposition I could, not as I should have liked but as compelled by the limited time available ; for it is a wise plan to cut one's coat according to one's cloth, when one cannot add more even if one wishes." End of the debate.

" O but as for you," said Catulus, " so far as I can judge, you have gathered together the whole of the points with such genius, that you appear not to have learnt from the Greeks but to be competent to instruct the Greeks themselves in these subjects. For myself at all events it is a great satisfaction to have been admitted to share in your discourse ; and I only wish my son-in-law, your friend Hortensius, had been here. He, I am convinced, will come to the top in all the accomplishments that you have included in oratory."

9 " Will come ? " said Crassus ; " no, in my judgement he is there already, and I formed this judgement when he defended the cause of Africa in the Senate

causam defendit Africae, nuperque etiam magis cum
pro Bithyniae rege dixit.   Quam ob rem recte vides,
Catule, nihil enim isti adolescenti neque a natura
230 neque a doctrina deesse sentio.   Quo magis est tibi,
Cotta, et tibi, Sulpici, vigilandum ac laborandum ;
non enim ille mediocris orator vestrae quasi suc-
crescit aetati, sed et ingenio peracri et studio flag-
ranti et doctrina eximia et memoria singulari ; cui
quanquam faveo, tamen illum aetati suae praestare
cupio, vobis vero illum tanto minorem praecurrere
vix honestum est.

Sed iam surgamus, inquit, nosque curemus et
aliquando ab hac contentione disputationis animos
nostros curaque laxemus.

during my consulship, and even more so recently, when he spoke on behalf of the King of Bithynia. Consequently your view, Catulus, is correct, for I feel that the young man in question lacks no gift of 230 nature or of education. And this makes it all the more necessary for you, Cotta, and you, Sulpicius, to be watchful and diligent. For it is no ordinary orator who is growing up in the person of Hortensius to follow on after your generation, but one gifted with a very keen intelligence, ardent devotion to study, exceptional learning and an unrivalled memory; and though I favour him, nevertheless, while I am eager that he shall outstrip his own generation, still it would be hardly creditable for you that one so much your junior as he is should outstrip you.

" But now let us rise," he said, " and take some refreshment; this has been a very keen debate, and it is time to give our minds a rest from the strain."

DE FATO

Others apart sat on a hill retired
In thoughts more elevate, and reason'd high
Of providence, foreknowledge, will, and fate,
Fix'd fate, free will, foreknowledge absolute ;
And found no end, in wand'ring mazes lost.
MILTON, *Paradise Lost,* Book I.

INTRODUCTION

OF this essay only a part has come down to us ; a few quotations from the larger part which is lost occur in later writers. It belongs to the encyclopaedia of philosophy on the composition of which Cicero embarked, after the death of his daughter Tullia in February 45 B.C., as the best service that he could render to his fellow-countrymen now that he had retired from public life. He continued working at these writings until his return to the political arena in the autumn of 44 B.C. A scheme of them will be found in *De Divinatione*, ii. §§ 1-4, where it appears that *De Fato* is an appendix to the treatise on theology formed by the three books of *De Natura Deorum* and the two books of *De Divinatione*. The same is implied in the preface to *De Fato*, § 1 ; and it appears from § 2 that the book was written after the death of Caesar in March 44 B.C.

The work is in the shape of a dialogue held between Cicero and Hirtius, at Cicero's villa at Puteoli (Pozzuoli on the Bay of Naples). Hirtius had been a personal and political friend of Caesar, serving as his *legatus* in Gaul in 58 B.C., and was one of the ten praetors nominated by him in 46 B.C. After his praetorship he received Belgic Gaul as his province for 44 B.C., but governed it by deputy, and attended on Caesar at Rome. Caesar nominated him consul

189

CICERO

for 43 B.C. After Caesar's assassination Hirtius joined Antony, but was disgusted by his despotic arrogance, and retired to Puteoli, where he had a place near Cicero's. On 27th April 43 he fell in action against Antony, who was besieging Mutina. Though political opponents, Cicero and Hirtius were on very friendly terms as neighbours in the country, and had studious interests in common (*Ad Fam.* vii. 23, ix. 6, *De Fato* §§ 2, 3). Cicero had given lessons in oratory to Hirtius and Pansa, whom he used to call ' discipulos et grandes praetextatos ' (Suetonius, *De Rhet.* 1).

CONTENTS

The Introduction (§§ 1-4) implies that the book began with a discourse of Hirtius, but this is lost. What survives is part of Cicero's reply, but even this, as appears from § 41, is the second of two speeches made by him, the first having disappeared. The surviving fragment begins (§§ 6, 7) with the end of a refutation of the fatalism of Posidonius the Stoic, pupil of Panaetius and friend of Cicero. Posidonius had argued that the fact of omens shows that the future follows inevitably from the past ; Cicero replies that events may equally well be due to chance. He then (§§ 7-17) turns to the view of Chrysippus, the third head and second founder of the Stoic school, and argues that although external circumstances do affect character and conduct, the will is free. Chrysippus was countered by the logic of his contemporary, the Megarian Diodorus. Epicurus's ' swerve ' of the atom (§§ 18-23) is not required to avoid fatalism, since secondary causes are accidental ; and Carneades,

DE FATO

the Academic of the second century, is right in teaching (§§ 23-25) that free-will means freedom from external compulsion, not absence of rational motive. Indeed (26-30) fate truly means only universal causation, which in part is casual; it does not mean necessity, or imply fatalism and inaction. Volition (31-38) is a fact, and circumstances are only secondary causes of action. In fact (39-45) Chrysippus steered a middle course between fatalism and freedom, and inclined to the latter, which is supported by the psychology of volition and also that of perception. . . . (§§ 46-48) Epicurus's uncaused 'swerve' is meaningless.

EDITIONS

The text of this edition of *De Fato* is based on that in Nobbe's complete Cicero (Leipzig, 1827). Nobbe revised his book for a second edition (1850), and appended critical notes; those on *De Fato* are at p. 1387. There is an edition of *De Fato* with critical notes and a commentary by 'Henricus Alanus, Hibernicus' (London, 1839), and a Teubner text by Ax (Leipzig, 1938).

M. TULLI CICERONIS

DE FATO

1   I. . . . quia pertinet ad mores, quod ἦθος illi
vocant, nos eam partem philosophiae de moribus
appellare solemus, sed decet augentem linguam
Latinam, nominare moralem. Explicandaque vis est
ratioque enuntiationum, quae Graeci ἀξιώματα vocant;
quae de re futura cum aliquid dicunt deque eo quod
possit fieri aut non possit, quam vim habeant obscura
quaestio est, quam περὶ δυνατῶν philosophi appellant;
totaque est λογική, quam 'rationem disserendi' voco.
Quod autem in aliis libris feci, qui sunt de natura
deorum, itemque in eis quos de divinatione edidi, ut
in utramque partem perpetua explicaretur oratio, quo
facilius id a quoque probaretur quod cuique maxime
probabile videretur, id in hac disputatione de fato
2 casus quidam ne facerem impedivit. Nam cum essem
in Puteolano, Hirtiusque noster consul designatus

---

^a *i.e.* the department of philosophy termed Ethics, the
name being derived from *ēthos*, ' character.'
  ^b The term here means 'judgements,' not ' axioms.'
  ^c ' *About Things Possible*,' Theory of Possibilities.

192

MARCUS TULLIUS CICERO

DE FATO

1 I. . . . because it [a] relates to character, called in
Greek *ēthos*, while we usually term that part of
philosophy ' the study of character,' but the suitable
course is to add to the Latin language by giving
this subject the name of 'moral science.' It is also
necessary to expound the meaning and the theory
of propositions, called in Greek *axiōmata* [b] ; what
validity these have when they make a statement
about a future event and about something that may
happen or may not is a difficult field of inquiry,
entitled by philosophers *Peri Dynatōn* [c] ; and the
whole subject is *Logikē*, which I call ' the theory of
discourse.' The method which I pursued in other
volumes, those on the Nature of the Gods, and also
in those which I have published on Divination, was
that of setting out a continuous discourse both for
and against, to enable each student to accept for
himself the view that seems to him most probable ;
but I was prevented by accident [d] from adopting it
in the present discussion on the subject of Fate. For
I was at my place at Puteoli, [e] and my friend Hirtius,

Introduction : Latin terminology.

Scene and persons of dialogue.

---

[d] What is referred to does not appear.
[e] See Introduction, p. 189.

eisdem in locis, vir nobis amicissimus et eis studiis in quibus nos a pueritia viximus deditus, multum una eramus, maxime nos quidem exquirentes ea consilia quae ad pacem et ad concordiam civium pertinerent. Cum enim omnes post interitum Caesaris novarum perturbationum causae quaeri viderentur, eisque esse occurrendum putaremus, omnis fere nostra in eis deliberationibus consumebatur oratio, idque et saepe alias, et quodam liberiore quam solebat et magis vacuo ab interventoribus die, cum ille ad me venisset, primo ea quae erant cotidiana et quasi legitima nobis, de pace et de otio.

5 II. Quibus actis, Quid ergo ? inquit ille, quoniam oratorias exercitationes non tu quidem ut spero reliquisti, sed certe philosophiam illis anteposuisti, possumne aliquid audire ?

Tu vero, inquam, vel audire vel dicere ; nec enim, id quod recte existimas, oratoria illa studia deserui, quibus etiam te incendi, quamquam flagrantissimum acceperam, nec ea quae nunc tracto minuunt sed augent potius illam facultatem. Nam cum hoc genere philosophiae quod nos sequimur magnam habet orator societatem, subtilitatem enim ab Academia mutuatur et ei vicissim reddit ubertatem orationis et ornamenta dicendi. Quam ob rem,

194

the consul designate, a very close friend of mine and a devoted student of the subjects that have occupied my life from boyhood, was in the neighbourhood. Consequently we were a great deal together, being engrossed as we for our part were in seeking for a line of policy that might lead to peace and concord in the state. For since the death of Caesar it had seemed as if a search was being made for every possible means of causing fresh upheavals, and we thought that resistance must be offered to these tendencies. Consequently almost all our conversation was spent in considering those matters,—and this both on many other occasions and also, on a day less occupied by engagements than usual and less interrupted by visitors, Hirtius having come to my house, we began with our daily and regular topics of peace and tranquillity.

3   II. These dealt with, Hirtius remarked, " What now ?   I hope you have not actually abandoned your oratorical exercises, though you have undoubtedly placed philosophy in front of them ; well then, is it possible for me to hear something ? "

" Well," I said, " you can either hear something or say something yourself; for you are right in supposing that I have not abandoned my old interest in oratory,—indeed I have kindled it in you also, although you came to me an ardent devotee already ; and moreover my oratorical powers are not diminished by the subjects that I now have in hand, but rather increased. For there is a close alliance between the orator and the philosophical system of which I am a follower, since the orator borrows subtlety from the Academy and repays the loan by giving to it a copious and flowing style and rhetorical ornament

195

inquam, quoniam utriusque studii nostra possessio est, hodie utro frui malis optio sit tua.

Tum Hirtius: Gratissimum, inquit, et tuorum omnium simile ; nihil enim umquam abnuit meo 4 studio voluntas tua. Sed quoniam rhetorica mihi vestra sunt nota teque in eis et audivimus saepe et audiemus, atque hanc Academicorum contra propositum disputandi consuetudinem indicant te suscepisse Tusculanae disputationes, ponere aliquid ad quod audiam, si tibi non est molestum, volo.

An mihi, inquam, potest quidquam esse molestum quod tibi gratum futurum sit ? Sed ita audies ut Romanum hominem, ut timide ingredientem ad hoc genus disputandi, ut longo intervallo haec studia repetentem.

Ita, inquit, audiam te disputantem ut ea lego quae scripsisti ; proinde ordire. Considamus hic.

. . . .

5 III. . . . quorum in aliis, ut in Antipatro poeta, ut in brumali die natis, ut in simul aegrotantibus fratribus, ut in urina, ut in unguibus, ut in reliquis eiusmodi, naturae contagio valet, quam ego non tollo—vis est nulla fatalis ; in aliis autem fortuita quaedam esse possunt, ut in illo naufrago, ut in Icadio, ut in Daphita. Quaedam etiam Posidonius (pace

---

[a] Cicero is replying to the lost thesis of Hirtius, promised in § 4; indeed the words *in prima oratione*, § 40, seem to show that this is a second speech from Cicero, his first one being lost, with the rejoinder to it that Hirtius presumably made.

[b] Unknown, as is the Icadius mentioned in this sentence, and also the meaning of the other instances of divination here quoted.

This being so," I said, " as both fields of study fall
within our province, to-day it shall be for you to
choose which you prefer to enjoy."

" That is most kind of you," rejoined Hirtius, " and
exactly like what you do always ; for your willingness
never refuses anything to my inclination. But I am
acquainted with the rhetorical discourses of your
school, and have often heard and also often shall
hear you in them ; moreover your Tusculan Disputations show that you have adopted this Academic
practice of arguing against a thesis advanced ; consequently I am willing to lay down some thesis in
order that I may hear the counter-arguments, if this
is not disagreeable to you."

" Can anything be disagreeable to me," I said,
" that will be agreeable to you ? But you will hear
me speaking as a true Roman, as one who is nervous
in entering on this kind of discussion, and who is
returning to these studies after a long interval."

" I shall listen to your discourse in the same spirit
as I read your writings ; so begin. Let us sit down
here."

. . . .

. . . .

5   III. " . . . *a* in some of which, for instance in the
case of the poet Antipater,*b* in that of persons born
on the shortest day, or of brothers who are ill at the
same time, in the cases of urine and finger-nails
and other things of that kind, natural connexion
operates, and this I do not exclude—it is not a
predestined compelling force at all ; but in other
cases there can be some elements of chance, for
instance with the shipwrecked sailor we spoke of, or
Icadius, or Daphitas. Some cases even seem (if the

*All omens
ambiguous ;
no proof
of fate.*

197

magistri dixerim) comminisci videtur; sunt quidem[1]
absurda. Quid enim ? si Daphitae fatum fuit ex equo
cadere atque ita perire, ex hocne equo, qui cum equus
non esset nomen habebat alienum ? aut Philippus
hasne in capulo quadrigulas vitare monebatur ? quasi
vero capulo sit occisus. Quid autem magnum aut
naufragum illum sine nomine in rivo esse lapsum—
quamquam huic quidem hic scribit praedictum in
aqua esse pereundum ? ne hercule Icadii quidem
praedonis video fatum ullum ; nihil enim scribit ei
6 praedictum : quid mirum igitur ex spelunca saxum
in crura eius incidisse ? puto enim, etiam si Icadius
tum in spelunca non fuisset, saxum tamen illud
casurum fuisse, nam aut nihil est omnino fortuitum
aut hoc ipsum potuit evenire fortuna. Quaero igitur
(atque hoc late patebit), si fati omnino nullum nomen
nulla natura nulla vis esset, et forte temere casu aut
pleraque fierent aut omnia, num aliter ac nunc
eveniunt evenirent ? Quid ergo attinet inculcare
fatum, cum sine fato ratio omnium rerum ad naturam
fortunamve referatur ?

7   IV. Sed Posidonium sicut aequum est cum bona

---

[1] quidem *Davisius :* inquam quidem *codd. :* quidem
inquam *Moser.*

---

[a] Posidonius.
[b] Daphitas was an epigrammatist, who tricked the oracle
at Delphi by asking it whether he should find his horse;
being answered that he should, he rejoined that he had
never had a horse. He was punished by Attalus, king of
Pergamum, by being thrown from a rock called The Horse
(Hippos).
[c] Philip of Macédon had been warned by an oracle to
beware of a chariot, and would never ride in one ; but the

master [a] will excuse my saying so) to be the invention
of Posidonius ; at all events they are ridiculous.   For
consider : suppose it was Daphitas's destiny to fall
off his horse and meet his end in that way, was it
off this horse, which as it was not a real horse had a
name that did not belong to it ? [b] or was it against
these little four-in-hands on the sword-hilt that Philip
used to be warned to be on his guard ? [c] just as if
it was the hilt of a sword that killed him !   Again,
what is there remarkable about that nameless shipwrecked sailor's having fallen into a brook ? although
in his case indeed our authority does write that he
had been warned that he was to meet his end in the
water.   Even in the case of the brigand Icadius I
swear I can't see any trace of destiny ; for the story
6 does not say that he had any warning, so that if a
rock from the roof of a cave did fall on his legs, what
is there surprising about it ? for I suppose that even
if Icadius had not been in the cave at the time, that
rock would have fallen all the same, since either
nothing at all is fortuitous or it was possible for this
particular event to have happened by fortune.   What
I want to know therefore is (and this is a matter that
will have a wide bearing), if there were no such word
at all as fate, no such thing, no such force, and if
either most things or all things took place by mere
casual accident, would the course of events be different from what it is now ?   What is the point then
of harping on fate, when everything can be explained by reference to nature and fortune without
bringing fate in ?
7   IV. " But let us give Posidonius the polite dis-

sword with which he was assassinated (336 B.C.) had a
chariot-race carved in ivory on its hilt.

gratia dimittamus, ad Chrysippi laqueos revertamur. Cui quidem primum de ipsa rerum contagione respondeamus, reliqua postea persequemur. Inter locorum naturas quantum intersit videmus : alios esse salubres, alios pestilentes, in aliis esse pituitosos et quasi redundantes, in aliis exsiccatos atque aridos ; multaque sunt alia quae inter locum et locum plurimum differant. Athenis tenue caelum, ex quo etiam[1] acutiores putantur Attici, crassum Thebis, itaque pingues Thebani et valentes. Tamen neque illud tenue caelum efficiet ut aut Zenonem quis aut Arcesilam aut Theophrastum audiat, neque crassum ut Nemea[2] potius quam Isthmo[3] victoriam petat. Diiunge[4] longius : quid enim loci natura afferre potest ut in porticu Pompeii potius quam in campo ambulemus ? tecum quam cum alio ? Idibus potius quam Kalendis ? Ut igitur ad quasdam res natura loci pertinet aliquid, ad quasdam autem nihil, sic affectio astrorum valeat si vis ad quasdam res, ad omnes certe non valebit. At enim quoniam in naturis hominum dissimilitudines sunt, ut alios dulcia alios subamara delectent, alii libidinosi alii iracundi aut crudeles aut superbi sint, alii a[5] talibus vitiis abhorreant,—quoniam igitur, inquit, tantum natura a

8

---

[1] etiam : v.l. omnes. [2] Nemeae ? Rackham.
[3] in Isthmo ? Rackham. [4] diiungo cod. unus.
[5] a addidit Lambinus.

---

[a] One of a group of public buildings built near the Campus Martius by Pompey ; in one stood his statue, at the base of which Caesar was murdered.

missal that he deserves and return to the subtleties
of Chrysippus. And first let us answer him on the
actual influence of connexion ; the other points we
will go on to afterwards. We see the wide difference
between the natural characters of different localities :
we notice that some are healthy, others unhealthy,
that the inhabitants of some are phlegmatic and as
it were overcharged with moisture, those of others
parched and dried up ; and there are a number of
other very wide differences between one place and
another. Athens has a rarefied climate, which is
thought also to cause sharpness of wit above the
average in the population ; at Thebes the climate is
dense, and so the Thebans are stout and sturdy. All
the same the rarefied air of Athens will not enable
a student to choose between the lectures of Zeno,
Arcesilas and Theophrastus, and the dense air of
Thebes will not make a man try to win a race at Nemea
8 rather than at Corinth. Carry the distinction further:
tell me, can the nature of the locality cause us to
take our walk in Pompey's Porch [a] rather than in the
Campus ? in your company sooner than in someone
else's ? on the 15th of the month rather than on the
1st ? Well then, just as the nature of the locality
has some effect on some things but none on others,
so the condition of the heavenly bodies may if you
like influence some things, but it certainly will not
influence everything. You will say that inasmuch
as there are differences in the natures of human
beings that cause some to like sweet things, others
slightly bitter things, and make some licentious and
others prone to anger or cruel or proud, while others
shrink in horror from vices of that sort, therefore, we
are told, inasmuch as there is so wide a difference

natura distat, quid mirum est has dissimilitudines **ex**
differentibus causis esse factas ?

9 V. Haec disserens qua de re agatur et in quo
causa consistat non videt. Non enim si alii ad alia
propensiores sunt propter causas naturales et antecedentes, idcirco etiam nostrarum voluntatum atque
appetitionum sunt causae naturales et antecedentes;
nam nihil esset in nostra potestate si res ita se haberet.
Nunc vero fatemur, acuti hebetesne, valentes im-
becilline simus, non esse id in nobis, qui autem ex
eo cogi putat ne ut sedeamus quidem aut ambulemus voluntatis esse, is non videt quae quamque rem res consequatur. Ut enim et ingeniosi et
tardi ita nascantur, antecedentibus causis, itemque
valentes et imbecilli, non sequitur tamen ut etiam
sedere et ambulare et rem agere aliquam principa-

10 libus causis definitum et constitutum sit. Stil-
ponem, Megaricum philosophum, acutum sane hominem et probatum temporibus illis accepimus. Hunc
scribunt ipsius familiares et ebriosum et mulierosum
fuisse, neque haec scribunt vituperantes sed potius
ad laudem, vitiosam enim naturam ab eo sic edomi-
tam et compressam esse doctrina ut nemo umquam
vinolentum illum, nemo in eo libidinis vestigium
viderit. Quid ? Socratem nonne legimus quemadmodum notarit Zopyrus physiognomon, qui se profite-
batur hominum mores naturasque ex corpore oculis

between one nature and another, what is there surprising in the view that these points of unlikeness
result from different causes ?

9   V. " In putting forward this view Chrysippus fails and the will modifies the character which controls action.
to see the question at issue and the point with which
the argument is dealing.   For it does not follow that
if differences in men's propensities are due to natural
and antecedent causes, therefore our wills and desires
are also due to natural and antecedent causes;
for if that were the case, we should have no freedom
of the will at all.   But as it is, though we admit that
it does not rest with ourselves whether we are quick-
witted or dull, strong or weak, yet the person who
thinks that it necessarily follows from this that even
our choice between sitting still and walking about is
not voluntary fails to discern the true sequence of
cause and effect.   For granted that clever people
and stupid people are born like that, owing to antecedent causes, and that the same is true of the strong
and the weak, nevertheless it does not follow that
our sitting and walking and performing some action

10 are also settled and fixed by primary causes.   The
Megarian philosopher Stilpo, we are informed, was
undoubtedly a clever person and highly esteemed in
his day.   Stilpo is described in the writings of his
own associates as having been fond of liquor and of
women, and they do not record this as a reproach
but rather to add to his reputation, for they say that
he had so completely mastered and suppressed his
vicious nature by study that no one ever saw him the
worse for liquor or observed in him a single trace of
licentiousness.   Again, do we not read how Socrates
was stigmatized by the ' physiognomist' Zopyrus,
who professed to discover men's entire characters and

vultu fronte pernoscere ? stupidum esse Socratem
dixit et bardum quod iugula concava non haberet
—obstructas eas partes et obturatas esse dicebat;
addidit etiam mulierosum, in quo Alcibiades cachin-
11 num dicitur sustulisse. Sed haec ex naturalibus
causis vitia nasci possunt, exstirpari autem et funditus
tolli, ut is ipse qui ad ea propensus fuerit a tantis
vitiis avocetur, non est positum in naturalibus causis,
sed in voluntate studio disciplina; quae tollentur[1]
omnia si vis et natura fati ex divinationis ratione
firmabitur.

VI. Etenim si est divinatio, qualibusnam a per-
ceptis artis proficiscitur ('percepta' appello quae
dicuntur Graece θεωρήματα)? Non enim credo nullo
percepto aut ceteros artifices versari in suo munere
aut eos qui divinatione utantur futura praedicere.
12 Sunt igitur astrologorum percepta huiusmodi: ' Si
quis (verbi causa) oriente Canicula natus est, is in mari
non morietur.' Vigila, Chrysippe, ne tuam causam,
in qua tibi cum Diodoro valente dialectico magna
luctatio est, deseras. Si enim est verum quod ita
conectitur, ' Si quis oriente Canicula natus est, in

---

[1] *Rackham :* tolluntur *codd.*

[a] See *Tusculans* iv. 37. Socrates admitted that the char-
acter-reader had told his natural propensities correctly, but
said that they had been overcome by philosophy.

[b] *Ars* means 'a science,' theoretical or practical, a
systematized collection of facts; the term survives at the
universities in the title *Magister Artium,* which meant
'qualified teacher of the sciences.' *Scientia* means 'knowledge,' a psychological term, denoting a state or action of
the mind.

natures from their body, eyes, face and brow ? he said that Socrates was stupid and thick-witted because he had not got hollows in the neck above the collar-bone—he used to say that these portions of his anatomy were blocked and stopped up ; he also added that he was addicted to women—at which Alci-
11 biades is said to have given a loud guffaw ![a] But it is possible that these defects may be due to natural causes ; but their eradication and entire removal, recalling the man himself from the serious vices to which he was inclined, does not rest with natural causes, but with will, effort, training ; and if the potency and the existence of fate is proved from the theory of divination, all of these will be done away with.

VI. " Indeed, if divination exists, what pray is the nature of the scientific [b] observations (I use the term ' observations ' to render *theōrēmata*) which are its source ? For I do not believe that those who prac-tise divination dispense entirely with the use of observation in foretelling future events, any more than do the practitioners of all the other sciences in
12 pursuing their own function. Well then, here is a specimen of the observations of the astrologers : ' If (for instance) a man was born at the rising of the dogstar, he will not die at sea.' Keep a good look-out, Chrysippus, so as not to leave your position un-defended ; you have a great tussle about it with that stalwart logician Diodorus.[c] For if the connexion of propositions ' If anyone was born at the rising of the dogstar, he will not die at sea ' is true, the

Divination implies a necessary sequence of events.

[c] Head of the Megarian School *c.* 300 B.C., known as ὁ διαλεκτικός.

mari non morietur,' illud quoque verum est, 'Si
Fabius oriente Canicula natus est, Fabius in mari non
morietur.' Pugnant igitur haec inter se, Fabium
oriente Canicula natum esse et Fabium in mari moriturum, et quoniam certum in Fabio ponitur natum
esse eum Canicula oriente, haec quoque pugnant, et
esse Fabium et in mari esse moriturum. Ergo haec
quoque coniunctio est ex repugnantibus, 'Et est
Fabius et in mari Fabius morietur,' quod ut propositum
est ne fieri quidem potest. Ergo illud, 'Morietur in
mari Fabius,' ex eo genere est quod fieri non potest.
Omne igitur quod falsum dicitur in futuro, id fieri
13 non potest. VII. At hoc, Chrysippe, minime vis,
maximeque tibi de hoc ipso cum Diodoro certamen
est. Ille enim id solum fieri posse dicit quod aut sit
verum aut futurum sit verum, et quidquid futurum
sit id dicit fieri necesse esse et quidquid non sit
futurum id negat fieri posse. Tu et quae non sint
futura posse fieri dicis, ut frangi hanc gemmam etiam
si id numquam futurum sit, neque necesse fuisse
Cypselum regnare Corinthi quamquam id millesimo
ante anno Apollinis oraculo editum esset. At si ista
comprobabis divina praedicta, et quae falsa in futuris
dicentur in eis habebis ut ea fieri non possint (ut si
dicatur Africanum Karthagine non esse[1] potiturum),
et si vere dicatur de futuro idque ita futurum sit,

[1] non esse *add. Alanus* (ut si . . . potiturum *secl. edd.*).

---

[a] What particular member (if any) of this large and distinguished clan is referred to is not known.

[b] Scipio Africanus Minor took Carthage 146 B.C. He was
found dead in his bed at Rome, 129 B.C., and it was generally

following connexion is also true, ' If Fabius ᵃ was born at the rising of the dogstar, Fabius will not die at sea.' Consequently the propositions ' Fabius was born at the rising of the dogstar ' and ' Fabius will die at sea ' are incompatible, and since that he was born at the rising of the dogstar is predicated with certainty in the case of Fabius, the propositions ' Fabius exists ' and ' Fabius will die at sea ' are also incompatible. Therefore also ' Fabius exists and Fabius will die at sea ' is a conjunction of incompatibles, which as propounded is an impossibility. Therefore the proposition ' Fabius will die at sea ' belongs to the class of impossibilities. Therefore every false proposition about the future is an im-

13 possibility. VII. But this is a view that you, Chrysippus, will not allow at all, and this is the very point about which you are specially at issue with Diodorus. He says that only what either is true or will be true is a possibility, and whatever will be, he says, must necessarily happen, and whatever will not be, according to him cannot possibly happen. You say that things which will not be are also ' possible '—for instance it is possible for this jewel to be broken even if it never will be—, and that the reign of Cypselus at Corinth was not necessary although it had been announced by the oracle of Apollo a thousand years before. But if you are going to sanction divine prophecies of that sort, you will reckon false statements as to future events (for instance a prophecy that Africanus was not going to take Carthage ᵇ) as being in the class of things impossible, and also, if a thing is truly stated about the future and it will be

Chrysippus denies Diodorus's identification of 'possible' with 'necessary';

thought that he had been murdered (cf. § 18), but this was never proved.

dicas esse necessarium est[1]; quae est tota Diodori
14 vobis inimica sententia.   Etenim si illud vere conectitur, ' Si oriente Canicula natus es, in mari non
morieris,' primumque quod est[2] in conexo, ' Natus es
oriente Canicula,' necessarium est (omnia enim vera
in praeteritis necessaria sunt, ut Chrysippo placet
dissentienti a magistro Cleanthe, quia sunt immutabilia nec in falsum e vero praeterita possunt
convertere[3]) — si igitur quod primum in conexo est
necessarium est, fit etiam quod sequitur necessarium.
Quamquam hoc Chrysippo non videtur valere in omnibus ; sed tamen si naturalis est causa cur in mari
Fabius non moriatur, in mari Fabius mori non potest.
15   VIII. Hoc loco Chrysippus aestuans falli sperat
Chaldaeos ceterosque divinos, neque eos usuros esse
coniunctionibus ut ita sua percepta pronuntient, ' Si
quis natus est oriente Canicula, is in mari non
morietur,' sed potius ita dicant, ' Non et natus est
quis oriente Canicula et is in mari morietur.'   O
licentiam iocularem ! ne ipse incidat in Diodorum,
docet Chaldaeos quo pacto eos exponere percepta
oporteat.   Quaero enim, si Chaldaei ita loquantur ut
negationes infinitarum coniunctionum potius quam
infinita conexa ponant, cur idem medici, cur geo-
metrae, cur reliqui facere non possint ?   Medicus in

---

[1] est *add. Rackham.*   [2] est *add. Moser.*
[3] *v.l.* converti.

so, you would have to say that it is so ; but the whole
of this is the view of Diodorus, which is alien to your
14 school. For if the following is a true connexion, ' If
you were born at the rising of the dogstar you will
not die at sea,' and if the first proposition in the connexion, ' You were born at the rising of the dogstar,'
is necessary (for all things true in the past are necessary, as Chrysippus holds, in disagreement with his
master Cleanthes, because they are unchangeable
and because what is past cannot turn from true
into false)—if therefore the first proposition in the
connexion is necessary, the proposition that follows
also becomes necessary. Although Chrysippus does
not think that this holds good universally ; but all
the same, if there is a natural cause why Fabius
should not die at sea, it is not possible for Fabius to
die at sea.

15   VIII. " At this point Chrysippus gets nervous and but this
expresses a hope that the Chaldaeans and the rest of denial is
the prophets are mistaken, and that they will not refuted by
employ conjunctions of propositions putting out their logic.
observations in the form ' If anyone was born at the
rising of the dogstar he will not die at sea,' but rather
will say ' It is not the case both that some person
was born at the rising of the dogstar and that that
person will die at sea.' O what amusing presump-
tion ! to avoid falling into the hands of Diodorus himself he tutors the Chaldaeans as to the proper form
in which to set out their observations ! For I ask
you, if the Chaldaeans adopt the procedure of setting
forth negations of indefinite conjunctions rather than
indefinite sequences, why should it not be possible
for doctors and geometricians and the other profes-
sions to do likewise ? Take a doctor to begin with :

primis quod erit ei perspectum in arte non ita proponet, ' Si cui venae sic moventur, is habet febrem,' sed potius illo modo, ' Non et venae sic cui[1] moventur et febrem is non habet.' Itemque geometres non ita dicet, ' In sphaera maximi orbes medii inter se dividuntur,' sed potius illo modo, ' Non et sunt in sphaera maximi orbes et hi non medii inter se dividuntur.'

16 Quid est quod non possit isto modo ex conexo transferri ad coniunctionum negationem ? Et quidem aliis modis easdem res efferre possumus. Modo dixi, ' In sphaera maximi orbes medii inter se dividuntur ' ; possum dicere ' Si in sphaera maximi orbes erunt,' possum dicere ' Quia in sphaera maximi orbes erunt.' Multa genera sunt enuntiandi, nec ullum distortius quam hoc quo Chrysippus sperat Chaldaeos contentos Stoicorum causa fore. Illorum tamen nemo ita loquitur ; maius est enim has contortiones orationis quam signorum ortus obitusque perdiscere.

17 IX. Sed ad illam Diodori contentionem quam περὶ δυνατῶν appellant revertamur, in qua quid valeat id quod fieri possit anquiritur. Placet igitur Diodoro id solum fieri posse quod aut verum sit aut verum futurum sit. Qui locus attingit hanc quaestionem, nihil fieri quod non necesse fuerit, et quid-

---

[1] non . . . sic cui *Müller :* non ei (*vel* enim) venae sic *codd.*

---

[a] See § 1 note *c.*

he will not set forth a scientific principle that he has ascertained in this form, ' If a person's pulse is so and so, he has got a fever,' but rather as follows, ' It is not the case both that a person's pulse is so and so and that he has not got a fever.' And similarly a geometrician will not speak as follows, ' The greatest circles on a sphere bisect each other,' but rather as follows, ' It is not the case both that there are certain circles on the surface of a sphere that are the greatest and that these circles do not bisect each other.'

16 What is there that cannot be carried over in that sort of way from the form of a necessary consequence to that of a negation of conjoined statements ? And in fact we can express the same thing in other ways. Just now I said ' The greatest circles on a sphere bisect each other '; but it is possible for me to say ' If certain circles on a sphere are the greatest,' and it is possible for me to say ' Because certain circles on a sphere will be the greatest.' There are many ways of stating a proposition, and none is more twisted round than this one, which Chrysippus hopes that the Chaldaeans will accommodate the Stoics by accepting. Yet none of the Chaldaeans really use that sort of language, for it is a bigger task to familiarize oneself with these contorted modes of expression than with the risings and settings of the constellations.

7 IX. " But let us go back to the argument of Diodorus already mentioned, which they term *Peri Dynatōn*,[a] in which the meaning of the term ' possible ' is investigated. Well, Diodorus holds that only what either is true or will be true is possible. This position is connected with the argument that nothing happens which was not necessary, and that

Diodorus's theory restated and upheld

quid fieri possit, id aut esse iam aut futurum esse,
nec magis commutari ex veris in falsa ea posse quae
futura sint quam ea quae facta sint; sed in factis
immutabilitatem apparere, in futuris quibusdam,
quia non appareat,[1] ne inesse quidem videri, ut in
eo qui mortifero morbo urgeatur verum sit ' Hic
morietur hoc morbo,' at hoc idem si vere dicatur in
eo in quo vis morbi tanta non appareat, nihilo minus
futurum sit. Ita fit ut commutatio ex vero in falsum
ne in futuro quidem ulla fieri possit. Nam ' Morietur
Scipio ' talem vim habet ut, quamquam de futuro
dicitur, tamen id non possit convertere[2] in falsum ;
18 de homine enim dicitur, cui necesse est mori. Sic
si diceretur, ' Morietur noctu in cubiculo suo Scipio
vi oppressus,' vere diceretur, id enim fore diceretur
quod esset futurum, futurum autem fuisse ex eo
quia factum est intellegi debet. Nec magis erat
verum ' Morietur Scipio ' quam ' Morietur illo modo,'
nec magis[3] necesse mori Scipionem quam illo modo
mori, nec magis immutabile ex vero in falsum
' Necatus est Scipio ' quam ' Necabitur Scipio '; nec,
cum haec ita sint, est causa cur Epicurus fatum
extimescat et ab atomis petat praesidium easque de

---

[1] *edd. :* appareret *codd.*
[2] *v.l.* converti.   [3] *Ramus :* minus.

---

[a] See § 13 note *b.*

whatever is possible either is now or will be, and
that it is no more possible for things that will be to
alter than it is for things that have happened; but
that whereas in the things that have happened this
immutability is manifest, in some things that are
going to happen, because their immutability is not
manifest, it does not appear to be there at all, and
consequently, while the statement 'This man will
die of this disease' is true in the case of a man
who is suffering from a deadly disease, if this same
statement is made truly in the case of a man in whom
so violent an attack of the disease is not manifest, none
the less it will happen. It follows that no change
from true to false can occur even in the case of
the future. For 'Scipio will die' has such validity
that although it is a statement about the future it
cannot be converted into a falsehood, for it is a
statement about a human being, who must inevitably
18 die. If the form of the statement had been 'Scipio
will die by violence in his bedroom at night,'[a] the
statement in that form would have been a true one,
for it would have been a statement that a thing was
going to happen that was going to happen, and that
it was going to happen is a necessary inference from
the fact that it did happen. Neither was 'Scipio
will die' any truer than 'Scipio will die in that
manner,' nor was it more inevitable for Scipio to die
than it was for him to die in that manner, nor was it
more impossible for the statement 'Scipio has been
murdered' to change from a truth to a falsehood than
for the statement 'Scipio will be murdered'; nor, Never-
these things being so, is there any reason for Epi- theless
Epicurus's
curus's standing in terror of fate and seeking pro- 'swerve'
tection against it from the atoms and making them needless
to avoid

via deducat, et uno tempore suscipiat res duas
inenodabiles, unam ut sine causa fiat aliquid—, ex quo
exsistet ut de nihilo quippiam fiat, quod nec ipsi
nec cuiquam physico placet—alteram ut, cum duo
individua per inanitatem ferantur, alterum e regione
19 moveatur, alterum declinet. Licet enim Epicuro,
concedenti omne enuntiatum aut verum aut falsum
esse, non vereri ne omnia fato fieri sit necesse ; non
enim aeternis causis naturae necessitate manantibus
verum est id quod ita enuntiatur, ' Descendet[1] in
Academiam Carneades,' nec tamen sine causis, sed
interest inter causas fortuito antegressas et inter
causas cohibentes in se efficientiam naturalem. Ita
et semper verum fuit ' Morietur cum duo et septua-
ginta annos vixerit, archonte Pytharato,' neque tamen
erant causae fatales cur ita accideret, sed quod ita
20 cecidit[2] certe casurum[3] sicut cecidit fuit. Nec
ei qui dicunt immutabilia esse quae futura sint nec
posse verum futurum convertere[4] in falsum, fati necessitatem confirmant, sed verborum vim interpretantur;
at qui introducunt causarum seriem sempiternam,

---

[1] *Loercher :* descendit.
[2] *Bremius :* cecidisset.
[3] ⟨serie⟩ certa ⟨causarum⟩ casurum *edd.*
[4] *v.l.* converti.

---

[a] Epicurus held that, as the atoms fall vertically through
space at the same velocity, they would never meet, were it
not that any one of them occasionally makes an entirely
uncaused swerve, thus sometimes coming into collision with
other atoms and ultimately producing one of the clusters of
atoms of which visible things consist. Such a swerve taking

swerve out of the perpendicular,[a] and entertaining simultaneously two utterly inexplicable propositions, one that something takes place without a cause— from which it will follow that something comes out of nothing, which neither Epicurus nor any natural philosopher allows—, the other that when two atoms are travelling through empty space one moves in a

19 straight line and the other swerves. For it is not necessary for Epicurus to fear lest, when he admits that every proposition is either true or false, all events must necessarily be caused by fate ; for the truth of a proposition of the form ' Carneades will go down to the Academy ' is not due to an eternal stream of natural and necessary causation, and yet nevertheless it is not uncaused, but there is a difference between causes accidentally precedent and causes intrinsically containing a natural efficiency. Thus it is the case *both* that the statement ' Epicurus will die in the archonship of Pytharatus,[b] at the age of seventy-two,' was always true, *and* also that nevertheless there were no fore-ordained causes why it should so happen, but, because it did so fall out, it was certainly going to

20 fall out as it actually did.[c] Moreover those who say that things that are going to be are immutable and that a true future event cannot be changed into a false one, are not asserting the necessity of fate but explaining the meaning of terms ; whereas those who bring in an everlasting series of causes rob the

place among the atoms of a man's mind is what is known to his consciousness as an act of arbitrary volition : this was Epicurus's method of proving the freedom of the will. See §§ 21 ff. and Lucretius ii. 216 ff.

[b] 270 B.C.

[c] Editors emend the text to give ' was going to befall by a definite series of causes.'

ei mentem hominis voluntate libera spoliatam necessitate fati devinciunt.

X. Sed haec hactenus; alia videamus. Concludit
enim Chrysippus hoc modo : ' Si est motus sine causa,
non omnis enuntiatio (quod ἀξίωμα dialectici appellant) aut vera aut falsa erit, causas enim efficientes
quod non habebit id nec verum nec falsum erit ;
omnis autem enuntiatio aut vera aut falsa est ;
21 motus ergo sine causa nullus est. Quod si ita est,
omnia quae fiunt causis fiunt antegressis ; id si ita
est, omnia fato fiunt ; efficitur igitur fato fieri quaecumque fiant.' Hic primum si mihi libeat assentiri
Epicuro et negare omnem enuntiationem aut veram
esse aut falsam, eam plagam potius accipiam quam
fato omnia fieri comprobem ; illa enim sententia
aliquid habet disputationis, haec vero non est tolera-
bilis. Itaque contendit omnes nervos Chrysippus ut
persuadeat omne ἀξίωμα aut verum esse aut falsum.
Ut enim Epicurus veretur ne, si hoc concesserit,
concedendum sit fato fieri quaecumque fiant (si enim
alterutrum ex aeternitate verum sit, esse id etiam
certum, et si certum, etiam necessarium : ita et
necessitatem et fatum confirmari putat), sic Chrysippus metuit ne, si non obtinuerit omne quod enun-
tietur aut verum esse aut falsum, non teneat omnia
22 fato fieri et ex causis aeternis rerum futurarum. Sed
Epicurus declinatione atomi vitari fati necessitatem
putat ; itaque tertius quidam motus oritur extra

---

^a See § 1 note *b*.

human mind of freewill and fetter it in the chains of a fated necessity.

X. " But enough of these subjects ; let us examine others. For Chrysippus argues thus : ' If uncaused motion exists, it will not be the case that every proposition (termed by the logicians an *axiōma* ^a) is either true or false, for a thing not possessing efficient causes will be neither true nor false ; but every proposition is either true or false ; therefore uncaused 21 motion does not exist. If this is so, all things that take place take place by precedent causes ; if this is so, all take place by fate ; it therefore follows that all things that take place take place by fate.' At this point, in the first place if I chose to agree with Epicurus and to say that not every proposition is either true or false, I would rather suffer that nasty knock than agree that all events are caused by fate ; for the former opinion has something to be said for it, but the latter is intolerable. Accordingly Chrysippus exerts every effort to prove the view that every *axiōma* is either true or false. For just as Epicurus is afraid that if he admits this he will also have to admit that all events whatever are caused by fate (on the ground that if either of two alternatives is true from all eternity, that alternative is also certain, and if it is certain it is also necessary. This, he thinks, would prove both necessity and fate), similarly Chrysippus fears that if he fails to maintain that every proposition is either true or false he will not carry his point that all things happen by fate and spring 22 from eternal causes governing future events. But Epicurus thinks that the necessity of fate is avoided by the swerve of an atom ; and so in addition to gravity and impact there arises a third form of

Chrysippus proved fates by formal logic.

Epicurus's 'swerve' as basis for free-will

217

pondus et plagam, cum declinat atomus intervallo
minimo (id appellat ἐλάχιστον). Quam declinationem sine causa fieri, si minus verbis, re cogitur
confiteri ; non enim atomus ab atomo pulsa declinat,
nam qui potest pelli alia ab alia si gravitate feruntur
ad perpendiculum corpora individua rectis lineis, ut
Epicuro placet ? sequitur autem[1] ut, si alia ab alia
numquam depellatur, ne contingat quidem alia aliam;
ex quo efficitur, etiam si sit atomus eaque declinet,
declinare[2] sine causa.

23　　Hanc Epicurus rationem induxit ob eam rem quod
veritus est ne, si semper atomus gravitate ferretur
naturali ac necessaria, nihil liberum nobis esset, cum
ita moveretur animus ut atomorum motu cogeretur.
Id Democritus auctor atomorum accipere maluit,
necessitate omnia fieri, quam a corporibus individuis
naturales motus avellere. XI. Acutius Carneades,
qui docebat posse Epicureos suam causam sine hac
commenticia declinatione defendere. Nam cum
docerent esse posse quemdam animi motum volun-
tarium, id fuit defendi melius quam introducere
declinationem, cuius praesertim causam reperire
non possent; quo defenso facile Chrysippo possent
resistere, cum enim concessissent motum nullum
esse sine causa, non concederent omnia quae fierent
fieri causis antecedentibus, voluntatis enim nostrae
24 non esse causas externas et antecedentes. Communi

---

[1] autem *Davisius :* enim *cum codd. Usener, Plasberg.*
[2] *v.l.* declinare eam, *sed cf. § 24 fin.*

---

[a] *i.e.* asserted dogmatically, not put as an inference from
the atomic theory.

motion, when the atom swerves sideways a minimal space (termed by Epicurus *elachiston*). Also he is compelled to profess in reality, if not quite explicitly, that this swerve takes place without cause ; for the atom does not swerve in consequence of being struck by another atom, since how can impact between them take place if they are indivisible bodies travelling perpendicularly in straight lines by the force of gravity, as Epicurus holds ? but it follows that if one is never driven aside by another, one will never even meet another ; the consequence is that, even granting that the atom exists and that it swerves, the swerve is uncaused.

23   " The reason why Epicurus brought in this theory was his fear lest, if the atom were always carried along by the natural and necessary force of gravity, we should have no freedom whatever, since the movement of the mind was controlled by the movement of the atom. The author of the atomic theory, Democritus, preferred to accept the view that all events are caused by necessity, rather than to deprive the atoms of their natural motions. XI. Carneades showed greater insight : his doctrine was that the school of Epicurus could have maintained its cause without this fictitious swerve. For it would have been better for the dogma of the possibility of some voluntary movement of the mind to be maintained [a] than for them to introduce the swerve, especially as they were unable to invent a cause for it ; and by maintaining that dogma they could easily have withstood Chrysippus, for in admitting that no motion is uncaused they would not have been admitting that all events are due to antecedent causes, as they would have said that there are no external and antecedent

proved needless by Carneades : free-will means volition without external cause.

igitur consuetudine sermonis abutimur cum ita dicimus, velle aliquid quempiam aut nolle sine causa ; ita
enim dicimus sine causa ut dicamus sine externa et
antecedente causa, non sine aliqua. Ut cum vas inane
dicimus, non ita loquimur ut physici, quibus inane
esse nihil placet, sed ita ut verbi causa sine aqua,
sine vino, sine oleo vas esse dicamus, sic, cum sine
causa animum moveri dicimus, sine antecedente et externa causa moveri, non omnino sine causa dicimus.
De ipsa atomo dici potest, cum per inane moveatur
gravitate et pondere, sine causa moveri, quia nulla
25 causa accedat extrinsecus ; rursus autem, ne omnes
a physicis[1] irrideamur si dicamus quidquam fieri sine
causa, distinguendum est et ita dicendum, ipsius
individui hanc esse naturam ut pondere et gravitate
moveatur, eamque ipsam esse causam cur ita feratur. Similiter ad animorum motus voluntarios non
est requirenda externa causa ; motus enim voluntarius
eam naturam in se ipse continet ut sit in nostra
potestate nobisque pareat, nec id sine causa, eius
26 enim rei causa ipsa natura est. Quod cum ita sit,
quid est cur non omnis pronuntiatio aut vera aut
falsa sit, nisi concesserimus fato fieri quaecumque
fiant ? Quia futura vera, inquit, non possunt esse

---

[1] a physicis *edd. :* physici *codd.* (homines *vel* omnibus a
pro omnes *edd.*, omnes physici rideant nos *Müller*).

24 causes of our volition. Therefore when we use the
expression 'Somebody wishes (or does not wish) something without cause,' we are perverting the accepted
convention of language ; for we are using the phrase
' without cause ' in the sense of ' without an external
and antecedent cause,' not ' without a cause of some
kind.' Just as when we say that a vessel is empty
we do not use the expression in the sense in which it
is used by the natural philosophers, who hold that
no absolute vacuum exists, but we employ it to mean
that the vessel has (for example) no water in it, or
wine, or oil, similarly when we say that the mind
moves without cause we mean that it moves without
an antecedent external cause, not without any cause
at all. Motion without cause can be predicated of
the atom itself in moving through void by reason of
gravity and weight, because there is no additional
25 cause from outside ; but on the other hand, for fear
lest we all be laughed at by the natural philosophers
if we say that anything takes place without a cause,
a distinction must be made, and the matter must be
put in this way, that it is the nature of the atom itself
to be kept in motion by weight and gravity, and that
its nature is itself the cause of its travelling in this
manner. Similarly no external cause need be sought
to explain the voluntary movements of the mind ;
for voluntary motion possesses the intrinsic property
of being in our power and of obeying us, and its
obedience is not uncaused, for its nature is itself the
6 cause of this. This being so, what is the reason
why every proposition is not either true or false, if we
do not allow that whatever takes place is caused by
fate ? The reason is, says he, that future things that
have not got causes *why* they will be in the future

Universal
causation
implies fate,
but not
necessity :
some
causes are
fortuitous ;

ea quae causas cur futura sint non habent ; habeant
igitur causas necesse est ea quae vera sunt ; ita cum
evenerint, fato evenerint. XII. Confectum negotium,
siquidem tibi concedendum est aut fato omnia fieri
27 aut quidquam posse fieri sine causa. An aliter haec
enuntiatio vera esse potest,[1] ' Capiet Numantiam
Scipio,' nisi ex aeternitate causa causam serens hoc
erit effectura ? an hoc falsum potuisset esse si esset
sexcentis saeculis ante dictum ? Et si tum non esset
vera haec enuntiatio, ' Capiet Numantiam Scipio,'
ne illa quidem eversa vera est haec enuntiatio,
' Cepit Numantiam Scipio.' Potest igitur quicquam
factum esse quod non verum fuerit futurum esse ?
Nam ut praeterita ea vera dicimus quorum superiore
tempore vera fuerit instantia, sic futura quorum con-
sequenti tempore vera erit instantia, ea vera dicemus.
28 Nec si omne enuntiatum aut verum aut falsum est,
sequitur ilico esse causas immutabiles, easque aeter-
nas, quae prohibeant quidquam secus cadere atque
casurum sit. Fortuitae sunt causae quae efficiant, ut
vere dicantur quae ita dicentur, ' Veniet in senatum
Cato,' non inclusae in rerum natura atque mundo ;
et tamen tam est immutabile venturum, cum est
verum, quam venisse (nec ob eam causam fatum aut
necessitas extimescenda est) ; etenim erit confiteri
necesse ' Si haec enuntiatio, " Veniet in Tusculanum

---

[1] potest *Rackham :* non potest *codd.*

cannot be true ; therefore those that are true must necessarily have causes ; accordingly when they have occurred they will have occurred by fate. XII. That ends the business, inasmuch as you are bound to admit either that everything takes place by fate or that

27 something can take place without a cause. Consider the statement 'Scipio will take Numantia'[a]: if an external chain of interlinked causes is not going to bring this about, can it be true[b] in any other manner? could it have been false if it had been said innumerable ages ago? And if the statement 'Scipio will take Numantia' had not been true then, even after Numantia has fallen the statement 'Scipio has taken Numantia' is not true either. Therefore is it possible for anything to have happened that was not previously going to be true ? For just as we speak of past things as true that possessed true actuality at some former time, so we speak of future things as true that will possess true actuality at some following

28 time. Yet it does not immediately follow from the fact that every statement is either true or false that there are immutable causes, eternally existing, that forbid anything to fall out otherwise than it will fall out. The causes which bring it about that statements of the form 'Cato will come into the Senate' are true statements, are fortuitous, they are not inherent in the nature of things and the order of the universe; and nevertheless 'he will come,' when true, is as immutable as 'he has come' (though we need not on that account be haunted by fear of fate or necessity), for it will necessarily be admitted that if the statement 'Hortensius will come to his place

---

[a] Scipio (*cf.* § 13 note) took Numantia in Spain 133 B.C.
[b] The MSS. give 'can it be not true.'

Hortensius," vera[1] non est, sequitur ut falsa sit.'
Quorum isti neutrum volunt ; quod fieri non potest.

Nec nos impediet illa ignava ratio quae dicitur ;
appellatur enim quidam a philosophis ἀργὸς λόγος,
cui si pareamus nihil omnino agamus in vita. Sic
enim interrogant : ' Si fatum tibi est ex hoc morbo
convalescere, sive medicum adhibueris sive non ad-
29 hibueris convalesces ; item, si fatum tibi est ex hoc
morbo non convalescere, sive tu medicum adhibueris
sive non adhibueris non convalesces ; et alterutrum
fatum est ; medicum ergo adhibere nihil attinet.'
XIII. Recte genus hoc interrogationis ignavum atque
iners nominatum est, quod eadem ratione omnis e
vita tolletur actio. Licet etiam immutare, ut fati
nomen ne adiungas et eamdem tamen teneas sententiam, hoc modo : ' Si ex aeternitate verum hoc fuit,
" Ex isto morbo convalesces," sive adhibueris medicum sive non adhibueris convalesces ; itemque, si ex
aeternitate falsum hoc fuit, " Ex isto morbo[2] convalesces," sive adhibueris medicum sive non adhibu-
30 eris non convalesces ' ; deinde cetera. Haec ratio a
Chrysippo reprehenditur. Quaedam enim sunt, inquit,
in rebus simplicia, quaedam copulata ; simplex est,
' Morietur illo die Socrates ' ; huic, sive quid fecerit
sive non fecerit, finitus est moriendi dies. At si ita
fatum est,[3] ' Nascetur Oedipus Laio,' non poterit
dici, ' sive fuerit Laius cum muliere sive non fuerit ' ;

---

[1] *v.l.* verum . . . falsum (*sic edd. quidam, et* hoc enuntiatum *pro* haec enuntiatio).

[2] morbo *edd. :* morbo non *codd.*   [3] *Madvig :* erit.

---

[a] On a spur of Mons Albanus, ten miles S.E. of Rome,
near Frascati.

[b] The Latin is a translation of the Greek term that follows.
224

at Tusculum '[a] is not true, it follows that it is false.
Our opponents hold that it is neither ; which is impossible.

"Nor shall we for our part be hampered by what
is called the 'idle argument'[b]—for one argument is
named by the philosophers the *Argos Logos*, because
if we yielded to it we should live a life of absolute
inaction. For they argue as follows : 'If it is fated
for you to recover from this illness, you will recover
29 whether you call in a doctor or do not ; similarly, if
it is fated for you not to recover from this illness, you
will not recover whether you call in a doctor or do
not ; and either your recovery or your non-recovery
is fated ; therefore there is no point in calling in
a doctor.' XIII. This mode of arguing is rightly
called 'idle' and indolent, because the same train
of reasoning will lead to the entire abolition of action
from life. It is even possible to alter the form by not
introducing the word 'fate' and yet to retain the
same meaning, thus : 'If the statement "You will
recover from that illness" has been true from all
eternity, you will recover whether you call in a doctor
or do not ; and similarly if the statement "You will
recover from that illness" has been false from all
eternity, you will not recover whether you call in a
doctor or not '—the conclusion following as before.
30 This argument is criticized by Chrysippus. For, he
says, there exist in actuality two classes of facts,
simple and complex. An instance of a simple fact
is 'Socrates will die at a given date' ; in this case,
whether he does some action or does not do it, the day
of his death has been determined. But if it is fated
that 'Laius will have a son Oedipus,' it will not be
possible for the words 'whether Laius mates with a

Marginal notes:

and the existence of fate does not mean inaction:

action is fated, as well as its object.

copulata enim res est et confatalis : sic enim appellat
quia ita fatum sit, et concubiturum cum uxore Laium
et ex ea Oedipum procreaturum : ut si esset dictum,
' Luctabitur Olympiis Milo,' et referret aliquis, ' Ergo
sive habuerit adversarium, sive non habuerit luctabitur,' erraret ; est enim copulatum ' luctabitur,'
quia sine adversario nulla luctatio est.   Omnes igitur
istius generis captiones eodem modo refelluntur. ' Sive
tu adhibueris medicum sive non adhibueris, convalesces ' captiosum ; tam enim est fatale medicum
adhibere quam convalescere. Haec, ut dixi, confatalia ille appellat.

31   XIV. Carneades genus hoc totum non probabat
et nimis inconsiderate concludi hanc rationem puta-
bat.   Itaque premebat alio modo, nec ullam adhibe-
bat calumniam ; cuius erat haec conclusio : ' Si omnia
antecedentibus causis fiunt, omnia naturali colligatione conserte contexteque fiunt ; quod si ita est,
omnia necessitas efficit ; id si verum est, nihil est in
nostra potestate.   Est autem aliquid in nostra potestate.   At, si omnia fato fiunt, omnia causis antecedentibus fiunt.   Non igitur fato fiunt quaecumque
32 fiunt.'   Haec[1] artius astringi ratio non potest.
Nam si quis velit idem referre, atque ita dicere, ' Si
omne futurum ex aeternitate verum est, ut ita certe
eveniat quemadmodum sit futurum, omnia necesse
est colligatione naturali conserte contexteque fieri,'

[1] hoc *Turnebus.*

---

[a] συνειμαρμένον.
[b] This famous wrestler won six times at Olympia in the
later years of the 6th cent. B.C.

woman or does not ' to be added, for the matter is complex and ' condestinate '[a]—he gives that name to it because he thinks it is fated both that Laius will lie with a wife and that he will beget Oedipus by her: in the same way as, supposing it were said that ' Milo [b] will wrestle at Olympia ' and somebody replied ' If so, he will wrestle whether he has an opponent or not,' he would be wrong; for ' will wrestle ' is a complex statement, because there can be no wrestling without an opponent. Therefore all captious arguments of that sort can be refuted in the same way. ' You will recover whether you call in a doctor or do not ' is captious, for calling in a doctor is just as much fated as recovering. These connected events, as I said, are termed by Chrysippus ' condestinate.'

31 XIV. " Carneades refused to accept this class of things entirely, and held the view that the line of argument in question was not quite accurately thought out. In consequence he used to put his case in another manner, and did not employ any trickery; his argument ran like this : ' If everything takes place with antecedent causes, all events take place in a closely knit web of natural interconnexion; if this is so, all things are caused by necessity; if this is true, nothing is in our power. But something is in our power. Yet if all events take place by fate, there are antecedent causes of all events. Therefore it is not the case that whatever events take place take 32 place by fate.' This line of argument cannot be made more rigidly conclusive. For if anybody chose to repeat the same point and to put it thus, ' If all that will be is from eternity true, so that it must certainly turn out as it will be, events necessarily take place in a closely knit web of natural interconnexion,'

Carneades held that volition disproves fate, and that only necessary results can be predicted.

nihil dicat. Multum enim differt utrum causa
naturalis ex aeternitate futura vera efficiat an etiam
sine aeternitate naturali futura quae sint ea vera
esse possint intellegi. Itaque dicebat Carneades ne
Apollinem quidem futura posse dicere nisi ea quorum
causas natura ita contineret ut ea fieri necesse esset.
33 Quid enim spectans deus ipse diceret Marcellum
eum qui ter consul fuit in mari esse periturum ? erat
quidem hoc verum ex aeternitate, sed causas id
efficientes non habebat. Ita ne praeterita quidem
ea quorum nulla signa tamquam vestigia exstarent
Apollini nota esse censebat, quanto[1] minus futura,
causis enim efficientibus quamque rem cognitis posse
denique sciri quid futurum esset ; ergo nec de Oedi-
pode potuisse Apollinem praedicere nullis in rerum
natura causis praepositis cur ab eo patrem interfici
necesse esset, nec quidquam eiusmodi. XV. Quo-
circa si Stoicis qui omnia fato fieri dicunt consenta-
neum est huiusmodi oracula ceteraque quae ad divi-
nationem pertinent[2] comprobare, eis[3] autem qui quae
futura sunt ea vera esse ex aeternitate dicunt non
idem dicendum est, vide ne non eadem sit illorum

[1] *v.l.* quo.

[2] pertinent *: v.l.* dicuntur *:* pertinere dicuntur *edd. nonnulli,* a divinatione ducuntur *Madvig.*

[3] eis *:* ⟨de⟩ eis *? Rackham.*

[a] M. Claudius Marcellus, consul 166, 155 and 152 B.C.,

he would be talking nonsense. For it makes a great deal of difference whether a natural cause, existing from all eternity, renders future things true, or things that are going to be in the future can be understood to be true even without any natural eternity. Accordingly Carneades used to say that not even Apollo could tell any future events except those whose causes were so held together by nature 33 that they must necessarily happen. For what consideration could lead the god himself to say that the Marcellus who was three times consul was going to die at sea?[a] this had indeed been true from all eternity, but it had no efficient causes. Therefore Carneades held the view that Apollo had no knowledge even of these past events which had left behind them no trace of their passage—how much less had he knowledge of future events, for only by knowing the efficient causes of all things was it possible to know the future; therefore it was impossible for Apollo to foretell the fate of Oedipus when there were no causes fore-ordained in the nature of things making it necessary for him to murder his father, nor could he foretell anything of the sort. XV. Hence if, while it is consistent for the Stoics, who say that all things happen by fate, to accept oracles of this sort and all the other things connected with divination, yet the same position cannot be held by[b] those who say that the things which are going to happen in the future have been true from all eternity, observe that their case is not the same as

Hence the Academy cannot defend prophecy, which assumes necessary causation.

[a] was shipwrecked in 148 B.C. when going on an embassy to Masinissa, king of Numidia.

[b] Perhaps the Latin should be altered to give ' the same cannot be said about.'

causa et Stoicorum ; hi enim urgentur angustius,
34 illorum ratio soluta ac libera est.   Quodsi concedatur
nihil posse evenire nisi causa antecedente, quid proficiatur si ea causa non ex aeternis causis apta dicatur ?[1]
Causa autem ea est quae id efficit cuius est causa,
ut vulnus mortis, cruditas morbi, ignis ardoris.   Itaque non sic causa intellegi debet ut quod cuique antecedat id ei causa sit, sed quod cuique efficienter
antecedat, nec quod in campum descenderim id
fuisse causae cur pila luderem, nec Hecubam causam
interitus fuisse Troianis quod Alexandrum genuerit,
nec Tyndareum Agamemnoni quod Clytaemnestram.
Hoc enim modo viator quoque bene vestitus causa
35 grassatori fuisse dicetur cur ab eo spoliaretur.   Ex
hoc genere illud est Ennii,

> utinam ne in nemore Pelio securibus
> caesae accidissent abiegnae ad terram trabes!

Licuit vel altius, ' Utinam ne in Pelio nata ulla umquam esset arbor ! ' etiam supra, ' Utinam ne esset
mons ullus Pelius ! ' similiterque superiora repetentem regredi infinite licet.

> Neve inde navis inchoandi exordium
> cepisset.

Quorsum haec praeterita ? quia sequitur illud,

<hr />

[1] *v.l.* ducatur.

<hr />

[a] Ennius adapted Euripides's *Medea*, which begins :

> εἴθ' ὤφελ' Ἀργοῦς μὴ διαπτάσθαι σκάφος
> Κόλχων ἐς αἶαν κυανέας Ξυμπληγάδας,
> μηδ' ἐν νάπαισι Πηλίου πεσεῖν ποτε
> τμηθεῖσα πεύκη μηδ' ἐρετμῶσαι χέρας
> ἀνδρῶν ἀριστέων οἳ τὸ πάγχρυσον δέρας
> Πελίᾳ μετῆλθον· οὐ γὰρ ἂν δέσποιν' ἐμὴ
> Μήδεια πύργους γῆς ἔπλευσ' Ἰωλκίας,
> ἔρωτι θυμὸν ἐκπλαγεῖσ' Ἰάσονος.

Pĕlion or Pēlios was a mountain range in Thessaly.

that of the Stoics ; for their position is more limited and narrow, whereas the Stoic theory is untrammelled 34 and free. Even if it be admitted that nothing can happen without an antecedent cause, what good would that be unless it be maintained that the cause in question is a link in an eternal chain of causation ? But a cause is that which makes the thing of which it is the cause come about—as a wound is the cause of death, failure to digest one's food of illness, fire of heat. Accordingly ' cause ' is not to be understood in such a way as to make what precedes a thing the cause of that thing, but what precedes it effectively : the cause of my playing tennis was not my going down into the Campus, nor did Hecuba's giving birth to Alexander make her the cause of the death of Trojans, nor was Tyndareus the cause of Agamemnon's death because he was the father of Clytemnestra. For on those lines a well-dressed traveller also will be said to have been the cause of the high-35 wayman's robbing him of his clothes. To this class of expression belongs the phrase of Ennius [a]—

Distinction between circumstances and efficient causes.

> Would that in Pelius' glade the pine-tree beams
> Had never fallen to earth by axes hewn !

He might have gone even further back, ' Would that no tree had ever grown on Pelius ! ' and even further, ' Would that no Mount Pelius existed ! ' and similarly one may go on recalling preceding events in infinite regress.

> Nor thence had made inception of the task
> Of laying down a ship.

What is the point of recounting these past events ? because what follows is this :

    nam numquam era errans mea domo ecferret pedem
    Medea, animo aegra, amore saevo saucia,

non erat[1] ut eae res causam afferrent amoris.

36   XVI. Interesse autem aiunt utrum eiusmodi quid
sit sine quo aliquid effici non possit an eiusmodi quo
aliquid effici necesse sit. Nulla igitur earum est
causa, quoniam nulla eam rem sua vi efficit cuius
causa dicitur; nec id sine quo quippiam non fit causa
est, sed id quod cum accessit id cuius causa est efficit
necessario. Nondum enim ulcerato serpentis morsu
Philocteta quae causa in rerum natura continebatur
fore ut is in insula Lemno linqueretur? post autem
37 causa fuit propior et cum exitu iunctior. Ratio igitur
eventus aperuit[2] causam; sed ex aeternitate vera
fuit haec enuntiatio, ' Relinquetur in insula Philoctetes,' nec hoc ex vero in falsum poterat convertere.[3]
Necesse est enim in rebus contrariis duabus—contraria autem hoc loco ea dico quorum alterum ait
quid, alterum negat—ex eis igitur necesse est invito
Epicuro alterum verum esse, alterum falsum, ut
' Sauciabitur Philocteta ' omnibus ante saeculis verum
fuit, ' Non sauciabitur ' falsum; nisi forte volumus
Epicureorum opinionem sequi, qui tales enuntiationes

       [1] erat *addidit Rackham.*
       [2] *Rackham :* aperit *codd.*
       [3] *v.l.* converti.

---

      [a] The Latin text is here corrupt.
   [b] Modern logic terms such propositions ' contradictory.'

> For were it so, my roving royal mistress,
> Medea, from her home had ne'er set forth,
> Heartsick and by love's cruel weapon wounded.

It was not the case that those events brought the cause of love.[a]

36 XVI. " But they declare that there is a difference whether a thing is of such a kind that something cannot be effected without it, or such that something must necessarily be effected by it. None of the causes mentioned therefore is really a cause, since none by its own force effects the thing of which it is said to be the cause ; nor is that which is a condition of a thing's being effected a cause, but that of which the access necessarily produces the thing of which it is the cause. For at the time when the snake-bite had not yet caused Philoctetes to be afflicted with a sore, what cause was contained in the nature of things that would bring it to pass that he would be marooned on the Isle of Lemnos ? whereas afterwards the cause was nearer and more closely

37 connected with his death. Therefore it was the principle underlying the result that revealed the cause ; but the proposition ' Philoctetes will be marooned on an island ' had been true from all eternity, and this could not be turned from a truth into a falsehood. For it is necessary that of two contrary propositions—by contrary I here mean propositions one of which affirms something and the other denies it[b] —of these two propositions therefore it is necessary, *pace* Epicurus, that one should be true and the other false ; for example, ' Philoctetes will be wounded ' was true, and ' Philoctetes will not be wounded ' false, for the whole of the ages of the past ; unless perhaps we choose to follow the opinion of the Epi-

233

nec veras nec falsas esse dicunt, aut, cum id pudet,
illud tamen dicunt, quod est impudentius, veras esse
ex contrariis disiunctiones, sed quae in his enuntiata
38 sint,[1] eorum neutrum esse verum. O admirabilem
licentiam et miserabilem inscientiam disserendi ! Si
enim aliquid in eloquendo nec verum nec falsum est,
certe id verum non est; quod autem verum non est,
qui potest non falsum esse ? aut quod falsum non
est, qui potest non verum esse ? Tenebitur igitur[2] id
quod a Chrysippo defenditur, omnem enuntiationem
aut veram aut falsam esse ; ratio ipsa coget et ex
aeternitate quaedam esse vera et ea non esse nexa
causis aeternis et a fati necessitate esse libera.

39 XVII. Ac mihi quidem videtur, cum duae sententiae fuissent veterum philosophorum, una eorum
qui censerent omnia ita fato fieri ut id fatum vim
necessitatis afferret, in qua sententia Democritus,
Heraclitus, Empedocles, Aristoteles fuit, altera eorum
quibus viderentur sine ullo fato esse animorum motus
voluntarii, Chrysippus tamquam arbiter honorarius
medium ferire voluisse,—sed applicat se ad eos potius
qui necessitate motus animos[3] liberatos volunt ; dum
autem verbis utitur suis, delabitur in eas difficultates
40 ut necessitatem fati confirmet invitus. Atque hoc,
si placet, quale sit videamus in assensionibus, quas

---

[1] *Rackham :* essent *codd.*
[2] igitur *addit Lambinus* (ergo *Davisius*).
[3] animorum *Davisius.*

cureans, who say that propositions of this sort are
neither true nor false, or else, when ashamed of that,
they nevertheless make the still more impudent
assertion that disjunctions consisting of contrary
propositions are true, but that the statements contained in the propositions are neither of them true.
38 What marvellous effrontery and pitiable ignorance
of logical method! For if anything propounded is
neither true nor false, it certainly is not true ; but
how can something that is not true not be false, or
how can something that is not false not be true ? We
shall therefore hold to the position maintained by
Chrysippus, that every proposition is either true or
false ; reason itself will insist *both* that certain
things are true from all eternity *and* that they are
not involved in a nexus of eternal causes but are
free from the necessity of fate.

39   XVII. " And my own view at all events is that, as
between the two opinions held by the old philosophers, on the one hand the opinion of those who
deemed that everything takes place by fate in the
sense that this fate exercises the force of necessity
—the opinion to which Democritus, Heraclitus,
Empedocles and Aristotle adhered—and on the other
hand the opinion of those who held that the movements of the mind are voluntary and not at all controlled by fate, Chrysippus stood as unofficial umpire
and wished to strike a compromise,—though as a
matter of fact he inclines to adhere to those who hold
that the mind is released from all necessity of motion ;
but in employing formulae peculiar to himself he
slips into such difficulties that against his will he
40 lends support to the necessity of fate.   And let us
if you please examine the nature of this doctrine in

*Chrysip-
pus's view
half-way
between
necessity
of fate and
freedom
of will.*

*Psychology
of volition.*

235

prima oratione tractavi. Eas enim veteres illi quibus omnia fato fieri videbantur vi effici et necessitate dicebant. Qui autem ab eis dissentiebant, fato assensiones liberabant negabantque fato assensionibus adhibito necessitatem ab his posse removeri ; eique ita disserebant : ' Si omnia fato fiunt, omnia fiunt causa antecedente ; et si appetitus, illa etiam quae appetitum sequuntur ; ergo etiam assensiones. At si causa appetitus non est sita in nobis, ne ipse quidem appetitus est in nostra potestate ; quod si ita est, ne illa quidem quae appetitu efficiuntur sunt sita in nobis. Non sunt igitur neque assensiones neque actiones in nostra potestate. Ex quo efficitur ut nec laudationes iustae sint nec vituperationes nec honores nec supplicia.' Quod cum vitiosum sit, probabiliter concludi putant non omnia fato fieri quaecumque fiant.

41 XVIII. Chrysippus autem cum et necessitatem improbaret et nihil vellet sine praepositis causis evenire, causarum genera distinguit, ut et necessitatem effugiat et retineat fatum. ' Causarum enim,' inquit, ' aliae sunt perfectae et principales, aliae adiuvantes et proximae ; quam ob rem cum dicimus omnia fato fieri causis antecedentibus, non hoc intellegi volumus, causis perfectis et principalibus, sed causis adiuvantibus[1] et proximis.' Itaque illi rationi quam paullo ante conclusi sic occurrit : si omnia fato

[1] adiuvantibus *Davisius :* adiuvantibus antecedentibus *codd.*

---

[a] In the lost part of the dialogue.

connexion with the topic of assent, which I treated in my first discourse.[a] Those old philosophers who held that everything takes place by fate used to say that assent is given perforce as the result of necessity. On the other hand those who disagreed with them released assent from bondage to fate, and maintained that if assent were made subject to fate it would be impossible to dissociate it from necessity. They argued as follows : ' If all things take place by fate, all things take place with an antecedent cause ; and if desire is caused, those things which follow desire are also caused ; therefore assent is also caused. But if the cause of desire is not situated within us, even desire itself is also not in our power ; and if this is so, those things which are caused by desire also do not rest with us. It follows therefore that neither assent nor action is in our power. From this it results that there is no justice in either praise or blame, either honours or punishments.' But as this is erroneous, they hold that it is a valid inference that not everything that takes place takes place by fate.

41   XVIII. " But Chrysippus, since he refused on the one hand to accept necessity and held on the other hand that nothing happens without fore-ordained causes, distinguishes different kinds of causation, to enable himself at the same time to escape necessity and to retain fate. ' Some causes,' he says, ' are perfect and principal, others auxiliary and proximate. Hence when we say that everything takes place by fate owing to antecedent causes, what we wish to be understood is not perfect and principal causes but auxiliary and proximate causes.' Accordingly he counters the argument that I set out a little time ago by saying that, if everything takes

His distinction of causes as (1) principal, (2) auxiliary leaves desire in our power

fiant, sequi illud quidem ut omnia causis fiant antepositis, verum non principalibus et perfectis sed adiuvantibus et proximis. Quae si ipsae non sunt in
nostra potestate, non sequitur ut ne appetitus quidem
sit in nostra potestate. At hoc sequeretur si omnia
perfectis et principalibus causis fieri diceremus, ut,
cum hae causae non essent in nostra potestate, ne
42 ille quidem esset in nostra potestate. Quam ob
rem qui ita fatum introducunt ut necessitatem
adiungant, in eos valebit illa conclusio ; qui autem
causas antecedentes non dicent perfectas neque
principales, in eos nihil valebit. Quod enim dicantur
assensiones fieri causis antepositis, id quale sit facile
a se explicari putat ; nam quamquam assensio non
possit fieri nisi commota viso, tamen cum id visum
proximam causam habeat, non principalem, hanc
habet rationem, ut Chrysippus vult, quam dudum
diximus, non ut illa quidem fieri possit nulla vi extrinsecus excitata (necesse est enim assensionem viso
commoveri), sed revertitur ad cylindrum et ad turbinem suum, quae moveri incipere nisi pulsa non
possunt ; id autem cum accidit, suapte natura quod
superest et cylindrum volvi et versari turbinem
43 putat. XIX. ' Ut igitur,' inquit, ' qui protrusit cylindrum dedit ei principium motionis, volubilitatem
autem non dedit, sic visum obiectum imprimet illud
quidem et quasi signabit in animo suam speciem,

ᵃ To render φαντασία, which refers to any of the senses,
Cicero commonly uses *visum*, which properly denotes the
effect of an object on the sense of sight.

ᵇ This illustration from the motion of an agricultural roller
(κύλινδρος) and a child's top (στρόβιλος), here assigned to
Chrysippus, is not recorded elsewhere.

place by fate, it does indeed follow that everything takes place from antecedent causes, but not from principal and perfect but auxiliary and proximate causes. And if these causes themselves are not in our power, it does not follow that desire also is not in our power. On the other hand if we were to say that all things happen from perfect and principal causes, it would then follow that, as those causes are not in our power, desire would not be in our power either. Hence the train of argument in question will be valid against those who introduce fate in such a manner as to make it involve necessity; but it will have no validity against those who do not allege perfect and principal causes as antecedent. For they think that they can easily explain the meaning of the statement that assent takes place from pre-ordained causes; for although assent cannot take place unless prompted by a sense-presentation,[a] nevertheless since that presentation supplies a proximate and not a principal cause, this, according to Chrysippus, is explained by the theory which we stated just now, not indeed proving that assent can take place without being aroused by any external force (for assent must necessarily be actuated by our seeing an object), but Chrysippus goes back to his roller and spinning-top, which cannot begin to move unless they are pushed or struck, but which when this has happened, he thinks, continue to move of their own nature, the roller rolling forward and the top spinning round.[b]

43 XIX. 'In the same way therefore,' he says, 'as a person who has pushed a roller forward has given it a beginning of motion, but has not given it the capacity to roll, so a sense-presentation when it impinges will it is true impress and as it were seal its appearance and also 'assent' to sense-presentations as representing the objects.

239

sed assensio nostra erit in potestate, eaque, quemadmodum in cylindro dictum est, extrinsecus pulsa
quod reliquum est suapte vi et natura movebitur.
Quod si aliqua res efficeretur sine causa antecedente,
falsum esset omnia fato fieri ; sin omnibus quaecumque fiunt verisimile est causam antecedere, quid
afferri poterit cur non omnia fato fieri fatendum sit ?
modo intellegatur quae sit causarum distinctio ac
44 dissimilitudo.' Haec cum ita sint a Chrysippo explicata, si illi qui negant assensiones fato fieri,
fateantur tamen eas sine[1] viso antecedente fieri,
alia ratio est ; sed si concedunt anteire visa nec tamen
fato fieri assensiones quod proxima illa et continens
causa non moveat assensionem, vide ne idem dicant.
Neque enim Chrysippus, concedens assensionis proximam et continentem causam esse in viso positam,
eam[2] causam ad assentiendum necessariam esse con-
cedet, ut, si omnia fato fiant, omnia fiant causis antecedentibus et necessariis ; itemque illi qui ab hoc
dissentiunt confitentes non fieri assensiones sine prae-
cursione visorum, dicent, si omnia fato fierent eiusmodi ut nihil fieret nisi praegressione causae, con-
fitendum esse fato fieri omnia ; ex quo facile intel-

---

[1] sine *Lambinus :* non sine *codd.*
[2] eam *Turnebus :* neque eam *codd.*

on the mind, but the act of assent will be in our power, and as we said in the case of the roller, though given a push from without, as to the rest will move by its own force and nature. If some event were produced without antecedent cause, it would not be true that all things take place by fate ; but if it is probable that with all things whatever that take place there is an antecedent cause, what reason will it be possible to adduce why we should not have to admit that all things take place by fate ?—only provided that the nature of the distinction and difference between 44 causes is understood.' As this is the form in which These theory these doctrines are set out by Chrysippus, if the defended. people who deny that acts of assent take place by fate nevertheless would admit that those acts take place without an antecedent sense-presentation, it is a different theory ; but if they allow that sense-presentations come first, yet nevertheless acts of assent do not take place by fate, because assent is not prompted by the proximate and contiguous cause stated, surely this comes to the same thing. For Chrysippus, while admitting that the proximate and contiguous cause of assent is situated in a perceived object, will not admit that this cause is necessary for the act of assenting, so that if all things take place by fate all things take place from antecedent and necessary causes ; and also the thinkers who disagree with him in admitting that assent does not take place without the previous passage of sensory images will similarly say that, if everything were caused by fate in such a manner that nothing did take place without the precedent occurrence of a cause, it would have to be admitted that all things take place by fate ; and from this it is easy to understand that

lectu est, quoniam utrique patefacta atque explicata
sententia sua ad eumdem exitum veniant, verbis eos,
45 non re dissidere.   Omninoque cum haec sit distinctio,
ut quibusdam in rebus vere dici possit cum hae
causae antegressae sint non esse in nostra potestate
quin illa eveniant quorum causae fuerint, quibusdam
autem in rebus causis antegressis in nostra tamen
esse potestate ut illud[1] aliter eveniat, hanc distinc-
tionem utrique approbant ; sed alteri censent quibus
in rebus cum causae antecesserint non[2] sit in nostra
potestate ut aliter illa eveniant, illas fato fieri, quae
autem in nostra potestate sint, ab his fatum abesse. . . .
46   XX. Hoc modo hanc causam disceptari oportet,
non ab atomis errantibus et de via declinantibus praesidium petere. ' Declinat,' inquit, ' atomus.' Primum cur ? aliam enim quandam vim motus habebunt
a Democrito impulsionis quam plagam ille appellat,
a te, Epicure, gravitatis et ponderis. Quae ergo
nova causa in natura est quae declinet atomum (aut
num sortiuntur inter se quae declinet, quae non ?)
aut cur minimo declinent intervallo, maiore non, aut
cur declinent uno minimo, non declinent duobus aut
47 tribus ?   Optare hoc quidem est, non disputare. Nam
neque extrinsecus impulsam atomum loco moveri
et declinare dicis, neque in illo inani per quod

---

[1] illud : aliud *codd. plurimi.*
[2] non *Creuzer :* ita ut non *codd.*

since both parties, when their opinion has been developed and unfolded, come to the same ultimate
position, the difference between them is one of words
45 and not of fact. And putting it broadly, inasmuch
as the distinction can be made that whereas in some
things it can truly be said that when certain antecedent causes have occurred it is not in our power to
prevent certain results of which they were the causes
from happening, yet in some things, although antecedent causes have occurred, it is nevertheless within
our power to make the event turn out otherwise,—
this distinction is approved by both sides ; but one
of the two schools holds that although fate does
govern those matters in which when antecedent
causes have occurred it is not in our power to make
the results turn out otherwise, yet fate is not present
in the case of matters which are in our power. . . .

46 XX. "This is the proper method of discussing
this question,—one should not seek assistance from
atoms that roam and swerve out of their path. 'The
atom does swerve,' he says. In the first place what
causes the swerve ? for the motive force that they
will get from Democritus is a different one, a driving
force termed by him a 'blow'; from you, Epicurus,
they will get the force of gravity or weight. What
fresh cause therefore exists in nature to make the
atom swerve (or do the atoms cast lots among them
which is to swerve and which not ?) or to serve as the
reason for their making a very small swerve and not
a large one, or for their making one very small swerve
and not two or three swerves ? This is wishful think-
47 ing, not investigation. For you do not say that the
atom moves its position and swerves owing to being
driven by an external force, nor that there has been

Epicurus's
'uncaused
swerve'
unnecessary
to rebut
fatalism,
and
meaning-
less.

243

feratur atomus quidquam fuisse causae cur ea non e
regione ferretur, nec in ipsa atomo mutationis aliquid
factum esse[1] quam ob rem naturalem sui ponderis
motum non teneret. Ita cum attulisset nullam causam
quae istam declinationem efficeret, tamen aliquid sibi
dicere videtur cum id dicat quod omnium mentes
48 aspernentur ac respuant. Nec vero quisquam magis
confirmasse[2] mihi videtur non modo fatum verum
etiam necessitatem et vim omnium rerum sustulisse-
que motus animi voluntarios, quam hic qui aliter
obsistere fato fatetur se non potuisse nisi ad has
commenticias declinationes confugisset. Nam ut
essent atomi, quas quidem esse mihi probari nullo
modo potest, tamen declinationes istae numquam
explicarentur ; nam si atomis ut gravitate ferantur
tributum est necessitate naturae, quod omne pondus
nulla re impediente moveatur et feratur necesse est,
illud quoque necesse est, declinare, quibusdam atomis,
vel si volunt omnibus, naturaliter ?[3] . . .

[1] *Davisius :* est.
[2] *Rackham :* confirmare *codd.*
[3] *punctum Rackham.*

any factor in the void through which the atom travels to cause it not to travel in a straight line, nor that any change has taken place in the atom itself to cause it not to retain the natural motion of its own weight. Accordingly although he introduced no cause to occasion this swerve of yours, nevertheless he thinks that he is talking sense when he is saying something 48 that all men's minds scornfully reject. And in truth no one in my opinion has done more to uphold not only fate but also an all-controlling necessity, or to abolish voluntary movements of the mind, than has this philosopher who confesses that he has been unable to withstand fate in any other way than by taking refuge in these fictitious swerves. For if one granted the existence of the atoms, although I for my part find it entirely impossible to accept that they do exist, nevertheless there would never be any explanation of those swerves that you talk of; for if it is owing to a necessity of nature that the atoms are assigned the property of travelling by force of gravity, because every heavy body must necessarily move and travel when nothing hinders it, is that alleged swerve also necessary for some atoms, or, if they choose, for all, in the order of nature ? . . ."

FRAGMENTA HUIUS LIBRI

1. *Gellius, Noct. Attic. vii. 2. 15.* M. *Cicero in libro quem de fato conscripsit, cum quaestionem istam diceret obscurissimam esse et implicatissimam, Chrysippum quoque philosophum non expedisse se in ea ait his verbis :* Chrysippus, aestuans laboransque quonam pacto[1] explicet et fato omnia fieri et esse aliquid in nobis, intricatur hoc modo.

2. *Servius ad Vergil. Aen. iii. 376—' volvitque vices.' Definitio fati secundum Tullium, qui ait :* Fatum est conexio rerum per aeternitatem se invicem tenens, quae suo ordine et lege sua[2] variatur, ita tamen ut ipsa varietas habeat aeternitatem.

3. *Augustinus, De Civitate Dei v. 8. Illi quoque versus Homeri huic sententiae suffragantur, quos Cicero in Latinum vertit :*

> tales sunt hominum mentes quali pater ipse
> Iuppiter auctiferas lustravit lumine terras.

Nec in hac quaestione auctoritatem haberet poetica

---

[1] pacto *suppl. edd.*
[2] sua *add. Ax.*

FRAGMENTS OF *DE FATO*

1. In the book that he wrote on the subject of fate Marcus Cicero says that the question which you raise is very obscure and involved, and he remarks that the philosopher Chrysippus also had not cleared up his position with regard to it. Cicero's words are ' Chrysippus, finding himself quite at sea in the difficulty of how to explain his combination of universal fatalism with human free-will, ties himself up in the following knot.'

2. (Jove) ' plies the turns of fortune.' A definition of fate according to Tully, who says : ' Fate is the interconnexion of events that alternates continuously throughout eternity, varying in conformity with a law of its own and an order of its own, yet in such a manner that this variation is itself eternal.'

3. This view [a] is also supported by those verses of Homer, which Cicero renders in Latin :

> The minds of men are such as is the light
> Wherewith the fruitful earth has been illumined
> By Father Jove himself.

Nor would the view of a poet on this question have

---

will, which guides men when they are willing to comply and draws them on when they are unwilling.

Cicero translates *Odyssey* xviii. 136 f. :

τοῖος γὰρ νόος ἐστὶν ἐπιχθονίων ἀνθρώπων
οἷον ἐπ' ἦμαρ ἄγῃσι πατὴρ ἀνδρῶν τε θεῶν τε.

sententia ; sed quoniam Stoicos dicit vim fati afferentes istos ex Homero versus solere usurpare, non de illius poetae sed illorum philosophorum opinione tractatur, cum per istos versus quos disputationi adhibent quam de fato habent quid sentiant esse fatum apertissime declaratur, quoniam Iovem appellant, quem summum deum putant, a quo connexionem dicunt pendere fatorum.

4. *Macrobius, Saturnalia iii. 16. 3 sq. Et ne vilior sit testis poeta, accipite assertore Cicerone in quo honore fuit hic piscis apud P. Scipionem Africanum illum et Numantinum. Haec sunt in dialogo de fato verba Ciceronis :* Nam cum esset apud se ad Lavernium Scipio unaque Pontius, allatus est forte Scipioni acupenser, qui admodum raro capitur sed est piscis, ut ferunt, in primis nobilis. Cum autem Scipio unum et alterum ex eis qui eum salutatum venerant invitavisset pluresque etiam invitaturus videretur, in aurem Pontius, Scipio, inquit, vide quid agas : acupenser iste paucorum hominum est.

---

[a] *Cf.* §§ 13 note, 27 note.
[b] Otherwise unknown ; as also is the application that Cicero made of this anecdote in his argument.

DE FATO (FRAGMENTS)

authority ; but since he (Cicero) says that the Stoics are in the habit of quoting those verses of Homer when adducing the power of fate, the matter being treated is not the opinion of that poet but of those philosophers, as the verses referred to which they introduce into their discussion of the subject of fate serve to show very clearly what they consider fate to be, since they call it Jove, whom they deem the supreme deity, from whom they say that the linked chain of the fates is suspended.

4. And lest the poet should be too cheap a witness, ^{The} learn on the affirmation of Cicero the honour in which ^{sturgeon.} this fish stood with the famous Publius Scipio,[a] the victor of Africa and Numantia. These are Cicero's words in his dialogue on fate : ' Scipio was at his place at Lavernium, and Pontius [b] was staying with him, when there happened to arrive for Scipio a present of a sturgeon, a fish not often caught, but said to be extremely highly valued. Scipio invited one or two of the people who had called to pay their respects to stay to dinner, and seemed to be going to invite more, so Pontius whispered to him : " Mind what you are doing, Scipio ; your sturgeon is a dish for a few." '

PARADOXA STOICORUM

INTRODUCTION

This book consists of six short essays setting out the most striking ethical doctrines of the Stoic school of philosophy : that virtue is the sole good, and the sole requisite for happiness; that all good deeds are equally meritorious and all bad deeds equally heinous; that folly is insanity and slavery, wisdom the only freedom and the only riches. In other writings Cicero criticizes these doctrines as extravagant and pedantic —see especially *De Finibus* iv. 74-77 and *Pro Murena* 60-66; but in his preface here, § 4, he expresses his warm acceptance of them.

Not that the author regards these essays as serious works on philosophy ; he merely presents them as amusing popularizations of the recondite teachings of the Stoics (§ 4). He sets out and explains their doctrines in familiar language, defends them by popular arguments, sometimes hardly more than a play upon words, and illustrates them with anecdotes from history and even with allusions to contemporary life, especially to its extravagant display of wealth. No. IV is a hardly veiled attack on Clodius (see § 32 note *b*), who is doubtless also in mind in No. II. No. V satirizes costly luxury and affectation of connoisseurship in collecting works of art : Cicero here probably aims at Lucullus who fought against Mithri-

dates; and he doubtless elsewhere has in mind his rival at the bar, Hortensius, the champion of the optimates. No. VI has been supposed to be an exposure of the methods of Licinius Crassus the triumvir and multimillionaire, who speculated in contracts for public works; but § 43 is against this, as public opinion did not condemn money-making in the case of a member of the equestrian order, to which Crassus belonged.

The book hardly represents a single piece of work. The preface, addressed to Marcus Brutus, alludes (§ 1) to Cato in terms that show that he was still alive, or at all events that news of his death, which took place in Africa in April 46 B.C., had not yet reached Cicero; but it was written (§ 5) when the long nights of winter were over, and after another work, also dedicated to Brutus: this was *De Claris Oratoribus*, which contains allusions dating its composition as early in the year 46. But the essays themselves must have been begun some years earlier: No. IV was presumably written before the death of Clodius, and No. VI before that of Marcus Crassus, if it refers to him. It appears then that Cicero after his arrival in Rome from Brundisium amused himself by finishing and sending to his friend a series of rhetorical trifles that he had by him already.

M. TULLII CICERONIS

PARADOXA STOICORUM

PROOEMIUM

1 Animadverti, Brute, saepe Catonem avunculum tuum cum in senatu sententiam diceret locos graves ex philosophia tractare abhorrentes ab hoc usu forensi et publico, sed dicendo consequi tamen ut illa etiam 2 populo probabilia viderentur. Quod eo maius est illi quam aut tibi aut nobis, quia nos ea philosophia plus utimur quae peperit dicendi copiam et in qua dicuntur ea quae non multum discrepant ab opinione populari, Cato autem, perfectus mea sententia Stoicus, et ea sentit quae non sane probantur in vulgus et in ea est haeresi quae nullum sequitur florem orationis neque dilatat argumentum sed minutis interrogatiunculis quasi punctis quod pro- 3 posuit efficit. Sed nihil est tam incredibile quod non

---

ᵃ See Introduction, p. 253.
ᵇ τόποι, see p. 256, note a.
ᶜ *Interrogatio*, ἐρώτημα, denotes properly a syllogistic argument with each step put as a question to which the adversary

MARCUS TULLIUS CICERO

PARADOXA STOICORUM

PREFACE

1 I have often noticed, Brutus,[a] that your uncle Cato when making a speech in the Senate deals with weighty arguments [b] drawn from philosophy which do not conform with our usual practice in the law-courts and the assembly, but that nevertheless his oratory succeeds in making such things acceptable even to the
2 general public. And this is a greater achievement for him than it would be either for you or for me, because we make more use of the system of philosophy which is the parent of oratorical fluency and which contains doctrines not greatly differing from ordinary modes of thought, whereas Cato, in my view a perfect specimen of a Stoic, holds opinions that by no means meet with the acceptance of the multitude, and moreover belongs to a school of thought that does not aim at oratorical ornament at all or employ a copious mode of exposition, but proves its case by
3 means of tiny little interrogatory pin-pricks.[c] But nothing is so difficult to believe that oratory cannot

must assent; but the Greek term is often used simply to mean 'proof,' including one that proceeds categorically.

dicendo fiat probabile, nihil tam horridum tam in-
cultum quod non splendescat oratione et tamquam
excolatur. Quod cum ita putarem, feci etiam auda-
cius quam ille ipse de quo loquor. Cato enim dumtaxat de magnitudine animi de continentia de morte
de omni laude virtutis de dis immortalibus de caritate patriae Stoice solet oratoriis ornamentis adhibitis
dicere ; ego tibi illa ipsa quae vix in gymnasiis et in
otio Stoici probant ludens conieci in communes locos.[a]

4 Quae quia sunt admirabilia contraque opinionem
omnium (ab ipsis etiam παράδοξα appellantur), ten-
tare volui possentne proferri in lucem, id est in
forum, et ita dici ut probarentur, an alia quaedam
esset erudita alia popularis oratio : eoque scripsi
libentius quod mihi ista παράδοξα quae appellant
maxime videntur esse Socratica longeque verissima.

5 Accipies igitur hoc parvum opusculum lucubratum
his iam contractioribus noctibus, quoniam illud
maiorum vigiliarum munus[c] in tuo nomine apparuit,
et degustabis genus exercitationum earum quibus
uti consuevi, cum ea quae dicuntur in scholis θετικῶς[d]
ad nostrum hoc oratorium transfero dicendi genus.
Hoc tamen opus in acceptum ut referas nihil postulo ;

---

[a] κοινοὶ τόποι, ' common places ' in the Aristotelian
sense, *i.e.* arguments of general application, not inferences
from particular cases ; but Cicero tends to use the term of
proofs set out for general acceptance, in popular form, as
here, and so it approximates to the sense of ' commonplace.'

[b] *admirabilia*, the accepted rendering of παράδοξα, see *De
Finibus* iv. 47.

[c] *Brutus, seu De Claris Oratoribus*, an essay in dialogue
form on the ideal public speaker.

[d] *i.e.* technically : a *thesis* was a ' proposition ' laid down
to be proved by logical argument.

make it acceptable, nothing so rough and uncultured as not to gain brilliance and refinement from eloquence. And holding this opinion I have acted even more boldly than the person I am speaking of himself. For Cato at all events follows the Stoic practice of employing the embellishments of eloquence when he is discoursing on grandeur of mind, or self-control, or death, or the glory of virtue in general, or the immortal gods, or love of country ; but I for my part have amused myself by throwing into common form,[a] for your benefit, even those doctrines which the Stoics scarcely succeed in proving in the retirement of the schools

4 of philosophy. These doctrines are surprising,[b] and they run counter to universal opinion—the Stoics themselves actually term them *paradoxa* ; so I wanted to try whether it is possible for them to be brought out into the light of common daily life and expounded in a form to win acceptance, or whether learning has one style of discourse and ordinary life another ; and I wrote with the greater pleasure because the doctrines styled *paradoxa* by the Stoics appear to me to be in the highest degree Socratic,

5 and far and away the truest. You will therefore receive this brief little essay, the lamplight production of the nights that are now growing shorter, since the former occupation of my longer watches has already appeared in your name[c] ; and you will sample a class of exercises that I have made a practice of employing when transposing things expressed in the schools of philosophy in the form of logical demonstration[d] into this oratorical style of discourse that is my own. All the same, I make no demand that you should place this work to my credit, for it is

CICERO

non enim est tale ut in arce poni possit quasi Minerva
illa Phidiae, sed tamen ut ex eadem officina exisse
appareat.

PARADOXON I

Ὅτι μόνον τὸ καλὸν ἀγαθόν.

Quod honestum sit id solum bonum esse.

6 Vereor ne cui vestrum ex Stoicorum[1] hominum
disputationibus, non ex meo sensu deprompta haec
videatur oratio; dicam quod sentio tamen, et dicam
brevius quam res tanta poscit.[2]

Numquam mehercule ego neque pecunias istorum
neque tecta magnifica neque opes neque imperia
neque eas quibus maxime astricti sunt voluptates
in bonis rebus aut expetendis esse duxi, quippe cum
viderem rebus his circumfluentes ea tamen desiderare
maxime quibus abundarent. Neque enim umquam
expletur nec satiatur cupiditatis sitis, neque solum
ea qui habent libidine augendi cruciantur sed etiam
amittendi metu.

7 In quo equidem continentissimorum hominum
maiorum nostrorum saepe requiro prudentiam, qui
haec imbecilla et commutabilia[3] verbo bona putaverunt appellanda cum re ac factis longe aliter iudicavis-

---

[1] Socraticorum *Baiter et Kayser.*
[2] poscit *Rackham :* dici poscit *codd.*
[3] commutabilia pecuniae membra *codd. :* om. *Bentley.*

---

[a] The colossal gold and ivory statue of Athena in the
Parthenon at Athens.
[b] A contemptuous reference to ordinary men of the
world.

not conceivable that it could be enshrined in the citadel like the famous Minerva [a] of Phidias, but nevertheless it is possible that it should seem to have come from the same workshop.

PARADOX I

That only what is morally noble is good.

6 I am afraid that some of you may think that this essay is derived from the discussions of the Stoic school and not from my own thinking ; still, I will state what I think, and will state it more briefly than a subject of such magnitude demands.

For my own part I protest that I have never deemed either the money of these people [b] or their splendid houses or their resources or their official powers or the pleasures that hold them most closely prisoners as counting among good things or things desirable, since I have noticed that although surrounded by floods of these things they nevertheless felt themselves most lacking in the things of which they had an overflowing quantity. For appetite has a thirst that is never fully and completely sated, and they are not only tortured by the lust of increasing their possessions but also by the fear of losing them.

7 And herein I often remark the absence of the wisdom of our ancestors, who were persons of the greatest self-restraint, and who thought that these unreliable and transitory things deserved only the nominal title of ' goods,' since they had formed an entirely different estimate of them in substance and reality.

259

sent. Potestne bonum cuiquam malo esse, aut potest
quisquam in abundantia bonorum ipse esse non bonus?
Atqui ista omnia talia videmus ut etiam improbi
8 habeant et obsint probis. Quam ob rem licet irrideat
si quis vult, plus apud me tamen vera ratio valebit
quam vulgi opinio, neque ego umquam bona perdidisse dicam si qui pecus aut supellectilem amiserit,
neque non saepe laudabo sapientem illum, Biantem
ut opinor, qui numeratur in septem, cuius cum
patriam Prienen cepisset hostis ceterique ita fugerent
ut multa de suis rebus secum asportarent, cum esset
admonitus a quodam ut idem ipse faceret, ' Ego
vero,' inquit, ' facio, nam omnia mecum porto mea.'
9 Ille haec ludibria fortunae ne sua quidem putavit
quae nos appellamus etiam bona.

' Quid est igitur,' quaeret aliquis, ' bonum ? ' Si
quod[1] recte fit et honeste et cum virtute id bene
fieri vere dicitur, quod rectum et honestum et cum
virtute est id solum opinor bonum.

10 Sed haec videri possunt odiosiora cum lentius
disputantur: vita atque factis illustranda sunt
summorum virorum haec quae verbis subtilius quam
satis est disputari videntur. Quaero enim a vobis
num ullam cogitationem habuisse videantur ei qui
hanc rempublicam tam praeclare fundatam nobis
reliquerunt aut argenti ad avaritiam aut amoenitatum
ad delectationem aut supellectilis ad delicias aut

---

[1] *Bentley :* quid *codd.*

[a] Of Priene in Ionia, *fl.* 550 B.C.

Can a thing that is a good be for anybody an evil ? or can anybody amidst an abundance of goods be himself not good ? Yet all that list of things we see to be of such a nature that even wicked men possess them and that virtuous men derive harm from them.
8 On that account though anyone who likes is at liberty to laugh at me, yet with me true reason will carry more weight than the opinion of the common herd, and I for my part shall never say that anybody who has lost cattle or furniture has suffered a loss of goods, and moreover I shall often praise that wise man, Bias [a] I think it was, who is reckoned as one of the Seven, who, when his native place Priene had been taken by the enemy and the rest of the people although flying were carrying away many of their chattels with them, met somebody's suggestion that he himself should do the same with the reply, ' But I am doing so, for I carry all my belongings with
9 me.' Bias refused to think of these toys of fortune, which we actually call goods, as even among his belongings.

' What then *is* good ? ' somebody will ask. An action rightly done, and honourably, and virtuously, is truly said to be a good action, and I deem good only what is right and honourable and virtuous.

10 But these views may possibly seem somewhat repellant when they are discussed too coolly. They need to have light thrown upon them by the life and actions of men of eminence : wordy discussion of them seems to be excessive subtlety. For I ask you, do the men who so gloriously founded this republic and bequeathed it to us appear to have had any thought of money to gratify their avarice or of beautiful grounds for their delight or of furniture for their

11 epularum ad voluptates ? Ponite ante oculos unum
quemque—regum vultis a Romulo ? vultis post libe-
ram civitatem ab eis ipsis qui liberaverunt eam ?
Quibus tandem gradibus Romulus escendit in caelum,
eisne quae isti bona appellant, an rebus gestis atque
virtutibus ? Quid ? a Numa Pompilio minusne gratas
dis immortalibus capedines ac fictiles hirnulas fuisse,
quam filicatas aliorum pateras arbitramur ? Omitto
reliquos, sunt enim omnes pares inter se praeter
12 Superbum. Brutum si quis roget quid egerit in
patria liberanda, si quis item reliquos eiusdem consilii socios quid spectaverint quid secuti sint, num
quis exsistat cui voluptas cui divitiae cui denique
praeter officium fortis et magni viri quidquam aliud
propositum fuisse videatur ? Quae res ad necem
Porsennae C. Mucium impulit sine ulla spe salutis
suae ? quae vis Coclitem contra omnes hostium copias
tenuit in ponte solum ? quae patrem Decium, quae
filium devota vita immisit in armatas hostium copias ?
quid continentia C. Fabricii, quid tenuitas victus M'.
Curii sequebatur, quid duo propugnacula belli Punici
Cn. et P. Scipiones, qui Karthaginiensium adven-

ᵃ Leader in the expulsion of the Tarquins, 510 B.C., and
first consul.

ᵇ Mucius entered the Etruscan camp to kill King Porsena,
was captured, and proved his determination by holding his
right hand in a sacrificial fire till it was destroyed (hence
his name Scaevola, ' Left-handed '). The king let him go
free, and abandoned the invasion.

ᶜ Horatius Cocles held the Pons Sublicius against the
Etruscan troops of King Porsenna until the Romans had
destroyed the bridge behind him, and then swam back across
the Tiber.

ᵈ Both rallied their troops by courting death in battle, the
one against the Latins, 340 B.C., and the other against the
Gauls, 295 B.C.

11 gratification or banquets for their pleasure ? Place them before your eyes one by one—will you start with Romulus among the Kings, or will you start after the liberation of the state with the liberators themselves ? What pray was the ladder by which Romulus climbed to heaven ? did he rise by means of what your school call goods, or by his achievements and his virtues ? Or do we suppose that sacrificial cups and vessels of earthenware from Numa Pompilius were less acceptable to the immortal gods than the chased libation-bowls of others ? The rest I omit, for they are all on a par with one another, except

12 Tarquin the Proud. If one were to ask Brutus *a* what his object was in liberating his country, and similarly if one asked the remaining members of the same conspiracy what aim or goal they had in view, would anyone be found among them who would appear to have been aiming at pleasure or wealth or any other object beside the duty of a brave man and a hero ? What motive led Gaius Mucius *b* to attempt to kill Porsenna, without any hope of his own escape ? what power kept Cocles *c* on the bridge, confronting all the forces of the foe single-handed ? what power inspired the self-immolation of the elder or of the younger Decius, *d* and caused them to charge the armed forces of the foe ? what was the purpose of Gaius Fabricius's self-restraint, *e* or of Manius Curius's thrift and abstinence ? *f* or of the two bulwarks of the Punic War, Gnaeus and Publius *g* Scipio, who

---

e See § 48 note *a*.   *f* See §§ 38, 48 note *b*.
g Consul 218 B.C., encountered Hannibal in Cisalpine Gaul, and was wounded, only being rescued by the heroism of his son, the elder Africanus, the future conqueror of Hannibal. Publius and Gnaeus later carried on the war in Spain, 217–211 B.C.

tum corporibus suis intercludendum putaverunt, quid
Africanus maior, quid minor, quid inter horum aetates
interiectus Cato, quid innumerabiles alii—nam domes-
ticis exemplis abundamus ? cogitasse quidquam in
vita sibi expetendum nisi quod laudabile esset et
13 praeclarum videntur ? Veniant igitur isti irrisores
huius orationis ac sententiae, et iam vel ipsi iudicent
utrum se eorum[1] alicuius qui marmoreis tectis ebore
et auro fulgentibus qui signis qui tabulis qui caelato
auro et argento qui Corinthiis operibus[2] abundant,
an C. Fabricii qui nihil eorum habuit nihil habere
voluit, similes esse malint.

14   Atque haec quidem quae modo huc modo illuc
transferuntur facile adduci solent ut in rebus bonis
esse negent, illud arte tenent accurateque defendunt,
voluptatem esse summum bonum. Quae quidem
mihi vox pecudum videtur esse, non hominum. Tu,
cum tibi sive deus sive mater ut ita dicam rerum
omnium natura dederit animum quo nihil est praestantius neque divinius, sic te ipse abicies atque pro-
sternes ut nihil inter te atque quadrupedem aliquam
putes interesse ? Quicquamne bonum est quod non
15 eum qui id possidet meliorem facit ? ut enim est
quisque maxime boni particeps ita est laudabilis
maxime, neque est ullum bonum de quo non is qui
id habeat honeste possit gloriari. Quid autem est
horum in voluptate ? melioremne efficit aut lauda-

---

[1] *Rackham :* horum *codd.*   [2] aeribus ? *Rackham.*

---

[a] See § 48 note *c.*
[b] Cato Major, consul 195, censor 184 B.C.
[c] Perhaps the text should be altered to *aeribus,* ' bronzes,'
vessels of the Corinthian alloy of gold, silver and copper.
[d] See § 48 note *a.*

deemed it their duty to bar with their own bodies the onset of the Carthaginians? or of the elder or the younger [a] Africanus, or of Cato [b] who came between them in date? or of countless others—for we overflow with examples in our own history? do we suppose that they thought anything their proper aim in life save what they deemed to be worthy of praise 13 and renown? This being so, let your scoffers at this pleading and this verdict come and give judgement now, whether they would even themselves prefer to resemble one of the people rich to superfluity in houses of marble that shine with ivory and gold, in statues and pictures and chased gold and silver plate and Corinthian works of art,[c] or Gaius Fabricius [d] who possessed and who wished to possess none of them.

14 And albeit they can easily be induced to deny a place among things good to these things that are passed from hand to hand, now here, now there, yet they hold fast to the conviction, which they champion with zealous devotion, that the chief good is pleasure. But this to me appears to be the language of cattle, not of human beings. On you has been bestowed by God, or else by Nature, the universal mother as she may be called, the gift of intellect, the most excellent and the divinest thing that exists: will you make yourself so abject and so low an outcast as to deem that there is no difference between you and some four-footed animal? Is there any good thing 15 that does not make its owner better? for in proportion as each man is a partaker in the good, so is he also deserving of praise, and there is no good thing that is not a source of honourable pride to its possessor. But which of these characteristics belongs to pleasure? does it make one a better

biliorem virum ? an quisquam in potiundis voluptatibus gloriando se et praedicatione effert ? Atqui si voluptas quae plurimorum patrociniis defenditur in rebus bonis habenda non est, eaque quo est maior eo magis mentem e sua sede et statu demovet, profecto nihil est aliud bene et beate vivere nisi honeste et recte vivere.

PARADOXON II

Ὅτι αὐτάρκης ἡ ἀρετὴ πρὸς εὐδαιμονίαν.
In quo virtus sit ei nihil deesse ad beate vivendum.

16 Nec vero ego M. Regulum aerumnosum nec infelicem nec miserum umquam putavi ; non enim magnitudo animi eius excruciabatur a Poenis, non gravitas non fides non constantia non ulla virtus, non denique animus ipse, qui tot virtutum praesidio tantoque comitatu, cum corpus eius caperetur, capi certe ipse non potuit. C. vero Marium vidimus, qui mihi secundis in[1] rebus unus ex fortunatis hominibus, in[1] adversis unus ex summis viris videbatur, quo beatius esse mortali nihil potest.

17 Nescis, insane, nescis quantas vires virtus habeat ; nomen tantum virtutis usurpas, quid ipsa valeat ignoras. Nemo potest non beatissimus esse qui est totus aptus ex sese quique in se uno sua ponit omnia ; cui spes omnis et ratio et cogitatio pendet ex fortuna,

---

[1] in *bis om. nonnulli.*

---

[a] Taken prisoner in the First Punic War and sent back to Rome to arrange peace, but advised his country to reject the offer, and returned to Carthage, where (so the story goes) he was put to death with torture.

man or more praiseworthy ? or does anybody pride
himself upon and boast about and advertise his success in getting pleasures ? Yet if pleasure, which is
championed by the patronage of the largest number,
is not to be counted among things good, and if the
greater it is the more it dislodges the mind from its
own abode and station, assuredly the good and happy
life is none other than the life of honour and of
rectitude.

PARADOX II

That the possession of virtue is sufficient for happiness.

16 Nor indeed have I myself ever thought Marcus
Regulus *ᵃ* either wretched or unhappy or miserable ;
for the tortures of the Carthaginians did not affect
his greatness of mind or his dignity or loyalty or
constancy or any of his virtues, nor finally his mind
itself, for this, defended as it was by so great a retinue
of virtues, certainly could not possibly itself be taken
prisoner, although his body was.   But we have actually seen Gaius Marius, who appeared to me in his
prosperity to be one of fortune's favourites among
mankind and in his adversity one of the supreme
heroes, and that is the highest happiness that can
befall a mortal.

17 You know not, madman, you know not how
great is the strength that virtue possesses ; you
merely utter the name ' virtue,' you do not know
what virtue *itself* means.   No one can fail to be
supremely happy who relies solely on himself and
who places all his possessions within himself alone ;
whereas he whose hope and purpose and thought

huic nihil potest esse certi, nihil quod exploratum
habeat permansurum sibi unum diem. Eum tu
hominem terreto, si quem eris nactus, istis mortis
aut exilii minis ; mihi vero quidquid acciderit in tam
ingrata civitate ne recusanti quidem evenerit, non
modo non repugnanti. Quid enim ego laboravi aut
quid egi aut in quo evigilaverunt curae et cogitationes
meae, si quidem nihil peperi tale nihil consecutus sum
ut in[1] eo statu essem quem neque fortunae temeritas
18 neque inimicorum labefactaret iniuria ? Mortemne
mihi minitaris ut omnino ab hominibus, an exilium
ut ab improbis demigrandum sit ? Mors terribilis
est eis quorum cum vita omnia exstinguuntur, non
eis quorum laus emori non potest, exilium autem illis
quibus quasi circumscriptus est habitandi locus, non
eis qui omnem orbem terrarum unam urbem esse
ducunt. Te miseriae te aerumnae premunt omnes,
qui te beatum qui florentem putas ; tuae libidines te
torquent, tu dies noctesque cruciaris, cui nec sat est
quod est et id ipsum ne non sit diuturnum times ;
te conscientiae stimulant maleficiorum tuorum,
te metus exanimant iudiciorum atque legum ; quocumque aspexisti, ut furiae sic tuae tibi occurrunt
iniuriae quae te respirare non sinunt.

19 Quam ob rem ut improbo et stulto et inerti nemini
bene esse potest, sic bonus vir et fortis et sapiens
miser esse non potest. Nec vero cuius virtus mores-
que laudandi sunt eius non laudanda vita est, neque

[1] ut in *Rackham :* ut *codd.*

hang entirely on fortune can have nothing certain,
nothing that he is assured will remain with him for
a single day. That is the sort of person, if you come
upon one, for you to terrify with your threats of death
or of exile; but to me, in so ungrateful a country,
whatever happens will happen without even protest,
not merely without resistance, on my part. For what
have been my efforts or what my achievements, or
wherein have my anxious thoughts and meditations
passed whole nights of wakefulness, if I have indeed
produced and attained nothing to place me in a position that cannot be undermined by the heedlessness
of fortune or the wrong dealt me by my enemies?
18 Do you threaten me with death, to compel me to quit
the society of mankind entirely, or with exile, to make
me leave the wicked? Death is terrible to those
who in losing life lose everything, not to those whose
glory cannot die away; exile to those whose place of
domicile is encircled by a bounding line, not to those
who deem the whole world to be a single city. It is
you that are crushed by every misery and sorrow, who
think yourself happy and prosperous; it is you that
are tortured by your lusts, you that are in torment
day and night, who are not content with what you
have and who fear that even that may not be lasting;
you are goaded by the conscience-pricks of your ill
deeds, rendered faint by fear of the courts and of the
laws; wherever you turn your gaze, the wrongs that
you have done encounter you like furies, and will not
let you take a breath.
19 Wherefore as no wicked and foolish and idle man
can have well-being, so the good and brave and wise
man cannot be wretched. Nor yet can he whose
virtue and whose character deserve praise fail to live

porro fugienda vita quae laudanda est; esset autem
fugienda si esset misera. Quam ob rem quidquid est
laudabile, idem et beatum et florens et expetendum
videri debet.

PARADOXON III

Ὅτι ἴσα τὰ ἁμαρτήματα καὶ τὰ κατορθώματα.
Aequalia esse peccata et recte facta.

20 ' Parva,' inquis, ' res est.' At magna culpa; nec
enim peccata rerum eventu sed vitiis hominum meti-
enda sunt; in quo peccatur id potest aliud alio maius
esse aut minus, ipsum quidem illud peccare quoquo
verteris unum est. Auri navem evertat gubernator
an paleae, in re aliquantulum, in gubernatoris inscitia
nihil interest. Lapsa est libido in muliere ignota:
dolor ad pauciores pertinet quam si petulans fuisset
in aliqua generosa ac nobili virgine, peccavit vero
nihilominus, si quidem est peccare tamquam transire
lineas, quod cum feceris culpa commissa est; quam
longe progrediare cum semel transieris, ad augendam
culpam nihil pertinet. Peccare certe licet nemini;
quod autem non licet, id hoc uno tenetur si arguitur
non licere; id si nec maius nec minus umquam fieri

---

[a] This technical term of Greek ethics means literally a
success due to correct calculation, just as the opposite means
literally a failure, mistake, bad shot.

a life that is praiseworthy, and further, a life that is praiseworthy is not a life to flee from ; yet it would be a life to flee from if it were wretched. Therefore whatever is praiseworthy must also be deemed to be happy and prosperous and desirable.

PARADOX III

That transgressions are equal and right actions [a] *equal.*

20 You say, ' It is a small matter.' But it is a great offence ; for transgressions are not to be measured by their results but by the vices of the persons transgressing. The occasion of the transgression may be more important or less important in one case than in another, but the act of transgressing is itself one, whichever way you twist it. Whether a helmsman capsizes a ship with a cargo of bullion or a barge laden with chaff makes some little difference in the result, but none in respect of the helmsman's incompetence. Passion has made a slip in the case of a woman of no position : in this case resentment extends to fewer persons than if it had played the wanton with some maiden who was a lady of high birth, but it has transgressed none the less, since to transgress is to cross over the lines, which once done, an offence has been committed ; how much farther you go when once you have crossed the line has no effect in increasing the offence. It is unquestionable that transgression is not allowed to anybody ; but what is not allowed depends only upon the single point of being proved not to be allowed ; if this fact of not being allowed cannot ever become greater or smaller, since

potest, quoniam in eo est peccatum si non licuit,
quod semper unum et idem est, quae ex eo peccata
21 nascuntur aequalia sint oportet. Quod si virtutes
pares sunt inter se, paria esse etiam vitia necesse est ;
atqui pares esse virtutes nec bono viro meliorem nec
temperante temperantiorem nec forti fortiorem nec
sapiente sapientiorem posse fieri facillime potest per-
spici. An virum bonum dices qui depositum nullo
teste cum lucrari impune posset auri pondo decem
reddiderit, si idem in decem milibus[1] non[2] fecerit ?
aut temperantem qui se in aliqua libidine continuerit,
22 in aliqua effuderit ? Una virtus est consentiens cum
ratione et perpetua constantia, nihil huc addi potest
quo magis virtus sit, nihil demi ut virtutis nomen
relinquatur. Etenim si benefacta recte facta sunt
et nihil recto rectius, certe ne bono quidem melius
quicquam inveniri potest. Sequitur igitur ut etiam
vitia sint paria, si quidem pravitates animi recte vitia
dicuntur. Atqui quoniam pares virtutes sunt. recte
facta quando a virtutibus proficiscuntur paria esse
debent, itemque peccata quoniam ex vitiis manant
sint aequalia necesse est.
23 'A philosophis,' inquis, 'ista sumis.' Metuebam
ne a lenonibus diceres. 'Socrates disputabat isto
modo.' Bene hercle narras, nam istum doctum et

---

[1] *Manutius :* milibus pondo auri *codd.*
[2] non *dett. :* non idem *codd. cet.*

---

[a] διαστροφαί (also rendered 'perversitates'), since what is
not straight is crooked, and degrees of crookedness do not
matter.

the action's being a transgression consists in its not having been allowed, the transgressions springing from the fact of non-allowance must necessarily be
21 equal.   And if virtues are equal to one another, vices also must necessarily be equal to one another ; but it can very easily be seen that virtues are equal, and that no one can be better than a good man or more temperate than a temperate man or braver than a brave man or wiser than a wise man.   Will you call a man good who pays back ten pounds of gold when as the money had been entrusted to him without a witness he could easily have pocketed it without punishment, if he fails to do the same in the case of a sum of ten thousand pounds ? or temperate, who restrains himself in one sort of excess but lets himself
22 go in another ?   Virtue in harmony with reason and unbroken constancy is one—nothing can be added to it to make it virtue in a greater degree, and nothing can be taken away from it and yet the name of virtue be left to it.   In fact if good deeds are deeds done rightly, and if nothing is more right than that which is right, undoubtedly also nothing can be found that is better than that which is good.   It follows therefore that vices also are equal, inasmuch as vices are correctly termed ' deformities *a* of the mind.'   But inasmuch as virtues are equal, right actions must be equal, since they proceed from the virtues, and similarly transgressions must necessarily be equal since they emanate from vices.
23   ' You get those doctrines of yours from the philosophers,' say you.   I was afraid you would say ' From the panders.'   ' That is the fashion in which Socrates used to argue.'   Bravo !   your history is most welcome, for it is recorded that the person you

273

sapientem virum fuisse memoriae traditum est. Sed
tamen quaero ex te, quando verbis inter nos con-
tendimus non pugnis, utrum de bonis est quaerendum
quid baiuli atque operarii an quid homines doctissimi
senserint ? praesertim cum hac sententia non modo
verior sed ne utilior quidem hominum vitae reperiri
ulla possit. Quae vis enim est quae magis arceat
homines ab improbitate omni quam si senserint
nullum in delictis esse discrimen, aeque peccare se si
privatis ac si magistratibus manus afferant, quamcumque in domum stuprum intulerint eamdem esse
labem libidinis ?

24 ' Nihilne igitur interest ' (nam hoc dicet aliquis)
' patrem quis enecet an servum ? ' Nuda ista si
ponas, iudicari qualia sint non facile possunt : patrem
vita privare si per se scelus est, Saguntini qui parentes
suos liberos emori quam servos vivere maluerunt par-
ricidae fuerunt. Ergo et parenti nonnumquam adimi
vita sine scelere potest et servo saepe sine iniuria
non potest. Causa igitur haec non natura distinguit ;
quae quoniam utro accessit id fit propensius, si utro-
25 que adiuncta sit paria fiant necesse est. Illud tamen
interest, quod in servo necando, si id fit iniuria, semel

---

a In Spain; taken by Hannibal 219 B.C. As Livy tells
the story, the leading men when its capture was imminent
made a bonfire into which they threw all the gold and silver
in the city, many throwing themselves also into the flames.

274

cite was a learned and a wise man. But nevertheless
I put to you the question, as the bout between us is
one of words and not of fisticuffs,—on matters of moral
good ought we to inquire what is the opinion of
porters and labourers, or of persons of the highest
learning ? especially as this opinion is not only the
truest that can be discovered but even the most
serviceable for the conduct of life. For what power
is there that gives people a better safeguard against
all wickedness than the conviction that there is no
difference between offences, that they transgress as
much if they lay hands on private citizens as if on
high officers of state, that the pollution of licentiousness is the same whatever be the home into which
they introduce outrage ?

24 'Then does it make no difference ' (this is what
somebody will say) ' whether a man murders his
father or a slave ? ' If you posit those cases without qualification, their real nature cannot easily be
judged ; if to rob a father of life is in itself a crime,
the people of Saguntum *a* who chose that their own
parents should all die free men rather than live as
slaves were guilty of parricide. Therefore it is both
sometimes possible to deprive a parent of life without crime and also not often possible to kill a slave
without wrongdoing. Consequently it is the motive
that distinguishes these actions, not the nature of
the action ; and since to whichever action the motive
attaches, that action is the more readily committed,
if the motive is linked with both actions, they must
25 necessarily become equal to one another. Nevertheless there is the difference that, whereas in the
case of the murder of a slave if the action is done
without justification it is a single transgression, in

275

peccatur, in patris vita violanda multa peccantur:
violatur is qui procreavit, is qui aluit, is qui erudivit,
is qui in sede ac domo atque in republica collocavit;
multitudine peccatorum praestat eoque poena maiore
dignus est. Sed nos in vita non quae cuique peccato
poena sit sed quantum cuique liceat spectare debemus : quidquid non oportet scelus esse, quidquid
non licet nefas putare.[1] 'Etiamne in minimis rebus ?'
Etiam, si quidem rerum modum fingere non pos-
26 sumus, animorum modum tenere possumus. Histrio
si paulum se movit extra numerum aut si versus
pronuntiatus est syllaba una brevior aut longior,
exsibilatur exploditur: in vita tu qui omni gestu
moderatior omni versu aptior esse debes, una[2] syllaba
te peccare dices ? Poetam non audio in nugis peccantem[3]: in vitae societate audiam civem digitis
peccata dimetientem sua—'si visa sint breviora,
leviora videantur ?' Breviora[4] qui possint videri, cum
quidquid peccatur perturbatione peccetur rationis
atque ordinis, perturbata autem semel ratione et ordine
nihil possit addi quo magis peccari posse videatur ?

---

[1] putare *Rackham :* putare debemus *codd.*
[2] una *Rackham :* ut *aut* ut in *codd.*
[3] peccantem *add. Rackham.*
[4] breviora *add. Rackham.*

laying violent hands on the life of one's father many transgressions are committed: violence is done to the author of one's being, to him who gave us nurture and education and a place in his house and home and in the state ; the parricide stands first in the number of his transgressions and therefore deserves a greater penalty. But in the conduct of life we ought not to consider what penalty belongs to each transgression but how much is permitted to each person : we ought to deem whatever is wrong a crime, whatever is not permitted a sin. ' Even in the smallest things ? ' Yes, inasmuch as we are not able to impose regulation on things, but are able to 26 regulate our minds. If an actor makes a movement that is a little out of time with the music, or recites a verse that is one syllable too short or too long, he is hissed and hooted off the stage : in real life, will you, whose conduct ought to be more carefully controlled than any stage.gesture, more accurately proportioned than any verse of poetry, say that you only transgress by a single syllable ? I will not listen to a poet when he transgresses in trifles : am I to listen to a citizen when he measures off on his fingers his transgressions in the intercourse of life— ' if they appear smaller in size, they appear less in gravity ? ' How could they appear smaller in size, when every transgression is a transgression caused by the dislocation of system and order, but when system and order have once been dislocated nothing further can be added to make a greater degree of transgression appear possible ?

CICERO

PARADOXON IV

Ὅτι πᾶς ἄφρων μαίνεται.
Omnem stultum insanire.

27 Ego vero te non stultum, ut saepe, non improbum, ut semper, sed dementem esse et insanire[1] ... rebus ad victum necessariis esse invictum potest, sapientis animus magnitudine consilii, tolerantia fortunae, rerum humanarum contemptione, virtutibus denique omnibus ut moenibus septus, vincetur et expugnabitur? Qui ne civitate quidem pelli potest. Quae est enim civitas? omnisne conventus etiam ferorum et immanium? omnisne etiam fugitivorum ac latronum congregata unum in locum multitudo? Certe negabis. Non igitur erat illa tum civitas cum leges in ea nihil valebant, cum iudicia iacebant, cum mos patrius occiderat, cum ferro pulsis magistratibus senatus nomen in republica non erat; praedonum ille concursus et te duce latrocinium in foro constitutum et reliquiae coniurationis a Catilinae furiis ad tuum scelus furoremque conversae non civitas erat.

28 Itaque pulsus ego civitate non sum quae nulla erat: arcessitus in civitatem sum, cum esset in republica consul qui tum nullus fuerat, esset senatus qui tum occiderat, esset consensus populi liberi, esset iuris

---

[1] esse et insanire . . . *Rackham :* insanire (*aut erasa*) *codd.*

---

a Doubtless the author has Clodius in mind: see Introduction, p. 252 and p. 282 note *b*.
b Some clauses have been lost in the Latin.
c In 58 B.C. during the Clodian upheaval. It was a

PARADOX IV

That every foolish man is mad.

27   But I will prove that you [a] are being, not foolish—
that you often are,—not wicked—that you are always,
—but out of your mind and mad. . . . can possibly
be unconquered by . . .,[b] things necessary for life,
yet shall the mind of the wise man, walled and fortified
as it is by grandeur of purpose, by endurance of
fortune, by contempt for human affairs, in short by
all the virtues, be conquered and taken by storm?
Why, it cannot even be banished into exile from the
state. For what is a state? every collection even of
uncivilized savages? every multitude even of run-
aways and robbers gathered into one place? Not
so, you will certainly say. Therefore our community
was not a state at a time when laws had no force in
it, when the courts of justice were abased, when
ancestral custom had been overthrown, when the
officers of government had been exiled and the name
of the senate was unknown in the commonwealth;
that horde of bandits and the brigandage that under
your leadership was a public institution, and the
remnants of conspiracy that had turned from the
frenzies of Catiline to your criminal insanity, was not
28 a state. Accordingly I was not exiled [c] from the
state, which did not exist, but I was summoned to
the state by the existence in our commonwealth of
a consul, who had previously been non-existent, a
senate, which had previously fallen, a free and unani-

favourite paradox of Cicero that his retirement was not
' exile,' and in fact the sentence of exile was not passed until
after he had left Rome.

et aequitatis, quae vincula sunt civitatis, repetita memoria.

Ac vide quam ista tui latrocinii tela contempserim. Iactam et immissam a te nefariam in me iniuriam semper duxi, pervenisse ad me numquam putavi, nisi forte cum parietes disturbabas aut cum tectis sceleratas faces inferebas meorum aliquid ruere aut
29 deflagrare arbitrabare. Nihil neque meum est neque cuiusquam quod auferri quod eripi quod amitti potest. Si mihi eripuisses divinam animi mei constantiam, si[1] conscientiam[2] meis curis vigiliis consiliis stare te invitissimo rempublicam, si huius aeterni beneficii immortalem memoriam delevisses, multo etiam magis si illam mentem unde haec consilia manarunt,[3] mihi eripuisses tum ego accepisse me confiterer iniuriam! Sed si haec nec fecisti nec facere potuisti, reditum mihi gloriosum iniuria tua dedit, non exitum calamitosum.

Ergo ego semper civis, et tum maxime cum meam salutem senatus exteris nationibus ut civis optimi commendabat : tu ne nunc quidem, nisi forte idem esse hostis et civis potest. An tu civem ab hoste natura ac loco, non animo factisque distinguis ?
30 Caedem in foro fecisti, armatis latronibus templa tenuisti, privatorum domos, aedes sacras incendisti : cur hostis Spartacus si tu civis ? Potes autem tu esse

---

[1] si *add. Rackham.*
[2] conscientiam *add. Moser.*
[3] *Rackham :* manarant *codd.*

---

[a] Thracian brigand, headed army of escaped slaves that overran Italy 73–71 B.C., till defeated by Crassus.

mous people, and memories once more recalled of
justice and equity that are the bonds of the state.

And see how I despised those weapons of your
banditry! That a wicked outrage had been hurled
and aimed at me by you I always believed, but I
never thought that it had reached me—unless perhaps
when you were demolishing walls of houses and flinging
your scoundrelly torches upon roofs you fancied that
some portion of my property was falling in ruin or in
29 flames. Nothing belongs to me or to anybody that can
be carried away or plundered or lost. If you had
plundered from me my heaven-sent firmness of mind,
or the knowledge that it was my devotion and watch-
fulness and policy which much against your will were
keeping the commonwealth standing—if you had
obliterated the undying recollection of this everlasting public service,—even much more if you had
robbed me of the intellect that was the source from
which this policy emanated,—then I would admit
that I had suffered an outrage ! But if you neither
did these things nor could do them, your outrage
bestowed on me a glorious return, not a disastrous
departure.

Therefore I for my part was a citizen all the time,
and most of all when the senate commended me, as
a citizen of the highest worth, to the protection of
foreign peoples, but you are not one even now,
unless perchance the same man can be an enemy and
a citizen. Do you distinguish a citizen from an
enemy by race and by locality, not by character and
30 conduct ? You caused a massacre in the forum, you
held the temples with armed brigands, you burnt
private persons' houses and consecrated buildings :
if you are a citizen what makes Spartacus [a] an enemy ?

civis propter quem aliquando civitas non fuit, et me
tuo nomine appellas cum omnes meo discessu ex-
sulasse rempublicam putent? Numquamne, homo
amentissime, te circumspicies? numquam nec quid
facias considerabis nec quid loquare? Nescis exilium
scelerum esse poenam, meum illud iter ob praeclaris-
31 simas res a me gestas esse susceptum? Omnes
scelerati atque impii (quorum tu te ducem esse
profiteris) quos leges esilio affici volunt exules sunt
etiam si solum non mutarunt : an cum omnes leges
te exulem esse iubeant, non appellet inimicus? ' Qui
cum telo fuerit ': ante senatum tua sica deprehensa
est ; ' qui hominem occiderit ': tu plurimos occidisti ;
' qui incendium fecerit ': aedes nympharum manu
tua deflagravit ; ' qui templa occupaverit ': in foro
32 castra posuisti. Sed quid ego communes leges pro-
fero, quibus omnibus es exul? familiarissimus tuus
de te privilegium tulit ut si in opertum Bonae Deae
accessisses exulares ; at te id fecisse etiam gloriari
soles. Quomodo igitur tot legibus in exilium eiectus
nomen exulis non perhorrescis? ' Romae sum,'
inquis. Et quidem in operto fuisti. Non igitur ubi
quisque erit eius loci ius tenebit si ibi eum legibus
esse non oportebit.

ᵃ This doubtless means ' an assassin hired by you.'
ᵇ Earth-goddess, deity of chastity, worshipped by Vestals.
Yearly rites celebrated by women, in the house of a praetor ;
profaned by P. Clodius, who entered Caesar's house disguised
as a woman, 62 B.C.

But can you be a citizen if owing to you at one period no state existed, and do you designate me by the appellation that belongs to you, although everybody thinks that with my departure the commonwealth went into exile ? O maddest of mankind, will you never look around you ? will you never consider what you are doing, or what you are saying ? Do you not know that exile is a penalty for crime, but that that journey of mine was undertaken on account of the

31 glorious deeds that I had accomplished ? All impious criminals (whose leader you openly profess yourself to be) whom the laws wish to be punished with exile are exiles, even if they have not left the country : would not an enemy term you ' exile ' when all the laws ordain that you are to be one ? ' A person found with a weapon ' : your dagger [a] was detected in front of the senate-house ; ' who has killed a man ' : you have killed a great many ; ' who has caused a fire ' : your hand set fire to the Temple of the Nymphs and it was burnt down ; ' who has seized temples ' : you encamped in the forum. But why need I

32 quote the universal principles of law, by all of which you are an exile ? your closest intimate carried a special bill with regard to you, to punish you with exile if you intruded on the secret shrine of the Good Goddess [b] ; but you actually make a habit of boasting that you did so. As therefore so many laws have flung you into exile, how is it you do not fear and dread the name of exile ? ' I am at Rome,' you say. Yes, and in fact you were in the secret shrine. Therefore a man will not have the rights of the particular place where he happens to be if by law he ought not to be there.

CICERO

PARADOXON V

Ὅτι μόνος ὁ σοφὸς ἐλεύθερος καὶ πᾶς ἄφρων δοῦλος.
Solum sapientem esse liberum, et omnem stultum servum.

33 Laudetur vero hic imperator aut etiam appelletur aut hoc nomine dignus putetur : imperator quo modo ? aut cui tandem hic libero imperabit, qui non potest cupiditatibus suis imperare ? Refrenet primum libidines, spernat voluptates, iracundiam teneat, coerceat avaritiam, ceteras animi labes repellat ; tum incipiat aliis imperare cum ipse improbissimis dominis dedecori ac turpitudini parere desierit : dum quidem his obediet, non modo imperator sed liber habendus omnino non erit.

Praeclare enim est hoc usurpatum a doctissimis—quorum ego auctoritate non uterer si mihi apud aliquos agrestes haec habenda esset oratio ; cum vero apud prudentissimos loquar quibus haec inaudita non sunt, cur ego simulem me si quid in his studiis operae posuerim perdidisse ?—dictum est igitur ab eruditissimis viris nisi sapientem liberum 34 esse neminem. Quid est enim libertas ? potestas vivendi ut velis. Quis igitur vivit ut vult nisi qui recta sequitur, qui gaudet officio, cui vivendi via considerata atque provisa est, qui ne legibus quidem propter metum paret sed eas sequitur atque colit

284

PARADOX V

That only the wise man is free, and that every foolish man is a slave.

33 But granted that this person is lauded as commander-in-chief, or even that he is so styled, or is deemed worthy of that title : commander in what sense ? or to what free man will this person possibly issue commands, who cannot command his own desires ? First let him curb his lusts, despise pleasures, restrain his angry temper, control his avarice, repulse all the other defilements of the mind ; let him start commanding others only when he has himself left off obeying those most unprincipled masters, unseemliness and turpitude : so long as he is subservient to these, he will be altogether unworthy to be deemed not merely a commander but even a free man.

For an excellent dictum is current among people of the greatest learning—whose authority I should not employ if I had to deliver this discourse before persons of no cultivation, but as I am speaking in the presence of people of the highest wisdom, to whom these doctrines are no novelty, why should I pretend that I have wasted any trouble that I may have spent in these studies ?—well, it has been said by men of the greatest erudition that no one is free save the 34 wise man. For what is freedom ? the power to live as you will. Who then lives as he wills except one who follows the things that are right, who delights in his duty, who has a well-considered path of life mapped out before him, who does not obey even the laws because of fear but follows and respects them

285

quia id salutare maxime esse iudicat, qui nihil dicit
nihil facit nihil cogitat denique nisi libenter ac libere,
cuius omnia consilia resque omnes quas gerit ab ipso
proficiscuntur eodemque referuntur, nec est ulla res
quae plus apud eum polleat quam ipsius voluntas
atque iudicium ? cui quidem etiam quae vim habere
maximam dicitur fortuna ipsa cedit, si, ut sapiens
poeta dixit, suis ea cuique fingitur moribus. Soli
igitur hoc contingit sapienti ut nihil faciat invitus,
35 nihil dolens, nihil coactus. Quod etsi ita esse pluribus
verbis disserendum est, illud tamen et breve et con-
fitendum est, nisi qui ita sit affectus esse liberum
neminem. Servi igitur omnes improbi, servi ! Nec
hoc tam re est quam dictu inopinatum atque mirabile.
Non enim ita dicunt eos esse servos ut mancipia
quae sunt dominorum facta nexu aut aliquo iure
civili ; sed si servitus sit, sicut est, obedientia fracti
animi et abiecti et arbitrio carentis suo, quis neget
omnes leves omnes cupidos omnes denique improbos
esse servos ?

36   An ille mihi liber cui mulier imperat, cui leges
imponit, praescribit iubet vetat quod videtur, qui
nihil imperanti negare potest, nihil recusare audet ?
poscit, dandum est ; vocat, veniendum ; eiicit, ab-
eundum ; minatur, extimescendum. Ego vero istum
non modo servum sed nequissimum servum, etiam

ᵃ *Manners makyth man.* The Latin is not quite a literal
quotation, not being in verse ; the author is not known.
286

because he judges that to be most conducive to health, whose every utterance and action and even thought is voluntary and free, whose enterprises and courses of conduct all take their start from himself and likewise have their end in himself, there being no other thing that has more influence with him than his own will and judgement? to whom indeed Fortune, whose power is said to be supreme, herself submits—if, as the wise poet said, she is moulded for each man by his manners.[a] It therefore befalls the wise man alone that he does nothing against his will nor with 35 regret nor by compulsion. And though this is a truth that deserves to be discussed at greater length, it is nevertheless a dictum at once brief and indisputable that no one is free save him who has this disposition. All wicked men are slaves therefore, slaves! Nor is this really so startling a paradox as it sounds. For they do not mean that they are slaves in the sense of chattels that have become the property of their lords by assignment for debt or some law of the state; but if slavery means, as it does mean, the obedience of a broken and abject spirit that has no volition of its own, who would deny that all lightminded and covetous people and indeed all the vicious are really slaves?

36 Or can I think a man free who is under the command of a woman, who receives laws from her, and such rules and orders and prohibitions as she thinks fit, who when she commands can deny her nothing and dares refuse her nothing? she asks—he must give; she calls—he must come; she throws him out —he must go; she threatens—he must tremble. For my part I hold that such a fellow deserves to be called not only a slave but a very vile slave, even

si in amplissima familia natus sit, appellandum
puto.

Atque ut in magna familia servorum[1] sunt alii
lautiores ut sibi videntur servi sed tamen servi,
atrienses ac topiarii, pari stultitia sunt quos signa
quos tabulae quos caelatum argentum quos Corinthia
opera[2] quos aedificia magnifica nimio opere delectant.
Et ' sumus,' inquiunt, ' civitatis principes.' Vos
vero ne conservorum quidem vestrorum principes
37 estis ; sed ut in familia qui tractant ista, qui tergunt
qui ungunt qui verrunt qui spargunt, non honestissimum locum servitutis tenent, sic in civitate qui
se istarum rerum cupiditatibus dediderunt ipsius servitutis locum paene infimum obtinent. ' Magna,'
inquis, ' bella gessi, magnis imperiis et provinciis
praefui.' Gere igitur animum laude dignum. Aetio-
nis tabula te stupidum detinet aut signum aliquod
Polycleti. Mitto unde sustuleris et quomodo habeas :
intuentem te admirantem clamores tollentem cum
video, servum te esse ineptiarum omnium iudico.
38 ' Nonne igitur sunt ista festiva ? ' Sint, nam nos
quoque oculos eruditos habemus ; sed obsecro te, ita
venusta habeantur ista non ut vincula virorum sint
sed ut oblectamenta puerorum. Quid enim censes ?
si L. Mummius aliquem istorum videret matellionem

---

[1] servorum *Rackham :* stultorum *codd.*
[2] aera *? Rackham.*

---

[a] See § 13 note *c.*
[b] His most celebrated picture was the marriage of Alexander and Roxana.   [c] Argive sculptor, *fl.* 452–412 B.C.
[d] Consul 146 B.C., conquered Greece, destroying Corinth ;

though he were born in a family of the greatest
splendour.

And as in a great family other slaves are (as they
fancy themselves) of a higher class, but all the
same they are slaves,—the major-domo, the land-
scape-gardener,—equally foolish are the people who
take excessive delight in statues and pictures and
chased silver and Corinthian works of art[a] and
magnificent buildings. And they say, ' It is we who
are the chief people in the state.' On the contrary,
you are not actually even the chief among your
37 fellow-slaves ; but as in the household those who
handle articles of that sort or dust or oil or sweep or
sprinkle them do not hold the most honourable rank
of slavery, so in the state those who have given themselves up to coveting that sort of thing occupy almost
the lowest place in the slave-order itself. You say,
' I have carried on great wars and governed great
dominions and provinces.' If so, carry a spirit deserving of praise. You stand gaping spell-bound
before a picture of Aetion[b] or a statue of Polyclitus.[c] I pass over the question where you got it
from and how you come to have it, but when I see
you gazing and marvelling and uttering cries of
admiration, I judge you to be the slave of every
38 foolishness. ' Then are not those kinds of things
delightful ? ' Granted that they are, for we also have
trained eyes ; but I beg of you, do let the charm that
those things are deemed to possess make them serve
not as fetters for men but as amusements for children.
For what do you suppose ? if Lucius Mummius[d] saw
one of you people handling with eager, covetous

ship-captains conveying unique works of art to Rome were
put under bond to replace any lost with others as good.

Corinthium cupidissime tractantem, cum ipse totam
Corinthum contempsisset, utrum illum civem excellentem an atriensem diligentem putaret ? Re-
vivescat M'. Curius aut eorum aliquis quorum in villa
ac domo nihil splendidum nihil ornatum fuit praeter
ipsos, et videat aliquem summis populi beneficiis
usum barbatulos mullos exceptantem de piscina et
pertractantem et muraenarum copia gloriantem :
nonne hunc hominem ita servum iudicet ut ne
in familia quidem dignum maiore aliquo negotio
putet ?

39   An eorum servitus dubia est qui cupiditate peculii
nullam condicionem recusant durissimae servitutis ?
Hereditatis spes quid iniquitatis in serviendo non
suscipit ? quem nutum locupletis orbi senis non ob-
servat ?   Loquitur ad voluntatem, quidquid denuntiatum est facit, assectatur assidet muneratur : quid
horum est liberi, quid denique non servi inertis ?

40   Quid ? iam illa cupiditas quae videtur esse libe-
ralior, honoris imperii provinciarum, quam dura est
domina, quam imperiosa, quam vehemens ! Cethego
homini non probatissimo servire coegit eos qui sibi
esse amplissimi videbantur, munera mittere, noctu
venire domum ad eum, Praeciae denique supplicare :
quae servitus est si haec libertas existimari potest ?

ᵃ See § 48 note b.
  ᵇ A comrade of Catiline. The underhand influence in
public affairs of his mistress Praecia is described by Plutarch,
Lucullus, ch. 6.

looks a little Corinthian pot, whereas he himself had despised the whole of Corinth, would he have thought him a distinguished citizen, or an industrious major-domo? Let Manius Curius [a] return to life, or one of those whose country house and town mansion contained no splendour or decoration except their own personalities, and let him see a man who has enjoyed the highest benefits that the nation bestows catching mullets with their little beards out of his fish-pond and feeling them all over, and priding himself on his large supply of lampreys : would he not put this person down as a slave whom he would not even deem capable of any specially important function in his establishment ?

39   Or is there any doubt about the slavery of people who are so covetous of cash that they refuse no condition of the hardest servitude ? The hope of a legacy—what harshness of service does it not undertake ? what nod from a rich old man without children does it not attend to ? It makes conversation when it suits him, executes all his commissions, follows him about, sits at his side, makes him presents : which of these is the action of a free man ? which indeed does not mark an indolent slave ?

40   Well, next take the class of desire that does seem more worthy of a free man, the ambition for office and military command and governorships : what a hard mistress she is, how domineering, how headstrong ! She compelled people who thought themselves very distinguished to slave for Cethegus,[b] not a very estimable person ; to send him presents, to wait upon him at his own house by night, even to present their humble entreaties to Praecia : if this can be deemed freedom, what is slavery ?

Quid ? cum cupiditatum dominatus excessit et
alius est dominus exortus ex conscientia peccatorum
timor, quam est illa misera quam dura servitus !
adolescentibus paullo loquacioribus est serviendum,
omnes qui aliquid scire videntur tamquam domini
timentur. Iudex vero quantum habet dominatum,
quo timore nocentes afficit ! an non est omnis metus
41 servitus ? Quid valet igitur illa eloquentissimi viri
L. Crassi copiosa magis quam sapiens oratio ? ‘ Eri-
pite nos ex servitute ’ : quae est ista servitus tam
claro homini tamque nobili ? omnis animi debilitati
et humilis et fracti timiditas servitus est. ‘ Nolite
sinere nos cuiquam servire ’ : in libertatem vindi-
cari vult ? minime ; quid enim adiungit ? ‘ nisi
vobis universis ’ : dominum mutare, non liber esse
vult. ‘ Quibus et possumus et debemus ’ : nos
vero siquidem animo excelso et alto et virtutibus
exaggerato sumus nec debemus nec possumus ; tu
posse te dicito, quoniam quidem potes, debere ne
dixeris, quoniam nihil quisquam debet nisi quod est
turpe non reddere.

Sed haec hactenus : ille videat quomodo imperator
esse possit, cum eum ne liberum quidem esse ratio
et veritas ipsa convincat.

---

^a Perhaps the speech by which L. Crassus made his name
at the age of 21 (119 B.C.), when prosecuting (on what charge
is not known) C. Cabirius Carbo. Carbo anticipated conviction by suicide.
^b See § 33.

Again, when the mastership of the desires is over, and another master has arisen—fear, springing from a guilty conscience,—what a wretched and what a hard slavery that is ! it means having to truckle to young people that are a little too talkative, and fearing as one's masters all the people who seem to know something. Then what a powerful master is a judge ! what fear he inspires in the guilty ! and is not all 41 fear slavery ? What is the value therefore of that oration,[a] marked by more fluency than wisdom, delivered by a man of the greatest eloquence, Lucius Crassus ? 'Rescue us from slavery': what slavery does this mean, as affecting so famous and distinguished a person ? all the timidity of a weakened and humbled and broken spirit is slavery. 'Do not allow us to be in slavery to anybody ': does he want to be emancipated in the literal sense ? by no means ; for what does he add next ? 'except to your entire body ': he wants to change masters, not to be free. 'Whose servants we both can be and ought to be.' We on the contrary, as we have a high and lofty spirit, exalted by the virtues, neither ought to be nor can be ; but for your part by all means say that you can, inasmuch as that is the case, but do not say that you ought, inasmuch as no one owes any service save what it is dishonourable not to render.

But enough of this subject : let the person in question[b] see to it how he can possibly be commander-in-chief when reason and truth herself prove him to be not even free.

CICERO

PARADOXON VI

῞Οτι μόνος ὁ σοφὸς πλούσιος.
Solum sapientem esse divitem.

42 Quae est ista in commemoranda pecunia tua tam
insolens ostentatio? solusne tu dives? Pro di immortales! egone me audivisse aliquid et didicisse
non gaudeam? Solusne dives? Quid si ne dives
quidem? quid si pauper etiam? Quem enim intellegimus divitem, aut hoc verbum in quo homine
ponimus? opinor in eo cui tanta possessio est ut
ad liberaliter vivendum facile contentus sit, qui nihil
43 quaerat nihil appetat nihil optet amplius. Animus
oportet tuus te[1] iudicet divitem, non hominum sermo
neque possessiones tuae. Nihil sibi deesse putat,
nihil curat amplius, satiatus est aut contentus etiam
pecunia? concedo, dives es. Sin autem propter avi-
ditatem pecuniae nullum quaestum turpem putas
(cum isti ordini ne honestus quidem possit esse ullus),
si cotidie fraudas decipis poscis pacisceris aufers
eripis, si socios spolias aerarium expilas, si testamenta
amicorum exspectas aut ne exspectas quidem atque
ipse supponis, haec utrum abundantis an egentis
44 signa sunt? Animus hominis dives, non arca appellari solet: quamvis illa sit plena, dum te inanem
videbo, divitem non putabo. Etenim ex eo quantum
cuique satis est metiuntur homines divitiarum mo-

---

[1] te *dett.* : se *cett.*

PARADOX VI

That the wise man alone is rich.

42   What is the meaning of that insolent boastfulness
of yours in speaking of your money ? Are you alone
rich ? Gracious heavens, am not I to exult in having
heard and learnt something ? Are you alone rich ?
What if you are not rich at all ? what if you are
actually poor ? For whom are we to understand as
being rich, or to what person are we to apply this
term ? I suppose to the person who owns so much
property that for the purpose of living liberally he is
easily contented, the person who looks for and aims
43 at and desires nothing further. It is your own mind
that ought to pronounce you rich, not the talk of
your neighbours, nor your possessions. Does it think
that it lacks nothing, and not trouble about anything
further, is it fully satisfied or even merely contented
with your money ? then, I admit, you are rich. But
if you are so greedy for money that you think no
mode of profit-making base (though really for your
rank none can be even respectable), if every day you
cheat and trick and ask and bargain and plunder and
snatch, if you defraud your partners and pillage the
treasury, if you are in wait for your friends' wills, or
don't even wait for them but foist in forged ones
yourself, are these the marks of a man of overflowing
44 wealth or of one in need ? It is a person's mind to
which the term ' rich ' is usually applied, not his
money-box : although that is full, I shall not think
you rich as long as I see you yourself empty. In
fact people measure the amount of wealth in accordance with what is sufficient for each individual. Has

dum. Filiam quis habet? pecunia est opus; duas?
maiore; plures? maiore etiam; si, ut aiunt Danao,
quinquaginta sint filiae, tot dotes magnam quaerunt
pecuniam! Quantum enim cuique opus est ad id
accommodatur, ut ante dixi, divitiarum modus; qui
igitur non filias plures sed innumerabiles cupiditates
habet quae brevi tempore maximas copias exhaurire
possint, hunc quo modo ego appellabo divitem cum
45 ipse etiam egere se sentiat? Multi[1] te audierunt
cum diceres neminem esse divitem nisi qui exercitum
alere posset suis fructibus, quod populus Romanus
tantis vectigalibus iampridem vix potest. Ergo hoc
proposito numquam eris dives ante quam tibi ex tuis
possessionibus tantum reficietur ut eo tueri sex
legiones et magna equitum ac peditum auxilia possis.
Iam fateris igitur non esse te divitem cui tantum
desit ut expleas id quod exoptas; itaque istam pau-
pertatem vel potius egestatem ac mendicitatem tuam
46 numquam obscure tulisti. Nam ut eis qui honeste
rem quaerunt mercaturis faciendis, operis dandis, publicis sumendis, intellegimus opus esse quaesito,
sic qui videt domi tuae pariter accusatorum atque in-
dicum consociatos greges, qui nocentes et pecuniosos
reos eodem te actore corruptelam iudicii molientes,
qui tuas mercedum pactiones in patrociniis, inter-
cessiones pecuniarum in coitionibus candidatorum,
dimissiones libertorum ad fenerandas diripiendasque

---

[1] multi *Rackham :* multi ex, *aut* multa ex *codd.*

---

[a] Mythical king of Argos, married his 50 daughters to
the 50 sons of his brother Aegyptus; 49 of the brides
murdered their husbands.

[b] Pliny, *Nat. Hist.* xxxiii. 47 assigns this saying to M.
Crassus, with whom indeed the object of Cicero's satire here
might well have been identified on general grounds also.

a man a daughter ? he needs money. Two ? more
money. More than two ? more money still. And
if a man were to have fifty daughters, like Danaus *a*
in the story, fifty dowries call for a lot of money !
For the measure of a man's wealth, as I said before,
corresponds to the amount that he individually requires ; therefore how is a person who possesses, not
several daughters, but desires past counting, which are
capable of draining dry the largest resources in a
short time, to receive from me the title of rich, when
45 he himself feels that he is actually needy ? Many
persons have heard you say that nobody is rich except
a person who is able with his own income to maintain
an army *b* ; a thing which the Roman people with all
its revenues has long been scarcely able to do. It
follows from this premiss that you will never be rich
before you derive a sufficient return from your possessions to enable you to keep six legions and large
auxiliary forces of cavalry and infantry. Therefore
you are now admitting that you are not rich, as you
fall so far short of being able to satisfy your full
desires ; and accordingly you have never made any
secret of the poverty or rather the beggarly destitu-
46 tion which you endure. For just as we are aware
that those who seek wealth in an honourable manner,
by mercantile enterprises or by undertaking contracts or farming taxes, require to gain money, so anybody seeing the gangs of prosecutors and informers
all herded together at your house, the guilty and
rich men on trial likewise at your prompting plotting
some plan to seduce a jury, your bargains for profits
in defending actions, guaranteeings of sums of money
in coalitions between candidates, dispatchings of
freedmen to drain with usury and to plunder the

297

provincias, qui expulsiones vicinorum, qui latrocinia
in agris, qui cum servis cum libertis cum clienti-
bus societates, qui possessiones vacuas, qui proscrip-
tiones locupletium, qui caedes municipiorum, qui
illam Sullani temporis messem recordetur, qui tot[1]
testamenta subiecta, tot[2] sublatos homines, qui
denique omnia venalia, delectum decretum, alienam
suam sententiam, forum domum, vocem silentium,
quis hunc non putet confiteri sibi quaesito opus esse ?
cui autem quaesito opus sit, quis umquam hunc vere
47 dixerit divitem ? etenim divitiarum est fructus in
copia, copiam autem declarat satietas rerum atque
abundantia ; quam tu quoniam numquam assequere
numquam omnino es futurus dives.

Meam autem quoniam pecuniam contemnis (et
recte, est enim ad vulgi opinionem mediocris, ad
tuam nulla, ad meam modica), de me silebo, de re
48 loquar. Si censenda nobis atque aestimanda res sit,
utrum tandem pluris aestimemus pecuniam Pyrrhi
quam Fabricio dabat an continentiam Fabricii qui
illam pecuniam repudiabat ? utrum aurum Samni-
tum an responsum M'. Curii ? hereditatem L. Paulli
an liberalitatem Africani qui eius hereditatis Q.

---

[1] tot *add. Rackham.*   [2] tot *Rackham :* tot qui *codd.*

---

[a] King of Epirus, supported Tarentum against Rome by
invading Italy and Sicily, 280 B.C. Fabricius Luscinus was
sent to him to negotiate an exchange of prisoners, and
rejected his attempts to buy him over to his service.
[b] M'. Curius Dentatus, consul 290 B.C., conquered the
Samnites, after 49 years of war. A Samnite embassy once
found him at his farm-house roasting turnips on the hearth;

provinces, dislodgements of neighbours, landgrab-bings, partnerships with slaves and freedmen and clients, empty properties, proscriptions of wealthy men, massacres of the free towns, and who remembers the notorious harvest reaped in the period of Sulla, the many wills forged, the many persons put out of the way, and finally the universal corruption—re-cruiting, ordinances, another man's vote, his own vote, the public courts, the home, utterance, silence, all on sale,—who would not deem that this person confesses his need of gain ? But who can ever have correctly described a person who needs to make gain 47 as a wealthy man ? For the value of wealth consists in abundance, and abundance means a full and over-flowing supply of goods ; and as this will never be attained by you, you will never be a wealthy man at all.

But as my money meets with your scorn, and rightly (for to the ideas of the common public it is moderate, to yours, non-existent, to mine a modest sum), I will be silent about myself and speak about 48 the subject of property. If we are to hold an assess-ment and a valuation of property, pray shall we set a higher value on the money of Pyrrhus [a] that he offered to Fabricius or on the self-restraint of Fabricius who put that money away from him ? on the gold of the Samnites or the reply of Manius Curius ? [b] the bequest of Lucius Paullus or the generosity of Africanus [c] who surrendered his own

he refused their presents, saying he preferred ruling over the owners of gold to owning it himself. See also §§ 12, 38.

[c] Scipio Minor, victor of Third Punic War, younger son of Aemilius Paullus, conqueror of Macedon, but adopted by the son of the elder Africanus the conqueror of Hannibal.

Maximo fratri partem suam concessit? haec profecto quae sunt summarum virtutum pluris aestimanda sunt quam illa quae sunt pecuniae. Quis
igitur, si quidem ut quisque quod plurimi sit possi-
deat ita ditissimus habendus sit, dubitet quin in
virtute divitiae sint, quoniam nulla possessio, nulla
vis auri et argenti pluris quam virtus aestimanda est?

49 O di immortales! non intellegunt homines quam
magnum vectigal sit parsimonia! venio enim iam
ad sumptuosos, relinquo istum quaestuosum. Capit
ille ex suis praediis sescenta sestertia, ego centena
ex meis : illi aurata tecta in villis et sola marmorea
facienti et signa tabulas supellectilem[1] vestem infinite concupiscenti non modo ad sumptum ille est
fructus sed etiam ad fenus exiguus, ex meo tenui
vectigali detractis sumptibus cupiditatis aliquid etiam
redundabit. Uter igitur est divitior, cui deest an
cui superat? qui eget an qui abundat? cuius possessio quo est maior eo plus requirit ad se tuendam,

50 an quae suis se viribus sustinet? Sed quid ego de
me loquor qui morum ac temporum vitio aliquantum
etiam ipse fortasse in huius saeculi errore verser?
M'. Manilius patrum nostrorum memoria (ne semper
Curios et Luscinos loquamur) pauper tandem fuit?
habuit enim aediculas in Carinis et fundum in Labi-
cano. Nos igitur divitiores qui plura habemus?

[1] *Lambinus :* supellectilem et *codd.*

---

[a] Say £5300 and £880 gold.
[b] See § 48 notes *a* and *b*.
[c] Consul in first year of Third Punic War, 149 B.C. ; celebrated jurist.
[d] A fashionable residential region between the Caelian
and Esquiline Hills, now S. Pietro in Vincoli.
[e] Labicum in the Alban Hills, 15 miles S.E. of Rome.

share of that bequest to his brother Quintus Maximus ? Assuredly the latter form of wealth in each case, the possession of supreme virtue, is to be valued higher than the former, the ownership of money. Assuming therefore that we ought to count each man most wealthy in proportion as he owns the property that is worth most, who could doubt that riches consist in virtue, since no possession, no quantity of gold and silver is to be valued higher than virtue ?

49 Great heavens, cannot people realize how large an income is thrift ! for I now come to the spenders of money and leave your profiteer who makes it. Yonder landlord's rents bring him in 600 sestertia, mine 100 [a] ; but as he adorns his country houses with gilt ceilings and marble floors and has an unlimited covetousness for statues, pictures, furniture and clothes, that return is scanty not only for his expenditure but even for the interest on his debts ; whereas my narrow income will actually show a certain balance left over after the expenses of my tastes have been deducted. Which of us then is richer, the one who has a deficit or the one who has a surplus ? the one who is in need or the one who has plenty ? the one who requires more to keep him going the larger his property is, or the one 50 who maintains himself by his own resources ? But why do I talk about myself, who owing to the fault of our habits and of the times am possibly even myself somewhat involved in the present generation's error ? Within our own fathers' memory (that we may not be always talking of Curii and Luscini [b]), pray was Manius Manilius [c] a poor man ? for he had a small town house on the Keels [d] and a farm near Labicum.[e] Are we therefore richer, who own more property ?

301

Utinam quidem ! sed non aestimatione census verum
51 victu atque cultu terminatur pecuniae modus.   Non
esse cupidum pecunia est, non esse emacem vectigal
est ; contentum vero suis rebus esse maximae sunt
certissimaeque divitiae.

Etenim si isti callidi rerum aestimatores prata et
areas quasdam magno aestimant quod ei generi pos-
sessionum minime quasi noceri potest, quanti est
aestimanda virtus quae nec eripi nec subripi potest
umquam, neque naufragio neque incendio amittitur,
nec vi tempestatum nec temporum perturbatione
52 mutatur ! Qua praediti qui sunt soli sunt divites,
soli enim possident res et fructuosas et sempiternas,
solique (quod est proprium divitiarum) contenti sunt
rebus suis, satis esse putant quod est, nihil appetunt,
nulla re egent, nihil sibi deesse sentiunt, nihil requirunt.   Improbi autem et avari, quoniam incertas atque in casu positas possessiones habent et plus semper
appetunt nec eorum quisquam adhuc inventus est
cui quod haberet esset satis, non modo non copiosi
ac divites sed etiam inopes ac pauperes existimandi
sunt.

I only wish we were ! but it is one's mode of life and one's culture, not one's valuation for rating, that
51 really fixes the amount of one's money. Not to be covetous is money, not to love buying things is an income ; in fact contentment with one's own possessions is a very large and perfectly secure fortune !

Indeed if your skilled valuers set a high value on particular rural and urban sites for the reason that this class of property is least liable to damage, how great a value should be set on virtue, of which one can never be robbed or cheated, and which is not lost by shipwreck or fire, or affected by the violence
52 of storms or by stormy periods in politics ! Those endowed with virtue alone are rich, for they alone possess property that both produces profit and lasts for ever, and they alone have the special characteristic of wealth—contentment with what is theirs ; they think what they have got is enough and seek for nothing more, they want nothing, think that they lack nothing, need nothing. Whereas the wicked and the covetous, as the property that they own is uncertain and depends on chance, and as they are always seeking to get more and not one of them was ever hitherto found who was content with what he had, are to be deemed not only not well-off and rich but actually needy and poor.

DE PARTITIONE ORATORIA

INTRODUCTION

THE *De Partitione Oratoria*, " Of the Classification of Rhetoric "—or, as the title is also recorded, *Partitiones Oratoriae,* "The Divisions (διαιρέσεις) of Oratory " —is a brief but detailed essay on the art of oratory, designed for the instruction of Cicero's son Marcus Tullius. It is based on the system of rhetoric of the Middle Academy, and it takes the form of a dialogue, in which the questions of young Cicero are answered by his father. It is the most purely scientific of all Cicero's writings on rhetoric, and the technical terms employed make the meaning occasionally rather obscure. Its authenticity has been challenged, but it is repeatedly quoted as Cicero's by Quintilian without any expression of doubt.

The scene of the dialogue is not specified, but we may doubtless place it at Cicero's villa at Tusculum. He says at the beginning of the work that it was written when he was completely at leisure, having at last been able to leave Rome. This may be taken to indicate the end of 46 B.C. or the beginning of the following year, shortly before the death of Tullia and the departure of young Marcus to study at Athens as his father had done before him. The young student would be nineteen years old. He had already served in Pompey's army in Greece. As to his later career, on the death of Caesar in 44 B.C., he joined the

republican party, and held a commission in the forces of Brutus in Macedonia, fought at Philippi, and after the defeat fled to Sextus Pompeius in Sicily. When peace was concluded three years later he shared in the general amnesty, and was actually the colleague of Octavian in the consulship in 30 B.C.

The present treatise falls into three parts, which deal respectively with a speaker's personal resources in point of matter and style, the structure of a speech, and the various subjects available for treatment.

I (§ 5) *Vis oratoris* : the functions of an orator are (1) *inventio*, the discovery of arguments designed to convince or to influence the audience—arguments either elicited from the evidence or inherent in the facts of the case ; (2) *collocatio* (§ 9), the arrangement of the arguments in a manner suited to the nature of the speech—according as it is to be delivered in a court of law, or in a deliberative assembly, or for the purpose of display ; (3) *elocutio* (§ 16)—varieties of style are analysed ; and finally, (§ 25) (4) *actio*, graces of delivery, and (5) *memoria* are briefly glanced at.

II (§ 27) *Oratio* : the structure of a speech comprises four divisions, (1) *exordium*, the introduction, aimed at securing a favourable attention ; (2) (§ 31) *narratio*, the statement of the case, which must be clear, convincing and attractive; (3a) (§ 33) *confirmatio*, proof of the case by arguments from probability, by definition (§ 41) of the essential properties of the facts and by explanation of the quality of the action with which the case is concerned, together with (3 b) (§ 44) *reprehensio*, refutation of the opponent's case, and (3 c), (§ 45) rules for the development of the argument and for the handling of witnesses ; (4), (§ 52) *peroratio*, the summing up, which

consists of (*a*) amplification and (*b*) recapitulation (§ 59) of the arguments already advanced.

III (§ 61) *Quaestio*, the matter at issue ; this is either (1) *infinita*, " undefined," *i.e.* a general discussion of a theoretical or practical topic, not dealing with particular persons or occasions—in this case it is called a *propositum*, " thesis," or *consultatio*, " debate," —or (2) *finita*, " limited," *i.e.* dealing with a particular person or subject, when it is called *causa*—though this is really a subdivision of the former. (1) An *infinita quaestio* (§ 62) is of two kinds—*cognitio*, dealing with the existence, essential nature and qualities of the thing dealt with, and *actio* (§ 67), discussing the means and method by which something can be obtained or avoided. (2) A *finita quaestio* (§ 69) is of three kinds, (i) *genus demonstrativum*, a speech in praise or in depreciation of a person's character—there follows (§ 75) a discussion of the virtues and vices ; (ii) *genus deliberativum* (§ 83), delivered in a public assembly on a matter of policy, when the motives of men's actions must be analysed by means of a scale of values ; and (iii) *genus iudiciale* (§ 98), a speech in a lawsuit ; the lines to be taken by the prosecution (§ 101) are tabulated and points for treatment detailed —questions of fact, the moral qualities of the parties, the meaning of documents, etc. Corroborative evidence (§ 114) must be produced—hints are given for handling witnesses and for their examination under torture. Then (§ 119) lines of defence are indicated, countering the above. Both parties can support their case (§ 123) by means of defining legal terms and by the use of other commonplaces of pleading, *e.g.* moral considerations. Suggestions are added (§ 132) for dealing with documents produced in evidence and
308

with disputes as to the meaning of the law and as to considerations of equity.

In conclusion (§ 139) it is urged that the study of logic and of moral science forms an essential part of the education of an orator.

M. TULLII CICERONIS

DE PARTITIONE ORATORIA

1   I. Cicero Filius. Studeo, mi pater, Latine ex te audire ea quae mihi tu de ratione dicendi Graece tradidisti—si modo tibi est otium, et si vis.

Cicero Pater. An est, mi Cicero, quod ego malim quam te quam doctissimum esse ? Otium autem primum est summum, quoniam aliquando Roma exeundi potestas data est ; deinde ista tua studia vel maximis occupationibus meis anteferrem libenter.

2   C. F. Visne igitur, ut tu me Graece soles ordine interrogare, sic ego te vicissim eisdem de rebus Latine interrogem ?

C. P. Sane, si placet. Sic enim et ego te meminisse intellegam quae accepisti et tu ordine audies quae requires.

3   C. F. Quot in partes distribuenda est omnis doctrina dicendi ?

C. P. In tres.

C. F. Cedo quas ?

MARCUS TULLIUS CICERO

CLASSIFICATION OF ORATORY

1   I. CICERO JUNIOR. Father, I should like you to give Introduc-
tion.
me in Latin the information that you have imparted
to me in Greek about the theory of rhetoric—that is if
you are at leisure, and if you wish to do so.

CICERO SENIOR. Is there anything, my boy, that I
could wish more than that you should be as accomplished a scholar as possible ? And, as for leisure, in
the first place I have plenty of that now that I have
at last obtained an opportunity of going out of town;
and in the second place, I would gladly give your
oratorical studies precedence over even the most
important engagements of my own.

2   C. JUN. Well then, are you agreeable to my adopting your method, and putting to you a series of questions in Latin about the same subjects as you examine
me upon in Greek ?

C. SEN. By all means if you like, as that procedure
will enable me to see that you have remembered
your previous lesson, and you will be able to obtain
information on the points you raise *seriatim*.

3   C. JUN. Into how many parts ought the theory of Theory of
Rhetoric:
three
divisions,
with sub-
divisions.
rhetoric as a whole to be divided ?

C. SEN. Three.

C. JUN. Pray tell me what they are.

L   311

C. P. Primum in ipsam vim oratoris, deinde in orationem, tum in quaestionem.

C. F. In quo est ipsa vis ?

C. P. In rebus et verbis. Sed et res et verba invenienda sunt et collocanda—proprie autem in rebus invenire, in verbis eloqui dicitur, collocare autem, etsi est commune, tamen ad inveniendum refertur. Vox, motus, vultus atque omnis actio eloquendi comes est, earumque rerum omnium custos est memoria.

4 C. F. Quid ? orationis quot sunt partes ?

C. P. Quattuor. Earum duae valent ad rem docendam, narratio et confirmatio, ad impellendos animos duae, principium et peroratio.

C. F. Quid ? Quaestio quasnam habet partes ?

C. P. Infinitam, quam consultationem appello, et definitam, quam causam nomino.

5 II. C. F. Quoniam igitur invenire primum est oratoris, quid quaeret ?

C. P. Ut inveniat quemadmodum fidem faciat eis quibus volet persuadere et quemadmodum motum eorum animis afferat.

C. F. Quibus rebus fides fit ?

C. P. Argumentis, quae ducuntur ex locis aut in re ipsa insitis aut assumptis.

C. F. Quos vocas locos ?

C. P. Eos in quibus latent argumenta.

---

[a] *i.e.*, a general inquiry, a debate as to principle or method.

C. Sen. First, the speaker's personal resources, second the speech, and third the question.

C. Jun. In what do the speaker's personal resources consist ?

C. Sen. In matter and in language. But both matter and language have to be found and have to be arranged—although the term ' invention ' is used specially of the matter and ' delivery ' of the language, but arrangement, though belonging to both, nevertheless is applied to invention. With delivery go voice, gesture, facial expression and general bearing, and all of these are in the keeping of memory.

4 C. Jun. Next the speech—into how many parts does it fall ?

C. Sen. Four parts. Two of them, the statement of the facts and the proof, serve to establish the case, and two, the exordium and the peroration, to influence the mind of the audience.

C. Jun. Next, what exactly are the divisions of the question ?

C. Sen. One unlimited, which I call a discussion,[a] and the other limited, to which I give the name of a cause.

5 II. C. Jun. Inasmuch then as the first of the speaker's functions is to invent, what will be his aim ?

C. Sen. To discover how to convince the persons whom he wishes to persuade and how to arouse their emotions.

C. Jun. What things serve to produce conviction ?

C. Sen. Arguments, which are derived from topics that are either contained in the facts of the case itself or are obtained from outside.

C. Jun. What do you mean by topics ?

C. Sen. Pigeonholes in which arguments are stored.

I. The speaker's functions : (1) invention of arguments to convince or to influence.

C. F. Quid est argumentum ?

C. P. Probabile inventum ad faciendam fidem.

6 C. F. Quomodo igitur duo genera ista dividis ?

C. P. Quae sine arte putantur, ea remota appello, ut testimonia.

C. F. Quid insita ?

C. P. Quae inhaerent in ipsa re.

C. F. Testimoniorum quae sunt genera ?

C. P. Divinum et humanum : divinum, ut oracula, ut auspicia, ut vaticinationes, ut responsa sacerdotum, haruspicum, coniectorum, humanum, quod spectatur ex auctoritate et ex voluntate et ex oratione aut libera aut expressa : in quo insunt scripta, pacta, promissa, iurata, quaesita.

7 C. F. Quae sunt quae dicis insita ?

C. P. Quae infixa sunt rebus ipsis, [tum ex toto, tum ex partibus, tum ex notatione, tum ex eis rebus quae quodammodo affectae sunt ad id de quo quaeritur et ad id totum de quo disseritur ; tum definitio adhibetur, tum partium enumeratio, tum notatio verbi ; ex eis autem rebus quae quodammodo affectae sunt ad id de quo quaeritur alia coniugata appellantur [alia]¹ ex genere, alia ex forma, alia ex similitudine, alia ex differentia, alia ex contrario, alia ex coniunctis, alia ex antecedentibus, alia ex consequentibus, alia ex repugnantibus, alia ex causis, alia ex effectis, alia ex comparatione maiorum aut

¹ *Rackham.*

C. Jun. What is an argument ?

C. Sen. A plausible device to obtain belief.

6 C. Jun. How then do you distinguish between the two kinds of arguments you speak of ?

C. Sen. Arguments thought of without using a system I term arguments from outside, for instance the evidence of witnesses.

C. Jun. What do you mean by internal arguments ?

C. Sen. Those inherent in the actual facts of the case.

C. Jun. What kinds of evidence are there ?

C. Sen. Divine and human. Divine evidence is for instance oracles, auspices, prophecies, the answers of priests and augurs and diviners ; human evidence is what is viewed in the light of authority and inclination and things said either freely or under compulsion—the evidence that includes written documents, pledges, promises, statements made on oath or under examination.

7 C. Jun. What do you mean by internal arguments ?

C. Sen. Those that are inherent in the facts themselves, [sometimes derived from the whole, sometimes from parts, sometimes from their designation, sometimes from things in some way related to the point under investigation and to the whole of the subject under discussion ; sometimes definition is employed, sometimes enumeration of the parts, sometimes etymology ; and of the things related in some way to the matter under investigation some are termed generically related, others formally, others by similarity, others by difference, others as contraries, others as connected, or as precedent, or as consequent, or as contrary, or causally, or in effect, or by

315

parium aut minorum :]¹ ut definitio, ut contrarium,
ut ea quae sunt ipsi contrariove eius aut similia aut
dissimilia aut consentanea aut dissentanea : ut ea
quae sunt quasi coniuncta aut ea quae sunt quasi
pugnantia inter se : ut earum rerum de quibus agitur
causae, aut causarum eventus, id est, quae sunt
effecta de causis : ut distributiones, ut genera
partium generumve partes : ut primordia rerum et
quasi praecurrentia, in quibus inest aliquid argumenti : ut rerum contentiones, quid maius, quid par,
quid minus sit, in quibus aut naturae rerum aut
facultates comparantur.

8   III. C. F. Omnibusne igitur ex his locis argumenta sumemus ?

C. P. Immo vero scrutabimur et quaeremus ex
omnibus : sed adhibebimus iudicium ut levia semper
reiiciamus, nonnumquam etiam communia praetermittamus et² non necessaria.

C. F. Quoniam de fide respondisti, volo audire de
motu.

C. P. Loco³ quidem quaeris, sed planius quod vis
explicabitur cum ad orationis ipsius quaestionum-
que rationem venero.

9   C. F. Quid sequitur igitur ?

C. P. Cum inveneris, collocare : cuius⁴ in infinita
quaestione ordo est idem fere quem exposui locorum ; in definita autem adhibenda sunt illa etiam
quae ad motus animorum pertinent.

---

¹ [tum ex toto . . . aut minorum] *Ernesti.*
² [communia] praetermittamus [et] *Ernesti.*
³ *Ernesti :* loco tu *aut* tu loco.
⁴ [cuius] *Ernesti.*

ᵃ The passage bracketed is apparently an interpolation.
it is an abbreviation of *Topica* §§ 8-20.

comparison with things greater or equal or smaller] *a* ;
for instance definition, antithesis, things either like
or unlike or consistent or inconsistent with the thing
itself or with its antithesis ; things that are as it were
mutually connected or mutually hostile ; the causes of
the things under discussion, or the consequences of
those causes, that is the things produced by the
causes ; or distributions or classes of sections or
sections of classes ; or the elements and so to speak
pre-conditions of things that contain some factor of
argument ; or comparisons of things, distinguishing
the greater, equal and less in magnitude,—the pro-
cedures in which either the essences or the potenti-
alities of things are compared.

8   III. C. Jun. Shall we then derive arguments from
all the topics you specify ?

C. Sen. Say rather that we shall examine them and
seek for arguments from them all ; but we shall use
our judgement always to reject those of little value and
also sometimes to pass over those that are of general
application and not intimately related to our case.

C. Jun. As you have answered my inquiry as to
convincing, I wish to be told about arousing emotion.

C. Sen. Your inquiry is it is true not out of place,
but what you want will be explained more clearly
when I come to the theory of the actual speech and
of inquiries.

9   C. Jun. What is the next step then ?

C. Sen. Having found your arguments, to put them (2) Arrange-
together ; and in an unlimited inquiry the order of ment of
arrangement is almost the same as that in the arrange- arguments :
ment of topics which I have explained ; but in a
limited inquiry we must also employ the means
designed to excite the emotions.

C. F. Quomodo igitur ista explicas ?

C. P. Habeo communia praecepta fidem faciendi et commovendi. Quoniam fides est firma opinio, motus autem animi incitatio aut ad voluptatem aut ad molestiam aut ad metum aut ad cupiditatem (tot enim sunt motus genera, partes plures generum singulorum), omnem collocationem ad finem accommodo quaestionis. Nam est in proposito finis fides, in causa et fides et motus. Quare cum de causa dixero, in qua est propositum, de utroque dixero.

10 C. F. Quid habes igitur de causa dicere ?

C. P. Auditorum eam genere distingui. Nam aut auscultator est modo qui audit aut disceptator, id est, rei sententiaeque moderator : ita ut aut delectetur aut statuat aliquid. Statuit autem aut de praeteritis, ut iudex, aut de futuris, ut senatus. Sic tria sunt genera, iudicii, deliberationis, exornationis— quae quia in laudationes maxime confertur, proprium habet iam ex eo nomen.

1⅃ IV. C. F. Quas res sibi proponet in istis tribus generibus orator ?

C. P. Delectationem in exornatione, in iudicio aut saevitiam aut clementiam iudicis, in suasione autem aut spem aut reformidatiónem deliberantis.

318

C. Jun. How then do you explain these ?

C. Sen. I have a set of instructions adapted both for producing conviction and for exciting emotion. As a conviction is a firmly established opinion, while emotion is the excitement of the mind to either pleasure or annoyance or fear or desire—for there are all these kinds of emotion and each kind has several divisions—, I adapt the whole method of arrangement to the purpose of the inquiry ; for the purpose of the statement is to convince, and that of the case is both to convince and to excite emotion. Consequently when I have dealt with the case, which contains the statement, I shall have spoken of them both.

10 C. Jun. What have you to say then about the case ? speeches judicial, deliberative or for display.

C. Sen. I say that it varies according to the class of the audience. For a member of the audience is either merely a hearer or an arbitrator, *i.e.* an estimator of fact and opinion ; consequently it must aim either at giving pleasure to the hearer or at causing him to make some decision. But he makes a decision either about things that are past, as a judge does, or about things in the future, as the senate does ; so there are these three divisions, dealing with judgement, with deliberation and with embellishment ; the latter has obtained its special name from the fact that it is particularly employed in panegyrics.

11 IV. C. Jun. What objects will the speaker put before him in the three kinds of style you mention ?

C. Sen. In embellishment, he will aim at giving pleasure ; in judgement, at arousing either severity or clemency in the judge ; in persuasion, at inspiring either hope or alarm in a member of a deliberative body.

C. F. Cur igitur exponis hoc loco genera controversiarum ?

C. P. Ut rationem collocandi ad finem cuiusque accommodem.

12   **C. F.** Quonam tandem modo ?

C. P. Quia quibus in orationibus delectatio finis est varii sunt ordines collocandi. Nam aut temporum servantur gradus aut generum distributiones, aut a minoribus ad maiora ascendimus aut a maioribus ad minora delabimur : aut haec inaequabili varietate distinguimus, cum parva magnis, simplicia coniunctis, obscura dilucidis, laeta tristibus, incredibilia probabilibus inteximus, quae in exornationem cadunt omnia.

13   **C. F.** Quid ? in deliberatione quid spectas ?

C. P. Principia vel non longa vel saepe nulla ; sunt enim ad audiendum qui deliberant sua causa parati. Nec multum sane saepe narrandum est ; est enim narratio aut praeteritarum rerum aut praesentium, suasio autem futurarum. Quare ad fidem et ad motum adhibenda est omnis oratio.

14   **C. F.** Quid ? in iudiciis quae est collocatio ?

C. P. Non eadem accusatoris et rei, quod accusator rerum ordinem prosequitur et singula argumenta quasi hasta in manu collocata vehementer proponit, concludit acriter, confirmat tabulis, decretis, testi-

C. Jun. Why then do you set out the classes of cases at this point ?

C. Sen. So that I may adjust my scheme of arrangement to the purpose of each.

12 C. Jun. How so pray ?

C. Sen. Because in speeches the purpose of which is to give pleasure there are various methods of arrangement. For we either keep to chronological order or to arrangement in classes; or we ascend from smaller matters to larger, or glide down from larger ones to smaller ; or we group these with complete irregularity, intertwining small matters with great ones, simple with complicated, obscure with clear, cheerful with gloomy, incredible with probable—all of these methods falling under the head of embellishment.

13 C. Jun. Well, what do you aim at in the case of deliberation ?

C. Sen. Opening passages either brief or often absent altogether—for members of a deliberative body are prepared to listen for their own sake. Nor indeed in many cases is much narration needed ; for narrative deals with matters past or present, but persuasion deals with the future. Consequently the whole of the speech must be applied to convincing and arousing emotion.

14 C. Jun. Well, what is the system of arrangement in judicial cases ?

C. Sen. It is not the same for the prosecutor as for the defendant, because the prosecutor follows the order of the facts and after arranging his series of arguments ready in his hand like a spear, states them vehemently, draws his conclusions freely, supports them with documents and decrees and the evidence

321

moniis, accuratiusque in singulis commoratur ; per-
orationisque praeceptis, quae ad incitandos animos
valent, et in reliqua oratione paullulum digrediens de
cursu dicendi utitur et vehementius in perorando.
Est enim propositum ut iratum efficiat iudicem.

15 V. C. F. Quid faciendum est contra reo ?

C. P. Omnia longe secus. Sumenda principia ad
benevolentiam conciliandam ; narrationes aut ampu-
tandae quae laedunt, aut relinquendae si totae sunt
molestae ; firmamenta ad fidem posita aut per se
diluenda aut obscuranda aut degressionibus obru-
enda ; perorationes autem ad misericordiam con-
ferendae.

C. F. Semperne igitur ordinem collocandi quem
volumus tenere possumus ?

C. P. Non sane ; nam auditorum aures moderantur oratori prudenti et provido, et quod respuunt
immutandum est.

16 C. F. Expone deinceps quae ipsius orationis verborumque praecepta sint.

C. P. Unum igitur genus est eloquendi sua sponte
fusum, alterum conversum[1] atque mutatum. Prima
vis est in simplicibus verbis, in coniunctis secunda.
Simplicia invenienda sunt, coniuncta collocanda. Et
simplicia verba partim nativa sunt, partim reperta :
nativa ea quae significata sunt sensu, reperta quae

[1] *Rackham :* versum.

---

[a] *Peroratio* properly denotes any rhetorical harangue
summing up the argument and enforcing it by an appeal
to feeling, but it was of course specially used of the conclusion of a speech, as in §§ 4, 52.

of witnesses, and dwells upon them in detail with greater precision, employing the principles of perorating[a] that are effective in arousing feeling, both in the rest of his speech when he diverges a little from his line of discourse, and with greater vehemence in the concluding peroration. For his object is to make the judge angry.

15 V. C. Jun. What must the defendant do on the other side ?

C. Sen. His entire procedure must be widely different. His opening remarks must be chosen for the purpose of securing goodwill ; narrations must either be cut down if they are tiresome, or dropped altogether if they are entirely wearisome ; corroborations put forward to carry conviction must either be done away with as a separate item, or thrown into the background, or covered up with digressions ; while peroration passages must be devoted to securing compassion.

C. Jun. Shall we always be able to keep to the plan of arrangement that we desire ?

C. Sen. Certainly not ; the prudent and cautious speaker is controlled by the reception given by his audience—what it rejects has to be modified.

16 C. Jun. Next expound the rules applying to the speech itself and to its style of diction.

C. Sen. There is one kind of oratory that flows on spontaneously, and another that inverts and modifies. The first resource consists in single words, and the second in combinations of words. Single words require discovering, combination calls for arrangement. Also single words are some of them natural and some invented. Natural words are ones that are indicated by the meaning ; invented words are made out of the

(marginal note:) (3) diction: vocabulary and structure of sentence, aiming at brilliance or charm or interest;

323

ex his facta sunt et novata aut similitudine aut imitatione aut inflexione aut adiunctione verborum.

17 Atque etiam est haec distinctio in verbis—altera natura, tractatione altera : natura, ut sint alia sonantiora, grandiora, leviora et quodammodo nitidiora, alia contra ; tractatione autem, cum aut propria sumuntur rerum vocabula aut addita ad nomen aut nova aut prisca aut ab oratore modificata et inflexa quodammodo—qualia sunt ea quae transferuntur aut immutantur aut ea quibus tamquam abutimur aut ea quae obscuramus, quae incredibiliter tollimus quaeque mirabilius quam sermonis consuetudo patitur ornamus.

18 VI. C. F. Habeo de simplicibus verbis : nunc de coniunctione quaero.

C. P. Numeri quidam sunt in coniunctione servandi, consecutioque verborum. Numeros aures ipsae metiuntur, ne aut non compleas verbis quod proposueris aut redundes ; consecutio autem, ne generibus, numeris, temporibus, personis, casibus perturbetur oratio. Nam ut in simplicibus verbis quod non est Latinum, sic in coniunctis quod non

19 est consequens vituperandum est. Communia autem simplicium coniunctorumque sunt haec quinque quasi lumina, dilucidum, breve, probabile, illustre, suave. Dilucidum fit usitatis verbis propriis, dispositis aut circumscriptione conclusa aut intermissione aut concisione verborum. Obscurum autem aut longitudine aut contractione orationis aut

former, and are coined either by similarity or imitation
17 or modification or combination of words. And also
there is the further distinction among words that
some exist by nature and others by usage. Words
are formed by nature so as to be some of them
more sonorous, grander, smoother and in some way
more brilliant, and others the contrary ; and words
are formed by usage when the proper terms for
things are employed, or epithets added to the noun,
or terms that are new or archaic or altered and
modified in some way by the speaker—as for instance
words used metaphorically or metonymically, or
those which we so to say misuse, or those which we
degrade or extravagantly elevate and deck out in
greater splendour than the custom of ordinary conversation allows.

18 VI. C. Jun. Well, I understand about single words,
so now I want to be told about combination of words.

C. Sen. In combining words the things that have
to be observed are certain rhythms, and sequence.
Rhythms are judged by the ear itself, to secure one
against either failing to fill out the verbal scheme one
has proposed or being over-full ; while sequence
guards the style against irregularity of gender,
number, tense, person or case. For neglect of
sequence in combinations of words is just as much to
19 be censured as bad Latinity in single words. But the
following five ornaments belong in common both to
single words and to combinations of words : lucidity,
brevity, acceptability, brilliance, charm. Lucidity is
secured by using the accepted words in their proper
meanings, arranged either in rounded periods or in
short clauses and divisions. Obscurity is caused by
either length or abridgement of style or ambiguity

ambiguitate aut inflexione atque immutatione verborum. Brevitas autem conficitur simplicibus verbis semel una quaque re dicenda, nulli rei nisi ut dilucide dicas serviendo. Probabile autem genus est orationis si non nimis est comptum atque expolitum, si est auctoritas et pondus in verbis, si sententiae vel graves vel aptae opinionibus hominum et moribus.

20 Illustris autem oratio est si et verba gravitate delecta ponuntur et translata et superlata et ad nomen adiuncta et duplicata et idem significantia atque ab ipsa actione atque imitatione rerum non abhorrentia. Est enim haec pars orationis quae rem constituat paene ante oculos, is enim maxime sensus attingitur : sed ceteri tamen, et maxime mens ipsa moveri potest. Sed quae dicta sunt de oratione dilucida, cadunt in hanc illustrem omnia; est enim pluris[1] aliquanto illustre quam illud dilucidum : altero fit ut intellegamus, altero vero ut videre videamur.

21 Suave autem genus erit dicendi primum elegantia et iucunditate verborum sonantium et lenium, deinde coniunctione quae neque asperos habeat concursus neque disiunctos atque hiantes et sit circumscripta non longo anfractu sed ad spiritum vocis apto habeatque similitudinem aequalitatemque verborum; tum ex contrariis sumpta verbis,[2] crebra crebris, paria paribus respondeant : relataque ad idem verbum et geminata [atque duplicata][3] vel etiam saepius iterata

---

[1] *Rackham :* plus.   [2] [verbis] *Ernesti.*
　　　　　　　　　[3] *Ernesti.*

or modification of words or metonymy. Brevity is
achieved by expressing each separate idea once, in
simple terms, and by paying no attention to anything
but clearness of expression. The acceptable kind of
oratory is when it is not too decorative and polished,
if the words contain authority and weight, and if the
views put forward are either weighty or in conformity
20 with the opinions and customs of mankind. The
style is brilliant if the words employed are chosen
for their dignity and used metaphorically and in
exaggeration and adjectivally and in duplication and
synonymously and in harmony with the actual action
and the representation of the facts. For it is this
department of oratory which almost sets the fact before the eyes—for it is the sense of sight that is most
appealed to, although it is nevertheless possible for
the rest of the senses and also most of all the mind
itself to be affected. But the things that were said
about the clear style all apply to the brilliant style. For
brilliance is worth considerably more than the clearness above mentioned. The one helps us to understand what is said, but the other makes us feel that we
21 actually see it before our eyes. As for the charming
kind of style, it will be achieved first by the pleasing
elegance of a sonorous and smooth vocabulary, and
secondly by combinations of words that avoid both
rough collisions of consonants and gaping juxta-
positions of vowels, and are enclosed not in lengthy
clauses but ones adapted to the breath of the voice,
and that possess uniformity and evenness of vocabulary ; then the choice of words must employ contrary
terms, repetition answering to repetition and like to
like, and the words must be arranged to come back
to the same word and in pairs and doublets or even

ponantur, constructioque verborum tum coniunctioni-
22 bus copuletur, tum dissolutionibus relaxetur.   Fit
etiam suavis oratio cum aliquid aut invisum aut
inauditum aut novum dicas.   Delectat enim quidquid est admirabile, maximeque movet ea quae
motum aliquem animi miscet oratio, quaeque significat oratoris ipsius amabiles mores : qui exprimun-
tur aut significando iudicio ipsius et[1] animo humano
ac liberali, aut inflexione sermonis cum aut augendi
alterius aut minuendi sui causa alia dici ab oratore,
alia existimari videntur, idque comitate fieri magis
quam vanitate.   Sed multa sunt suavitatis praecepta
quae orationem aut magis obscuram aut minus
probabilem faciant ; itaque etiam hoc loco nobis est
ipsis quid causa postulet iudicandum.
23   VII. C. F. Reliquum est igitur ut dicas de conversa oratione atque mutata.

C. P. Est itaque id genus totum situm in commutatione verborum : quae simplicibus in verbis ita
tractatur ut aut ex verbo dilatetur aut in verbum
contrahatur oratio—ex verbo cum aut proprium aut
idem significans aut factum verbum in plura verba
diducitur, ex oratione cum aut definitio ad unum
verbum revocatur aut assumpta verba removentur
aut[2] circuitus diriguntur aut in coniunctione fit
24 unum verbum ex duobus; in coniunctis autem verbis
triplex adhiberi potest commutatio, non verborum

---

[1] *v.l.* ex.
[2] *Rackham :* aut in.

more numerous repetitions, and the construction must
be now linked together by conjunctions and now dis-
22 connected by asyndeton. It will also give the style
charm to employ some unusual or original or novel
expression. For anything that causes surprise gives
pleasure, and the most effective style is one that
stirs up some emotion in the mind, and that indicates
amiability of character in the speaker himself ; and
amiability of character is expressed either by his
indicating his own judgement and humanity and
liberality of mind, or by the modification of the style
when it appears that the speaker for the sake of
magnifying a second party or disparaging himself is
saying something different from what he actually
thinks, and that he is doing this more out of good
nature than insincerity. But there are many rules
for charm that render the style either less lucid or less
convincing ; consequently in this department also we
have to use our own judgement as to what the case
requires.

23 VII. C. Jun. It remains therefore for you to speak
of the inverted and modified style.

C. Sen. Well, the whole of this class consists in the
modification of words : which in respect of single
words is handled in such a manner that a phrase
is either expanded out of a word or contracted into a
word—out of a word when either the proper word or
a synonym or a coined word is split up into several
words, out of a phrase when either an explanation
is reduced to a single word or epithets are discarded
or circumlocutions replaced by direct language or
24 two words are combined to make a single word ; while
in words combined in sentences a three-fold modification is available, by altering not the words but merely

329

sed ordinis tantummodo, ut cum semel dictum sit directe sicut natura ipsa tulerit, invertatur ordo et idem quasi sursum versus retroque dicatur, deinde idem intercise atque permixte. Eloquendi autem exercitatio maxime in hoc toto convertendi genere versatur.

25   C. F. Actio igitur sequitur, ut opinor.

C. P. Est ita : quae quidem oratori et cum rerum et cum verborum momentis commutanda maxime est. Facit enim et dilucidam orationem et illustrem et probabilem et suavem non verbis sed varietate vocum, motu corporis, vultu, quae plurimum valebunt si cum orationis genere consentient eiusque vim ac varietatem subsequentur.

26   C. F. Num quidnam de oratore ipso restat ?

C. P. Nihil sane praeter memoriam, quae est gemina litteraturae quodammodo et in dissimili genere persimilis. Nam ut illa constat ex notis litterarum et ex eo in quo imprimuntur illae notae, sic confectio memoriae tamquam cera locis utitur et in his imagines ut litteras collocat.

27   VIII. C. F. Quoniam igitur vis oratoris omnis exposita est, quid habes de orationis praeceptis dicere ?

C. P. Quattuor esse eius partes, quarum prima et postrema ad motum animi valet—is enim initiis est

their order, with the result that after the statement
has been made once in a direct form as prompted by
mere instinct, the order is inverted and the same
thing is said as it were upside down or the other
way round, and then the same thing in a piece-
meal and mixed up form. Practice in speaking is
specially occupied in the whole of this division, that
of inversion.

25 C. Jun. Well then, the next topic, I suppose, is (4) delivery;
delivery.

C. Sen. Yes; and it is most important for the
speaker to modify his delivery in correspondence with
the variations of his matter and also of his language.
For he invests his speech with lucidity, brilliance, convincingness and charm not by his language but by
changes of voice, by gestures and by glances, which
will be most efficacious if they harmonize with the
class of speech and conform to its effect and its variety.

26 C. Jun. Have you anything else remaining to (5) memory
mention in relation to the speaker himself?

C. Sen. Well, nothing except memory, which is in
a manner the twin sister of written script, and is very
similar to it in a dissimilar field. For just as script
consists of marks indicating letters and of the material
on which those marks are imprinted, so the structure
of memory, like a wax tablet, employs ' topics,' and
in these stores images which correspond to the letters
in written script.

27 VIII. C. Jun. Well then, the exposition of the II. Struc-
faculty of the speaker has now been completed; so ture of
what have you to say about the rules that govern a speech.
speech?

C. Sen. That a speech consists of four divisions, of
which the first and the last are the parts that serve for

et perorationibus concitandus—, secunda, narratio, et
tertia, confirmatio, fidem facit orationi. Sed amplificatio quamquam habet proprium locum, saepe etiam
primum, postremum quidem fere semper, tamen
reliquo in cursu orationis adhibenda est, maximeque
cum aliquid aut confirmatum est aut reprehensum.
Itaque ad fidem quoque vel plurimum valet; est
enim amplificatio vehemens quaedam argumentatio,
ut illa docendi causa sit, haec commovendi.

28   C. F. Perge igitur ordine quattuor istas mihi partes
explicare.

C. P. Faciam, et a principiis primum ordiar,
quae quidem ducuntur aut ex personis aut ex rebus
ipsis; sumuntur autem trium rerum gratia: ut
amice, ut intellegenter, ut attente audiamur. Quorum
primus locus est in personis nostris, disceptatorum,
adversariorum; e quibus initia benevolentiae con-
ciliandae comparantur aut meritis nostris efferendis[1]
aut dignitate aut aliquo genere virtutis, et maxime
liberalitatis, officii, iustitiae, fidei, contrariisque rebus
in adversarios conferendis, et cum eis qui disceptant
aliqua coniunctionis aut causa aut spe significanda:
et si in nos aliquod odium offensiove collocata sit,
tollenda ea minuendave aut diluendo aut extenu-

[1] efferendis *add. Kayser.*

arousing emotion—for introductions and perorations must appeal to the emotions—, while the second division, narrative, and the third, proof, are the parts that procure belief in what is said. But amplification, although it has a special place of its own, often even occupying the first place and almost always coming at the end, nevertheless ought to be employed in the rest of the course of the speech, and particularly when some statement has either been supported or challenged. Consequently it is also very effective for securing credence, inasmuch as amplification is a sort of forcible method of arguing, argument being aimed at effecting proof, amplification at exercising influence.

28   C. Jun. Proceed then and explain your four divisions to me *seriatim*.

C. Sen. I will, and I will start first from the introductory passages, which are derived either from the persons or from the facts of the case, and which are employed for three purposes : to secure for us a friendly hearing, an intelligent hearing and an attentive hearing. The first of these topics consists in our own personality and those of the judges and of our opponents : from which the first steps to secure goodwill are achieved by extolling our own merits or worth or virtue of some kind, particularly generosity, sense of duty, justice and good faith, and by assigning the opposite qualities to our opponents, and by indicating some reason for or expectation of agreement with the persons deciding the case ; and by removing or diminishing any odium or unpopularity that has been directed against ourselves, either by doing away with it or diminishing it or by diluting it or by weakening it or by setting something against it or

(1) Introduction, to secure audience's goodwill, understanding and attention.

29 ando aut compensando aut deprecando. Intellegenter autem ut audiamur et attente, a rebus ipsis
ordiendum est. Sed facillime auditor discit et quid
agatur intellegit si complectare a principio genus
naturamque causae, si definias, si dividas, si neque
prudentiam eius impedias confusione partium nec
memoriam multitudine ; quaeque mox de narratione
dilucida dicentur, eadem etiam huc poterunt recte
30 referri. Ut attente autem audiamur, trium rerum
aliqua consequemur ; nam aut magna quaedam pro-
ponemus aut necessaria aut coniuncta cum ipsis apud
quos res agetur. Sit autem hoc etiam in praeceptis,
ut si quando tempus ipsum aut res aut locus aut
interventus alicuius aut interpellatio aut ab adversario dictum aliquod, et maxime in perorando,
dederit occasionem nobis aliquam ut dicamus aliquid
ad tempus apte, ne derelinquamus ; et quae suo
loco de amplificatione dicemus, multa ex his poterunt
ad principiorum praecepta transferri.

31 IX. C. F. Quid ? in narratione quae tandem conservanda sunt ?

C. P. Quoniam narratio est rerum explicatio et
quaedam quasi sedes ac fundamentum constituendae
fidei, ea sunt in ea servanda maxime quae etiam in
reliquis fere dicendi partibus : quae partim sunt

29 by making an apology. To secure an intelligent and an attentive hearing, we must start from the actual facts themselves. But it is easiest for the hearer to learn them and to understand the matter at issue if you include in your opening a statement of the class and nature of the case and define it and divide it into parts, and do not handicap his intelligence by confusing and mixing up the parts with one another nor his memory by making them too numerous ; and the same set of rules that will shortly be given as to clearness in the narration will be able with propriety

30 to be transferred to this matter also. Then we shall secure an attentive hearing by employing one or other of three methods—we shall advance considerations that are either of great importance or inevitable or have some connexion with the actual members of the court. But it must also be included among the rules that if ever the actual occasion or the circumstances or the place, or some person's intervention or interruption, or some statement of our adversary's, especially if it was made in his peroration, gives us an opportunity to make a telling point at the right moment, we must not lose the opportunity ; and much of what we shall say about amplification at the place belonging to it will be able to be transferred to the rules for the exordium.

31 IX. C. Jun. Well, what then are the rules to be observed in the statement of the case ? (2) Statement of case.

C. Sen. Well, the statement is an explanation of the facts and as it were a base and foundation for the establishment of belief. Consequently special attention must be given in this part to the rules that must also be observed in almost all the rest of the divisions of a speech ; rules that are partly indispensable and

necessaria, partim assumpta ad ornandum. Nam ut
dilucide probabiliterque narremus, necessarium est,
32 sed assumimus etiam suavitatem. Ergo ad dilucide
narrandum eadem illa superiora explicandi et illustrandi praecepta repetemus, in quibus est brevitas
ea quae[1] saepissime in narratione laudatur, de qua
supra dictum est. Probabilis autem erit si personis,
si temporibus, si locis ea quae narrabuntur consentient : si cuiusque facti et eventi causa ponetur :
si testata dici videbuntur, si cum hominum auctoritate,[2] si cum lege, cum more, cum religione coniuncta :
si probitas narrantis significabitur, si antiquitas, si
memoria, si orationis veritas, et vitae fides. Suavis
autem narratio est quae habet admirationes, exspecta-
tiones, exitus inopinatos, interpositos motus animorum, colloquia personarum, dolores, iracundias,
metus, laetitias, cupiditates. Sed iam ad reliqua
pergamus.
33　C. F. Nempe ea sequuntur quae ad faciendam
fidem pertinent.

C. P. Ita est : quae quidem in confirmationem et
reprehensionem dividuntur. Nam in confirmando
nostra probare volumus, in reprehendendo redarguere
contraria. Quoniam igitur omne quod in controversiam venit, id aut an[3] sit necne[4] aut quid sit aut
quale sit quaeritur, in primo coniectura valet, in
altero definitio, in tertio ratio.

34　C. F. Teneo istam distributionem : nunc coniec-
turae locos quaero.

---

[1] *v.l.* eaque.
[2] *Rackham :* opinione auctoritate (opinione vel auct. *Schol.*).
　[3] an *om. vulg.*　　　[4] *Schol. v.l.* necne sit.

partly adopted for the purpose of embellishment. For clarity and convincingness in the statement of the case
32 are essential, but we also add charm. Consequently to secure clarity of statement we shall go back to the same rules for exposition and elucidation that we gave above, which rules must include the quality of brevity spoken of above, which is most frequently applauded in the statement of the case. And the statement will be convincing if the facts narrated are in accordance with the persons, the times and the places ; if we set out the cause of every action and occurrence ; if what we say appears to be based on evidence, and to be in agreement with the judgement of mankind, and with law and custom and religion ; if it indicates honesty in the speaker, integrity, memory, truth in speech and loyalty in conduct. And a statement has the quality of charm when it comprises causes for surprise and suspense and unexpected issues, with an inter-mixture of human emotions, dialogues between people, and exhibitions of grief, rage, fear, joy, and desire. But now let us go on to the matters that remain.

33   C. Jun. Obviously the next point is the means directed to securing credence.

C. Sen. Yes : and these fall into two divisions, con-firmation and refutation. The aim of confirmation is to prove our own case and that of refutation is to refute the case of our opponents. The question in regard to every matter that comes into dispute is either as to its reality or its identity or its qualities ; consequently in considering the first point inference is a valid method, on the second definition and on the third ratiocination.

34   C. Jun. I grasp the distinction you mean ; and now I want to know the topics employed by inference.

(3 a) Proof of case (i.) by inference from prob-ability in regard to persons, places, times, and actions;

X. C. P. In verisimilibus et in propriis rerum notis
posita est tota. Sed appellemus docendi gratia
verisimile quod plerumque ita fiat, ut adolescentiam
procliviorem esse ad libidinem ; propriae autem
notae argumentum quod numquam aliter fit certum-
que declarat, ut fumus ignem. Verisimilia reperiuntur ex partibus et quasi membris narrationis ; ea
sunt in personis, in locis, in temporibus, in factis, in
eventis, in rerum ipsarum negotiorumque naturis.
35 In personis naturae primum spectantur, valetudinis,
figurae, virium, aetatis, marium, feminarum : atque
haec quidem in corpore[1] ; animi autem aut quemadmodum affecti sint virtutibus, vitiis, artibus, inertiis,
aut quemadmodum commoti cupiditate, metu, voluptate, molestia. Atque haec quidem in natura spectantur. In fortuna genus, amicitiae, liberi, propinqui,
affines, opes, honores, potestates, divitiae, libertas,
36 et ea quae sunt eis contraria. In locis autem et illa
naturalia, maritimi an remoti a mari, plani an mon-
tuosi, leves an asperi, salubres an pestilentes, opaci
an aprici, et illa fortuita, culti an inculti, celebres
an deserti, coaedificati an vasti, obscuri an rerum
gestarum vestigiis nobilitati, consecrati an profani.
37 XI. In temporibus autem praesentia [et][2] praeterita
[et][3] futura cernuntur : in his ipsis vetusta, recentia,
instantia, paullo post aut aliquando futura. Insunt
etiam in temporibus illa quae temporis quasi naturam

---

[1] [marium . . . corpore] *Kayser.*
[2] *Kayser.*   [3] *Kayser.*

X. C. SEN. Inference is based entirely on probabilities and on the essential characteristics of things.
But let us for the sake of conveying our meaning
define the term ' probable ' as ' that which usually
occurs in such and such a way '—for example that
youth is more prone to self-indulgence ; while an
essential characteristic gives a proof that is never
otherwise and that supplies an indication that is
certain, as smoke is a certain indication of fire. Probabilities are obtained from the parts or ' members '
of the statement ; these deal with persons, places,
times, actions, occurrences—the natures of the actual
35 facts and transactions.   In the case of persons we
first examine their natural attributes of health, figure,
strength, age, and sex—male or female—, which are
in the body ; while as to the mind we note either
men's conditions in respect of virtues and vices, arts
and sciences or the lack of these, or else their reactions
to the emotions of desire, fear, pleasure and annoyance.   And whereas these are qualities observed in
men's natures, their circumstances comprise birth,
friendships, children, relations, connexions, resources,
office, power, riches, freedom and the opposites of
36 these.   In the case of places too there are both natural
qualities—on the coast or inland, flat or mountainous,
smooth or rugged, salubrious or unhealthy, shady or
sunny, and accidental qualities—cultivated or uncultivated, inhabited or deserted, built up or open,
obscure or famous for historic monuments, con-
37 secrated or secular.   XI. Under the head of times we
observe present, past and future, and their sub-
divisions—long past or recent, immediately impend-
ing or going to happen in the near or remoter future.
Also among specifications of time are the terms that

notant, ut [hiems, ver, aestas, auctumnus aut][1] anni
tempora, ut mensis, ut dies, [ut][2] nox, hora, [tem-
pestas][3] quae sunt naturalia : fortuita autem sacri-
38 ficia, festi dies, nuptiae. Iam facta et eventus aut
consilii sunt aut imprudentiae, quae est aut in casu
aut in quadam animi permotione : casu cum aliter
cecidit ac putatum sit, permotione cum aut oblivio
aut error aut metus aut aliqua cupiditatis causa per-
movit. Est etiam in imprudentia necessitas ponenda.
Rerum autem bonarum et malarum tria sunt genera,
nam aut in animis aut in corporibus aut extra esse
possunt. Huius igitur materiae ad argumentum
subiectae perlustrandae animo partes erunt omnes,
et ad id quod agetur ex singulis coniectura capienda.
39 Est etiam genus argumentorum aliud quod ex facti
vestigiis sumitur, ut telum, cruor, clamor editus,
titubatio, permutatio coloris, oratio inconstans,
tremor, ceterorum[4] aliquid quod sensu percipi possit ;
etiamsi praeparatum aliquid, si communicatum cum
40 aliquo, si postea visum, auditum, indicatum. Verisimilia autem partim singula movent suo pondere,
partim etiamsi videntur esse exigua per se, multum
tamen cum sunt coacervata proficiunt. Atque in his
verisimilibus insunt nonnumquam etiam certae rerum
et propriae notae. Maximam autem facit fidem ad
similitudinem veri primum exemplum, deinde intro-
ducta rei similitudo ; fabula etiam nonnumquam, etsi
est incredibilis, tamen homines commovet.

---

[1] *Kayser.*   [2] *Kayser.*   [3] *Kayser.*
[4] ceterorum *? Warmington :* et eorum.

denote the nature of the time, such as the seasons of the year, month, day or night, hour,—which are natural periods ; while accidental occasions are sacri-

38 fices, holidays, weddings. Again actions and occurrences are either matters of design or unintentional, the latter depending either on accident or on some psychological factor : on accident when something unexpected happens, on psychology when the occurrence is the result of forgetfulness or of a mistake or of fear or of some motive of desire. Necessity also may be classed under the unintentional. Then goods and evils are of three kinds, for they can be either in the mind or in the body or outside us. With this material therefore supplied as a basis for the argument it will be necessary to pass all the parts of it in mental review and arrive at an inference from each in turn with reference to the matter that will be under

39 consideration. There is also another kind of argument that is taken from the mere indications of an action, for instance a weapon, blood, a cry, a stumble, change of colour, stammering, trembling, or anything else that can be perceived by the senses : also some sign of preparation or of communication with somebody, or

40 something seen or heard or hinted later on. As to probabilities, these in some cases carry their own weight intrinsically, and in others even if they seem to be slight in themselves nevertheless go a long way when combined together. Also among these probabilities there are sometimes also marks that are certain and peculiar to the things. But the greatest corroboration is supplied to a probable truth by first an example, next the introduction of a parallel case; and also sometimes an anecdote, even though it be a tall story, nevertheless has an effect on people.

Grades of probability.

41 XII. C. F. Quid ? definitionis quae ratio est et quae via ?

C. P. Non dubium est id quidem quin definitio genere declaretur et proprietate quadam aut etiam communium frequentia ex quibus proprium quid sit eluceat. Sed quoniam de propriis oritur plerumque magna dissensio, definiendum est saepe ex contrariis, saepe etiam ex dissimilibus, saepe ex paribus. Quam ob rem descriptiones quoque sunt in hoc genere saepe aptae et enumeratio consequentium, in primisque commovet explicatio vocabuli ac nominis.

42 C. F. Sunt exposita iam fere ea quae de facto quaeque de facti appellatione quaeruntur. Nempe igitur ea restant quae, cum factum constet et nomen, qualia sint vocatur in dubium.

C. P. Est ita ut dicis.

C. F. Quae sunt igitur in eo genere partes ?

C. P. Aut iure factum depellendi aut ulsciscendi doloris gratia, aut pietatis aut pudicitiae aut religionis aut patriae nomine, aut denique necessitate, **43** inscitia, casu. Nam quae motu animi et perturbatione facta sine ratione sunt, ea defensionem contra crimen in legitimis iudiciis non habent, in liberis disceptationibus habere possunt. Hoc in genere, in quo quale sit quaeritur, [ex controversia][1] iure et

[1] *Schütz.*

41   XII. C. Jun. Well, what is the principle and the
method of definition ?

    C. Sen. It is at all events clear that a definition is
an explanation in the form of a statement of the class
to which a thing belongs and of some special property
that distinguishes it, or else a collection of common
properties among which what its special property is
comes into view. But as there usually arises a great
deal of disagreement about special properties, we
often have to adopt the method of definition by means
of opposites and also often by means of unlike or of
like objects. Consequently in this class of argument descriptions are also frequently appropriate, and
enumerations of consequences, and a specially effective
method is the explanation of a term or a name.

(ii.) proof of case by definition of essential properties of the facts :

42   C. Jun. This practically completes the exposition
of the questions raised about the act committed and
about its proper designation. Presumably therefore
there now remain those questions as to quality
which arise when both the action and its name have
been settled.

(iii.) proof by consideration of the quality of the action ;

    C. Sen. Yes, that is so.

    C. Jun. What then are the divisions in this class of
consideration ?

    C. Sen. Either that the deed was rightly done for
the sake of avoiding or avenging pain or in the name
of piety or modesty or religious scruple or patriotism,
or finally because of necessity or ignorance or accident.

43 For actions done owing to emotion and mental dis-
turbance and therefore irrational afford no lines of
defence against the charge in a court of law, but they
can provide a defence in a free debate. In this kind
of debate, in which the question at issue is as to the
quality of the action, the inquiry usually is based on

recte necne actum sit quaeri solet : quorum disputatio ex locorum descriptione sumenda est.

44 C. F. Age sis ergo, quoniam in confirmationem et reprehensionem diviseras orationis fidem, et dictum de altero est, expone nunc de reprehendendo.

C. P. Aut totum est negandum quod in argumentatione adversarius sumpserit, si fictum aut falsum esse possis docere, aut redarguenda ea quae pro verisimilibus sumpta sint : primum dubia sumpta esse pro certis, deinde etiam in perspicue falsis eadem posse dici, tum ex eis quae sumpserit non effici quod velit. Accidere autem oportet singula : sic universa frangentur. Commemoranda sunt etiam exempla quibus simili in disputatione creditum non sit, conquerenda conditio communis periculi si ingeniis hominum criminosorum sit exposita vita innocentium.

45 XIII. C. F. Quoniam unde inveniuntur quae ad fidem pertinent habeo, quemadmodum in dicendo singula tractentur exspecto.

C. P. Argumentationem quaerere videris, quae est[1] argumenti explicatio [: quae sumpta ex eis locis qui sunt expositi conficienda et distinguenda dilucide est].[2]

C. F. Plane istuc ipsum desidero.

46 C. P. Est ergo (ut supra dictum est) explicatio argumenti argumentatio : sed ea conficitur cum

---

[1] *v.l.* sit.   [2] *Ernesti.*

---

[a] Presumably an interpolation.

a dispute as to whether the action was done lawfully and rightly or not ; and a line to adopt in discussing these points must be taken from the list of topics.

44 C. Jun. Come then, please, inasmuch as you had divided the section of the speech dealing with proof into confirmation and refutation, and the former has been dealt with, now explain about the method of refuting. (3 b) Refutation of opponent's case.

C. Sen. Either you must deny the whole of what your opponent has assumed in arguing his case, if you are able to show that it is imaginary or untrue, or you must rebut the statements that he has assumed as probable, and must show, first that doubtful points have been taken for certain, next that the same statements can also be made in the case of things manifestly false, and then that the results that he desires do not follow from his assumptions. But the proper way is to whittle them away one by one, and thus the whole of them will be demolished. Also you must recall examples which in a similar dispute have not obtained credence; and you must deplore the general state of danger that will prevail if the life of innocent people is exposed to the clever tricks of calumniators.

45 XIII. C. Jun. Now that I know where to find means of obtaining credence, I next want to be told how each successive topic is to be handled in speaking. (3 c) Development of argument and handling of witnesses.

C. Sen. I take it that what you desire to hear about is ratiocination, which is the process of developing the argument. [This process, derived from the topics that have been set forth, requires completing and clarifying in detail.[a]]

C. Jun. Clearly that is exactly what I require.

46 C. Sen. Well then, ratiocination as I said just now, is the process of developing the argument ; but this

sumpseris aut non dubia aut probabilia ex quibus id
efficias quod aut dubium aut minus probabile per se
videtur. Argumentandi autem duo sunt genera,
quorum alterum ad fidem directo spectat, alterum se
inflectit ad motum. Dirigitur cum proposuit aliquid
quod probaret sumpsitque ea quibus niteretur, atque
his confirmatis ad propositum se rettulit atque con-
clusit. Illa autem altera argumentatio quasi retro
et contra : prius sumit quae vult eaque confirmat,
deinde id quod proponendum fuit permotis animis
47 iacit ad extremum. Est autem illa varietas in argumentando et non iniucunda distinctio, ut cum in-
terrogamus nosmet ipsi aut percunctamur aut
imploramus[1] aut optamus—quae sunt cum aliis compluribus sententiarum ornamenta. Vitare autem
similitudinem poterimus non semper a proposito
ordientes, et si non omnia disputando confirmabimus,
breviterque interdum quae erunt satis aperta
ponemus quodque ex his efficietur, si id apertum
sit, non habebimus necesse semper concludere.

48   XIV. C. F. Quid ? illa quae sine arte appellantur,
quae iamdudum assumpta dixisti, ecquonam modo[2]
artis indigent ?

C. P. Illa vero indigent, nec eo dicuntur sine arte
quod ita sunt, sed quod ea non parit oratoris ars sed

---

[1] *v.l.* imperamus.
[2] *v.l.* ecquonam modo, ecquonam! oco.

process is achieved when you have assumed either indubitable or probable premises from which to draw a conclusion that appears in itself either doubtful or less probable. And there are two kinds of ratiocination, one of which aims directly at convincing and the other devotes itself to exciting feeling. It proceeds directly, when it has put forward a proposition to prove, and has chosen the arguments to support its case, and after establishing these has returned to the proposition and drawn the conclusion ; but the other form of ratiocination proceeds in the opposite way, backward : it first assumes the premises that it wants and establishes these, and then after exciting emotion throws in at the end what ought to have been pre-
47 mised at the start. Ratiocination also permits the following variety of methods, a not unpleasing divergence, when we put a question to ourselves or cross-examine ourselves or make an appeal or express a desire—forms of expression which with a great many others serve to decorate our sentences. But we shall be able to avoid monotony by not always starting from the point we are making, and if we do not prove all our points by advancing arguments, and sometimes lay down quite shortly statements that will be sufficiently obvious, and do not always hold it necessary formally to draw the conclusion that will follow from them, if it is obvious.

48 XIV. C. Jun. Well, as to the rules that are styled not matters of science, which you said have been adopted long ago, do they as a matter of fact require some degree of scientific method ?

C. Sen. They do indeed, and they are not called unscientific because they really are so, but because they are not engendered by the science of the speaker, but

foris ad se delata tamen arte tractat, et maxime in
49 testibus. Nam et de toto genere testium quam id
sit infirmum saepe dicendum est, et argumenta rerum
esse propria, testimonia voluntatum, utendumque
est exemplis quibus testibus creditum non sit ; et
de singulis testibus, si natura vani, si leves, si cum
ignominia, si spe, si metu, si iracundia, si miseri-
cordia impulsi, si praemio, si gratia adducti ; com-
parandique superiore cum auctoritate testium quibus
50 tamen creditum non sit. Saepe etiam quaestionibus
resistendum est, quod et dolorem fugientes multi in
tormentis ementiti persaepe sint morique malue-
rint falsum fatendo quam[1] infitiando dolere ; multi
etiam suam vitam neglexerint ut eos qui eis[2] cariores
quam ipsi sibi essent liberarent, alii autem aut natura
corporis aut consuetudine dolendi aut metu supplicii
ac mortis vim tormentorum pertulerint, alii ementiti
sint in eos quos oderant.[3] Atque haec exemplis
51 firmanda sunt. Neque est obscurum, quin, quoniam
in utramque partem sunt exempla et item ad coniecturam faciendam loci, in contrariis contraria sint
sumenda. Atque etiam incurrit alia quaedam in
testibus et in quaestionibus ratio ; saepe enim ea
quae dicta sunt si aut ambigue aut inconstanter aut

---

[1] *v.l.* quam verum. [2] *Rackham :* his.
[3] alii ementiti . . . oderant *ante* alii autem . . . pertulerint *tr. ? Warmington.*

---

[a] 'and others . . . hated' should perhaps be transposed
to come before ' while others aided . . . ' above.
348

he receives them from outside, yet all the same he handles them with science, and particularly in dealing

49 with the evidence of witnesses. He often has to declare how unreliable all witnesses are as a class, and to say that proofs are matters of fact but the evidence of witnesses is a matter of personal inclinations, and he must cite instances of witnesses who were not believed ; and he must also run down particular witnesses, if they are men of unreliable character, or frivolous, or under a cloud, or actuated by hope or fear or anger or pity, or influenced by hope of reward or by gratitude ; and they must be compared with witnesses of higher authority who have nevertheless

50 not been given credence. It is also often necessary to oppose the use of examination under torture, on the grounds that many men under torture in the desire to escape from pain have very often told utter lies, and have preferred to die while confessing what was false rather than to suffer pain by denying it, and that many have even disregarded their own life in order to secure the freedom of persons dearer to them than themselves ; while others aided either by bodily physique or habituation to pain or actuated by fear of punishment and death have endured violent torture to the end, and others have given false evidence against those whom they hated.[a] And these state-

51 ments must be supported by instances. Nor is it hard to see that, as there are instances telling in either direction and also opportunities for making a conjecture, contrary instances must be taken in contrary cases. And there is also occasion for another method in dealing with witnesses and examinations : frequently, when statements have been made that were ambiguous, or inconsistent, or incredible, or even

349

incredibiliter dicta sunt aut etiam aliter ab alio dicta, subtiliter reprehenduntur.

52 XV. C. F. Extrema tibi pars restat orationis, quae posita in perorando est, de qua sane velim audire.

C. P. Facilior est explicatio perorationis. Nam est divisa in duas partes, amplificationem et enumerationem. Augendi autem et hic est proprius locus in perorando, et in cursu ipso orationis declinationes ad amplificandum dantur confirmata re aliqua aut 53 reprehensa. Est igitur amplificatio gravior quaedam affirmatio quae motu animorum conciliet in dicendo fidem. Ea et verborum genere conficitur et rerum. Verba ponenda sunt quae vim habeant illustrandi nec ab usu sint abhorrentia, gravia, plena, sonantia, iuncta, facta, cognominata, non vulgata, superlata, in primisque translata ; nec in singulis verbis sed in continentibus soluta, quae dicuntur sine coniunctione, 54 ut plura videantur. Augent etiam relata verba, iterata, duplicata, et ea quae ascendunt gradatim ab humilioribus[1] ad superiora ; omninoque semper quasi naturalis et non explanata oratio, sed gravibus referta verbis, ad augendum accommodatior. Haec igitur in verbis, quibus actio vocis, vultus et gestus congruens et apta ad animos permovendos accommodanda est. Sed et in verbis et in actione causa erit tenenda et pro re agenda ; nam haec quia videntur

---

[1] *Schütz :* humilioribus verbis.

discrepant with statements made by someone else, the method is to meet them with a mere refutation.

52 XV. C. Jun. You still have the last part of the speech left, which consists in delivering a peroration, and I should certainly like to hear about that.

C. Sen. The peroration is an easier matter to explain. It falls into two divisions, amplification and re-capitulation. But enlargement not only has a special place here in the peroration, but also in the actual course of the speech opportunities occur, when something has been proved or refuted, for turning aside to 53 amplify. Amplification therefore is a sort of weightier affirmation, designed to win credence in the course of speaking by arousing emotion. This is accomplished both by the nature of the language used and by that of the facts adduced. Words must be employed that are powerfully illuminating without being inconsistent with ordinary usage, weighty, full, sonorous, com-pounds, coinages, synonyms, unhackneyed, exag-gerated, and above all used metaphorically. This as to single words ; in the sentences the words must be disconnected—*asyndeton* as it is called— so as to make 54 them seem more numerous. Enlargement is also effected by repetition, iteration, doubling of words, and a gradual rise from lower to higher terms ; and in general a natural style as it were, not smoothed down but filled out with weighty terms, is always more suitable for enlargement. These points then as to the language, to which must be adjusted a suitable management of the voice, countenance and gestures, designed to arouse the emotions. But both in the matter of language and in that of delivery careful consideration must be given to the case, and the line taken must be appropriate ; for language and delivery

(4) Perora-tion : (a) amplifica-tion, various methods of;

351

perabsurda cum graviora sunt quam causa fert,
diligenter quid quemque deceat iudicandum est.
55 XVI. Rerum amplificatio sumitur eisdem ex locis
omnibus quibus illa quae dicta sunt ad fidem ; maximeque definitiones valent conglobatae et consequentium frequentatio et contrariarum et dissimilium
et inter se pugnantium rerum conflictio, et causae,
et ea quae sunt de causis orta, maximeque similitudines et exempla ; fictae etiam personae, muta
denique loquantur ; omninoque ea sunt adhibenda, si
causa patitur, quae magna habentur, quorum est
56 duplex genus : alia enim magna natura videntur,
alia usu—natura, ut caelestia, ut divina, ut ea quorum
obscurae causae, ut in terris mundoque admirabilia
quae sunt, ex quibus similibusque, si attendas, ad
augendum permulta suppetunt ; usu, quae videntur
hominibus aut prodesse aut obesse vehementius,
quorum sunt genera ad amplificandum tria. Nam
aut caritate moventur homines, ut deorum, ut
patriae, ut parentum, aut amore, ut fratrum, ut
coniugum, ut liberorum, ut familiarium, aut honestate,
ut virtutum, maximeque earum quae ad communi-
onem hominum et liberalitatem valent. Ex eis et
cohortationes sumuntur ad ea retinenda, et in eos a
quibus ea violata sunt odia incitantur et miseratio
57 nascitur. XVII. [Proprius locus est augendi in his

seem quite ridiculous when they are weightier than what the case can carry, and consequently care must be taken to judge what suits each particular case. 55 XVI. Amplification of the facts is obtained from all the same topics from which were taken the statements made to secure credence ; and very effective are accumulations of definitions, recapitulation of consequences, juxtaposition of contrary, discrepant and contradictory statements, and statements of causes and their consequences, and especially analogies and instances ; and also imaginary persons and even dumb objects must speak ; and in general, if the case allows, one must introduce matters that are supposed to be of high importance, these being of two kinds : 56 some things seem important by nature, others in our experience of them ; examples of the former are heavenly and divine objects, things whose causes are obscure, the wonders of the earth and the sky, from which and from similar things, if you give your mind to them, plenty of topics for enlargement are forthcoming ; examples of the latter are things that appear to be exceptionally advantageous or detrimental to mankind, of which there are three kinds available for amplification—inasmuch as men are moved either by love, for instance love of the gods, love of country, love of parents ; or by affection, for instance for their brothers and wives and children and households ; or by moral considerations, for instance respect for the virtues and especially for those virtues that promote human fellow-feeling and generosity. These supply exhortations to hold fast to them, and also arouse hatred for those who violate them, and they engender 57 compassion. XVII. [A special topic for enlargement is supplied in the loss of these matters or the danger

rebus aut amissis aut amittendi periculo.][1] Nihil est
enim tam miserabile quam ex beato miser, et hoc
totum quidem moveat, si bona ex fortuna quis cadat,
et a quorum caritate divellatur, quae amittat aut
amiserit, in quibus malis sit futurusve sit exprimatur
breviter—cito enim arescit lacrima, praesertim in
alienis malis ; nec quidquam in amplificatione nimis
enucleandum est, minuta est enim omnis diligentia ;
hic autem locus grandia requirit.

58   Illud iam est iudicii, quo quaque in causa genere
utamur augendi. In illis enim causis quae ad delectationem exornantur ei loci tractandi sunt qui movere
possunt exspectationem, admirationem, voluptatem ;
in cohortationibus autem bonorum ac malorum
enumerationes et exempla valent plurimum. In
iudiciis accusatori fere quae ad iracundiam, reo
plerumque quae ad misericordiam pertinent ; nonnumquam tamen accusator misericordiam movere
debet et defensor iracundiam.

59   Enumeratio reliqua est, nonnumquam laudatori,
suasori non saepe, accusatori saepius quam reo
necessaria. Huius tempora duo sunt, si aut memoriae
diffidas eorum apud quos agas vel intervallo temporis
vel longitudine orationis, aut frequentatis firmamentis orationis et breviter expositis vim est habitura

[1] *Kayser.*

----

[a] This sentence appears to be an interpolation.

of losing them.[a]] For there is no object so pitiable as the unhappy man who once was happy, and indeed the whole topic may provide an emotional appeal, if a man falls from good fortune and an account is given both of the persons whose affection is reft from him and of the losses he is suffering or has suffered and the evils which encompass or are going to encompass him—a brief account, for a tear is quickly dried, especially when shed for the misfortunes of others; and in amplification no point must be too minutely elaborated, for all elaboration is petty, whereas this topic calls for treatment on the grand scale.

58 Next discretion must be used as to what kind of enlargement to employ in each case. For in the cases that are being handled in a decorative style, for the purpose of giving pleasure, we should employ the topics that are capable of arousing anticipation, wonder and delight; but in exhortations, enumerations and instances of things good and evil will have most effect. In trials, the prosecutor must chiefly employ topics that conduce to anger and the defendant for the most part those that conduce to compassion; although occasionally it is necessary for the prosecutor to excite compassion and the defendant anger.

59 There remains enumeration, which in panegyrics is required sometimes and in deliberative speeches seldom, while in judicial oratory it is more often necessary for the prosecutor than for the defendant. There are two occasions for its employment, when owing to the lapse of time or the length of your speech you distrust the memory of your audience, and when your case will be strengthened by recapitulating and briefly setting forth the main points of your argu-

(b) recapitulation.

355

60 causa maiorem. Et reo rarius utendum est, quod ponenda sunt contraria, quorum dissolutio in brevitate lucebit, aculei pungent. Sed erit in enumeratione vitandum ne ostentatio memoriae suscepta videatur esse puerilis. Id effugiet qui non omnia minima repetet sed brevia singula attingens pondera rerum ipsa comprehendet.

61 XVIII. C. F. Quoniam et de ipso oratore et de oratione dixisti, expone eum mihi nunc quem ex tribus extremum proposuisti, quaestionis locum.

C. P. Duo sunt, ut initio dixi, quaestionum genera, quorum alterum finitum temporibus et personis, causam appello, alterum infinitum nullis neque personis neque temporibus notatum propositum voco. Sed est consultatio quasi pars causae quaedam et controversiae : inest enim infinitum in definito, et 62 ad illud tamen referuntur omnia. Quam ob rem prius de proposito dicamus, cuius genera sunt duo—cognitionis alterum ; eius scientia est finis, ut verine sint sensus : alterum actionis, quod refertur ad efficiendum quid, ut si quaeratur quibus officiis amicitia colenda sit. Rursus superioris genera sunt tria : sit necne, quid sit, quale sit. Sit necne, ut

---

^a *Propositum* = θέσις, represented above by *consultatio*, § 4; ee notes there and at § 68.

^b *Consultatio*, a synonym for *propositum*, *cf.* § 4.

^c These correspond to our terms ' pure science ' and ' applied ' or ' practical ' science.

60 ment. Also the defendant should employ enumeration more rarely, because his business is to produce counter-arguments, the effectiveness of which as retorts will shine out and their sting have full effect in brevity. But care must be taken in enumeration to avoid the appearance of childishness involved in embarking on a parade of one's powers of memory. This danger will be escaped by one who does not repeat all his very small points, but while briefly touching on them one by one brings into focus the actual values of the facts.

61 XVIII. C. Jun. Well, you have spoken about both the speaker himself and the speech, so now expound to me the topic that you put forward last of the three, that of the question.

III. The question : (1) either a general thesis, theoretical or practical;

C. Sen. Questions, as I said at the beginning, are of two kinds ; one kind is limited by its referring to particular occasions and persons, and this I call a cause ; and the other is unlimited, that is, marked by no persons or occasions, and this I designate a thesis.[a] In a manner of speaking however a discussion [b] is a division of a cause and a dispute, for what is limited contains an element that is unlimited, and all matters contained in the former

62 have a reference nevertheless to the latter. Let us therefore first speak about the thesis. Of this there are two kinds [c] : one is a matter of learning—its object (a) is knowledge, for instance, whether the reports of the senses are true ; the other is a matter of action—which is directed to doing something, for instance if it is asked what are the services by which friendship has to be cultivated. Then again the former, knowledge, falls into three classes—(1) does a thing exist or does it not ? (2) what is it ? (3) what are its

ius in naturane sit an in more ; quid autem sit,
sitne ius id quod maiori parti sit utile ; quale autem
63 sit, iuste vivere sit necne utile. Actionis autem duo
sunt genera—unum ad persequendum aliquid aut
declinandum, ut quibus rebus adipisci gloriam possis
aut quomodo invidia vitetur, alterum quod ad aliquod commodum usumque refertur, ut quemadmodum sit respublica administranda aut quemadmodum
64 in paupertate vivendum. Rursus autem ex cognitionis consultatione, ubi sit necne sit aut fuerit
futurumve sit quaeritur, unum genus est quaestionis,
possitne aliquid effici ? ut cum quaeritur, ecquisnam
perfecte sapiens esse possit ? alterum, quemadmodum quidque fiat, ut quonam pacto virtus pariatur,
naturane an ratione an usu ? Cuius generis sunt
omnes in quibus, ut in obscuris naturalibusque
quaestionibus, causae rationesque rerum explicantur.
65 XIX. Illius autem generis in quo quid sit id de quo
agitur quaeritur duo sunt genera, quorum in altero
disputandum est, aliud an idem sit, ut pertinacia et
perseverantia, in altero autem descriptio generis
alicuius et quasi imago exprimenda est, ut qualis sit
66 avarus aut quid sit superbia. Tertio autem in genere,
in quo quale sit quaeritur, aut de honestate aut de
utilitate aut de aequitate dicendum est. De honestate sic, ut honestumne sit pro amico periculum aut

qualities ? The first is the question of reality—*e.g.* does justice exist in nature or is it merely a convention ? The second one of definition—*e.g.* is justice the advantage of the majority ? The third is a question of quality—*e.g.* is it advantageous to live justly or

63 is it not ? Action, on the other hand has two (*b*) kinds : one aims at obtaining or avoiding something, for instance, by what means can one win fame, or how can envy be avoided ? the other is directed to some advantage and utility, for instance, how should the state be administered, or how should one conduct

64 one's life in poverty ? And again, under the consideration of learning, (1) in cases where it is inquired whether a thing is (or was, or will be) or not, (*a*) one class of question is, ' Is a certain result possible ? ' for instance when it is asked whether it is possible for anybody to be perfectly wise ; and (*b*) the other class is, ' How is a particular result produced ? ' for instance ' In what manner is virtue engendered, by nature or by reason or by practice ? ' To this class (*b*) belong all the inquiries in which the causes and reasons of things are unfolded—as for instance in

65 metaphysics and natural science. XIX. Then (2) the class in which it is inquired what the thing under consideration is has two divisions : in one of these (*a*) the point to be debated is the question of difference or identity :—for instance is pertinacity the same thing as perseverance ?—while in the other (*b*) the description and so to say pattern of a particular class has to be expressed, *e.g.* what sort of person is a

66 miser, or what is pride ? Then (3) in the third class, in which the quality of an object is sought for, we have to discuss either honour or utility or equity. An instance of a question of honour is—is it honourable

invidiam subire ; de utilitate autem sic, ut sitne
utile in republica administranda versari ; de aequitate vero sic, ut sitne aequum amicos cognatis anteferre. Atque in hoc eodem genere in quo quale sit
quaeritur exoritur aliud quoddam disputandi genus.
Non enim simpliciter solum quaeritur quid honestum
sit, quid utile, quid aequum, sed etiam ex comparatione, quid honestius, quid utilius, quid aequius,
atque etiam, quid honestissimum, quid utilissimum,
quid aequissimum ; cuius generis illa sunt quae
praestantissima sit dignitas vitae.

Atque ea quidem quae dixi cognitionis sunt omnia.
67 Restant actionis, cuius alterum est praecipiendi genus
quod ad rationem officii pertinet, ut quemadmodum
colendi sint parentes, alterum autem ad sedandos
animos et oratione sanandis, ut in consolandis
maeroribus, ut in iracundia comprimenda aut in
timore tollendo aut in cupiditate minuenda. Cui
quidem generi contrarium est disputandi genus ad
eosdem illos animi motus, quod in amplificanda
oratione saepe faciendum est, vel gignendos vel
concitandos. Atque haec fere est partitio consultationum.
68 XX. C. F. Cognovi : sed quae ratio sit in his
inveniendi et disponendi requiro.

C. P. Quid ? tu aliamne censes et non eamdem
quae est exposita, ut ex eisdem locis ad fidem et
ad inveniendum ducantur omnia ? Collocandi autem

to undergo danger or unpopularity for the sake of a friend ? One of utility—does it pay to go in for politics ? One of equity—is it equitable to place one's friends before one's relations ? And in this same class containing the inquiry into the quality of a thing there arises another kind of debate. For the question asked is not only the simple inquiry, what is honourable, what is useful, what is equitable, but it also involves comparison—what is *more* honourable or useful or equitable, and also what is *most* honourable or useful or equitable—a class of consideration which comprises the things that constitute the supreme value of life.

67 The matters I have specified are all matters of learning. There remain (*b*) matters of action. Of these one division is that of instruction related to the theory of duty, for instance the proper mode of paying respect to parents, and the other division is concerned with the healing influence of oratory in calming the minds of men, for instance in offering consolation for sorrow or controlling anger or assuaging fear or diminishing desire. And the opposite of this division is the class of argument aimed at either engendering or stimulating those same emotions, which it is frequently proper to do in amplifying a speech. These then virtually are the departments into which discussions are divided.

68 XX. C. JUN. I understand ; but I want to know what is the method of discovery and arrangement that is to be followed in these departments.

C. SEN. Well, surely you agree that it is identical with the method that has been set out, to draw all the materials for convincing and discovering arguments from the same topics ? And as for arrange-

quae est exposita in aliis ratio, eadem huc trans-
fertur.

C. F. Cognita igitur omni distributione proposi-
tarum consultationum, causarum genera restant.

69   C. P. Admodum ; et earum quidem forma duplex
est, quarum altera delectationem sectatur audien-
tium,[1] alterius ut obtineat, probet et efficiat[2] quod
agit, omnis est suscepta contentio. Itaque illud
superius exornatio dicitur, quod cum latum genus
esse potest saneque varium, unum ex eo delegimus,
quod ad laudandos claros viros suscipimus et ad
improbos vituperandos. Genus enim nullum est
orationis quod aut uberius ad dicendum aut utilius
civitatibus esse possit aut in quo magis orator in
cognitione virtutum vitiorumque versetur. Reliquum autem genus causarum aut in provisione
posteri temporis aut in praeteriti disceptatione
versatur, quorum alterum deliberationis est, alterum

70 iudicii. Ex qua partitione tria genera causarum
exstiterunt, unum quod a meliori parte laudationis
est appellatum, deliberationis alterum, tertium
iudiciorum. Quam ob rem de primo primum, si placet,
disputemus.

C. F. Mihi vero placet.

XXI. C. P. Ac laudandi vituperandique rationes,
quae non ad bene dicendum solum sed etiam ad
honeste vivendum valent, exponam breviter, atque
a principiis exordiar et laudandi et vituperandi.

71   Omnia enim sunt profecto laudanda quae coniuncta cum virtute sunt, et quae cum vitiis, vitu-
peranda. Quam ob rem finis alterius est honestas,

---

[1] *Schol. :* aurium.   [2] [probet et efficiat] *? Rackham.*

[a] The two terms used to render θέσις, see § 61 notes *a* and
b, are here in the Latin combined in one phrase.

ment, the same method that has been set out in the other divisions must be transferred to this one.

C. Jun. Now therefore that we know the whole of the scheme of theses or considerations,[a] there remains the classification of causes. or (2) a particular subject:

69 C. Sen. Exactly. And causes have a double form : one aims at giving pleasure to the audience, the other aims solely at maintaining, proving and establishing its case. Consequently the former is called embellishment ; this can be a wide department and have very varied forms, so we have chosen one form of it, the form that we adopt for panegyrics on distinguished men and for censuring the wicked. For there is no class of oratory capable of producing more copious rhetoric or of doing more service to the state, nor any in which the speaker is more occupied in recognizing the virtues and vices. The remaining class of cases is occupied either in forecasting the future or in discussing the past—one of which subjects is a matter of deliberation and the other a matter

70 of judgement. This classification has given us three kinds of cases, one designated from its more important section laudatory oratory, the second deliberative oratory and the third judicial oratory. Consequently, if you are agreeable, let us discuss the first kind first.

C. Jun. I am quite agreeable.

XXI. C. Sen. I will give a brief account of the principles of awarding praise and blame, which have a value not only for good oratory but also for right conduct ; and I will begin with the first principles both of laudation and of vituperation. either (i.) a panegyric speech:

71 Clearly everything associated with virtue deserves praise and everything associated with vice deserves blame ; consequently praise is aimed at moral excel- laudable qualities and the reverse;

CICERO

alterius turpitudo. Conficitur autem genus hoc
dictionis narrandis exponendisque factis sine ullis
argumentationibus, ad animi motus leniter trac-
tandos magis quam ad fidem faciendam aut confir-
mandam accommodate. Non enim dubia firmantur
sed ea quae certa aut pro certis posita sunt augen-
tur. Quam ob rem ex eis quae ante dicta sunt et
72 narrandi et augendi praecepta repetentur. Et quoniam in his causis omnis ratio fere ad voluptatem
auditoris et ad delectationem refertur, utendum erit
eis in oratione singulorum verborum insignibus quae
habent plurimum suavitatis : id est ut factis verbis
aut vetustis aut translatis frequenter utamur, et in
ipsa constructione verborum ut paria paribus et
similia similibus saepe referantur, ut contraria, ut geminata, ut circumscripta numerose, non ad similitudinem versuum, sed ad explendum aurium sensum,
73 apto quodam quasi verborum modo. Adhibenda-
que frequentius etiam illa ornamenta rerum sunt,
sive quae admirabilia et nec opinata, sive significata
monstris, prodigiis, oraculis, sive quae videbuntur
ei de quo agimus accidisse divina atque fatalia.
Omnis enim exspectatio eius qui audit et admiratio
et improvisi exitus habent aliquam in audiendo
74 voluptatem. XXII. Sed quoniam tribus in generibus
bona malave versantur, externis, corporis, animi,
prima sunt externa, quae ducuntur a genere : quo
breviter modiceque laudato aut si erit infame praeter-

364

lence and blame at moral baseness. But this kind of discourse consists in narrating and exhibiting past actions, without employing any argument, and its style is adapted to gently influencing the emotions rather than to achieving conviction and proof. For it does not establish propositions that are doubtful but amplifies statements that are certain, or advanced as being certain. Consequently what has been said already will supply rules both for narration and for amplification. And because virtually the whole method in these causes is directed to giving the audience pleasure and entertainment, in the style employment must be made of those brilliant touches in particular words which are such an extremely agreeable feature,—that means that we must frequently employ new coinages or archaisms or metaphors—, and in the actual construction of the words that we must use frequent repetitions of parallels and similes and contraries and doublets and rhythmic periods not designed to resemble verse but to satisfy the ear with what may be called a suitable verbal harmony. And an even more frequent use must be made of decorative details such as surprising or unexpected events or things foreshadowed by portents and prodigies and by oracles, or what will appear to be occurrences sent by heaven or by fate to the person of whom we shall be speaking. For any feeling of anticipation aroused in the hearer and surprise and unexpected issues have an element of pleasure in a recital. XXII. But as things good or evil occupy three classes, external goods, goods of the body and goods of the mind, the class to take first is that of external goods, which are headed by the man's family : this must be praised briefly and with

misso, si humile, vel praeterito vel ad augendam
eius quem laudes gloriam tracto ; deinceps si res
patietur de fortunis erit et facultatibus dicendum,
postea de corporis bonis, in quibus quidem quae
virtutem maxime significat facillime forma laudatur.
75 Deinde est ad facta veniendum, quorum collocatio
triplex est : aut enim temporum servandus est ordo
aut in primis recentissimum quodque dicendum aut
multa et varia facta in propria virtutum genera sunt
dirigenda.

Sed hic locus virtutum atque vitiorum latissime
patens ex multis et variis disputationibus nunc in
76 quamdam angustam et brevem concludetur. Est
igitur vis virtutis duplex ; aut enim scientia cernitur
virtus, aut actione. Nam quae prudentia, quae
calliditas, quaeque gravissimo nomine sapientia
appellatur, haec scientia pollet una ; quae vero
moderandis cupiditatibus regendisque animi motibus
laudatur, eius est munus in agendo : cui tempe-
rantiae nomen est. Atque illa prudentia in suis
rebus domestica, in publicis civilis appellari solet.
77 Temperantia autem in suas itidem res et in communes distributa est, duobusque modis in rebus
commodis discernitur, et ea quae absunt non expe-
tendo et ab eis quae in potestate sunt abstinendo.
In rebus autem incommodis est itidem duplex ;
nam quae venientibus malis obstat fortitudo, quae

moderation, or, if it is disgraceful, omitted, or if of low station, either passed over or so treated as to increase the glory of the person you are praising; next, if the facts permit, you must speak of his fortune and estate; and then of his personal endowments, among which it is easiest to praise a handsome appearance, as providing a very great indication of

75 virtue. Next one must come to the man's achievements, as to which there are three possible methods of arrangement: either one must keep their chronological order, or speak of the most recent first, or classify a number of different actions under the virtues to which they belong.

But as this topic of virtues and vices is of very wide virtues and extent, on this occasion it shall be summarized into a vices; single limited and brief discourse in place of a number

76 of different ones. Virtue has a twofold meaning, for it is exhibited either in knowledge or in conduct. The virtue that is designated prudence and intelligence and the most impressive name of all, wisdom, exercises its influence by knowledge alone; but the virtue applauded in moderating the desires and controlling the emotions has its function in action, and the name of this virtue is temperance. The virtue of prudence when displayed in a man's private affairs is usually termed personal sagacity and when in public

77 affairs political wisdom. Similarly temperance is directed both to one's own affairs and those of the community, and is manifested in two ways in respect of profitable things—in not seeking those which one has not got and in refraining from using those which are in one's power. In respect of unprofitable things temperance is similarly twofold: that which withstands coming evils is named fortitude, and that which

quod iam adest tolerat et perfert patientia nominatur.
Quae autem haec uno genere complectitur, magnitudo animi dicitur : cuius est liberalitas in usu
pecuniae, simulque altitudo animi in capiendis
incommodis et maxime iniuriis, et omne quod est
eius generis, grave, sedatum [non turbulentum].[1]

78 In communione autem quae posita pars est, iustitia
dicitur, eaque erga deos religio, erga parentes pietas,
vulgo autem bonitas, creditis in rebus fides, in
moderatione animadvertendi lenitas, amicitia in
benevolentia nominatur.

XXIII. Atque hae quidem virtutes cernuntur in
agendo. Sunt autem aliae quasi ministrae comi-
tesque sapientiae, quarum altera quae sint in disputando vera atque falsa quibusque positis quid
sequatur distinguit et iudicat, quae virtus omnis in
ratione scientiaque disputandi sita est ; altera autem

79 oratoria. Nihil enim est aliud eloquentia nisi
copiose loquens sapientia, quae ex eodem hausta
genere quo illa quae in disputando est, uberior est
atque latior et ad motus animorum vulgique sensus
accommodatior. Custos vero virtutum omnium
dedecus fugiens laudemque maxime consequens
verecundia est. Atque hi sunt fere quasi quidam[2]
habitus animi sic affecti et constituti ut sint singuli
inter se proprio virtutis genere distincti : a quibus
ut quaeque res gesta est, ita sit honesta necesse est
summeque laudabilis.

80 Sunt autem alii quidam animi habitus ad virtutem quasi praeculti et praeparati rectis studiis et

---

[1] [non turbulentum] *vel* [grave, sedatum] *edd.*
[2] quidam *edd. :* quidam ficti *aut* perfecti.

steadfastly endures present evil patience. But the virtue that embraces these qualities under a single head is called greatness of mind ; this includes liberality in the use of money and also loftiness of mind in accepting unprofitable things and especially wrongs, and every quality of this kind, dignified and

78 calm. The part of virtue displayed in society is called justice, and that manifested towards the gods religion, towards parents piety, or in general goodness, in matters of trust good faith, in moderating punishment mercy, in benevolence friendliness.

XXIII. These virtues so far are displayed in action. But there are others which are so to speak the handmaidens and companions of wisdom ; of these one is displayed in debate, distinguishing truth from falsehood and judging the logical consequence of given premisses—this virtue resides entirely in the method and science of debating ; while the sphere of the

79 other is oratory. For eloquence is nothing else but wisdom delivering copious utterance ; and this, while derived from the same class as the virtue above that operates in debate, is more abundant and wider and more closely adapted to the emotions and to the feelings of the common herd. But the guardian of all the virtues, which shuns disgrace and attains praise in the greatest degree, is modesty. These then practically are as it were habits of mind that are so characterized and constituted as to be mutually distinct from each other and each in a class of virtue belonging to itself ; and in proportion as a particular action is directed by them, so it must of necessity be morally good and supremely praiseworthy.

80 But there are certain other states of mind trained and prepared for virtue by proper studies and sciences,

artibus, ut in suis rebus studia litterarum, ut numerorum ac sonorum, ut mensurae, ut siderum, ut
equorum, ut venandi, ut armorum, in communibus
propensiora studia in aliquo genere virtutis praecipue
colendo aut divinis rebus deserviendo aut parentibus,
amicis, hospitibus praecipue atque insigniter dili-
81 gendis.   Atque haec quidem virtutum ; vitiorum
autem sunt genera contraria. Cernenda autem sunt
diligenter, ne fallant ea nos vitia, quae virtutem
videntur imitari.   Nam et prudentiam malitia et
temperantiam immanitas in voluptatibus asper-
nandis et magnitudinem animi superbia in nimis[1]
extollendis et despicientia in contemnendis honoribus
et liberalitatem effusio et fortitudinem audacia
imitatur et patientiam duritia immanis et iustitiam
acerbitas et religionem superstitio et lenitatem
mollitia animi et verecundiam timiditas et illam disputandi prudentiam concertatio captatioque verborum, et hanc oratoriam vim inanis quaedam proflu-
entia loquendi.   Studiis autem bonis similia videntur
82 ea quae sunt in eodem genere nimia.   Quam ob
rem omnis vis laudandi vituperandique ex his sumetur virtutum vitiorumque partibus ; sed in toto quasi
contextu orationis haec erunt illustranda maxime,
quemadmodum quisque generatus, quemadmodum
educatus, quemadmodum institutus moratusque
fuerit, et si quid cui magnum aut incredibile acciderit,
maximeque si id divinitus accidisse potuerit videri ;
tum quod quisque senserit, dixerit, gesserit ad ea
quae proposita sunt virtutum genera accommoda-
buntur, ex illisque eisdem inveniendi locis causae

[1] *Orelli :* animis.

as for instance among personal matters the study of literature, rhythms and music, mensuration and astronomy, riding and hunting and fencing ; and interests more important in the life of the community consisting in the special cultivation of some particular kind of virtue, or devotion to the service of religion, or outstanding and exceptional filial affection or friend-
81 ship or hospitality. These are the classes of virtues. Those of the vices are their opposites ; but careful attention must be given to them to save ourselves from being deceived by those vices which seem to imitate virtue. For cunning masquerades as prudence, boorish contempt for pleasure as temperance, pride in over-valuing honours and superciliousness in looking down on them as high-mindedness, profusion as liberality, audacity as bravery, savage hardness as endurance, harshness as justice, superstition as religion, softness as gentleness, timidity as modesty, verbal controversy and logic-chopping on the one hand as skilfulness in argument, and an empty flux of talk on the other as oratorical power. And again valuable studies are counterfeited by excesses in the
82 same department. Consequently all the resources of panegyric and reprehension will be adopted from these divisions of the virtues and vices ; but in the whole fabric of the speech the greatest attention is to be focussed on the quality of a person's breeding and upbringing and education and character ; and on any important or startling occurrence that a man has encountered, especially if this can appear to be due to the intervention of providence ; and then each individual's opinions and utterances and actions will be classified under the scheme of the virtues that has been propounded. and these same topics of

rerum et eventus et consequentia requirentur.
Neque vero mors eorum quorum vita laudabitur
silentio praeteriri debebit, si modo quid erit anim-
advertendum aut in ipso genere mortis aut in eis
rebus quae post mortem erunt consecutae.

83 XXIV. C. F. Accepi ista, didicique breviter non
solum quemadmodum laudarem alterum sed etiam
quemadmodum eniterer ut possem ipse iure laudari.
Videamus igitur deinceps in sententia dicenda quam
viam et quae praecepta teneamus.

C. P. Est igitur in deliberando finis utilitas, ad
quem omnia ita referuntur in consilio dando sententiaque dicenda ut illa prima sint suasori aut
dissuasori videnda, quid aut possit fieri aut non possit
et quid aut necesse sit aut non necesse. Nam et
si quid effici non potest, deliberatio tollitur quamvis
utile sit, et si quid necesse est (necesse autem id est
sine quo salvi liberive esse non possumus), id est
reliquis et honestatibus in civili ratione et commodis
84 anteponendum. Cum autem quaeritur quid fieri
possit, videndum etiam est quam facile possit; nam
quae perdifficilia sunt perinde habenda saepe sunt
ac si effici non possint. Et cum de necessitate
attendemus, etsi aliquid non necessarium videbitur,
videndum tamen erit quam sit magnum; quod enim

research will be drawn on to supply the causes and results and consequences of things. Nor yet will it be proper to pass over in silence the death of those persons whose life is going to be praised, in case of there being something noticeable either in the nature of their death itself or in the events that follow after death.

83   XXIV. C. Jun. You have given me brief instructions not merely as to how to praise another but also as to how to endeavour to be able to be deservedly praised myself. Let us then next see what course and what rules we are to follow in delivering an opinion.

or (ii.) a speech in debate: advice as to courses of action;

C. Sen. Well, the purpose in deliberating is to obtain some advantage, to which the whole procedure in giving advice and pronouncing an opinion is directed in such a manner, that the primary considerations to be kept in view by the giver of advice for or against a certain course are what action is or is not possible and what course is necessary or not necessary. For if a thing is unattainable, debate about it is cancelled, however advantageous it may be, and also if a thing is necessary—and a necessity is something that is an indispensable condition of our security or freedom—it must take precedence in public policy of all the remaining considerations, 84 alike of honour and of profit. But in process of inquiring what can be achieved we must also consider how easily it can be achieved ; for things that are of extreme difficulty ought in many cases to be deemed entirely impracticable. And when we are considering the question of necessity, even if something appears to be not necessary, we shall nevertheless have to consider how important it is ; for a thing that

85 permagnum est pro necessario saepe habetur. Itaque cum constet hoc genus causarum ex suasione et dissuasione, suasori proponitur simplex ratio, si et utile est et fieri potest, fiat, dissuasori duplex, una, si non utile est, ne fiat, altera, si fieri non potest, ne suscipiatur. Sic suasori utrumque docendum est, 86 dissuasori alterum infirmare sat est. Quare quoniam in his versatur omne consilium duobus, de utilitate ante dicamus, quae in discernendis bonis malisque versatur. Bonorum autem partim necessaria sunt, ut vita, pudicitia, libertas, partim non necessaria, ut liberi, coniuges, germani, parentes[1] : quorum alia sunt per se expetenda, ut ea quae sita sunt in officiis atque virtutibus, alia quod aliquid commodi efficiunt, 87 ut opes et copiae. Eorum autem quae propter se expetuntur partim honestate ipsa, partim commoditate aliqua expetuntur : honestate ea quae proficiscuntur ab eis virtutibus de quibus paullo ante est dictum, quae sunt laudabilia ipsa per se : commoditate autem aliqua quae sunt in corporis aut in fortunae bonis expetenda, quorum alia sunt quasi cum honestate coniuncta, ut honos, ut gloria, alia diversa, ut vires, forma, valetudo, nobilitas, divitiae, 88 clientelae. XXV. Est etiam quaedam quasi materies

---

[1] ut liberi . . . parentes *hic Orelli : ante* partim non necessaria *codd. : an secludendum ? Rackham.*

---

[a] The MSS. place 'for instance children . . . parents' before 'and some not necessary '; perhaps the words are an interpolation.

is of extremely great moment is often deemed to be
85 virtually necessary. Consequently as this class of
cases consists in advising or dissuading, one who
advises a certain course has available only a single line
of advice—if the thing is both advantageous and
feasible, do it ; whereas the dissuader has available
a double line—one, if the thing is not advantageous,
do not do it, the other, if it is impossible, do not
attempt it. Thus the adviser of a course has to prove
both the conditions, whereas it is enough for the dis-
86 suader to refute either one of them. Consequently
inasmuch as all deliberation is occupied with these
two considerations, let us first discuss that of advantage, which is concerned with distinguishing between
good things and bad things. Good things are some
of them necessary, for instance life, self-respect,
freedom, and some not necessary, for instance
children, wives, relations, parents.[a] The latter fall
into two classes : one, things desirable for their own
sake, as the objects in the sphere of the duties and the
virtues, the other, things such as wealth and resources,
87 that are means to something of value. But of things
desired for their own sake some are desired on
account of their intrinsic moral value and others
on account of some advantage they confer : desired
on account of their moral value are the objects discussed a little time before, which are praiseworthy
for themselves ; desired on account of some advantage
are such among bodily goods and goods of fortune as
are desirable. Of these some are in a manner combined with a certain moral value, for example honour,
glory ; while others are in a different class, for instance
strength, beauty, health, fame, wealth, dependents.
88 XXV. Moral goodness also has so to speak a subject-

subiecta honestati, quae maxime spectatur in
amicitiis. Amicitiae autem caritate et amore cernuntur ; nam cum deorum, tum parentum patriaeque
cultus eorumque hominum qui aut sapientia aut
opibus excellunt ad caritatem referri solet, coniuges
autem et liberi et fratres et alii quos usus familiari-
tasque coniunxit, quamquam etiam caritate ipsa,
tamen amore maxime continentur. In his igitur
rebus cum bona sint, facile est intellectu quae sint
89 contraria. Quodsi semper optima tenere possemus,
haud sane, quoniam quidem ea perspicua sunt, consilio multum egeremus. Sed quia temporibus, quae
vim habent maximam, persaepe evenit ut utilitas cum
honestate certet, earumque rerum contentio plerumque deliberationes efficit ne aut opportuna propter
dignitatem aut honesta propter utilitatem relin-
quantur, ad hanc difficultatem explicandam praecepta
90 referamus. Et quoniam non ad veritatem solum sed
etiam ad opiniones eorum qui audiunt accommodanda est oratio, hoc primum intellegamus, hominum
duo esse genera, alterum indoctum et agreste,
quod anteferat semper utilitatem honestati, alterum
humanum et politum, quod rebus omnibus dignitatem anteponat. Itaque huic generi laus, honor,
gloria, fides, iustitia, omnisque virtus, illi autem
alteri quaestus emolumentum fructusque proponitur.
Atque etiam voluptas, quae maxime est inimica
virtuti bonique naturam fallaciter imitando adulterat,

matter which is particularly visible in friendships. Friendships are manifested by esteem and by affection. Respect for the gods and for parents and country and for those persons who are eminent for wisdom or for wealth is customarily classed under esteem, whereas wives and children and brothers and other persons attached to us by association and familiarity are bound to us partly it is true by actual esteem but chiefly by affection. As then there are good things in these departments, it is easy to understand what 89 things are the opposite of good. If indeed it were in our power to possess the greatest goods always, it is quite certain that we should not be much in need of advice, inasmuch as they are obvious. But because circumstances, which are a very important factor, very often bring it about that utility is at variance with moral value, and as the opposition between these two factors usually produces debate, aimed at avoiding the sacrifice of advantages for the sake of what is worthy or of moral goodness for the sake of utility, let us record some rules for the solution of this 90 problem. And because it is necessary to adapt one's discourse to conform not only with the truth but also with the opinions of one's hearers, the first point that we must grasp is that mankind falls into two classes, one uninstructed and uncultivated, which always prefers utility to moral value, and other humane and cultivated, which places true worth above all other things. Consequently the latter class of people give the first place to distinction, honour, glory, good faith, justice and all the forms of virtue, while the former class put the profits and emoluments of gain first. And also pleasure, which is the greatest enemy of virtue and adulterates the true essence of the good

quam immanissimus quisque acerrime sequitur,
neque solum honestis rebus sed etiam necessariis
anteponit, in suadendo, cum ei generi hominum
consilium des, saepe sane laudanda est.

91 XXVI. Et illud videndum, quanto magis homines
mala fugiant quam sequantur bona. Nam neque
honesta tam expetunt quam devitant turpia ; quis
enim honorem, quis gloriam, quis laudem, quis ullum
decus tam umquam expetat quam ignominiam,
infamiam, contumeliam, dedecus fugiat ? quarum
rerum dolor gravis est testis genus hominum ad
honestatem natum, malo cultu pravisque opinionibus
corruptum. Quare in cohortando atque suadendo
propositum quidem nobis erit illud, ut doceamus
qua via[1] bona consequi malaque vitare possimus :
92 sed apud homines bene institutos plurimum de laude
et de honestate dicemus, maximeque ea virtutum
genera tractabimus quae in communi hominum
utilitate tuenda augendaque versantur. Sin apud
indoctos imperitosque dicemus, fructus, emolumenta,
voluptates vitationesque dolorum proferantur ; ad-
dantur etiam contumeliae atque ignominiae ; nemo
enim est tam agrestis quem non, si ipsa minus
honestas, contumelia tamen et dedecus magnopere
93 moveat. Quare quod ad utilitatem spectat ex eis
quae dicta sunt reperietur : quod autem, possit

---

[1] *Rackham :* vi.

by deceptive imitations, and which is most eagerly pursued by all the most uncivilized people, who place it in front of not only things of moral value but also necessaries, it will quite often have to receive your praise in advisory speeches, when you are giving counsel to persons of that class.

91   XXVI. And it must be noticed how much more energetically people fly from what is evil than they pursue what is good. Neither indeed do they seek after what is honourable so much as they try to avoid what is disgraceful. Who would seek to gain honour and glory and praise and any distinction so keenly as he flees from ignominy and discredit and contumely and disgrace ? The pain that these inflict gives weighty evidence that the human race was designed by nature for what is honourable, although it has been corrupted by bad education and erroneous opinions. Consequently, in exhorting and advising, although our aim will be to teach by what method it is possible for us to attain the good and avoid the 92 evil, nevertheless in addressing well educated people we shall speak most of glory and honour, and shall give our chief attention to the kinds of virtue that are exercised in protecting and increasing the common advantage of mankind. Whereas if we are speaking in the presence of the unlearned and ignorant, it is profits and rewards, pleasures and modes of avoiding pain that must be put forward ; and references to contumely and disgrace must also be added, for there is nobody so boorish that he is not deeply sensitive to contumely and disgrace, even though he be less 93 influenced by actual considerations of honour. Consequently what has been said will supply information as to considerations of utility, while practicability,

motives of action;

379

effici necne,[1] in quo etiam quam facile possit quamque expediat quaeri solet, maxime ex causis eis quae
quamque rem efficiant est videndum. Causarum
autem genera sunt plura ; nam sunt aliae quae ipsae
conficiunt, aliae quae vim aliquam ad conficiendum
afferunt. Itaque illae superiores conficientes vocentur, hae reliquae ponantur in eo genere ut sine his
94 confici non possit. Conficiens autem causa alia est
absoluta et perfecta per se, alia aliquid adiuvans et
efficiendi socia quaedam : cuius generis vis varia est,
et saepe aut maior aut minor, ut et illa quae maximam vim habet sola saepe causa dicatur. Sunt
autem aliae causae quae aut propter principium aut
propter exitum conficientes vocantur. Cum autem
quaeritur quid sit optimum factu, aut utilitas aut
spes efficiendi ad assentiendum impellit animos.

95 XXVII. Et quoniam de utilitate iam diximus, de
efficiendi ratione dicamus. Quo toto in[2] genere
quibuscum et contra quos et quo tempore et quo
loco quibus facultatibus armorum, pecuniae, socio-
rum, earumve rerum quae ad quamque rem efficien-
dam pertinent possimus uti requirendum est. Neque
solum ea sunt quae nobis suppetunt sed etiam illa
quae adversantur videnda ; et si ex contentione pro-
cliviora erunt nostra, non solum effici posse quae
suademus erit persuadendum sed curandum etiam
ut illa facilia, proclivia, iucunda videantur. Dis-
suadentibus autem aut utilitas labefactanda est aut

---

[1] *Ernesti :* possit necne possit.   [2] *v.l. om.* in.

with which are also usually included the questions of facility and of expediency, is chiefly to be looked at in the light of the causes productive of the various objects in view. Causes are of several kinds, some producing a result intrinsically and others contributing to its production. Let us call the former efficient causes, and class the latter as indispens-94 able accessory causes. An efficient cause is either absolute and complete in itself or auxiliary and associated in producing an effect; a force of the latter kind varies and is sometimes more and sometimes less effective, with the further consequence that the term ' cause ' often denotes only the most powerful cause. There are other causes which are called efficient either as being initiatory or as ultimate. When the question is raised what is the best thing to do, the motive causing acceptance of the solution is either expediency or hope of effective success.

95 XXVII. And as we have spoken about expediency already, let us discuss the meaning of efficiency. Under this general head we have to discover with whom and against whom and when and where it is in our power to employ what resources of arms and money and allies or of the things contributory to our effecting a particular result. And we must not only envisage the resources that we possess but the things that operate against us; and if on comparison the balance is on our side, we must not only persuade our audience that the course we advise is feasible but also take pains to make it appear easy and practicable and agreeable. On the other hand when arguing against a policy we have either to demolish the assertion of its expediency or to put forward the difficulties

efficiendi difficultates efferendae, neque aliis ex prae-
96 ceptis sed eisdem ex suasionis locis.   Uterque vero
ad augendum habeat exemplorum aut recentium
quo notiora sint aut veterum quo plus auctoritatis
habeant, copiam; maximeque sit in hoc genere
meditatus, ut possit vel utilia ac necessaria saepe
honestis vel haec illis anteferre.   Ad commovendos
autem animos maxime proficient, si incitandi erunt,
huiusmodi sententiae quae aut ad explendas cupiditates aut ad odium satiandum aut ad ulciscendas
iniurias pertinebunt;   sin autem reprimendi, de
incerto statu fortunae dubiisque eventis rerum
futurarum et retinendis suis fortunis si erunt
secundae, sin autem adversae, de periculo com-
monendi.   Atque hi quidem sunt perorationis loci.
97 Principia autem in sententiis dicendis brevia esse
debent;   non enim supplex ut ad iudicem venit
orator sed hortator atque auctor.   Quare proponere
qua mente dicat, quid velit, quibus de rebus dicturus
sit debet, hortarique ad se breviter dicentem audiendum.   Tota autem oratio simplex et gravis et sententiis debet ornatior esse quam verbis.

98   XXVIII. C. F. Cognovi iam laudationis et suasionis

in the way of carrying it out, and we must base our
arguments not on other principles but on the same
topics as those that have been employed in speaking
96 in favour of the proposal. But both proposer and
opposer must have a supply of precedents for the
purpose of amplification—either recent precedents,
so as to be more in general knowledge, or old ones so
as to carry more authority ; and the speaker must
have had a great deal of practice in this department,
so that he may be able very often to place considerations of expediency and necessity in front of
those of morality, or *vice versa.* If the audience
requires stimulating, the most effective kind of considerations for rousing them will be those concerned
with satisfying their desires or gratifying their hatred
or avenging their wrongs ; but if on the other hand
it is necessary to repress their impulses, they must be
warned as to the instability of fortune and the doubtful issues of the future, and if they are enjoying good
fortune, as to keeping it, or if bad, as to the danger
they are in. These then are the topics for the perora-
97 tion. The exordium in a statement of opinion ought
to be brief ; for the speaker does not come as a
suppliant, as he would in a court of law, but as giving
an exhortation and making a proposal. Consequently
he ought to set forth what he has in mind in speaking and what is his intention and what subjects
he is going to deal with, and to exhort his audience
to give his brief remarks a hearing. Moreover
the whole of the speech must be simple and
weighty, and more elaborate in its contents than in
its language.

98   XXVIII. C. Jun. Now I know the topics belonging
to a panegyric and to a speech in debate. I now look
to a panegyric and to a speech in debate. I now look *or* (iii.) a
speech in
an action

383 at law:

locos : nunc quae iudiciis accommodata sint exspecto, idque nobis genus restare unum puto.

C. P. Recte intellegis. Atque eius quidem generis
finis est aequitas, quae non simpliciter spectatur sed
ex comparatione nonnumquam, ut cum de verissimo
accusatore disputatur aut cum hereditatis sine lege
aut sine testamento petitur possessio, in quibus
causis quid aequius aequissimumve sit quaeritur ;
quas ad causas facultas petitur argumentationum ex
99 eis de quibus mox dicetur aequitatis locis. Atque
etiam ante iudicium de constituendo ipso iudicio
solet esse contentio, cum aut sitne actio illi qui agit
aut iamne sit aut num iam esse desierit aut illane
lege hisne verbis sit actio quaeritur. Quae etiamsi
ante quam res in iudicium venit aut concertata aut
diiudicata aut confecta non[1] sunt, tamen in ipsis
iudiciis permagnum saepe habent pondus cum ita
dicitur : plus petisti ; sero petisti ; non fuit tua
petitio ; non a me, non hac lege, non his verbis,
100 non hoc iudicio. Quarum causarum genus est
positum in iure civili quod est in privatarum[2] rerum
lege aut more positum ; cuius scientia neglecta ab
oratoribus plerisque nobis ad dicendum necessaria

---

[1] [non] *Lambinus.*
[2] *Kayser :* privatarum ac publicarum.

to you for the arguments appropriate to a court of law ; that, I believe, is the only kind of oratory that we still have left.

C. SEN. You are quite right. And the subject at which a speech of this kind aims is equity, which occasionally is envisaged not in simple form but by means of a comparison, as for example when the entire reliability of the prosecutor is enlarged upon, or when possession of an estate is sued for without the support of law or in the absence of a will ; in these cases, the question is raised as to what is more, or most, equitable ; and for these cases a ready supply of lines of argument is afforded by the topics deal-99 ing with equity that will soon be discussed. And even before the trial begins there is usually a dispute about the institution of the trial itself, when the question is raised whether the party taking proceedings has the right to do so, or has the right to do so yet, or has now ceased to have it, or whether action is open to him under the law cited, or in the terms employed. And even if these questions have not been raised or decided or settled before the case comes into court, nevertheless they often carry very great weight during the actual proceedings, when the statement is advanced, ' You have sued for an excessive amount,' or ' You have taken proceedings too late,' or ' The suit was not one for you to institute,' or ' I was not the party to be sued,' or ' not under this law,' or ' not in this form of words,' 100 or ' not before this court.' This class of cases comes under the principles of civil law embodied in some enactment or precedent governing private affairs ; and a knowledge of these principles although neglected by most pleaders appears to us to be indis-

385

videtur. Quare de constituendis actionibus, de[1] accipiendis subeundisque iudiciis, de excipienda iniquitate actionis, de comparanda aequitate, quod ea fere generis eius sunt ut quamquam in ipsum iudicium saepe delabantur tamen ante iudicium tractanda videantur, paullulum ea separo a iudiciis tempore magis agendi quam dissimilitudine generis. Nam omnia quae de iure civili aut de aequo et bono disceptantur cadunt in eam formam in qua quale quid sit ambigitur, de qua dicturi sumus ; quae in aequitate et iure maxime consistit.

101　　XXIX. In omnibus igitur causis tres sunt gradus ex quibus unus aliquis capiendus est, si plures non queas, ad resistendum. Nam aut ita constituendum[2] est ut id quod obiicitur factum neges, aut illud quod factum fateare neges eam vim habere atque id esse quod adversarius criminetur, aut si neque de facto neque de facti appellatione ambigi potest, id quod arguere neges tale esse quale ille dicat et rectum

102 esse quod feceris concedendumve defendas. Ita primus ille status et quasi conflictio cum adversario coniectura quadam, secundus autem definitione atque descriptione aut informatione verbi, tertius aequi et veri et recti et humani ad ignoscendum disputatione tractandus est. Et quoniam semper is qui defendit non solum resistat oportet aliquo statu

<hr />

[1] de *add. Rackham.*
[2] *Rackham :* consistendum.

pensable for a speaker. Consequently the subjects of instituting proceedings, securing or accepting a court, objecting to inequitable and obtaining equitable procedure, as they are mostly of such a kind that, although in fact they are often allowed to slip into the course of the actual proceedings, they ought nevertheless, as it appears, to be dealt with before the commencement of the case—these subjects I keep somewhat separate from the actual trials, in respect of the time of their being raised rather than owing to a difference of kind. For all discussions about legal principle or about equity and right fall under the class of cases in which the point debated is the nature of a particular matter, a class of cases which we are going to discuss, and which chiefly turns on equity and justice.

101   XXIX. In all cases therefore there are three stages, one of which must be taken, if you are unable to take more, to make a stand against. Either you must decide to deny that the action in question ever took place, or, if you admit that it did take place, to deny that it has the effect alleged and is the action that your opponent lays to your charge, or, if it is not possible to challenge either the action or the name applied to it, you must deny that the action with which you are charged is of the nature that he states and you must maintain that what you really did 102 was right, or permissible. Thus the first stand for joining issue with your opponent must be managed by employing a kind of conjecture, the second by using definition and paraphrase or explanation of a term, and the third by discussing equity, truth, right and humanity in forgiving. And since a defendant must always not only take his stand

Lines of prosecution.

387

aut infitiando aut definiendo aut aequitate oppo-
nenda sed etiam rationem subiiciat recusationis suae,
primus ille status rationem habet iniqui criminis,
ipsam negationem infitiationemque facti ; secundus
quod non sit in re quod ab adversario ponatur in
verbo ; tertius quod id recte factum esse defendat
quod sine ulla nominis controversia factum fatetur.

103 Deinde uni cuique rationi opponendum est ab
accusatore id quod si non esset in accusatione, causa
omnino esse non posset. Itaque ea quae sic referuntur continentia causarum vocentur : quamquam non
ea magis quae contra rationem defensionis afferuntur
quam ipsae defensionis rationes continent causas.
Sed distinguendi gratia rationem appellamus eam
quae affertur ab reo ad recusandum depellendi
criminis causa, quae nisi esset, quod defenderet non
haberet : firmamentum autem quod contra ad labe-
factandam rationem refertur, sine quo accusatio
stare non potest.

104 XXX. Ex rationis autem et[1] firmamenti con-
flictione et quasi concursu quaestio exoritur quaedam quam disceptationem voco : in qua quid veniat
in iudicium et de quo disceptetur quaeri solet. Nam
prima adversariorum contentio diffusam habet quaestionem ; ut in coniectura, ceperitne pecunias
Decius ; in definitione, minueritne maiestatem

---

[1] et *Rackham :* et ex.

on some definite position, employing either denial
or definition or the counterplea of equity, but must
also submit the line he adopts for his counterplea,
the first position mentioned above takes the line
of the injustice of the charge, a flat negation and
denial of the act alleged; the second a statement
that the real fact has not the same content that
your opponent places in the term; and the third, the
contention that the act which without any disputing
about its name he confesses was committed, was

103 a right act.   Then each successive argument must
be met by the prosecutor with the point the absence
of which in the charge would make the case an
absolute impossibility.   Consequently the matters
thus introduced may be called the key-points of a
case ;   although cases do not depend more on the
arguments adduced to counter the line of the defence
than on the actual lines of the defence.   But for the
sake of distinction let us apply the term ' reason ' to
the plea advanced by the defendant to take exception
for the purpose of repelling the charge, the absence
of which plea would leave him without a defence ;
while we will use ' corroboration ' to denote the
counter-consideration directed to undermine the
reason, and indispensable to the validity of the charge.

104   XXX. But the discrepancy and collision between
the reason and the corroboration gives rise to an
inquiry which I call the discussion—a section in
which it is usual to inquire what is the point at issue
in the suit and what is the subject under discussion.
For the first encounter between the opponents raises
some wide question, for example on a point of conjecture :   ' Did Decius take the money ? ' or of definition :   ' Was Norbanus's conduct treasonable ? ' or

Norbanus ; in aequitate, iurene occiderit Opimius
Gracchum.   Haec, quae primam contentionem
habent ex arguendo et resistendo, lata, ut dixi, et
fusa sunt ; rationum et firmamentorum contentio
adducit in angustum disceptationem.   Ea in coniectura nulla est ; nemo enim eius quod negat factum
rationem aut potest aut debet aut solet reddere.
Itaque in his causis eadem et prima quaestio, et
105 disceptatio est extrema.   In illis autem ubi ita
dicitur : ' Non minuit maiestatem quod egit de
Caepione turbulentius ; populi enim Romani dolor
iustus vim illam excitavit, non tribuni actio ; maiestas
autem, quoniam est magnitudo quaedam, populi
Romani in eius potestate ac iure retinendo aucta
est potius quam diminuta,' et ubi ita refertur :
' Maiestas est in imperii atque in nominis populi
Romani dignitate, quam minuit is qui per vim
multitudinis rem ad seditionem vocavit,' exsistit illa
disceptatio, minueritne maiestatem qui voluntate
populi Romani rem gratam et aequam per vim egerit.
106 In eis autem causis ubi aliquid recte factum aut
concedendum esse defenditur, cum est facti subiecta
ratio, sicut ab Opimio : ' Iure feci, salutis omnium
et conservandae reipublicae causa,' relatumque est
ab Decio : ' Ne sceleratissimum quidem civem sine
iudicio iure ullo necare potuisti,' oritur illa dis-

of equity : ' Was Opimius justified in taking Gracchus's life ? ' These questions which comprise the first encounter, based on argument and counterargument, are as I said of a wide and loose form ; but the encounter that employs reasons and corroborations brings the discussion into a narrow field. This does not depend on any inference, for it is not possible or necessary or usual for anybody to give a reason for an action which he denies. Consequently in these cases the first inquiry and the concluding

105 discussion are the same. But in the ones that run like this : ' His somewhat disorderly procedure in respect of Caepio involved no treason ; the violence in question was aroused by the just indignation of the public and not by the action of the tribune ; whereas the majesty of the Roman people, inasmuch as that means their greatness, was increased rather than diminished in the maintenance of its power and right,' and when the terms of reference are : ' Majesty resides in the dignity of high office and of the name of the Roman people, which was impaired by one who employed mob violence to promote sedition,' the question will arise whether one who with the consent of the Roman people employed violence to effect a result that was acceptable and equitable,

106 really diminished the majesty of the people. But in the cases in which the defence is that some action was right or permissible, when the reason for the action is submitted, as in the case of the explanation of Opimius : ' I acted rightly, for the sake of the general safety and the preservation of the state,' and Decius's rejoinder : ' You had no power or right of any kind to kill even the most criminal citizen without trial,' the discussion that arises is whether he had

391

ceptatio: potueritne recte salutis reipublicae causa
civem eversorem civitatis indemnatum necare. Ita
disceptationes eae quae in his controversiis oriuntur
quae sunt certis personis et temporibus notatae fiunt
rursus infinitae detractis et temporibus et personis, et
rursum ad consultationis formam rationemque revo-
107 cantur. XXXI. Sed in gravissimis firmamentis etiam
illa ponenda sunt, si qua ex scripto legis aut testa-
menti aut verborum ipsius iudicii aut alicuius stipu-
lationis aut cautionis opponuntur defensioni contraria. Ac ne hoc quidem genus in eas causas
incurrit quae coniectura continentur; quod enim
factum negatur, id argui non potest scripto. Ne in
definitionem quidem venit genere scripti ipsius;
nam etiamsi verbum aliquod de scripto definiendum
est quam vim habeat, ut cum ex testamentis quid
sit penus aut cum ex lege praedii quaeritur quae
sint ruta caesa, non scripti genus sed verbi inter-
108 pretatio controversiam parit. Cum autem aut[1]
plura significantur scripto propter verbi aut verborum ambiguitatem, ut liceat ei qui contra dicat
eo trahere significationem scripti quo expediat ac
velit, aut, si ambigue scriptum non sit, vel a verbis
voluntatem et sententiam scriptoris abducere vel
alio se eadem de re contrarie scripto defendere,
tum disceptatio ex scripti contentione exsistit, ut

[1] [aut] ? *Rackham.*

the power and the right for the sake of the safety of
the state to put to death a citizen who was a violent
revolutionary without his having been found guilty.
Consequently the discussions arising in these disputes that involve definite persons and occasions are
turned into unlimited discussions when the persons
and occasions are removed, and fall back into the
107 form and method of debates. XXXI. But among the
most weighty corroborations must also be placed
those that are produced in opposition to the defence
from the text of a law or a will or the formula of the
actual trial or some covenant or guarantee. But
even this class of argument is not available in cases
that are based on inference ; for a denial of an action
cannot be met by a written document. It does not
even enter into definition, owing to the nature of
actual documentary evidence : for even if the force
of a word in a written document has to be defined,
for instance, if the meaning of the term ' stock ' in
a will is asked, or in the law of landed property the
meaning of ' minerals and timber,' it is not the class
of the document but the interpretation of the
108 language that causes controversy. When however
either because of the ambiguity of a word or words a
written document has several meanings, so that it is
open to the party speaking on the other side to
interpret the sense of the document in the way that
pays him and that he wishes, or else, if the document
is not ambiguous, to twist the intention and the
meaning of the writer away from the words, or to
put forward in his defence some other document
about the same matter having the contrary sense,
then comes in the discussion based on dispute as to a
written document, leading in the case of ambiguously

in ambiguis disceptetur quid maxime significetur,
in scripti sententiaeque contentione, utrum potius
sequatur iudex, in contrariis scriptis, utrum magis
sit comprobandum.

109   Disceptatio autem cum est constituta, propositum
esse debet oratori quo omnes argumentationes
repetitae ex inveniendi locis coniiciantur.   Quod
quamquam satis est ei qui videt quid in quoque
loco lateat quique illos locos tamquam thesauros
aliquos argumentorum notatos habet, tamen ea
quae sunt certarum causarum propria tangemus.

110 XXXII. In coniectura igitur, cum est in infitiando
reus, accusatori haec duo prima sunt—sed accusa-
torem pro omni actore et petitore appello : possunt
enim etiam sine accusatione in causis haec eadem
controversiarum genera versari—sed haec duo sunt
ei prima, causa et eventus. Causam appello rationem
efficiendi, eventum id quod est effectum.   Atque
ipsa quidem partitio causarum paullo ante in suasionis

111 locis distributa est. Quae enim in consilio capiendo
futuri temporis praecipiebantur, quam ob rem aut
utilitatem viderentur habitura aut efficiendi facultatem, eadem qui de facto argumentabitur colligere
debebit, quam ob rem et utilia illi quem arguet
fuisse et ab eo effici potuisse demonstret. Utilitatis
coniectura movetur si illud quod arguitur aut spe

expressed documents to a discussion of what the most
probable meaning is, and in the case of a conflict
between the expression and the intention, which of
the two the court is to follow by preference, and in
documents that conflict with one another, which is
to be accepted in preference to the other.

109　　But when the line of discussion is decided upon, the
speaker must have before him a point of reference to
which to refer all the lines of argument obtained from
topics of invention. And although this is enough for
one who sees the hidden content of each topic and
who has the topics in question neatly labelled like
storehouses of arguments, we will nevertheless touch
on the subjects that are appropriate to certain cases.

*Invention
of topics.*

110　XXXII. In inference therefore, when the defendant's
position is to deny the charge, the two first lines to be
taken by the prosecutor—I will use that term for
every plaintiff or person who institutes proceedings,
for these same kinds of dispute can find a place even
in actions that do not involve making a charge—
well, these are the two first points for the prosecutor
to take, the cause and the result. By ' cause ' I
mean the reason for doing something and by ' result '
the thing done. And as for the actual classification
of causes, this was expounded a little earlier among

111　the topics of persuasion. For the arguments there re-
commended in taking counsel for the future, for the
purpose of making the policy appear likely to be
either profitable or easy to execute, will similarly
have to be employed by a person going to argue about
a past action, as a way of proving that the thing was
both advantageous for the person he will be exposing
and within his power to execute. The inference of
advantageousness is suggested if his motive for doing

*Considera-
tions of
motive.*

395

bonorum aut malorum metu fecisse dicitur, quod
eo fit acrius quo illa in utroque genere maiora
112 ponuntur. Spectant etiam ad causam facti motus
animorum, si ira recens, si odium vetus, si ulciscendi
studium, si iniuriae dolor, si honoris, si gloriae, si
imperii, si pecuniae cupiditas, si periculi timor, si
aes alienum, si angustiae rei familiaris : si audax,
si levis, si crudelis, si impotens, si incautus, si in-
sipiens, si amans, si commota mente, si vinolentus,
si cum spe efficiendi, si cum opinione celandi aut si
patefactum esset depellendi criminis, vel perrum-
pendi periculi, vel in longinquum tempus differendi :
aut si iudicii poena levior quam facti praemium :
aut si facinoris voluptas maior quam damnationis
113 dolor. His fere rebus facti suspicio confirmatur,
cum et voluntatis in reo causae reperiuntur et
facultas. In voluntate autem utilitas ex adeptione
alicuius commodi vitationeque alicuius incommodi
quaeritur, ut aut spes aut metus impulisse videatur,
aut aliquis repentinus animi motus, qui etiam citius
in fraudem quam ratio utilitatis impellit. Quam
ob rem sint haec dicta de causis.

114 C. F. Teneo, et quaero qui sint illi eventus quos
ex causis effici dixisti.

XXXIII. C. P. Consequentia quaedam signa praeteriti et quasi impressa facti vestigia : quae quidem

the action censured is alleged to have been either hope of benefits or fear of evils ; and this gains further point in proportion as prospects of greater importance

112 in either class are produced. Also emotions have a bearing on the cause of an action, in cases where there is a recent outburst of anger, a long-standing hatred, desire for revenge, resentment for injury, desire for honour or glory or power or money, fear of danger, debt, straitened circumstances : or if a man is audacious, or frivolous, or cruel, or impulsive, or rash, or foolish, or in love, or excited, or drunk, or hopeful of succeeding in or confident of concealing a crime or, if it is discovered, of repelling the charge or of sweeping the danger aside or putting it off for a long time : or in case the penalty for conviction is less than the profit made out of the deed : or in case the pleasure of doing it is greater than the pain of being

113 punished for it. These more or less are the considerations that support suspicions of guilt, when both motives for wishing the crime and means of committing it are discovered in the defendant. Under the head of wish we look for the profit of getting some advantage or of avoiding some disadvantage, so as to make it appear that the act was prompted by either hope or fear or by some sudden impulse, which is a motive for dishonesty that acts even more quickly than considerations of profit. Consequently let this conclude our remarks about motive.

114 C. Jun. I accept your statements, and I want to know what are the results that you spoke of as being the consequences of motives.

XXXIII. C. Sen. Subsequent indications of something that is past, the traces and imprint of a previous action ; these indeed are most powerful in

Corroborative evidence.

vel maxime suspicionem movent et quasi tacita sunt
criminum testimonia, atque hoc quidem graviora
quod causae communiter videntur insimulare et
arguere omnes posse quorum modo interfuerit
aliquid : haec proprie attingunt eos ipsos qui arguuntur, ut telum, ut vestigium, ut cruor, ut deprehensum
aliquid, quod ablatum ereptumve videatur, ut
responsum inconstanter, ut haesitatum, ut titubatum, ut cum aliquo visus ex quo suspicio oriatur,
ut eo ipso in loco visus in quo facinus, ut pallor, ut
tremor, ut scriptum aut obsignatum aut depositum
quippiam. Haec enim et talia sunt quae aut in re
ipsa aut etiam ante quam factum est aut postea
115 suspiciosum crimen efficiant. Quae si non erunt,
tamen causis ipsis et efficiendi facultatibus niti
oportebit, adiuncta illa disputatione communi, non
fuisse illum tam amentem ut indicia facti aut effugere
aut occultare non posset, ut ita apertus esset, ut
locum crimini relinqueret. Communis ille contra
locus, audaciam temeritati, non prudentiae esse
116 coniunctam. Sequitur autem ille locus ad augendum,
non esse exspectandum dum fateatur, argumentis
peccata convinci ; et hic etiam exempla ponentur.
117   XXXIV. Atque haec quidem de argumentis. Sin
autem erit etiam testium facultas, primum genus
erit ipsum laudandum, dicendumque ne argumentis
teneretur reus ipsum sua cautione effecisse, testes

exciting suspicion, and are silent evidence of guilt, evidence indeed carrying all the more weight because it seems able collectively to accuse and convict of the offence everybody in any way connected with it: these intimately touch the actual persons accused— for instance, a weapon, a footprint, blood; the discovery of some article that looks as if it had been taken away or snatched from the victim; an inconsistent answer, hesitation, stammering; having been seen in company with somebody who gives rise to suspicion, having been seen at the actual place where the crime was committed; looking pale, trembling; a writing or a sealed document or deposition. For these are the kind of things that whether part of the affair itself or even as prior or subsequent occurrences

115 render the charge suspicious. If they are not forthcoming, nevertheless one will have to rely on the actual motives and the opportunities for doing the deed, with the addition of the stock argument that the defendant assuredly was not so insane as to be incapable of either escaping or concealing the traces of his act, or as to be so open, or as to leave ground for the charge. Against this there is the stock argument that audacity goes with rashness and not with

116 prudence. Then follows the corroborative argument that we must not wait till the guilty man makes a confession, but that offences are proved by arguments; and at this point we shall also produce instances.

117   XXXIV. So much for arguments. If however evidence of witnesses is also available, we shall have to begin by praising witnesses as a class, and saying that the defendant has by his own precautions made it impossible to prove him guilty by arguments, but

Handling of witnesses.

399

effugere non potuisse ; deinde singuli laudentur
[quae autem essent laudabilia dictum est][1] ; deinde
etiam argumento firmo, quia tamen saepe falsum
est, posse recte non credi, viro bono et firmo sine
vitio iudicis non posse non credi ; atque etiam, si
obscuri testes erunt aut tenues, dicendum erit non
esse ex fortuna fidem ponderandam, aut eos esse
cuiusque locupletissimos testes qui id de quo agatur
facillime scire possint. Sin quaestiones habitae aut
postulatio ut habeantur causam adiuvabunt, con-
firmandum genus primum quaestionum erit, dicendum de vi doloris, de opinione maiorum, qui eam rem
118 totam nisi probassent certe repudiassent ; de institutis Atheniensium, Rhodiorum, doctissimorum hominum, apud quos etiam (id quod acerbissimum est)
liberi civesque torquentur ; de nostrorum etiam
prudentissimorum hominum institutis, qui cum de
servis in dominos quaeri noluissent, de incestu tamen,
et coniuratione quae facta me consule est,[2] quaerendum putaverunt. Irridenda etiam disputatio est
qua solent uti ad infirmandas quaestiones et meditata puerilisque dicenda. Tum facienda fides
diligenter esse et sine cupiditate quaesitum, dicta-

---

[1] *seclusit Rackham.*
[2] [et coniuratione . . . facta est] *? Rackham.*

---

[a] This reads like a gloss on ' praising witnesses as a class '
above.

[b] The Catilinarian conspiracy denounced by Cicero in
63 B.C. There appears to be no other evidence for the use
of torture during these proceedings. Cicero, *pro Deiotaro*
§ 3, merely states that the examination of slaves by torture
to give evidence against their master is not allowed, and *pro*

that he has not been able to avoid witnesses ; then you must praise the witnesses individually (praiseworthy characteristics have been mentioned) [a] ; then say even a strong argument can be rightly disbelieved, as it is often false nevertheless, but a virtuous man of strong character cannot be refused belief save by the fault of the judge. And also, if the witnesses are men of no position or of slender means, you must say that a man's reliability is not to be measured by his fortunes, or that the most reliable witnesses of any matter are the people in the best position to know the matter in question. If examination of witnesses held under torture or the demand to hold such examination is likely to help the case, you must first support that institution, and speak about the efficacy of pain, and about the opinion of our ancestors, who undoubtedly would have repudiated the whole thing if they had not approved of it ; and about the institutions of the Athenians and Rhodians, highly cultivated people, with whom even freemen and citizens—most shocking as this is—are put to the torture ; and also about the institutions of our fellow-countrymen, persons of supreme wisdom, who although they would not allow slaves to be tortured to give evidence against their masters, nevertheless approved the use of torture in cases of incest, and in the case of conspiracy [b] that occurred during my consulship. Also the contention usually employed to invalidate evidence under torture must be scouted as ridiculous, and pronounced to be doctrinaire and childish. Then you must produce confidence in the thoroughness and the impartiality

Milone § 59, he says that it is only permitted in trials for incest. The clause is perhaps an interpolation.

que quaestionis argumentis et coniectura ponderanda. Atque haec accusationis fere membra sunt.

119 XXXV. Defensionis autem primum infirmatio causarum : aut non fuisse, aut non tantas, aut non sibi soli, aut commodius potuisse idem consequi, aut non eis se esse moribus, non ea vita, aut nullos animi motus aut non tam impotentes fuisse. Facultatum autem infirmatione utetur si aut vires aut animum aut copias aut opes abfuisse demonstrabit, aut alienum tempus aut locum non idoneum, aut multos arbitros quorum crederet nemini : aut non se tam ineptum ut id susciperet quod occultare non posset, neque tam amentem ut poenas ac iudicia contem-

120 neret. Consequentia autem diluet exponendo non esse illa certa indicia facti quae etiam nullo admisso consequi possent, consistetque in singulis, et ea aut eorum quae ipse facta esse dicit propria esse defendet potius quam criminis, aut si sibi cum accusatore communia essent, pro periculo potius quam contra salutem valere debere ; testiumque et quaestionum genus universum et quod poterit in singulis ex reprehensionis locis de quibus ante dictum est

of the inquiry, and weigh the statements made under torture by means of arguments and inference. These then more or less are the constituent parts of a case for the prosecution.

119 XXXV. In the case for the defence the first point is the demolition of the argument from motives, showing that there were none, or not strong enough ones, or not merely selfish ones, or that the same object could have been secured in an easier way, or that the charge is not consistent with one's character or one's record, or that there were no motives or no sufficiently overpowering motives for the act. The defendant will take the line of proving his inability to commit the deed by showing that he lacked the requisite strength or courage or means or money, or that the time was inopportune or the place unsuitable, or that there were a number of people present, on none of whom he could rely for secrecy, or that he is not so simple as to embark on a course of conduct that he could not possibly keep secret nor so insane as to make light 20 of penalties and courts of law. Proof by inference he will dispose of by arguing that no certain evidence of a crime is afforded by later occurrences that might equally well happen even when no crime had been committed, and he will dwell on particular details, and urge either that they belong to the actions which he himself declares that he has committed rather than to the crime with which he is charged, or that they attach to himself and to the prosecutor equally and so ought to count in his defence rather than against his acquittal; and he will draw upon the topics of refutation previously discussed to disparage both in general and as far as he is able in detail evidence given by witnesses and under torture.

Lines of defence.

§ 44

403

121 refellet. Harum causarum **principia suspiciosa ad** acerbitatem ab accusatore ponentur, denuntiabiturque insidiarum commune periculum, excitabunturque animi ut attendant. Ab reo autem querela conflati criminis collectarumque suspicionum et accusatoris insidiae et item commune periculum proferetur, animique ad misericordiam allicientur et modice benevolentia iudicum colligetur. Narratio autem accusatoris erit quasi membratim gesti negotii suspiciosa explicatio, sparsis omnibus argumentis, obscuratis defensionibus ; defensori aut praeteritis aut obscuratis suspicionum argumentis rerum

122 ipsarum eventus erunt casusque narrandi. In confirmandis autem nostris argumentationibus infirmandisque contrariis saepe erunt accusatori motus animorum incitandi, reo mitigandi. Atque haec quidem utrique maxime in peroratione facienda—alteri frequentatione argumentorum et coacervatione universa, alteri, si plane causam redarguendo explicarit, enumeratione ut quidque diluerit **et** miseratione ad extremum.

123   XXXVI. C. F. Scire mihi iam videor quemadmodum coniectura tractanda sit. Nunc de definitione audiamus.

C. P. Communia dantur in isto genere accusatori defensorique praecepta. Uter enim definiendo

404

121 The suspicious sources of these motives will be set forward by the prosecutor to arouse bad feeling, and he will cry out against the general danger of conspiracy, and will stir up the jury to give it their attention. The defendant for his part will put forward a protest against a trumped-up charge and a parade of suspicions and against the prosecutor's plotting, and also will bring forward the danger to the community, and will try to arouse feelings of compassion and up to a point to attract the goodwill of the court. As to the narrative passage the prosecutor will make it a suspicious exposition of the business as transacted stage by stage, spreading out all his proofs and minimizing the lines of defence ; whereas the defendant will have to pass over or else minimize the arguments for suspicion, and recount the issues 122 and incidents of the actual facts. In corroborating one's own lines of argument and discounting those of one's opponents, in the case of the prosecutor it will often be necessary to arouse emotion and in the case of the defendant to allay it. This indeed is specially the line to be taken by both parties in their concluding passage—the one by recapitulating his arguments and bringing them to a general focus, and the other, supposing he has fully dealt with the case by his line of defence, by a repetition of his successive refutations, closing with an appeal for compassion.

123 XXXVI. C. Jun. I now feel that I undrsteand the proper way of handling conjectural inference. Now let us hear about definition.

C. Sen. The rules laid down in that department Definition. serve in common for the prosecutor and for the defendant. Victory is bound to go to the one who in

describendoque verbo magis ad sensum iudicis
opinionemque penetrarit, et uter ad communem
verbi vim et ad eam praeceptionem quam incohatam
habebunt in animis ei qui audient magis et propius
124 accesserit, is vincat necesse est. Non enim argumentando hoc genus tractatur sed tamquam explicando
excutiendoque verbo, ut si in reo pecunia absoluto
rursusque revocato praevaricationem accusator esse
definiat omnem iudicii corruptelam ab reo, defensor
autem non omnem sed tantummodo accusatoris
corruptelam ab reo : sit ergo haec contentio prima
verborum, in qua, etiamsi propius accedat ad consuetudinem mentemque sermonis defensoris definitio,
125 tamen accusator sententia legis nititur ; negat enim
probari oportere eos qui leges scripserint ratum
habere iudicium si totum corruptum sit, si unus
accusator corruptus sit non[1] rescindere : nititur
aequitate, ut utilitate[2] scribenda lex sit, quaeque
tum[2] complecteretur in iudiciis corruptis ea verbo
126 uno praevaricationis comprehendisse dicitur. Defensor autem testabitur consuetudinem sermonis, ver-
bique vim ex contrario reperiet, quasi ex vero
accusatore, cui contrarium est nomen praevari-

[1] *v.l. om.* non.
[2] utilitate . . . tum *lectio incertissima.*

[a] A variant reading omits ' not.'

his definition and analysis of a term has entered more deeply into the mind and the ideas of the judge, and who has arrived more completely and closely at the common meaning of the term and at the same tentative conception of it as that which his hearers
124 will have forming in their minds. For this kind of consideration does not proceed by developing an argument but by eliciting and explaining the meaning of a term, as for instance if it is the case of a defendant who has secured acquittal by means of bribery and then has again been called up for trial the prosecutor defines ' corrupt acquittal ' as meaning any corruption of the court by the accused party, but the defendant makes out that it does not apply to all corruption but only to the corruption of the prosecutor by the accused party ; consequently this would be primarily a verbal dispute, in which even if the defendant's definition comes nearer to the customary usage and meaning of the term, nevertheless the prosecutor relies on the intention
125 of the statute ; for he denies the necessity of proving that legislation which invalidates the verdict in a case in which the whole court has been bribed does not[a] rescind the verdict if a single person, the prosecutor, has taken a bribe : he relies on equity, arguing that the law should be drafted on the lines of the general advantage, and he maintains that actions which in that case would be covered by the term ' corruption of the courts ' it has included under the
126 one expression ' corrupt acquittal.' The defendant on the other hand will appeal to the customary usage of language and will draw the meaning of the word from its contrary, that is, ' true prosecutor,' the contrary of which is the term ' corrupter of the court ' ; and from

catoris; ex consequentibus, quod ea littera de
accusatore solet dari iudici[1]; ex nomine ipso, quod
significat eum qui in contrariis causis quasi vare[2]
esse positus videatur. Sed huic tamen ipsi confu-
giendum est ad aequitatis locos, ad rerum iudicata-
rum auctoritatem, ad finem aliquem periculi; com-
muneque sit hoc praeceptum, ut cum uterque definierit
quam maxime potuerit ad communem sensum vimque verbi, tum similibus exemplisque eorum qui ita
locuti sunt suam definitionem sententiamque con-
127 firmet. Atque accusatori in hoc genere causarum
locus ille communis, minime esse concedendum ut is
qui de re confiteatur verbi se interpretatione defendat; defensor autem et ea quam proposui
aequitate nitatur et ea cum secum faciat non re
sed depravatione verbi se urgeri queratur. Quo in
genere percensere poterit plerosque inveniendi locos;
nam et similibus utetur et contrariis et consequentibus quamquam uterque, tamen reus, nisi plane
128 erit absurda causa, frequentius. Amplificandi autem
causa, quae aut cum degredientur a causa dici volent[3]
aut cum perorabunt, haec vel ad odium vel ad
misericordiam vel omnino ad animos iudicum moven-
dos ex eis quae sunt ante posita sumentur, si modo
rerum magnitudo hominumve aut invidia aut dignitas
postulabit.

[1] solet dici ? *Rackham.*
[2] *v.l.* varie.   [3] *v.l.* solent.

[a] Perhaps the text should be emended, giving 'because
the term is customarily used about the prosecutor.'

what follows, because the term concerning the prosecutor is customarily applied to the judge [a]; and from the word itself, which means a person who appears to be placed all askew in contrary cases. But nevertheless even the defendant himself has to have recourse to points of equity, to the authority of previous judgements, and to the desirability of bringing the issue to some conclusion ; and a rule common to both parties should be that after each has done his best to produce a definition in conformity with the usual sense and signification of the term, he should then support his definition and interpretation by means of parallels and instances of persons who have used the term in that way. Also the prosecutor in this class of cases must employ the common topic that it is quite unpermissible for the person who admits the fact to defend himself by interpreting the meaning of a word ; whereas the defendant must rely on the plea of equity that I have put forward, and must complain that though equity is on his side he is being met not with fact but with the perversion of a word. Under this head he will be able to run through most of the topics of investigation ; for parallels and contraries and consequences, though employed by both sides, will be more frequently employed by the defendant, if his case is not to fall absolutely flat. The means available for amplification, which they will desire to employ either when making a digression from the case in hand or in the peroration, will be selected from those that were set out previously, for the purpose of exciting either hatred or pity or any other emotion in the minds of the judges, provided that the importance of the facts or either the unpopularity or the eminence of the persons so demands.

129   XXXVII. C. F. Habeo ista ; nunc ea quae cum quale sit quippiam disceptatur quaeri ex utraque parte deceat velim audire.

C. P. Confitentur in isto genere qui arguuntur se id fecisse ipsum in quo reprehenduntur, sed quoniam iure se fecisse dicunt, iuris est omnis ratio nobis explicanda. Quod dividitur in duas partes primas, naturam atque legem, et utriusque generis vis in divinum et humanum ius est distributa, quorum 130 aequitatis est unum, alterum religionis. Aequitatis autem vis est duplex, cuius altera directa et veri et iusti et ut dicitur aequi et boni ratione defenditur, altera ad vicissitudinem referendae gratiae pertinet, quod in beneficio gratia, in iniuria ultio nominatur. Atque haec communia sunt naturae atque legis, sed propria legis et ea quae scripta sunt et ea quae sine litteris aut gentium iure aut maiorum more retinentur. Scriptorum autem privatum aliud est, publicum aliud : publicum lex, senatusconsultum, foedus, privatum tabulae, pactum conventum, stipulatio. Quae autem scripta non sunt, ea aut consuetudine aut conventis hominum et quasi consensu obtinentur, atque etiam hoc in primis, ut nostros mores legesque tueamur quodammodo naturali iure praescriptum 131 est. Et quoniam breviter aperti fontes sunt quasi quidam aequitatis, meditata nobis ad hoc causarum

129 XXXVII. C. Jun. I take your meaning ; and now I should like you to tell me what are the appropriate questions to be raised on each side when the discussion turns on the exact nature of something.

C. Sen. That is the sort of case in which the parties Right and accused admit the commission of the actual action on wrong. account of which they are censured, but assert that they were acting rightly, so that we have to expound the entire theory of right. It divides into two primary sections, nature and law, and the force of each class is separated into divine right and human right, one being the field of equity and the other of 130 religion. Equity again has a twofold meaning, one of which rests on the straightforward principle of truth and justice, of the 'fair and good,' as the phrase is, while the other concerns the interchange of repayment, which in the case of a kindness is called gratitude and in the case of an injury retaliation. These things belong in common to nature and to law ; but peculiar to law are written rules of conduct and also the unwritten rules preserved by the law of nations or by ancestral custom. Of the written code part is private and part public ; the public code consists in laws, resolutions of the senate and treaties, while the private code includes deeds, formal covenants and contracts. The unwritten rules are maintained either by custom or by the conventions and virtual consensus of mankind, and, this also a point of primary import-ance, it is in a manner prescribed by natural principle that we shall preserve our own customs and laws. 131 And now that we have briefly disclosed as it were the fountain heads from which equity flows, it will be necessary for us in regard to this class of cases to have

o 2 411

genus esse debebunt ea quae dicenda erunt in
orationibus de natura, de legibus, de more maiorum,
de propulsanda iniuria, de ulciscenda, de omni parte
iuris.   Si imprudenter aut necessitate aut casu
quippiam fecerit quod non concederetur eis qui sua
sponte et voluntate fecissent, ad eius facti deprecationem ignoscendi petenda venia est quae sumetur
ex plerisque locis aequitatis.

Expositum est ut potui brevissime de omni controversiarum genere—nisi praeterea tu quid requiris.

132   XXXVIII. C. F. Illud equidem quod iam unum
restare video, quale sit cum disceptatio versatur in
scriptis.

C. P. Recte intellegis ; eo enim exposito munus
promissi omne confecero.   Sunt igitur ambigui duobus adversariis praecepta communia.   Uterque enim
hanc significationem qua utetur ipse dignam scriptoris prudentia esse defendet : uterque id quod
adversarius ex ambigue scripto intellegendum esse
dicet aut absurdum aut inutile aut iniquum aut
turpe esse defendet aut etiam discrepare cum
ceteris scriptis vel aliorum vel maxime si poterit
eiusdem ; quamque defendet ipse eam rem et sententiam quemvis prudentem et iustum hominem si

considered what it is proper to say in speeches on the subject of nature, law, ancestral custom, defence against wrong and retribution for it, and every department of right. If a man has carelessly or under compulsion or by accident committed an action that in the case of persons acting deliberately and voluntarily would not be permissible, for the purpose of pleading forgiveness for the action pardon must be sued for by a form of petition that will be taken from a number of topics of equity.

That concludes my exposition, made in the briefest form within my power, of the whole subject of controversies—unless you yourself have some further question to ask.

132   XXXVIII. C. Jun. Well, I have one question, the only point to my view that now remains—what is the nature of the case when the dispute turns on something in a written document ?

C. Sen. You see the position quite correctly ; when I have explained the point you raise, I shall have completed the whole liability of my undertaking. Well then, the rules as to a disputed meaning are common to the two opponents. Each will maintain that the interpretation on which he himself will base his case is worthy of the intelligence of the writer ; and each will maintain that the meaning that his opponents will say is to be derived from an ambiguous phrase in the document is either absurd or useless or unfair or disgraceful, or else that it is inconsistent with the rest of the writings either of other persons or most preferably, if it be possible to say so, of the same person ; and that the point of view that he will himself maintain would be what, if it were given as an open question, any wise and just

Handling of disputed documents.

413

ad[1] integrum daretur scripturum fuisse, sed planius ;
133 eamque sententiam quam significari posse dicet nihil
habere aut captionis aut vitii, contrariam autem si
probarint,[2] fore ut multa vitia, stulta, iniqua, contraria
consequantur. Cum autem aliud scriptor sensisse
videtur et aliud scripsisse, qui scripto nitetur, eum
re exposita recitatione uti oportebit, deinde instare
adversario, iterare, renovare, interrogare num aut
scriptum neget aut contra factum infitietur ; post
134 iudicem ad vim scripti vocet. Hac confirmatione
usus amplificet rem lege laudanda audaciamque
confutet eius qui, cum palam contra fecerit idque
fateatur, adsit tamen factumque defendat. Deinde
infirmet defensionem : cum adversarius aliud voluisse,
[aliud sensisse][3] scriptorem, aliud scripsisse dicat,
non esse ferendum a quoquam potius latoris sensum
quam a lege explicari : cur ita scripserit si ita non
senserit ? cur, cum ea quae plane scripta sint
neglexerit, quae nusquam scripta sint proferat ?
cur prudentissimos in scribendo viros summae stul-
titiae putet esse damnandos ? quid impedierit
scriptorem quo minus exciperet illud quod adversarius tamquam si exceptum esset ita dicit se

[1] ad *add. Rackham.*
[2] *Rackham :* probarit.
[3] aliud sensisse *vel* aliud voluisse *secl. edd.*

414

person would have written, but in a more downright
133 form ; and that the meaning which he will declare
possible to be intended contains no trace of trickery
or fault, whereas if they approve the opposite
interpretation, a great many faulty and foolish
and unfair and contrary implications will result in
consequence. When however the writer appears
to have meant one thing and written another, an
advocate relying on the written document after setting out the case will have to read the document to
the court, and then to turn upon his opponent and
reiterate and repeat his points and ask him whether
he denies the document or alternatively maintains
that it was not contravened by the action taken ; and
afterwards he must call the judge to consider the
134 force of the document. And when he has employed
this method of confirmation, he must amplify his case
by speaking in praise of the law, and must denounce
the effrontery of a person who, after openly breaking
it and while admitting he has done so, nevertheless
appears in court and defends his conduct. Then he
must undermine the case for the defence, by saying
that, whereas his opponent maintains that the writer
meant one thing and wrote another, it is intolerable
that the meaning of the legislator should be explained
by anybody rather than by the law : why did he
write like that if that was not his meaning ? why,
when his opponent has neglected clearly written
statements does he bring forward statements not to
be found in writing anywhere ? why does he
imagine that the wisest masters of drafting are to be
held guilty of supreme stupidity ? what prevented
the writer from inserting the exception which his
opponent professes to have followed as though it

415

135 secutum ?   Utetur exemplis eis quibus idem scriptor
aut, si id non poterit, quibus alii quod excipiendum
putarint exceperint.   Quaerenda etiam ratio est, si
qua poterit inveniri, quare non sit exceptum ; aut
iniqua lex aut inutilis futura dicetur, aut alia causa
obtemperandi, alia abrogandi : dissentire adversarii
vocem atque legis.   Deinde amplificandi causa de
conservandis legibus, de periculo rerum publicarum
atque privatarum cum aliis locis, tum in perorando
maxime graviter erit vehementerque dicendum.

136   XXXIX. Ille autem qui se sententia legis volun-
tateque defendet, in consilio atque in mente scriptoris,
non in verbis ac litteris vim legis positam esse
defendet, quodque nihil exceperit in lege laudabit,
ne diverticula peccatis darentur atque ut ex facto
cuiusque iudex legis mentem interpretaretur.   Deinde
erit utendum exemplis in quibus omnis aequitas perturbetur si verbis legum ac non sententiis pareatur.

137 Deinde genus eiusmodi calliditatis et calumniae
retrahatur in odium iudicis cum quadam invidiosa
querela.   Et si incidet imprudentiae causa quae non
ad delictum sed ad casum necessitatemve pertineat,
quod genus paullo ante attigimus, erit eisdem aequi-

35 were actually there? He will adduce instances in which the same writer, or, if that is not possible, in which other persons have made an exception that they thought to be necessary. He will also try to discover a reason, if any such can be found, to account for the exception's not having been made: he will declare that the law is unjust, or else certain to be ineffective, or that if there is one motive for obeying it there is another for repealing it; and that the statement of his opponent does not agree with that of the law. Then, for the purpose of amplification, both in other parts of the speech and particularly in the peroration he will enlarge in weighty and vigorous language on the duty of maintaining the laws and on the danger threatening both public and private affairs.

36 XXXIX. On the other hand one who bases his defence on the meaning and intention of the law will maintain that the force of the law resides in the purpose and intention of the person who drafted it and not in its words and letters, and will praise him for not having inserted any exceptions in the law, so as not to give hiding-places for offences and so that the judge should interpret the meaning of the law in the light of the action of the particular individual. Then he must introduce examples of cases where all equity will be thrown into confusion if the words of 37 the law are followed and not the meaning. Then he must arouse the hatred of the judge against cunning and chicanery of such a kind, with a note of resentful complaint in his voice. And if the facts admit the plea of lack of consideration in respect of not the offence but accident or necessity, a class of topic that we have touched on a little before, the same maxims of equity

Law and equity.

417

tatis sententiis contra acerbitatem verborum depre-
candum. Sin scripta inter se dissentient, tanta series
artis est et sic inter se sunt pleraque connexa et
apta, ut quae paullo ante praecepta dedimus ambigui
quaeque proxime sententiae et scripti, eadem ad
138 hoc genus causae tertium transferantur. Nam
quibus locis in ambiguo defendimus eam significationem quae nos adiuvat, eisdem in contrariis legibus
nostra lex defendenda est. Deinde est efficiendum
ut alterius scripti sententiam, alterius verba defen-
damus. Ita quae modo de scripto sententiaque
praecepta sunt, eadem huc omnia transferemus.

139 XL. Expositae sunt tibi omnes oratoriae partitiones, quae quidem e media illa nostra Academia
effloruerunt ; neque sine ea aut inveniri aut intellegi aut tractari possunt ; nam et partiri ipsum et
definire et ambigui partitiones dividere et argumentorum locos nosse et argumentationem ipsam concludere, et videre quae sumenda in argumentando
sint quidque ex eis quae sumpta sunt efficiatur, et
vera a falsis, verisimilia ab incredibilibus diiudicare
et distinguere aut male sumpta aut male conclusa
reprehendere, et eadem vel anguste disserere, ut
dialectici qui appellantur, vel, ut oratorem decet,

will have to be employed as a plea to counter the harshness of the actual words. Or if there is a discrepancy between the documents, such is the interconnexion of science and so closely are most things interrelated that the rules we gave a little before in regard to double meaning and those given just now § 134 as to sense and style can be transferred without 138 modification to this third class of case. For the same topics by means of which in a case of ambiguity we maintain the interpretation that helps ourselves, must also be employed in a case of inconsistency between different laws to maintain the law that is on our side. Then we must contrive to maintain the meaning of one document but the actual words of the other. In this manner we shall transfer here all the rules that we laid down just now in regard to written matter and § 132 to meaning.

139 XL. You now have had set before you all the departments of oratory, that is those which have sprung from our famous school, the Middle Academy. Nor can they be discovered or understood or employed without the aid of that school ; for the actual process of division, and those of defining and distinguishing the two different meanings of an ambiguous statement, and knowing topics of arguments and bringing the actual process of argument to a conclusion, and discerning what things are to be assumed in a line of argument and what consequence follows from these assumptions, and distinguishing and differentiating true from false and probable from untrustworthy statements or censuring bad assumptions or bad conclusions, and treating the same topics either with close analysis, as do those who are termed dialecticians, or with broad exposition, as befits an orator, all come

Conclusion: the orator should study logic and moral science.

419

late exprimere illius exercitationis et subtiliter dispu-
140 tandi et copiose dicendi artis[1] est. De bonis vero
rebus et malis, aequis, iniquis, utilibus, inutilibus,
honestis, turpibus quam potest habere orator sine
illis maximarum rerum artibus facultatem aut
copiam ? Quare haec tibi sint, mi Cicero, quae
exposui, quasi indicia fontium illorum : ad quos si
nobis[2] eisdem ducibus aliisve perveneris, tum et haec
ipsa melius et multo maiora alia cognosces.

C. F. Ego vero, ac magno quidem studio, mi pater ;
multisque ex tuis praeclarissimis muneribus nullum
maius exspecto.

[1] [artis] *Ernesti.*
[2] [nobis] *? Ruckham.*

under the exercises mentioned and are part of the science of subtle disputation and copious oratory.
40 Moreover what readiness of style or supply of matter can a speaker possess on the subject of good and bad, right and wrong, utility and inutility, virtue and vice, without knowing these sciences of primary importance ? Consequently the points I have expounded must serve you, my dear Cicero, as signposts indicating the way to those great fountains of wisdom ; at which if with our guidance continued or with that of others you succeed in arriving, you will thereupon achieve a better knowledge both of these and of other much more important matters.

C. Jun. I shall indeed, father, and with great eagerness ; and among the many signal services that you confer upon me I look forward to none more important.

INDEX TO *DE ORATORE*

Proper Names

(The references are to book and section. A few notes are added to supplement the information given in the text.)

Academia, school of Plato at Athens, i. 43, 45, 84, 98, iii. 62, 67 f., 75, 109 f., 145

Accius, iii. 27, 154, 158, 217, 219

Achilles, iii. 57

Achivi, iii. 165

Acidinus, ii. 260

Aculeo, cousin of Cicero, i. 191, ii. 2, 262

Acusilas, early Greek prose author, ii. 53

Aelius Lamia, ii. 262

Aelius Sextus, Paetus Catus, consul 198 B.C., i. 193, 198, 212, 240, iii. 133

Aelius Tubero, ii. 341, iii. 87

Aemilius Lepidus, ii. 287

Aemilius Paullus, ii. 272

Aemilius Porcina, i. 40, ii. 197

Aemilius Scaurus, i. 214, ii. 197, 203, 257, 265, 280, 283

Aeschines, orator, ii. 94, iii. 28, 213

Aeschines, philosopher, i. 45

Aeschylus, iii. 27

Aesopus, tragic actor, friend of Cicero, i. 259, iii. 102

Africa, iii. 167

Africanus, the elder, i. 211, 215, ii. 170, 250, 268, 341, iii. 87

Africanus, the younger, i. 211, ii. 106, 154, iii. 28

Agesilaus, iii. 139

Aglaophon, iii. 26

Aiaces, ii. 265

Aiax Telamonius, ii. 193

Alabanda, ii. 95

Albanum, ii. 224

Albius, ii. 281

Albucius, ii. 281, iii. 171

Alcibiades, ii. 93, iii. 139

Alexander, ii. 58, 341, iii. 141

Anaxagoras, iii. 56, 138

Antiochus III, ii. 75

Antiopa, ii. 155

Antipater, see Coelius

Antipater of Sidon, iii. 194

Antisthenes, iii. 62

Antistius, ii. 287

Antonius, M. (see Introduction), i. 24 etc.

Apelles, iii. 26

Apenninus, iii. 69

Apollo Pythius, i. 199
Apollonius of Alabanda, i. 75, 126, 130
Appius, ii. 284
Appuleia lex, ii. 107, 201
Aquilius, ii. 188, 194
Aratus of Soli in Cilicia, *fl.* 250 B.C., wrote astronomical poems, translated by Cicero, i. 69
Arcesilas, iii. 67, 80
Archimedes, iii. 132
Archytas, Pythagorean philosopher, iii. 139
Argonautae, i. 174
Aristides, ii. 341
Aristippus, iii. 62
Aristophanes of Byzantium, iii. 132
Aristoteles, i. 43, 49, 55, ii. 43, 58, 116, 160, 326, 332, 343, iii. 2, 62, 67, 71, 80, 141, 147, 193
Aristoxenus, iii. 132
Asclepiades, i. 62
Asellus, Ti. Claudius, tribune 139 B.C., ii. 258, 268
Athenae, i. 13, 45, 47, ii. 13, iii. 43
Atreus, iii. 217, 219
Attici, ii. 217
Aurifex, ii. 245

Balbi, iii. 78
Bestia, ii. 283
Brulla, iii. 88
Brutus, leader in expulsion of Tarquins, i. 37, ii. 225
Bucculeius, unknown, i. 179
Byzantii, ii. 217

Caepio, ii. 197 ff.
Caieta, on coast of Latium, ii. 22
Calchedonius, iii. 128
Callimachus, iii. 132
Callisthenes, ii. 58
Calvinus, ii. 249
Calvus, ii. 250
Canius, ii. 280
Capitolium, iii. 180, 214
Carbo, i. 40, ii. 9, 106, 165, iii. 10, 28
Carneades, founder of New Academy, i. 45, 49, ii. 155, 161, iii. 68, 71, 80, 147
Carthago, ii. 75, iii. 109
Carvilius, ii. 249
Cassandra, ii. 265
Castor, ii. 352
Cato, M. Porcius, consul 195 B.C., i. 171, 215, 227, ii. 1, iii. 135, 165, 252, 271, 279
Catones, ii. 290, iii. 56
Catulus, Q. Lutatius (see Introduction), ii. 12, iii. 9 etc.
Cento, ii. 286
Ceres, iii. 167
Charmadas, i. 45, 47, 84, 93, ii. 360
Charybdis, iii. 163
Chrysippus, third head of Stoic school, i. 50
Chrysis, ii. 327
Cicero, L., ii. 2
Cicero, M., grandfather of the author, ii. 265
Cilicia, i. 82, ii. 2
Cimbri, ii. 266
Cincius Alimentus, ii. 286
Claudii, i. 176

INDEX TO *DE ORATORE*

Claudius, Appius, ii. 246, 284

Clitomachus, i. 45

Coelius Antipater, consul 94 B.C., i. 117, ii. 54, 257, iii. 153

Congus, Iunius, antiquary, i. 256

Conon, iii. 139

Coponius, i. 180, ii. 140

Corax, Sicilian, rhetorician, *fl.* 5th century B.C., i. 91, iii. 81

Corinthii, ii. 262

Cornelius, P. Rufinus, consul 290 and 277 B.C., ii. 268

Coruncanius, iii. 56, 134

Cossi, ii. 98

Cotta, C. Aurelius (see Introduction), i. 25 etc.

Cotta, L. Aurelius, tr. pl. 103 B.C., ii. 197, iii. 42, 46

Crannon, ii. 352

Crantor, iii. 67

Crassus, L. Licinius (see Introduction), i. 24, iii. 1 etc.

Crassus, P., i. 170, 216, 239, ii. 262, 265, 269, iii. 10, 134, 171

Critias, ii. 93, iii. 139

Critolaus, i. 45, ii. 155, 160

Ctesiphon, iii. 213

Curio, C. Scribonius, consul 76 B.C., ii. 98

Curius, M'., i. 180, 238, 242, ii. 24, 140

Cynici, iii. 62

Cyrenaici, iii. 62

Damon, iii. 132

Decius, P., ii. 132, 135

Delphi, iii. 132

Demetrius, ii. 95

Demochares, ii. 95

Democritus of Abdera, originated atomic theory, i. 42, 49, ii. 194, 235, iii. 56

Demosthenes, i. 58, 88, 260, ii. 94, iii. 28, 71, 213

Didius, T., consul 98 B.C., ii. 197

Dinarchus, ii. 94

Dio, iii. 139

Diodorus, i. 45

Diogenes, ii. 155, 160

Dionysius, ii. 57

Diphilus, i. 136

Domitius, ii. 45, 227, 230

Draco, i. 197

Drusus, M. Livius, leader of reform party 91 B.C., i. 24, 97, iii. 2

Duronius, ii. 257, 274

Egilia, ii. 277

Egilius, ii. 277

Empedocles, *d.* 424 B.C., i. 217

Ennius, early Roman epic and tragic poet, i. 154, 198, ii. 156, 222, 276, iii. 27, 164, 167, 217

Epaminondas, Theban, defeated Spartans at Leuctra 371, and Mantinea 362 B.C., i. 211, ii. 341, iii. 139

Ephesus, ii. 75

Ephorus, ii. 57, 94, iii. 36

Eretria, iii. 62

Erillus of Carthage, pupil of Zeno the Stoic, iii. 62

425

INDEX TO *DE ORATORE*

Esquilina porta, ii. 276
Etruscus, iii. 10
Euclides, iii. 132
Euripides, iii. 27, 141
Euxinus pontus, i. 174

Fabianus Fornix, ii. 267
Fabius, i. 211, ii. 273, 290
Fabricius, opponent of Pyrrhus, ii. 268, 290, iii. 56
Fannius, C. Strabo, consul 122 B.C., ii. 270, iii. 183
Fimbria, ii. 91
Flaccus, M. Fulvius, ii. 285
Flavius, Cn., curule aedile, published *Fasti* 304 B.C., i. 186
Fufius, unknown, i. 179, ii. 91, iii. 50
Fulvius Nobilior, ii. 256
Furius Philus, ii. 154

Galba, Servius Sulpicius, defeated by Lusitanians 151 B.C., consul 144 B.C., i. 40, 58, 227, 239, 255, ii. 9, 263, iii. 28
Gallus, unknown, ii. 265 f.
Glaucia, ii. 249, 263, iii. 164
Gorgias, Plato's dialogue, in which rhetoric is identified with sophistry and contrasted with philosophy, i. 47, 103, iii. 59. 129
Gracchus, C., tribune 123 B.C., social reformer, i. 38, 154, ii. 106, 132, iii. 214, 225
Gracchus, Ti., i. 38, 211, ii. 106, 285
Graecia, i. 13, ii. 6
Graecia Magna, ii. 154, iii. 60
Granius, ii. 244, 254, 281

Gratidianus, M. Marius, i. 178, ii. 262

Hannibal, i. 210, ii. 75 f.
Hecuba, iii. 219
Helena, iii. 219
Hellanicus, early Greek prose author, ii. 53
Helvius Mancina, unknown, ii. 266, 274
Hercules, ii. 70
Hermodorus, first Greek architect employed at Rome, i. 62
Herodotus, ii. 55
Hierocles, ii. 95
Hippias, contemporary of Socrates, iii. 127
Hippocrates, iii. 132
Homerus, iii. 57
Hortensius, iii. 228, 230
Hostilius, unknown, i. 245
Hostilius Mancinus, i. 181, 238, ii. 137
Hyperides, Attic orator, 4th century B.C., i. 58, ii. 94, iii. 28
Hypsaeus, consul 125 B.C., i. 166

Isocrates, Attic orator, early 4th century B.C., ii. 10, 94, iii. 28, 36, 59, 139, 141, 173
Ithaca, i. 196
Iulius, C. (see Introduction), ii. 12 etc.
Iulius, L., iii. 10
Iunia, ii. 225

Laelia, iii. 45
Laelius Decumus, ii. 25

Laelius, friend of Scipio Africanus Minor, i. 35, 58, 211, 215, 255, 265, ii. 22, 154, 286, 341, iii. 28, 45

Lamia, L. Aelius, unknown, ii. 262, 269

Largus, ii. 240

Laurentum, on coast of Latium, ii. 22

Lentulus, P., princeps senatus, consul 162 B.C., i. 211

Lepidi, ii. 290

Lepidus, see Porcina

Lepidus, consul 187, censor 179 B.C., ii. 287

Libo, ii. 263

Licinia, iii. 8

Licinius Varus, P., praetor 208 B.C., ii. 250

Livius, see Salinator

Longinus, i. 256

Lucilius, earliest Roman satirist, *b.* 180 B.C., i. 72, ii. 25, 253, 284, iii. 86, 171

Lyceum, gymnasium near Athens, where Aristotle taught, i. 98.

Lycurgus of Athens, ii. 94

Lycurgus of Sparta, i. 58, 197, iii. 56

Lysias, Attic orator, *fl.* 393 B.C., i. 231, ii. 93, iii. 28

Lysippus, iii. 26

Lysis, iii. 139

Macedonia, i. 45

Magius, unknown, ii. 265

Mago, Carthaginian author of work on agriculture translated by order of Senate, i. 249

Mancinus, see Hostilius Mancinus

Manilius, M'., i. 212, 246, iii. 133

Manlius, Cn., consul 105 B.C., ii. 125

Manlius, L., ii. 260

Marcellus, i. 57, 176

Marcius Philippus, L., i. 24, ii. 220, 245, 249, 255, 316, iii. 2, 4

Marcius Rex, ii. 125

Marius, i. 66, ii. 196, 266, iii. 8

Mars, iii. 167

Martius Campus, ii. 257

Maximi, ii. 290

Maximus, Q. Fabius Cunctator, dictator against Hannibal 217 B.C., i. 210, ii. 273, 290

Megarici, iii. 62

Memmius, tribune 111 B.C., ii. 240, 264, 267, 283

Menecles, ii. 95

Menedemus, rhetorician, 85, 88

Metellus, Q., made Macedonia a Roman province 148 B.C., i. 215, ii. 167

Metrodorus, i. 45, ii. 360, 365, iii. 75

Minerva, ii. 73

Misenum, on coast of Latium, ii. 60

Mnesarchus, i. 45, 83

Mucius Scaevola, P., i. 166, 212, 217, 240, 244, ii. 52, 285

Mucius Scaevola, Q., the Augur (see Introduction), i. 24 etc.

Mucius Scaevola, Q., Pont. Max., i. 180, 229, 244, iii. 10

Mummius, unknown, ii. 268

Myro, iii. 26

Naevius, ii. 45

Narbonensis colonia, ii. 223

Nasica, consul 191 B.C., ii. 260, 276

Naucrates, writer of funeral orations, ii. 94, iii. 173

Navius, unknown, ii. 249

Neoptolemus, ii. 156, 257

Neptunus, iii. 167

Nero, C. Claudius, won at the battle of Metaurus when Hasdrubal was defeated, 207 B.C., ii. 248

Nicander, i. 69

Norbanus, ii. 89, 107, 164, 197 ff.

Novae Tabernae, ii. 266

Novius, writer of Atellan plays, ii. 255, 279, 285

Numa Pompilius, second king of Rome, i. 37, ii. 154, iii. 73, 197

Numantia in Spain, destroyed by Rome 133 B.C., i. 181

Numerius Furius, iii. 87

Nummius, ii. 257

Octavius, i. 166

Olympia, iii. 127

Opimius, L., ii. 106, 132, 134, 165

Opimius, Q., consul 154 B.C., ii. 277

Orata, see Sergius

Pacuvius, poet, nephew of Ennius, i. 246, ii. 155, 187, 193, iii. 27, 157

Palatium, ii. 263

Pamphilus, iii. 81

Panaetius, Stoic, friend of Scipio Africanus Minor, i. 45, 75, iii. 78

Paris, iii. 219

Paulus, Aemilius, censor 164 B.C., ii. 272

Peleus, iii. 57

Pelias, iii. 217

Pericles, i. 216, ii. 93, iii. 59, 71, 238

Peripatetici, school of Aristotle, i. 43, 45, iii. 62, 67, 102, 115

Perperna, consul 92 B.C., ii. 262

Persius, literateur, quaestor 146 B.C., ii. 25

Pherecydes of Scyros, early Greek prose author, 560 B.C., ii. 53

Phidias, ii. 73

Philippus of Macedon, ii. 341, iii. 141

Philippus, L. Marcius, see Marcius Philippus

Philistus, b. 430 B.C., exiled 386 B.C. by elder Dionysius, ii. 57, 94

Philo, i. 62, iii. 110

Philoctetes, iii. 141

Philolaus, iii. 139

Phoenix, iii. 57

Phormio, ii. 75 f.

Pictor, Q. Fabius, earlier contemporary of Cato, wrote in Greek, ii. 51

Pinarius, T., ii. 266

Pisistratus, iii. 137

Piso, M. Pupius, consul 61 B.C., Cicero's tutor in oratory, i. 104

Piso, unknown, ii. 265, 285

Pittacus, iii. 56

Plato, i. 28, 47, 49, 89, 217, 224, 233, ii. 194, iii. 15, 21, 60, 67, 129, 139, 190

Plautus, iii. 45

Poenus, iii. 153

Polemo, iii. 67

Polyclitus, ii. 70, iii. 26

Polydorus, iii. 219

Pompeius, Sextus, uncle of Pompeius Magnus, i. 67, iii. 78

Pompeius Phrygio, unknown, ii. 283

Pompeius Rufus, i. 168

Pomponius, iii. 50

Pomptinum, ii. 290

Pontidius, unknown, ii. 275

Popilia, ii. 44

Porcina, M. Aemilius Lepidus, consul 137 B.C., i. 40

Priamus, iii. 102, 217

Privernum, town in Latium, ii. 224

Prodicus, iii. 128

Protagoras, iii. 128

Prytaneum, town hall at Athens, i. 232

Publicius, C., unknown, ii. 271

Pyrgensis, ii. 287

Pyrrho, founder of Sceptic school, iii. 62

Pyrrhonei, iii. 62

Pythagoras, physical philosopher of Samos, *fl.* 550 B.C., i. 42, ii. 154, iii. 56, 139

Quintus Cicero, i. 1, 24, iii. 13

Rex, Q. Marius, consul 118 B.C., ii. 125

Rhodus, i. 75, ii. 3, 217

Romani Ludi, i. 24

Romulus, i. 37

Roscius, celebrated actor, i. 124, 129, 251, 254, 258, ii. 233, 242, iii. 102, 221

Rudini, iii. 168

Rusca, M. Pinarius, unknown, ii. 261

Rutilius, P. Rufus, tr. pl. 136 B.C., i. 181

Rutilius, P. Rufus, pupil of Stoic Panaetius, i. 227 f., ii. 280, 313

Sabini, i. 37

Salamis, ii. 193

Salii, iii. 197

Salinator, M. Livius, ii. 273

Samnites, ii. 325, iii. 86

Scaevola, P., nephew of the next, i. 166, 170, 212, 217, 240, 265, ii. 52, 285

Scaevola, Mucius, see under Mucius

Scaurus, i. 214, ii. 203, 257, 265, 280, 283

Scipio, i. 255, ii. 22, 249, 260, 262, 267, 280, iii. 56, 81, 134. See Africanus

Scipio Nasica Serapio, consul 138 B.C., ii. 285

Scopas, ii. 352

INDEX TO *DE ORATORE*

Scribonius, L., i. 227, ii. 263

Sempronii Gracchi, Ti. and C. (tribune 123 B.C., social reformer), i. 38

Sempronius, A., ii. 247

Septumuleius, ii. 269

Sergius Orata, i. 178

Servilius, M., ii. 261

Servius Tullius, sixth king of Rome, i. 37

Sextius, ii. 246

Siculi, ii. 217, 278, 280

Silus, M. Sergius Orator, quaestor 105 B.C., ii. 285

Simonides, ii. 299, 351, 357

Sirens, ii. 154

Socrates, i. 28, 42, 63, 204, ii. 270, iii. 15, 60 ff., 67, 78, 129, 139

Solon, i. 58, 197, iii. 56

Sophocles, iii. 27

Soranus, Q. Valerius (of Sora, near Arpinum in Latium), iii. 43

Speusippus, iii. 67

Staseas, i. 104, ii. 2

Statius, ii. 40, 257

Stoici, i. 43, 220, ii. 157, iii. 62, 65, 78

Sulpicius, P. Rufus (see Introduction), i. 25, iii. 11 etc.

Sulpicius Gallus, consul 166 B.C., i. 228

Syri, ii. 265

Syrtis, iii. 163

Tarentum, ii. 273

Tarracina, in Latium, ii. 240

Tauriscus, iii. 221

Telamo, ii. 193

Terentius Afer, ii. 172, 326

Terentius Vespa, ii. 253

Teucer, ii. 193

Thales, iii. 137

Themistocles, ii. 299, 351, iii. 59

Theophrastus, successor of Aristotle, i. 43, 49, 55, iii. 184, 221

Theopompus, ii. 57, 94, iii. 36

Theramenes, ii. 93, iii. 59

Thessalia, ii. 352

Thoria lex, iii. 284

Thrasymachus, iii. 59, 128

Thucydides, ii. 56, 93

Thyestes, iii. 219

Tibur, ii. 224, 263

Timaeus, ii. 58

Timotheus, iii. 139

Tisias, Sicilian, rhetorician, *fl.* 5th century B.C., i. 91

Titius Sextus, ii. 48, 253, 265, iii. 88

Tubero, lawyer and Stoic, ii. 341, iii. 87

Tusculanum, i. 24, 27, 98, 224, 265, ii. 13

Tyndaridae, ii. 352

Ulixes, iii. 69, 162

Valerius, iii. 86

Valerius Soranus, iii. 43

Vargula, ii. 244, 247

Varius, tribune 91 B.C., i. 117

Velleius, iii. 78

Velocius, iii. 86

INDEX TO *DE ORATORE*

Vespa Terentius, unknown, ii. 253
Vesta, iii. 10
Vigellius, iii. 78
Vopiscus, C. Iulius Caesar Strabo (see Introduction), iii. 30

Xenocrates, iii. 62, 67
Xenophon, ii. 58, iii. 139

Zeno of Citium, iii. 62
Zethus, ii. 156
Zeuxis, iii. 26

TOPICS

abiudicare, ii. 102
abnutare, iii. 164
absolutio, i. 130, *cf.* iii. 84
actio, i. 18, ii. 73, iii. 213, 227
actuose, iii. 102
addictus, ii. 255
adiudicare, ii. 129
agnationes, i. 173
album pontificum, ii. 52
alluviones, i. 173
amplificatio, i. 18, iii. 104
amplitudo, iii. 7
anapaestus, iii. 185
anteoccupatio, iii. 205
applicatio, i. 177
auceps, i. 236
aucupari, ii. 30, 256

calumnia, ii. 226
cavillatio, ii. 218, *cf.* iii. 122
centumvirales causae, i. 173 etc.
choreus, iii. 193
circumluviones, i. 173
clausulae, iii. 181, 183, 192 f.
clepsydra, iii. 138
coemptio, i. 237
commentari, iii. 86
commoratio, iii. 202, *cf.* 32

conclusio rationis, iii. 203
conclusio verborum, ii. 34, iii. 174
coniuncta, ii. 166
cor, iii. 61, *cf.* i. 198

decemviri, i. 58 etc.
declinatio, iii. 207
decoctus, iii. 103
deminutio, iii. 202
deprecatio, iii. 205
dinumeratio, iii. 207
dissimulatio, ii. 269, iii. 203
dithyrambus, iii. 185
divisor, ii. 257
duodecim scriptis ludere, i. 217

emblema, iii. 171
erctum, erciscere, i. 237
ethologi, ii. 242, 244
exsecratio, iii. 205
extenuare, iii. 102, *cf.* 202

geminatio, iii. 206
gestus, i. 225, ii. 223, iii. 220
gyrus, iii. 71

herous numerus, iii. 182
hortuli Epicureorum, iii. 63

imminutio, iii. 207
immutatio, iii. 167, 207

431

interpellatio, iii. 205
interspiratio, iii. 173, 198
irraucio, i. 259

lacinia, iii. 110

manubiae, iii. 10
memoria, i. 4, 18, ii. 36,
350 ff.

os, i. 175, ii. 29, 91, iii. 221

παρονομασία, ii. 250, *cf.* iii.
90, 96
planetae, iii. 178
postliminium, i. 182
provocatio, ii. 199, iii. 205

reprehensio, iii. 100, 207

sannio, ii. 251
soluta oratio, iii. 173, *cf.* 186
sophistae, iii. 127 ff.
surculum defringere, iii. 110
sus Minervam, ii. 233

Tabulae xii, i. 58, 167, 193,
195
transferre, iii. 149, 155, 157
trochaeus, iii. 182, 193

vermiculatus, iii. 171
versutiloquus, iii. 154
viscera, ii. 318

INDEX TO *DE FATO*

(The references are to sections.)

Academy, 3 f., 19
Agamemnon, 34
Alcibiades, 10
Alexander, 34
Antipater, 5 note
Apollo, 13, 32 f.
Arcesilaus, 7
Argos Logos, 28
Aristotle, 39
ars, 11 note
assent to sense-presentation, 43
Athens, 7
atomic theory, 23, 46 ff.
axiōmata, 1

Caesar, 2
Campus Martius, 8, 34
Canicula, 12, 15
Carneades, 19, 23, 31 f.
Carthage, 13
Cato, 28
causation, principal and proximate, 41
Chaldeans, 15 f.
Chrysippus, 1, 7, 12 ff., 20, 30, 38 f., 41 ff.
Cleanthes, 14
climate and character, 7
Clytemnestra, 34

confatalia, 30
contagio, 7
Corinth, 7, 13
cylindrus, 42
Cypselus, 13

Daphitas, 5 note
Democritus, 23, 39, 46
Diodorus, 12 f. note, **15**, 17
divination, 33
Divinatione, De, 1
Dynatón, Peri, 1, 17

elachiston, 22
Empedocles, 39
Ennius, 35
Epicurus, 18 f., 21 f., 37, 46
ēthos, 1

Fabius, 12 note, 14

Hecuba, 34
Heraclitus, 39
Hirtius (see p. 189), 2, etc.
Homer quoted, fr. 1
Hortensius, 28

Icadius, 5 note
ignava ratio, 28

433

INDEX TO *DE FATO*

Laius, 30
Lavernium, fr. 4
Lemnos, 36
logikē, 1

Marcellus, 33 note
Medea, 35
Milo, 30 note
minimum, 22
moral science, 1

Natura Deorum, De, 1
Nemea, 7
Numantia, 27

Oedipus, 30
oracles, 33

Paris, 34
Pelius, 34 note
Philip, 5
Philoctetes, 36 f.
Pompey's Porch, 8 note
Pontius, fr. 4 note
Posidonius (see p. 190), 5, 7
possibility, theory of, 1, 17
Puteoli, 2 note
Pytharatus, 19 note

scientia, 11 n.
Scipio, Publius Africanus Aemilianus, 13 note, 17 f., 27 note, fr. 4
Socrates, 10, 30
Stilpo (Megarian philosopher, late 3rd cent. B.C.), 10
Stoics, 16, 33, fr. 3
sturgeon, fr. 4
swerve of atoms, 18 ff., 46 ff.
syneimarmena, 30 n.

Thebes, 7
Theophrastus, 7
theōrēmata, 11
Troy, 34
turbo, 42
Tusculan Disputations, 4
Tusculum, 28 note
Tyndareus, 34

visum = *phantasia*, 42 note

Zeno (founder of Stoic school), 7
Zopyrus, 10 note

INDEX TO
PARADOXA STOICORUM

(The references are to sections. Notes on the proper names will be
found beneath the text.)

admirabilia = *paradoxa*, 4
Africanus Maior, 12
Africanus Minor, 12, 48
    (note)
ambition enslaves, 40

Bias, 8
Bona Dea, 32
Brutus, 1, Introduction p. 253
Brutus the tyrannicide, 12

Carinae, 50
Carthaginians, 12
Catiline, 27 ff.
Cato, 1 ff., 12
Cethegus, 40
Clodius, 32 (note), Intro-
    duction p. 252
Cocles, 12
Corinth, 38
Corinthian plate, 13, 36, 38
Crassus, L., 41
Crassus, M., Introduction p.
    253
Curius, Manius Dentatus, 12,
    38, 48 (note)

Danaus, 44

Decii, 12
dowries, 44

Echion, 37
equality of goods and of evils,
    20 ff.
exile of Cicero, 28

Fabricius, 12, 48 (note)
freedom, the true, 33 ff.

good, nature of, 6 ff.

Horatius Cocles, 12
Hortensius, Introduction p.
    253

Labicum, 50
lampreys, 35
Lucullus, Introduction p. 253
Luscini, 50
luxury enslaves, 36 ff.

Manilius, M., 50
Marius, 16
Minerva, 5
Mucius, C., 12
mullets, 38
Mummius, L., 30

Nature, mother, 14
Numa Pompilius, 11
Nymphs, Temple of, 31

paradoxa, 4
Paullus, L., 48
Phidias, 5
Polyclitus, 37
Porsenna, 12
Priene, 8
Pyrrhus, 48

Regulus, 16
riches, true, 42 ff.
Romulus, 11

Saguntum, 24
Samnites, 48
Scipiones, 12
Seven Sages, 8
slavery, true, 35 ff.
Socrates, 4, 23
Spartacus, 30
Stoicism, 2, 46

Tarquin, 11
thetika, 5

vice enslaves, 35

INDEX TO *DE PARTITIONE ORATORIA*

(The references are to sections.)

Academia, 139
actio, 3, 25, 67
aequitas, 98, 129
amplificatio, 52
argumentatio, 139
argumentum, 5, 34
attentio, 30

brevitas, 19, 32

Caepio, 105
causa, 69
collocatio, 9
confirmatio, 4, 33
coniectura, 4, 34, 133
coniunctio verborum, 18
consultatio, 64
conversa oratio, 23

Decius, 104 ff.
defensio, 119
definitio, 41
deliberatio, 10, 13, 83 ff.
dialectici, 139
dilucidum, 19, 32
disceptatio, 104
dispositio, 68
dissuasio, 85

efficiendi ratio, 95
enumeratio, 52, 59
exornatio, 10
explicatio, 46

illustris oratio, 20
insita, 5 ff.
inventio, 5, 68, 109
iudicium, 10, 14
iuris ratio, 129

Latinum, 18
laudatio, 69 ff.
lex, 136
loci, 5

maiestas, 105
motus, 8
motus animorum, 112

narratio, 4, 31
Norbanus, 104

Opimius, 104 ff.
orationis genera, 16
orationis partes, 4

penus, 107

437

INDEX TO *DE PARTITIONE ORATORIA*

peroratio, 4, 14, 52
praevaricator, 126
principium, 4
probabile, 19, 32

quaestio, 4, 50, 61, 117, 120

religio, 129
reprehensio, 33, 44
ruta caesa, 107

scripta, 132

simplicia verba, 16
suasio, 85
suavitas, 21, 32

testes, 48, 117 ff.
testimonia, 6

veri similia, 34, 40
virtus, 75 ff.
vitia, 81 ff.
vituperatio, 69 ff.

Printed in Great Britain by R. & R. Clark, Limited, *Edinburgh*

THE LOEB CLASSICAL LIBRARY

VOLUMES ALREADY PUBLISHED

LATIN AUTHORS

Ammianus Marcellinus. J. C. Rolfe. 3 Vols.

Apuleius : The Golden Ass (Metamorphoses). W. Adlington (1566). Revised by S. Gaselee.

St. Augustine : City of God. 7 Vols. Vol. I. G. E. McCracken. Vol. II. W. M. Green. Vol. III. D. Wiesen. Vol. IV. P. Levine. Vol. V. E. M. Sanford and W. M. Green. Vol. VI. W. C. Greene. Vol. VII. W. M. Green.

St. Augustine, Confessions of. W. Watts (1631). 2 Vols.

St. Augustine : Select Letters. J. H. Baxter.

Ausonius. H. G. Evelyn White. 2 Vols.

Bede. J. E. King. 2 Vols.

Boethius : Tracts and De Consolatione Philosophiae. Rev. H. F. Stewart and E. K. Rand. Revised by S. J. Tester.

Caesar : Alexandrian, African and Spanish Wars. A. G. Way.

Caesar : Civil Wars. A. G. Peskett.

Caesar : Gallic War. H. J. Edwards.

Cato and Varro : De Re Rustica. H. B. Ash and W. D. Hooper.

Catullus. F. W. Cornish ; Tibullus. J. B. Postgate ; and Pervigilium Veneris. J. W. Mackail.

Celsus : De Medicina. W. G. Spencer. 3 Vols.

Cicero : Brutus and Orator. G. L. Hendrickson and H. M. Hubbell.

Cicero : De Finibus. H. Rackham.

Cicero : De Inventione, etc. H. M. Hubbell.

Cicero : De Natura Deorum and Academica. H. Rackham.

Cicero : De Officiis. Walter Miller.

Cicero : De Oratore, etc. 2 Vols. Vol. I: De Oratore, Books I and II. E. W. Sutton and H. Rackham. Vol. II: De Oratore, Book III ; De Fato ; Paradoxa Stoicorum ; De Partitione Oratoria. H. Rackham.

Cicero : De Republica, De Legibus. Clinton W. Keyes.

THE LOEB CLASSICAL LIBRARY

CICERO: DE SENECTUTE, DE AMICITIA, DE DIVINATIONE. W. A. Falconer.

CICERO: IN CATILINAM, PRO MURENA, PRO SULLA, PRO FLACCO. New version by C. Macdonald.

CICERO: LETTERS TO ATTICUS. E. O. Winstedt. 3 Vols.

CICERO: LETTERS TO HIS FRIENDS. W. Glynn Williams, M. Cary, M. Henderson. 4 Vols.

CICERO: PHILIPPICS. W. C. A. Ker.

CICERO: PRO ARCHIA, POST REDITUM, DE DOMO, DE HA-RUSPICUM RESPONSIS, PRO PLANCIO. N. H. Watts.

CICERO: PRO CAECINA, PRO LEGE MANILIA, PRO CLUENTIO, PRO RABIRIO. H. Grose Hodge.

CICERO: PRO CAELIO, DE PROVINCIIS CONSULARIBUS, PRO BALBO. R. Gardner.

CICERO: PRO MILONE, IN PISONEM, PRO SCAURO, PRO FONTEIO, PRO RABIRIO POSTUMO, PRO MARCELLO, PRO LIGARIO, PRO REGE DEIOTARO. N. H. Watts.

CICERO: PRO QUINCTIO, PRO ROSCIO AMERINO, PRO ROSCIO COMOEDO, CONTRA RULLUM. J. H. Freese.

CICERO: PRO SESTIO, IN VATINIUM. R. Gardner.

[CICERO]: RHETORICA AD HERENNIUM. H. Caplan.

CICERO: TUSCULAN DISPUTATIONS. J. E. King.

CICERO: VERRINE ORATIONS. L. H. G. Greenwood. 2 Vols.

CLAUDIAN. M. Platnauer. 2 Vols.

COLUMELLA: DE RE RUSTICA, DE ARBORIBUS. H. B. Ash, E. S. Forster, E. Heffner. 3 Vols.

CURTIUS, Q.: HISTORY OF ALEXANDER. J. C. Rolfe. 2 Vols.

FLORUS. E. S. Forster; and CORNELIUS NEPOS. J. C. Rolfe.

FRONTINUS: STRATAGEMS AND AQUEDUCTS. C. E. Bennett and M. B. McElwain.

FRONTO: CORRESPONDENCE. C. R. Haines. 2 Vols.

GELLIUS. J. C. Rolfe. 3 Vols.

HORACE: ODES AND EPODES. C. E. Bennett.

HORACE: SATIRES, EPISTLES, ARS POETICA. H. R. Fairclough.

JEROME: SELECT LETTERS. F. A. Wright.

JUVENAL AND PERSIUS. G. G. Ramsay.

LIVY. B. O. Foster, F. G. Moore, Evan T. Sage, A. C. Schlesinger and R. M. Geer (General Index). 14 Vols.

LUCAN. J. D. Duff.

LUCRETIUS. W. H. D. Rouse. Revised by M. F. Smith.

MANILIUS. G. P. Goold.

MARTIAL. W. C. A. Ker. 2 Vols. Revised by E. H. Warminton.

MINOR LATIN POETS: from PUBLILIUS SYRUS to RUTILIUS NAMATIANUS, including GRATTIUS, CALPURNIUS SICULUS,

2

THE LOEB CLASSICAL LIBRARY

NEMESIANUS, AVIANUS, with " Aetna," " Phoenix " and other poems. J. Wight Duff and Arnold M. Duff.
OVID : THE ART OF LOVE AND OTHER POEMS. J. H. Mozley.
OVID : FASTI. Sir James G. Frazer.
OVID : HEROIDES AND AMORES. Grant Showerman. Revised by G. P. Goold.
OVID : METAMORPHOSES. F. J. Miller. 2 Vols.
OVID : TRISTIA AND EX PONTO. A. L. Wheeler.
PETRONIUS. M. Heseltine ; SENECA : APOCOLOCYNTOSIS. W. H. D. Rouse. Revised by E. H. Warmington.
PHAEDRUS AND BABRIUS (Greek). B. E. Perry.
PLAUTUS. Paul Nixon. 5 Vols.
PLINY : LETTERS, PANEGYRICUS. B. Radice. 2 Vols.
PLINY : NATURAL HISTORY. 10 Vols. Vols. I-V. H. Rackham. Vols. VI-VIII. W. H. S. Jones. Vol. IX. H. Rackham. Vol. X. D. E. Eichholz.
PROPERTIUS. H. E. Butler.
PRUDENTIUS. H. J. Thomson. 2 Vols.
QUINTILIAN. H. E. Butler. 4 Vols.
REMAINS OF OLD LATIN. E. H. Warmington. 4 Vols. Vol. I (Ennius and Caecilius). Vol. II (Livius, Naevius, Pacuvius, Accius). Vol. III (Lucilius, Laws of the XII Tables). Vol. IV (Archaic Inscriptions).
SALLUST. J. C. Rolfe.
SCRIPTORES HISTORIAE AUGUSTAE. D. Magie. 3 Vols.
SENECA : APOCOLOCYNTOSIS. Cf. PETRONIUS.
SENECA : EPISTULAE MORALES. R. M. Gummere. 3 Vols.
SENECA : MORAL ESSAYS. J. W. Basore. 3 Vols.
SENECA : NATURALES QUAESTIONES. T. H. Corcoran. 2 Vols.
SENECA : TRAGEDIES. F. J. Miller. 2 Vols.
SENECA THE ELDER M. Winterbottom. 2 Vols.
SIDONIUS : POEMS AND LETTERS. W. B. Anderson. 2 Vols.
SILIUS ITALICUS. J. D. Duff. 2 Vols.
STATIUS. J. H. Mozley. 2 Vols.
SUETONIUS. J. C. Rolfe. 2 Vols.
TACITUS : AGRICOLA AND GERMANIA. M. Hutton ; DIALOGUS. Sir Wm. Peterson. Revised by R. M. Ogilvie, E. H. Warmington, M. Winterbottom.
TACITUS : HISTORIES AND ANNALS. C. H. Moore and J. Jackson. 4 Vols.
TERENCE. John Sargeaunt. 2 Vols.
TERTULLIAN : APOLOGIA AND DE SPECTACULIS. T. R. Glover; MINUCIUS FELIX. G. H. Rendall.
VALERIUS FLACCUS. J. H. Mozley.
VARRO : DE LINGUA LATINA. R. G. Kent. 2 Vols.

THE LOEB CLASSICAL LIBRARY

VELLEIUS PATERCULUS AND RES GESTAE DIVI AUGUSTI.
F. W. Shipley.
VIRGIL. H. R. Fairclough. 2 Vols.
VITRUVIUS: DE ARCHITECTURA. F. Granger. 2 Vols.

GREEK AUTHORS

ACHILLES TATIUS. S. Gaselee.
AELIAN: ON THE NATURE OF ANIMALS. A. F. Scholfield.
3 Vols.
AENEAS TACTICUS, ASCLEPIODOTUS AND ONASANDER. The
Illinois Greek Club.
AESCHINES. C. D. Adams.
AESCHYLUS. H. Weir Smyth. 2 Vols.
ALCIPHRON, AELIAN AND PHILOSTRATUS: LETTERS. A. R.
Benner and F. H. Fobes.
APOLLODORUS. Sir James G. Frazer. 2 Vols.
APOLLONIUS RHODIUS. R. C. Seaton.
THE APOSTOLIC FATHERS. Kirsopp Lake. 2 Vols.
APPIAN: ROMAN HISTORY. Horace White. 4 Vols.
ARATUS. Cf. CALLIMACHUS: HYMNS AND EPIGRAMS.
ARISTIDES. C. A. Behr. 4 Vols. Vol. I.
ARISTOPHANES. Benjamin Bickley Rogers. 3 Vols. Verse
trans.
ARISTOTLE: ART OF RHETORIC. J. H. Freese.
ARISTOTLE: ATHENIAN CONSTITUTION, EUDEMIAN ETHICS.
VIRTUES AND VICES. H. Rackham.
ARISTOTLE: THE CATEGORIES. ON INTERPRETATION. H. P.
Cooke; PRIOR ANALYTICS. H. Tredennick.
ARISTOTLE: GENERATION OF ANIMALS. A. L. Peck.
ARISTOTLE: HISTORIA ANIMALIUM. A. L. Peck. 3 Vols.
Vols. I and II.
ARISTOTLE: METAPHYSICS. H. Tredennick. 2 Vols.
ARISTOTLE: METEOROLOGICA. H. D. P. Lee.
ARISTOTLE: MINOR WORKS. W. S. Hett. " On Colours,"
" On Things Heard," " Physiognomics," " On Plants,"
" On Marvellous Things Heard," " Mechanical Prob-
lems," " On Invisible Lines," " Situations and Names of
Winds," " On Melissus, Xenophanes, and Gorgias."
ARISTOTLE: NICOMACHEAN ETHICS. H. Rackham.
ARISTOTLE: OECONOMICA AND MAGNA MORALIA. G. C.
Armstrong. (With METAPHYSICS, Vol. II.)
ARISTOTLE: ON THE HEAVENS. W. K. C. Guthrie.

THE LOEB CLASSICAL LIBRARY

ARISTOTLE : ON THE SOUL, PARVA NATURALIA, ON BREATH. W. S. Hett.

ARISTOTLE : PARTS OF ANIMALS. A. L. Peck ; MOVEMENT AND PROGRESSION OF ANIMALS. E. S. Forster.

ARISTOTLE : PHYSICS. Rev. P. Wicksteed and F. M. Cornford. 2 Vols.

ARISTOTLE : POETICS ; LONGINUS ON THE SUBLIME. W. Hamilton Fyfe ; DEMETRIUS ON STYLE. W. Rhys Roberts.

ARISTOTLE : POLITICS. H. Rackham.

ARISTOTLE : POSTERIOR ANALYTICS. H. Tredennick ; TOPICS. E. S. Forster.

ARISTOTLE : PROBLEMS. W. S. Hett. 2 Vols.

ARISTOTLE : RHETORICA AD ALEXANDRUM. H. Rackham. (With PROBLEMS, Vol. II.)

ARISTOTLE : SOPHISTICAL REFUTATIONS. COMING-TO-BE AND PASSING-AWAY. E. S. Forster ; ON THE COSMOS. D. J. Furley.

ARRIAN : HISTORY OF ALEXANDER AND INDICA. 2 Vols. Vol. I. P. Brunt. Vol. II. Rev. E. Iliffe Robson.

ATHENAEUS : DEIPNOSOPHISTAE. C. B. Gulick. 7 Vols.

BABRIUS AND PHAEDRUS (Latin). B. E. Perry.

ST. BASIL : LETTERS. R. J. Deferrari. 4 Vols.

CALLIMACHUS : FRAGMENTS. C. A. Trypanis ; MUSAEUS : HERO AND LEANDER. T. Gelzer and C. Whitman.

CALLIMACHUS : HYMNS AND EPIGRAMS, AND LYCOPHRON. A. W. Mair ; ARATUS. G. R. Mair.

CLEMENT OF ALEXANDRIA. Rev. G. W. Butterworth.

COLLUTHUS. Cf. OPPIAN.

DAPHNIS AND CHLOE. Cf. LONGUS.

DEMOSTHENES I : OLYNTHIACS, PHILIPPICS AND MINOR ORATIONS : I-XVII AND XX. J. H. Vince.

DEMOSTHENES II : DE CORONA AND DE FALSA LEGATIONE. C. A. and J. H. Vince.

DEMOSTHENES III : MEIDIAS, ANDROTION, ARISTOCRATES, TIMOCRATES, ARISTOGEITON. J. H. Vince.

DEMOSTHENES IV-VI : PRIVATE ORATIONS AND IN NEAERAM. A. T. Murray.

DEMOSTHENES VII : FUNERAL SPEECH, EROTIC ESSAY, EXORDIA AND LETTERS. N. W. and N. J. DeWitt.

DIO CASSIUS : ROMAN HISTORY. E. Cary. 9 Vols.

DIO CHRYSOSTOM. 5 Vols. Vols. I and II. J. W. Cohoon. Vol. III. J. W. Cohoon and H. Lamar Crosby. Vols. IV and V. H. Lamar Crosby.

DIODORUS SICULUS. 12 Vols. Vols. I-VI. C. H. Oldfather. Vol. VII. C. L. Sherman. Vol. VIII. C. B. Welles. Vols.

THE LOEB CLASSICAL LIBRARY

IX and X. Russel M. Geer. Vols. XI and XII. F. R. Walton. General Index. Russel M. Geer.

DIOGENES LAERTIUS. R. D. Hicks. 2 Vols. New Introduction by H. S. Long.

DIONYSIUS OF HALICARNASSUS : CRITICAL ESSAYS. S. Usher. 2 Vols.

DIONYSIUS OF HALICARNASSUS : ROMAN ANTIQUITIES. Spelman's translation revised by E. Cary. 7 Vols.

EPICTETUS. W. A. Oldfather. 2 Vols.

EURIPIDES. A. S. Way. 4 Vols. Verse trans.

EUSEBIUS : ECCLESIASTICAL HISTORY. Kirsopp Lake and J. E. L. Oulton. 2 Vols.

GALEN : ON THE NATURAL FACULTIES. A. J. Brock.

THE GREEK ANTHOLOGY. W. R. Paton. 5 Vols.

THE GREEK BUCOLIC POETS (THEOCRITUS, BION, MOSCHUS). J. M. Edmonds.

GREEK ELEGY AND IAMBUS WITH THE ANACREONTEA. J. M. Edmonds. 2 Vols.

GREEK MATHEMATICAL WORKS. Ivor Thomas. 2 Vols.

HERODES. Cf. THEOPHRASTUS : CHARACTERS.

HERODIAN. C. R. Whittaker. 2 Vols.

HERODOTUS. A. D. Godley. 4 Vols.

HESIOD AND THE HOMERIC HYMNS. H. G. Evelyn White.

HIPPOCRATES AND THE FRAGMENTS OF HERACLEITUS. W. H. S. Jones and E. T. Withington. 4 Vols.

HOMER : ILIAD. A. T. Murray. 2 Vols.

HOMER : ODYSSEY. A. T. Murray. 2 Vols.

ISAEUS. E. S. Forster.

ISOCRATES. George Norlin and LaRue Van Hook. 3 Vols.

[ST. JOHN DAMASCENE]: BARLAAM AND IOASAPH. Rev. G. R. Woodward, Harold Mattingly and D. M. Lang.

JOSEPHUS. 9 Vols. Vols. I-IV. H. St. J. Thackeray. Vol. V. H. St. J. Thackeray and Ralph Marcus. Vols. VI and VII. Ralph Marcus. Vol. VIII. Ralph Marcus and Allen Wikgren. Vol. IX. L. H. Feldman.

JULIAN. Wilmer Cave Wright. 3 Vols.

LIBANIUS : SELECTED WORKS. A. F. Norman. 3 Vols. Vols. I and II.

LONGUS : DAPHNIS AND CHLOE. Thornley's translation revised by J. M. Edmonds ; and PARTHENIUS. S. Gaselee.

LUCIAN. 8 Vols. Vols. I-V. A. M. Harmon. Vol. VI. K. Kilburn. Vols. VII and VIII. M. D. Macleod.

LYCOPHRON. Cf. CALLIMACHUS : HYMNS AND EPIGRAMS.

LYRA GRAECA. J. M. Edmonds. 3 Vols.

LYSIAS. W. R. M. Lamb.

THE LOEB CLASSICAL LIBRARY

MANETHO. W. G. Waddell; PTOLEMY: TETRABIBLOS. F. E. Robbins.

MARCUS AURELIUS. C. R. Haines.

MENANDER. F. G. Allinson.

MINOR ATTIC ORATORS. 2 Vols. K. J. Maidment and J. O. Burtt.

MUSAEUS : HERO AND LEANDER. *Cf.* CALLIMACHUS : FRAGMENTS.

NONNOS : DIONYSIACA. W. H. D. Rouse. 3 Vols.

OPPIAN, COLLUTHUS, TRYPHIODORUS. A. W. Mair.

PAPYRI. NON-LITERARY SELECTIONS. A. S. Hunt and C. C. Edgar. 2 Vols. LITERARY SELECTIONS (Poetry). D. L. Page.

PARTHENIUS. *Cf.* LONGUS.

PAUSANIAS : DESCRIPTION OF GREECE. W. H. S. Jones. 4 Vols. and Companion Vol. arranged by R. E. Wycherley.

PHILO. 10 Vols. Vols. I-V. F. H. Colson and Rev. G. H. Whitaker. Vols. VI-X. F. H. Colson. General Index. Rev. J. W. Earp.
    Two Supplementary Vols. Translation only from an Armenian Text. Ralph Marcus.

PHILOSTRATUS : THE LIFE OF APOLLONIUS OF TYANA. F. C. Conybeare. 2 Vols.

PHILOSTRATUS : IMAGINES ; CALLISTRATUS : DESCRIPTIONS. A. Fairbanks.

PHILOSTRATUS AND EUNAPIUS : LIVES OF THE SOPHISTS. Wilmer Cave Wright.

PINDAR. Sir J. E. Sandys.

PLATO: CHARMIDES, ALCIBIADES, HIPPARCHUS, THE LOVERS, THEAGES, MINOS AND EPINOMIS. W. R. M. Lamb.

PLATO : CRATYLUS, PARMENIDES, GREATER HIPPIAS, LESSER HIPPIAS. H. N. Fowler.

PLATO : EUTHYPHRO, APOLOGY, CRITO, PHAEDO, PHAEDRUS. H. N. Fowler.

PLATO : LACHES, PROTAGORAS, MENO, EUTHYDEMUS. W. R. M. Lamb.

PLATO : LAWS. Rev. R. G. Bury. 2 Vols.

PLATO : LYSIS, SYMPOSIUM, GORGIAS. W. R. M. Lamb.

PLATO : REPUBLIC. Paul Shorey. 2 Vols.

PLATO : STATESMAN, PHILEBUS. H. N. Fowler ; ION. W. R. M. Lamb.

PLATO : THEAETETUS AND SOPHIST. H. N. Fowler.

PLATO : TIMAEUS, CRITIAS, CLITOPHO, MENEXENUS, EPISTULAE. Rev. R. G. Bury.

PLOTINUS. A. H. Armstrong. 6 Vols. Vols. I-III.

THE LOEB CLASSICAL LIBRARY

PLUTARCH : MORALIA. 17 Vols. Vols. I-V. F. C. Babbitt.
Vol. VI. W. C. Helmbold. Vol. VII. P. H. De Lacy and
B. Einarson. Vol. VIII. P. A. Clement, H. B. Hoffleit.
Vol. IX. E. L. Minar, Jr., F. H. Sandbach, W. C.
Helmbold. Vol. X. H. N. Fowler. Vol. XI. L. Pearson,
F. H. Sandbach. Vol. XII. H. Cherniss, W. C. Helmbold.
Vol. XIII, Parts 1 and 2. H. Cherniss. Vol. XIV. P. H.
De Lacy and B. Einarson. Vol. XV. F. H. Sandbach.
PLUTARCH : THE PARALLEL LIVES. B. Perrin. 11 Vols.
POLYBIUS. W. R. Paton. 6 Vols.
PROCOPIUS : HISTORY OF THE WARS. H. B. Dewing. 7 Vols.
PTOLEMY : TETRABIBLOS. *Cf.* MANETHO.
QUINTUS SMYRNAEUS. A. S. Way. Verse trans.
SEXTUS EMPIRICUS. Rev. R. G. Bury. 4 Vols.
SOPHOCLES. F. Storr. 2 Vols. Verse trans.
STRABO : GEOGRAPHY. Horace L. Jones. 8 Vols.
THEOPHRASTUS : CHARACTERS. J. M. Edmonds ; HERODES,
etc. A. D. Knox.
THEOPHRASTUS : DE CAUSIS PLANTARUM. G. K. K. Link and
B. Einarson. 3 Vols. Vol. I.
THEOPHRASTUS : ENQUIRY INTO PLANTS. Sir Arthur Hort.
2 Vols.
THUCYDIDES. C. F. Smith. 4 Vols.
TRYPHIODORUS. *Cf.* OPPIAN.
XENOPHON : ANABASIS. C. L. Brownson.
XENOPHON : CYROPAEDIA. Walter Miller. 2 Vols.
XENOPHON : HELLENICA. C. L. Brownson.
XENOPHON : MEMORABILIA AND OECONOMICUS. E. C. Mar-
chant ; SYMPOSIUM AND APOLOGY. O. J. Todd.
XENOPHON : SCRIPTA MINORA. E. C. Marchant and G. W.
Bowersock.

CAMBRIDGE, MASS.   LONDON
HARVARD UNIV. PRESS   WILLIAM HEINEMANN LTD.